HOUSING IN CAPITALIST SOCIETIES

For Tania and Karen

3

301

Housing in Capitalist Societies

CEDRIC PUGH

South Australian Institute of Technology

6

Gower

Published by
Gower Publishing Company Limited,
Westmead, Farnborough, Hampshire, England

 British Library Cataloguing in Publication Data

Pugh, Cedric
  Housing in capitalist societies.
  1. Housing policy
  2. Democracy
  I. Title
  301.5'4   HD7287.5
  ISBN 0-566-00336-8
        11-4-84

Printed by Itchen Printers Limited,
Southampton, England

Contents

v

Preface

Housing policies in the modern democracies are in transition. Some countries have widened and diversified government activity in housing; others have sought to make their housing subsidies more selective and readily controlled. All are responding to changing circumstances - to the new inflation, and to other social and economic developments. Housing policy needs to be co-ordinated with economic management, social policy, urban renewal, land development, administrative structures and intergovernmental relations. As those have changed, housing policies have had to change accordingly.

This book is about change, and the reform process. Change means that housing should be interpreted afresh, and changing perceptions and understandings of the subject are a key theme of this study. That cannot be a simple theme. Increasingly, housing is seen as requiring a simultaneous solution to problems of shelter, social equity, building efficiency, builders' financial needs and occupiers' financial needs, and urban and regional networks with complex relationships between housing and other physical, social and economic services. To understand the subject as the policy-makers are nowadays required to understand it, the study has to extend to the most general problems of economics, finance, social policy, urban policy and urban administration.

The method adopted in this book is analytical, historical and comparative. Using Britain as a basis for comparison, it draws material selectively from the experience of Australia, West Germany, The Netherlands, Norway, Sweden and the United States. Between them those countries offer a fascinating variety of diverse approaches to common problems, and also some similar approaches to diverse problems. They began the modern transitional period, in the 1960s, with various patterns of government and social and political attitudes to housing. They have responded to changing conditions in diverse ways. To study their housing policies is thus to learn something about their more general capacities for political and social and economic change. Some countries have invented and adapted better than others. Most progress in policy development has occurred in continental Europe. This book tries to show why.

During recent years there have been three approaches in studies of housing policy - a social needs emphasis, economic analyses based upon market or tax incentives, and evaluations of political support and development. This book does not fall precisely into any one of these categories, but broadly covers the three previous approaches with the source of its economics coming mainly from modern public and merit goods theory. By adopting this approach, the book tries to break down disciplinary boundaries in the social sciences and to draw its ideas widely for exposition, criticism and appreciation. Essentially it is a book about policy.

Housing is a large part of anybody's life. This study of it has certainly enriched my own experience of it, in more than merely

academic ways.   Earlier, I lived in a terraced house in London which
the authorities eventually condemned as a slum.   I have since
experienced life with the semi-detached English middle class, and the
suburban life of Boston, Washington D.C., and some other American
cities.   In the course of the research for this book I stayed in a
tenement renovated by a London local authority, a Swedish 'magic house',
a Norwegian timber cottage, a German 'eigenheim' and a Dutch family
home.   The book was written in a mobile home in Ferndown, Dorset, and
a Victorian stone villa in Adelaide, Australia.   All those housing
types assume great significance in current housing policies, as will be
evident in this study.

Acknowledgments

This work has been encouraged and assisted by friends and professionals in eight countries. Detailed debts are acknowledged at the end of chapters, as relevant. Some encouragement has been enduring, general and extremely valuable. Accordingly I am particularly grateful to: Maurice Broady, Jim Kemeny, Fred Raes, Hugo Priemus, Alex Ramsay and Hugh Stretton.

My research assistant, Peter Martin, contributed to some earlier studies in the course of which we began to formulate ideas for this wider study of comparative housing policies. The work was then begun when I was a visiting researcher at the University College of Swansea, and concluded at the University of Adelaide.

The sort of research represented here depends very heavily upon many and varied acts of co-operation and friendship. Family, friends, people and institutions, have responded helpfully and I am grateful for all the assistance I have received. I remain responsible for any errors and misconceptions in the work.

Finally, my appreciation is given to Maureen Williams and Cintra Amos who have typed competently and cheerfully. Bill Gibberd, who has been a vital source of encouragement and friendship, assisted in the final stages of co-ordination and preparation for final copy.

Cedric Pugh

TABLES

CHARTS

FIGURES

Glossary

This glossary does not include all the technical terms used in this study; others are explained in the text, and in Notes at the end of each chapter.

Building societies

Building societies originated in Britain as self-help, mutual associations which collected subscriptions from members to finance home ownership by means of lending to members. They have adapted to social change over a period of some 200 years and they have differentiated into a variety of specialised institutions. In modern times, their main housing role is in financing home ownership. See the notes on *permanent* and *terminating* societies.

Consumer Subsidies

Consumer subsidies are cash payments or vouchers (i.e., housing allowances) paid directly to households. They are contrasted with *production* subsidies which are grants and/or loans, originating in public finance and channelled into the construction of specific housing. In continental Europe, consumer subsidies are termed *subject* subsidies, and production subsidies are termed *object* subsidies. The French express the distinction most literally: production subsidies are *aide à la brique* and consumption subsidies are *aide à la personne*.

Co-operative Housing

Co-operative housing can refer to *tenure*, to the specific developer, or to specific aspects in the development and management of housing. As a form of tenure, it involves the ownership-in-common or co-ownership principle, and the rights and entitlements of individual co-operators depend upon the law and customs of particular countries. Co-operation embraces the mutual self-help and limited-profit principle. As was mentioned this can be used in any aspect of housing development (e.g., land acquisition, procurement of materials, planning, construction and management), or in the total housing process. See the notes on *tenure* and *co-ownership*.

Co-ownership

Co-ownership refers to sharing rights and entitlements in the equity of a property. It includes co-operative and other ownership-in-common forms, and it can be used in specific contracts in which the equity of a property is shared between a person/household and another party. See the notes on *co-operative housing*.

Cost-rent housing

Cost-rent housing is distinguished from housing rented at market values or under *rent controls*. The rents are based upon *historical costs* and the amortisation of loans.

Eigenheim

Eigenheim is a German term, used to denote a self-contained dwelling standing on its own ground and in freehold tenure. It represents a spirit of aspiration for home ownership and access to a 'luxury'.

Historical cost

Historical cost renting refers to rents which are based upon the original costs of construction, interest rates, amortisation of loans and subsidies specific to the dwelling. It is to be distinguished from market rents which follow the forces of demand, supply and (uncontrolled or unregulated) price determination. See notes on *rent control* and *rent regulation*.

Horizontal equity

Horizontal equity refers to the distribution of resources and their prices (e.g., housing) among members of the same class. Inequity occurs when for arbitrary reasons, similar people pay different prices.

Housing allowances

Housing allowances are cash payments or vouchers directed to households for expenditure on housing. They are usually geared to income, rent and needs standards, and sometimes they are controlled by ensuring that recipients occupy housing which meets specified physical standards. Housing allowances are a form of *consumer* subsidy, as distinct from production subsidies. See the note on *consumer subsidies*.

Implicit subsidies

Implicit subsidies do not show up conspicuously in public finance. Examples include the tax concessions on mortgage interest, the imputed rental value of owner-occupied housing and other property-related concessions in tax law.

Key money

Key money refers to payments made informally or illegally to get access to housing in short supply. Such payments were common in nineteenth-century London and in the 1960s in Stockholm, reflecting severe housing shortages.

Production subsidies

See the note on *consumer subsidies*.

Permanent societies

Permanent building societies are to be distinguished from *terminating* societies. They continue to attract investing and borrowing members; these are distinct groups in these societies. See the notes on *building societies* and *terminating societies*.

Public housing

Public housing is a term which is applied to housing constructed by
government housing authorities.   In Britain it includes local
government's *council* housing, housing owned by new town development
corporations, and more recently the term has been applied to housing
financed under the provisions of the Housing Corporation.   Public
housing means different things according to its cultural and
institutional context, a point which is elaborated in this study.   In
this book, the term is used to describe housing constructed under the
responsibility of government housing authorities.

Redevelopment

Redevelopment refers to rebuilding and reconstruction, usually after
sites have been cleared.   See the note on *rehabilitation*.

Rehabilitation

Rehabilitation refers to making good arrears of maintenance and/or
bringing existing housing up to modern standards of design and amenity.
In West Germany, the term *modernisation* is used to express the same
meaning.   During earlier periods, rehabilitation was more pejoratively
termed 'slum patching', reflecting the preference of policy makers for
slum clearance and redevelopment.   See the note on *redevelopment*.

Rent control

Rent control refers to a statutory fixing of maximum rents.   Sometimes
there is provision for indexation to costs, but usually changes are by
ad hoc decisions.   See the note on *rent regulation*.

Rent regulation

Rent regulation is to be distinguished from *rent control*.   Under
regulation provisions, rents are assessed in relationship to criteria
laid down in law and administered by officers and/or tribunals.
Compared with rent controls, there is more flexibility in altering
rents periodically or as conditions change.   See the note on *rent
control*.

Slum housing

Originally the term was used to describe places where 'low goings on'
occurred.   It is a rather indefinite term combining social, physical
and attitudinal judgements, and it is often used pejoratively.   In
modern times it is more precise and relevant to view older housing in
terms of arrears of maintenance and obsolescence, rather than as slum
housing.   Historically, the term 'slums' has been used as a
justification (not always well reasoned) for clearance and redevelopment policies.

Social housing

Social housing is a term which is used in continental Europe and
originally referred to housing directly assisted by government subsidies
and loans.   It includes public housing, but also other housing which is

government-assisted. The meaning of the term has changed as housing
policies have developed and altered. Once it referred to housing
provided for low-income and working-class groups. But as government
policies began to extend assistance through the community, social
housing has taken on a new and broadened meaning. This leaves the
term somewhat indefinite, and particularly because the notion of
subsidisation in housing raises many complications and problems of
interpretation. Nevertheless, there are good reasons for using the
term where the intent is to describe general classes of events rather
than highly specific economic definitions.

Standard housing

Standard housing is to be contrasted with *sub-standard* and *unfit*
housing. These terms originate in theories of slum clearance and in
definitions implanted in building regulations. Standard housing is
the sort the law permits or the sort which *social housing* regulations
define.

Sub-standard housing

Sub-standard housing is housing not meeting *standard* requirements, but
not sufficiently bad to be declared *unfit* in condemnation orders. See
the notes on *standard* and *unfit* housing.

Tenure

Tenure refers to rights and entitlements in which property is held.
In housing, the key tenures are: owner-occupier, rental, and
co-operative or co-ownership. See notes on *co-operative* and
co-ownership housing.

Terminating societies

Terminating building societies are to be distinguished from *permanent*
societies. They accumulate a fund from members' subscriptions until
each member has a loan, then the society terminates. In this form of
society, investing and borrowing members are the same people. See the
notes on *permanent societies* and *building societies*.

Twilight housing

Twilight housing is a term used to describe housing which policy makers
and town planners considered would fall into dilapidation in a decade
or so. The term was widely used in the 1960s to indicate housing
which would come within clearance and redevelopment provisions in the
future (about 10 years or so). Now that policy makers have accepted
the prior claims of *rehabilitation*, the term has lost some of its
earlier policy significance.

Unfit housing

Unfit housing is housing which can be condemned by authorities owing to
its danger to health and its bad sanitary arrangements. See the notes
on *standard* and *sub-standard* housing.

Urban renewal

Urban renewal in its widest sense covers all changes in the built
environment and their relationship to economic, social and political
issues.   Most attention is given to overt public policies which have
varied in objectives and emphasis.   Slum clearance was more directly
associated with housing whereas renewal covers all urban investments.
See the notes on *rehabilitation* and *redevelopment*.

Vertical equity

Vertical equity refers to the distribution of income and resources
(e.g., housing) among people at different levels of income.   Inequity
occurs when, for arbitrary reasons, lower income groups pay more or get
less for the same price.   See the note on *horizontal* inequity.

1 Introduction

The study of housing and housing policy is one of the most complex
areas of social analysis.   This is partly because housing is such a
complex good.   Questions of housing policy require a consideration of
issues beyond the confines of the dwelling-unit itself.   Its analysis
raises important issues in finance; legislation; political, social
and philosophical attitudes; resource allocation; intergovernmental
relations; professional and administrative practices; and planning.
Housing is diverse and complex.   Virtually all its parts are influenced
by government through such factors as social housing, subsidy payments
to voluntary organisations, tax policies, welfare assistance and
immigration.   Housing should be understood by its relationship to
public policy, not merely as a built form.   In their public policy
context housing issues will be differently perceived according to the
relative importance of objectives to each other and to non-housing
issues.   Technical and analytical studies of housing will also take on
diverse characteristics depending upon the theoretical and intellectual
assumptions which are adopted by researchers.

This particular study of housing is aimed at providing a broad basis
for understanding recent policy developments in modern democratic
societies.   Although it draws on technical research it does not set
out to add to it.   Instead, its view of housing is primarily social;
it draws upon social theory, history, public policy, economics and
public administration without being tied down exclusively to any of
these in particular.   This approach is suitable for understanding
housing policy development in its social and historical context, and
for assessing the general consequences of alternative courses of action.

A multitude of public policies impinge on and influence housing.
Among them it is not always easy to distinguish housing policy itself,
in its own right.   In Britain, for example, until the 1960s there has
been no comprehensive or co-ordinated housing policy in a broad sense.
What there has been for more than a century is a progression from
concern with issues such as public health, to a series of *ad hoc*
policies aimed at meeting perceived social need.   Social goals in
British housing have been primarily the concern of local government and
central government, and, unlike other countries, much of the expression
of social aims has been associated with public housing built by local
government.   During the last decade or so, Britain has taken steps
towards bringing other housing sectors, including owner-occupied and
private rental housing, into general housing policy reviews.

This widening of housing policy perspectives is not unique to Britain.
Donnison [1] has pointed out that most modern democratic societies have
experienced, or are likely to experience, a similar progression.   This
evolution can be viewed in three stages.   The first is a period of
concern motivated by the needs and problems of industrial development
and such things as public health problems stemming from poor housing
conditions.   Stage two can be seen as a period of concern with social
need in housing.   This is typically associated with *ad hoc* policies.

1

which leave private housing to the market, and direct social housing (not always effectively) at social need. There have been very diverse definitions of social need. [2] Stage three breaks down the dualism. Relationships between social housing and private housing become more competitive, the boundaries between government and private involvements become less clear-cut, the shape and character of government activities begin to change, and sometimes new institutions are created to fill gaps in housing finance, organisation and research. This marks a development towards national comprehensiveness and co-ordination in housing policy. Britain has been entering this phase, though with some problems from historically inherited policies which are not fully compatible with comprehensiveness in housing. Other countries are grappling with such difficulties as organisational structure, resource allocation and the revision of subsidies. The transition is usually accomplished by intense phases of political and administrative reform, generally precipitated by war, economic crises brought on by major depressions or inflations, or by an accumulation of problems arising from a sense of breakdown in housing and urban policies. Also, housing reform is normally closely associated in historical time and in analytical explanation with reforms in social and urban policies.

For those reasons studies of housing policy should always see it in relation to more general processes of reform.

HOUSING AND ITS WIDER ENVIRONMENT

Principles of modern economic theory put forward distinctions between private and social costs and benefits, which are inherent in the nature of goods and services. The total benefits of some goods are enjoyed 'exclusively' by an individual without effect upon third parties, and the benefits are accordingly 'private' to that consumer without 'spillover' or 'external' benefits for other individuals. The nature of other goods is such that, in the course of consumption by one individual, the benefits do spill over to others. Goods without 'spillover' effects are 'private', and those with indivisible 'external' benefits are 'public'. Some goods such as housing, have mixed private and public characteristics. [3] The private part of housing is the dwelling from which occupants enjoy the benefits of the house, which can be 'privatised' by excluding others from them, literally by closing the door on neighbours. Other aspects of housing have a 'public' or 'external' ('neighbourhood') value associated with them, experienced as benefits or costs, or in the case of housing as a net result of external benefits and external ('social') costs. The external effects quite clearly depend upon the characteristics of the immediate social and physical neighbourhood, and even more upon some wider total town or metropolitan area services and functions.

Modern economics and sociology have isolated, explained and valued the portions of 'private' and 'public' benefits associated with urban housing. Economic studies by Richardson [4] and Wilkinson [5] show the relative strength of external and locational influences in the value of housing in twentieth-century urban conditions. More specifically, distance from the city centre, social class and physical characteristics of the neighbourhood, and other external factors are large influences in projecting value into housing. Factors valued as part of the characteristics of the dwelling include its size, the number of rooms,

a private garden or garage space. Housing is thus valued for its
built form and for its relationship to surrounding social space and
urban services as well as for rights of tenure and its role as an
economic asset. Furthermore, it is one of the few social and economic
assets which 'internalises' the value of its externalities into its
price. Put another way, we can say the economic value of housing
includes resources built into its form, and the net balance of external
costs and benefits from the social and physical environment. Thus, it
is seen that housing policies and problems interact with an urban and
regional environment. [6]

This analytical view of housing and its historical or evolutionary
profile carries interesting implications. Housing is fixed in space
and it exists in localities where private investment and publicly
provided infrastructure are part of the local environment. Localities
will vary in their relationship to economic growth and to historical
patterns. These variations will require specific localised responses
in housing markets and policy. However, housing also contains wider
regional and national interests. These open up a variety of issues,
involving the balance of localisation, regionalisation, and
centralisation. [7] In another dimension, housing contains a width of
considerations in social, economic and physical spheres requiring the
development of useful inter-agency relationships. In short,
comprehensiveness in housing must be developed *between* levels of
government (the 'vertical' dimension) and *within* levels of government
(the 'horizontal' dimension).

THE LOW-INCOME HOUSING PROBLEM AND URBANISATION

Our conceptualisation of housing can be widened and deepened by looking
at some of Wilkinson's recent interpretations. [8] He combines three
components from urban economics to create an explanation of the
accessibility problems which impede the housing aspirations of
low-income groups. They are: (1) the relationship between housing
needs and life-cycle changes, [9] (2) the division of the housing
market into sub-markets distinguished by location, quality, tenure and
other factors, and (3) processes of growth and change in urban
development. It is argued that while low-income groups often want to
improve their housing standards, and to achieve self-fulfilment, they
are impeded by: lack of income, difficulties of access to housing
credit, limited opportunities to increase their earnings, and living in
locations with lower physical standards and insufficient social
investment by government. These barriers are impediments to
geographical, economic and social mobility. Wilkinson also argues
that rapid urban growth tends to divert housing resources to new and
more profitable upper-income housing. [10] Bring these points
together and it is established that there are deep-seated, complicated
economic reasons interacting within market processes and in public
finance which result in an accessibility problem for low-income groups.

The important feature of Wilkinson's conceptualisation is that it
takes a developmental or process view of housing and urbanisation, and
of their interdependence. It explains and sheds light on such issues
as homelessness, and the sources of justification for a broad
government role in housing and in urban processes. In fact, Wilkinson
sees the solutions to these problems in the area of controlling new

urban growth, of planning housing and industry as one concerted programme, and channelling resources for housing improvement into low-income areas.

Castells [11] presents a more radical explanation of relationships between housing and urbanisation. Using some Marxist ideas, he says that there is an inherent contradiction between the *planned* production of capitalism and its *unplanned* competitive relations. Urbanisation concentrates jobs and people, with resulting conflicts of interest in the allocation of land and in the use of urban space. Viewed in this way, the history of urban administration is characterised with attempts to resolve the inherent contradictions. Housing then becomes an object of social causes - via the advocacy from urban social action movements - and it thereby falls within government attention and provision, rather than being exclusively provided under private markets. Although viewed from this different theoretical perspective, like Wilkinson's, Castells' reasoning presents conclusions that government roles are drawn profoundly into housing, and that housing problems should be interpreted from the overall organisation and functioning of urban administration. Historically policy responses to inherent contractions have led to structural and professional reforms in urban administration.

The ideas from Wilkinson and Castells, and the conceptualisations they spring from, add further support to the earlier demonstration of the analytical connections between housing and the economic processes and conflicts in the wider urban network. Again, by combining these ideas with the notion of comprehensiveness in housing, we see the need to link housing and urban policies with the development of intergovernmental and interagency co-operation. These ideas strengthen the case for integrating housing policy with other urban and regional policies. The case is stronger still when the connections between housing, poverty and community development are considered.

HOUSING, POVERTY AND SOCIAL DEVELOPMENT

Jackson [12] draws upon the idea of *human capital*, recently developed in social economics, and gives it a particular significance for understanding poverty in modern society. He argues that in earlier industrial society where conditions were less complex, anti-poverty policies could be primarily aimed at providing a *flow* of income maintenance (in the form of cash social security benefits) so that groups at the risk of falling into poverty could maintain their needs for food and shelter. By contrast, in the greater complexity of modern society it is the capacity for *social functioning* which is the key aspect of poverty, and anti-poverty policies should now involve the investment of resources in education, training, modern health care and housing. In other words, an individual (or a family) will fall into relative poverty and deprivation if he or she does not possess adequate social investments (i.e., a *stock* of human capital) to function in employment, to maintain dependants, to engage in social life and to achieve standard life expectancies in ordinary circumstances. Then, taking the social rather than the individual viewpoint, avoidance of poverty depends upon providing accessible social investments as well as upon the more traditional income maintenance and social security schemes. This means that social policies, including aspects of housing policy,

4

should be aimed at changing those external conditions, and especially the liabilities, which individuals, families and groups may suffer.

More light is shed upon housing and its relationship to social and government roles by referring to the idea of *merit goods*, an idea elaborated by Head [13] and other modern theorists in public finance. The idea of merit goods is relevant to important spheres of social policy where goods or services are provided directly in-kind, rather than simply (indirectly) by means of social cash income. This is particularly relevant to health, education, libraries and housing.

Merit goods arguments involve critical scrutinies of individual-based choice and, sometimes, the substitution of this for social preference. The case for such substitution is not meant to be a general open-ended one for any sort of government role. It is limited to a basis where: (1) the knowledge of individuals is significantly imperfect, (2) the nature of the good or service in question is very complicated, (3) individuals' choices are distorted by the complexity and the diffuse 'externality' nature of some of the benefits, and (4) income distributional and poverty problems of a very special sort are present. As we have already seen, in housing some of the benefits are indirect, delayed and not readily amenable to accurate assessment among the general population. This problem is compounded in poor neighbourhoods where the opportunities which would otherwise exist from good urban services, are unavailable or undeveloped. The distribution of merit goods and access to them is important *per se*, beyond considerations of only a cash-income distribution.

These discussions point to the general need to co-ordinate housing, urban and social policies. This need to co-ordinate policies has come to the centre of modern issues in housing policy. For example, in Britain the gaps and the administrative separatism between housing and social services have been the objects of critical review by the Morris Committee. [14] The Central Policy Review Staff has reported upon the desirability of co-ordination in income maintenance, social services, health, education and training, employment, and urban and housing policy developments. [15] The idea of co-ordination is one of the key themes in this present study.

Jackson's perspectives on poverty and the merit goods arguments are clearly useful for understanding the widening scope and content of a modern social administration of housing. He draws attention especially to the capacity to pay for housing, the accessibility to a wide range of urban services and to employment opportunities, and social planning in urban and regional development. Each of these social concerns has influenced modern policy development in housing, and a brief reference to recent initiatives in Britain will highlight this.

Britain and other modern democratic countries have re-considered policies on rents and housing subsidies, especially in their relation-ship to capacity to pay. One indication of this is the introduction of a new form of *consumer* subsidy, the *housing allowance*. Housing allowances were introduced into Britain in 1972; they ease the capacity to pay problem among low-income groups and they give these groups wider choices than the traditional production subsidies which are tied to dwellings rather than to people and their capacity to pay. Looking at the wider social matters in the urban and regional

5

environment, we note that the effect of some urban processes and policies has been to distance some vulnerable groups from employment, to accentuate social segregation, and to undermine rather than to develop a sense of community. The concern to change these conditions in Britain has been recently reflected in official reports on older urban areas [16] and on race relations. [17] Other countries have also given attention to inner-urban problems and social segregation. Professional interest in social planning among social workers has revived during the last decade following critical sociological studies by Broady [18] and Gans. [19] These authors advocated the idea of social planning for new community development - the identification, planning and provision of services in social development, education, health, recreation and so on. In Britain this social planning entered into central policy significance in 1967, [20] and other countries have similarly acknowledged the growing significance of social development in urban and regional planning.

Sometimes social issues in housing are conceived, researched and given policy relevance from rather narrow viewpoints. It is necessary, therefore, to set down a note of caution and some discussion on the way housing-related social problems can be misconceived and referred to 'second order' rather than 'primary' explanations. Two examples, one from the United States and the other from Britain will illustrate the point.

In the United States during the 1960s some social research gave public housing a bad reputation by reason of its excessive social segregation, the bureaucratic characteristic of its management, and its identification as a residual repository for poor, black, welfare families. This led to a strong and popular case against public housing *per se*, and support for rent supplement and other schemes which were seen as alternatives to public housing. However, following experience with alternative programmes and a fuller understanding of the nature of housing, a more circumspect attitude began to develop in the 1970s. Now, it is evident that the alternatives contained their own distinctive economic and administrative problems, and the bad characteristics of public housing could be primarily explained by the economic, financial and policy framework within which it was administered. As this study will show, there are alternative and better ways of organising public housing, and some countries effectively express social aims in housing through more varied methods than those which are used in American public housing. Thus, general arguments against public housing *per se* are not particularly useful for policy purposes; what are needed are broader views and evaluations of the conditions under which public housing is administered.

In Britain, homelessness has emerged as a key social problem and it has attracted considerable research effort [21] and agitation. Sometimes it was argued that the problem would disappear if local government officials did not stigmatise the homeless, and if Parliament assigned the statutory responsibilities to local governments' housing functions rather than to their social services. However, a more adequate explanation for the causes of homelessness in Britain can be found in Hallett's comparative study of British and West German policies in rental housing. [22] British policy makers have undermined the supply of private rental housing, despite a strong demand for this housing in London and other cities. Furthermore, for a whole variety of basic economic and administrative reasons which are reviewed in Chapter 5, British public housing (inevitably) raises more expectations than it can fulfil. Under a different policy and resourcing framework, West Germany does not have homelessness in the sense which Britain experiences. Again, we can see that in housing, social problems are more adequately interpreted from the basis of a broadly-conceived set of economic, political and administrative factors.

Housing and its policy issues will be differently perceived according to the relative importance given to different objectives. Reciprocally, housing objectives will tend to be chosen and acted on according to the historical legacy of policies and administrative instruments. For Britain in particular, but also for other countries, this means that in its broadest context housing will often be viewed in *sectors* - the owner-occupier, the public housing and the private rental sectors. We shall now briefly examine the sectoral interpretation of the housing system.

HOUSING SECTORS

Housing analysts, and particularly British analysts, view the housing system in terms of complex, stratified and segregated sectors. Murie and his co-authors [23] have noted that British public policy in housing has operated along *tenure* lines via the divisions in the financing instruments and the direct form of government involvement in building, allocation and managing the public housing sector in its own right. From the sectoral perspective, it is possible to examine various social and economic aspects of housing. For example, patterns of mobility vary from sector to sector, some sectors are typically occupied by specific socio-economic groups, and some social problems are concentrated within sectors. Much recent social research in British housing and policy developments (e.g., rent regulations) have been conceived and explained from sectoral perspectives.

Choice, self-fulfilment and security of tenure are related to sectoral conditions; and tenure, in particular, has importance as a housing topic in its own right. Tenure has long-term economic consequences for households and this influences their relativities in income, wealth and life-cycle opportunities in housing and in social functioning. These consequences have wide ramifications in the social justice and equity aspects of housing policies, and especially in circumstances where it can be argued that the barriers to access among some housing sectors accentuate inequalities of income and wealth. Tenure-related equity in housing has become a key issue in most modern democracies, though, as we shall see, Norway and other European democracies achieve a greater general choice in tenure, dwelling type and participation in housing management than Britain and other countries which have created major separatism between owner-occupier, public and private rental housing.

One problem arising from the deeply entrenched separatism represented in housing sectors is the limitation on choice and opportunity. As Murie and his co-authors have shown, mobility among housing sectors in Britain takes on a *shuffling* characteristic, and within some sectors where many modern housing problems exist, the range of choice is limited indeed. All of this means that when we discuss marginal policy adjustments in housing and their impact upon housing opportunity, we should focus on the conditions of the sub-sector or the sub-market in which a given social group is housed. Although relative sectoral rigidity is an important characteristic of British housing, some changes do occur in the long term, and our understanding of the housing system is deepened by examining these factors which produce the changes.

For the household, the choice of tenure depends upon its economic circumstances, its stage in the life-cycle, its preferences, the relative cost of different tenures, and access to loan funds. Access to owner-occupier tenure normally depends upon obtaining mortgage loans, and this in turn will depend upon the credit worthiness of the household and its capacity to earn. Clearly, the middle and higher-income households and those in regular employment will find it easier than low-income families to enter this tenure. In fact, from the *historical* perspective, private rental housing and its conditions of tenure can be regarded as an investor's means of minimising his/her risks. For the working classes, employment was insecure, the ease of mobility was important in taking up employment opportunities as periodic booms and slumps altered these opportunities, and landlords could use eviction as a means of getting *market* rents. In modern times, tenants' rights and security are sometimes protected in legislation. These general conditions governing access to different tenures, and the relative credit worthiness of households largely explain the predominance of middle and higher-income groups in owner-occupier tenure. As we shall see in the discussions in Chapters 3, 4 and 6, tenure-related equity is a significant issue in modern policy development. Some of the historical justifications for public housing were in providing low-cost accommodation with security of tenure and better standards than most private rental housing. However, like other economic goods, public housing has been scarce, but unlike market goods it has been allocated on the basis of administrative and social criteria to establish priorities and conditions of access. Under the conditions prevailing in British public housing, it has been mainly used by young working-class households which have left the private rental sector and then spent much of their life in this tenure.

The private rental sector has experienced economic and management problems. For various historical reasons some sub-sectors have been subject to rent control and rent regulation policies which have cut back their economic **viability**. The loss of the mobile young to other sectors has left the poorer, the aged and racial minorities in significant parts of older urban housing, with the result that economic and other problems have been aggravated. Also, landlords tend to operate on a small scale with little incentive or motivation to achieve adequate standards of maintenance and improvement. In those cities and regions where housing demand has pressed hardest, significant portions of the private rental stock have been sold into owner-occupier tenure, and its consequent reduction in supply has added to the housing stress among low-income groups.

The sectoral view of housing thus illuminates some of Britain's housing problems. These problems give added significance to changes in the relative composition of different tenures during the last 25 years. The private rental sector has declined from 52 per cent of the stock to 15 per cent, whereas the owner-occupier sector has increased from 31 per cent to 55 per cent and public housing from 17 per cent to 30 per cent.

In other countries, the sectoral interpretation of housing issues is
also useful, but the specific issues vary.   For example, in Sweden and
The Netherlands a key concern in the 1970s has been the rapid expansion
of the owner-occupier sector with some attendant problems of rapidly
rising costs and tendencies towards social segregation.   These
countries are now experiencing affluence and a widening of opportunities
in housing which had hitherto expressed limited choice by reason of
chronic shortages and policy instruments which ran in favour of mass
rental housing.   Thus, although the sectoral interpretation of current
housing problems is generally useful, we should not regard those issues
which are significant concerns in Britain as common to other countries.
Policy instruments, housing finance and administration have been
developed differently in other countries.   These points will be taken
up in subsequent chapters, and tenure is reviewed critically from an
analytical perspective in Chapter 3.

HOUSING, INFLATION AND ECONOMIC GROWTH [24]

Inflation has various impacts upon housing, primarily through the
escalation of interest rates and in the increases in construction costs.
When housing construction is relatively labour intensive, the increases
in construction costs can be expected to outstrip the general price
index.   More significantly, the interest rate burden raises the
barriers to access in home ownership, it places pressure on some parts
of public expenditure (including housing subsidies), and it imposes
some flow-of-funds problems among financial intermediaries which provide
housing loans.   All of these difficulties have concerned policy-makers
during the recent period of severe inflation.   These difficulties have
coincided with other social and economic changes which impinge upon the
general prospects for economic growth, and particularly upon the housing
industry.   In the two decades 1950-1970 housing policies centred around
the need to increase the rate of new building to overcome chronic
shortages in the wake of wartime conditions and rapid urbanisation, but
by the mid-1970s the major shortages had been overcome and the housing
industry then had to face the prospect of lower or stable outputs and a
re-ordering of emphasis towards maintaining and managing the existing
stock.   These changes occurred at a time when there were more general
problems of slower economic growth during the 1970s and higher levels of
unemployment together with inflation.

   British experience with inflation in housing is revealed in the
following statistics. [25]   Whereas in the years 1963-1972, the cost of
typical new private housing was 3.25 greater than average annual manual
earnings and 2.55 greater than non-manual earnings, in 1973 the ratios
had risen respectively to 3.88 and 3.30.   Also, the increase in interest
rates heightened the difficulties with the result that the net payment
among average new borrowers increased from 12 per cent to 17.3 per cent
of income from 1967 to 1973, and owner-occupier housing was becoming
accessible only to high-income or double-income households.   The
deposit for first-time average-income buyers increased from 55 per cent
to 66 per cent of their annual incomes.   Or, to take another perspective, under the conventional sort of mortgaging arrangements, an escalation of interest rates from 6 per cent to 11 per cent reduces the
borrowing power from 3.3 of annual income to only 2.1.   These sort of
factors lead to a clamour for action to make housing more accessible to
first-time buyers.

The key difficulties spring from the escalation of interest rates. Interest rates mainly rise to compensate savers for the depreciation in the value of the loans, but interest rates do not adjust precisely to maintain real values of the loans because future rates of inflation are uncertain. From the borrowers' viewpoint, under the *credit foncier* type of mortgage instrument (i.e., the typical *fixed* instalment loan), the cost of finance is very high, thereby raising the barriers to entry and eliminating all but high-income households. Under these circumstances, some housing economists and policy-makers have sought reforms to housing finance in the form of low-start deferred payments schemes (and similar variants) to ease the burden of repayments in the early years. These kind of schemes are reviewed critically in Chapter 4.

Essentially, inflationary interest rates disturb the balance of relative equity and the risk bearing among savers, borrowers and financial intermediaries. The gainers are those who borrow before severe inflation takes hold and repay their loans at depreciated values; and the losers are savers, new borrowers, and those potential borrowers who are precluded from taking up loans because the costs are too high. Gaining and losing can also be related to an inflationary cycle. Early speculative gains may occur, but later speculation is cut off by the price increases which speculation induces and by rising interest rates. Thus, an inflation can bear housing costs strongly upwards on a spiral which then hits a ceiling and is followed by a rapidly slackening demand and unemployment in the construction industry.

Inflation also disturbs the relative costs of owner-occupier and private rental housing. [26] When inflation is absent and imputed rental values of owner-occupied housing are not taxed, then owner-occupier tenure is cheaper because the imputed rents are not taxed whereas renters' incomes are fully taxed. However, with the advent of high rates of inflation, capital gains become more significant and this can, theoretically, lower the cost of providing rental housing because investors can get some of their return from the capital gains and not just from the anticipated rents. This effect in favour of renting is compounded if interest rates, although rising, do not fully compensate for the depreciation in the value of loans. All of these theoretical consequences will be significant to the extent that they are empirically valid, and for their implications in policy. They will have greater general policy relevance in those countries which maintain a significant *market* rental sector.

It can be shown that if inflation disturbs the relative cost of owner-occupier and private rental tenures in the ways argued above, then some frequently advocated policies need to be reconsidered. For example, housing reformers often advocate the taxation of imputed rent on owner-occupier housing in order to neutralise its economic advantages. However, as we have seen, under inflation the relative cost advantage on new construction is likely to run in favour of private rental tenure. Consequently, the taxation of imputed rent in owner-occupier housing would add further cost disadvantages to that tenure. Now looking at private rental tenure, we have noted that inflation produces high capital gains which induce increases in new construction. This relative advantage can be erased by linking loan repayments to the general price index. In conclusion, if policy-makers are concerned with general tenure-related equity, then the taxation of imputed rent

and the indexation of loans should be considered simultaneously.
Also, these policy issues are made more complicated when non-market
rental sectors (e.g., public housing) are brought into review. The
tenants in new houses in these sectors have often been protected from
the full impacts of inflation by the device of pooling total revenues
and costs in consolidated accounts and cross-subsidising the costs
among older and more recently constructed housing. [27]

Governments will get caught up in all these housing-related aspects
of inflation, and the extent of their involvement will be diverse and
full of conflict. On one hand, inflation will raise barriers to
access, leading to a clamour for action to make housing available for
first-time buyers. Also, the government's assistance programmes will
meet pressures of higher cost. On the other hand, however, governments
will have responsibilities for managing the overall economy. These
conditions are likely to lead to a policy of cutting public expenditure
(including housing subsidies) and the further raising of interest rates.
The conflict is clear, but the issue of reconciling inflation, access to
housing and the low-income housing problem will create a call for some
policy review. In fact, during the severe inflation of the 1970s, the
situation forced some governments into making an interesting set of
co-ordinated reforms in housing subsidies, finance and resources.
These are discussed in Chapter 4.

As was mentioned, the recent problems precipitated by inflation have
coincided with a slowing down of general economic growth and with the
need to re-order priorities in housing. Until recently, the dominant
policy emphasis in housing was geared to setting target levels of
output to overcome chronic shortages. Looking at Britain, it is
significant that in 1951 there were 750,000 more households than
dwellings, whereas by 1976 the number of dwellings exceeded the number
of households by 500,000. [28] Similar patterns have emerged in other
modern democracies generally, with deep implications for the housing
industry and for policy. In the period 1950-1970, housing in the
modern democracies has accounted for between 5 per cent and 8 per cent
of national income, and in the range of 20 per cent to 25 per cent of
fixed capital formation. All the present indicators suggest that
housing will be a declining sector with ramifications for employment,
trade, and investment in other sectors which supply equipment and
resources for housing and home-making.

The changing nature of the housing sector has qualitative as well as
quantitative implications. Earlier concerns were for getting 'a roof
over the head', whereas modern housing demands extend to improving the
range and quality of urban services, including shopping, transport,
educational, health, social and recreational services. Interest in
urban renewal has revived, but with an emphasis upon modernising older
housing and neighbourhoods (i.e., rehabilitation) rather than on
clearance and redevelopment. Other issues coming into modern
prominence include raising the quality of housing management services in
rental housing, and deepening the involvement with the many-sided
aspects of social concerns in housing. All of these changes point
towards the need to develop new skills in housing administration.
Finally, mention should be made of the fact that as some countries (e.g.,
Sweden) overcome acute shortages, some transitional problems spring up.
In Sweden, this is reflected in the release of a pent-up demand for
owner-occupier tenure and houses with gardens; under the era of

shortages, policies and production ran in favour of rental flats in mass project housing. The changing social and economic conditions alter the framework within which housing choices are made, and for Sweden and other European democracies this means that choice is loosening and widening for some groups, with transitional pressures showing up in some sectors.

A LONG-TERM VIEW OF HOUSING AND URBAN CHANGE

Some useful insights can be obtained by taking a long-term view of housing change and urbanisation. The relationship between the time-distance costs of travel and incomes provides a key source for explaining urbanisation. In early industrial society, the time-distance costs of travel to work were high relative to wages, and most workers had to live in high-density living areas within walking distance of work. With the passing of time, improvements in urban transport and increases in incomes enabled the more affluent groups to live further from work. This created suburbanisation and in the twentieth century access to suburbia has spread down the income range, but large cities with some low-income groups living near the city centres indicate the historical patterns. However, modern manufacturing industry, and particularly some higher growth industries, have been suburbanising, thus disturbing some of the traditional relationships between residence and the relative proximity of various social groups to sources of employment. These urbanisation processes have left their distinctive policy issues and problems in housing history.

Although urban forms are shaped variously according to the way housing and land are allocated (see the discussions in Chapter 7) we can identify some general long-term tendencies where scope is given to private choices. In the context of private choice, suburbanisation partly represents a trend towards households consuming more housing and land space compared with higher-density living in early industrial society. Suburbia provides cheaper land compared with the more intensively used inner-urban land. The suburbanisation process exerts a downward pressure on the relative long-term price of urban land, but with some qualification in shorter term periods when conflicts between market and government regulatory instruments can push up the relative price of urban land. In large rapidly growing cities the suburbanisa- tion process can lead to expansive social segregation.

It was the extreme economic and social pressures of densely concentrated urban slums in the nineteenth century which pushed up the rent-income burdens and which made slums into a social cause, eventually leading to deeper government involvements with housing. Although twentieth-century suburbanisation reflects increasing affluence and a contrast with historical slum tenements, the modern process contains its own distinctive social and economic problems. Suburbanisation tends to select young mobile households, separate them from their earlier social and community ties, and settle them in socially homogeneous areas which often lack adequate urban facilities and a sense of community. By contrast, older areas have established facilities and some useful social interaction, except in those which are characterised with excessive transience. The problems in older areas tend to revolve around poverty, obsolescence and getting access to public finance to improve urban services, whereas the problems in suburbia are those of establishing

community development, making urban services conveniently accessible in
their locational respects, and achieving some social diversity. Again,
we can see that housing needs to be understood in its relationships to
history, to the development of social policies, to urban change, to
land development policies and to urban administration.

ALLOCATIONAL ISSUES IN HOUSING

In the widest sense, allocational issues in modern housing policies
include the resourcing of the dwelling, the services which the dwelling
provides (see below), urban services, land development, urban renewal,
some social policies, and some urban administration. The way
allocational issues are perceived and classified will vary with social
and economic change, and with new conceptualisations in housing. For
example, some earlier reference was made to the contrast between past
concerns which centred upon the need to increase the rate of new
building, in contrast to the modern emphasis upon managing the existing
stock.   Accordingly Isler [29] makes out a case for distinguishing
three categories in the allocation of resources to housing: (1) to the
capital cost of the dwelling, (2) to the costs of providing *housing
services* (extensions and alterations; utilities; fittings in bathrooms,
laundries, kitchens and storage areas; and heating and insulation), and
(3) to neighbourhood services. Accounting for housing resources in
these classifications can clearly be useful for managing existing
dwellings, estates and urban servicing. Also, these categories are
relevant for reviewing the impacts of rent policies and housing
allowances.

  Some long-standing dilemmas in allocating housing resources revolve
around the relationships between the market and public finance.
Modern democratic societies mix market and government mechanisms in
allocations to housing. As will be evident from the discussions
below, both the private and the public sectors have social and economic
justifications and their distinctive roles in housing, but problems
arise in achieving balance and co-ordination between them. In
continental Europe, there has been much thought and some reform in this
during the last decade or so, and in the United States some recent
research programmes have been deeply involved in technical and
analytical work on the relation between public policy and its impacts
upon housing markets.

  A greater role for the market mechanism has the advantage of
signalling where the allocation of resources to housing, among competing
uses, shall cease. The market can be used as an indicator of
preferences and purchasing power. It will determine a cut-off point
more clearly than some forms of subsidisation, which have been used in
European countries and in Australia to overcome housing shortages
caused by the virtual cessation of building in wartime, the rapid
decline in building during severe economic depressions and the rapid
rate of household formation through migration and natural population
increases. Though these shortages can be overcome by subsidisation, it
can ironically create its own 'shortages'. Because of social need,
subsidised housing has been provided at a lower consumer price than
non-subsidised housing [30] and sometimes the price difference is
substantial. Under such circumstances there is a continuing excess
demand for attractively priced housing. In other words, there is a

housing shortage.

On the other hand, inherent market processes often conceal results which are socially, politically or economically unacceptable. Some sections of the housing stock have seen contagious diseases associated with dirty environments. Elimination of these inhuman and socially costly [31] conditions has been a prime aim of housing reformers. These references are historical rather than modern, but reconciling the goal of providing standard housing to all households, with the low-income group's ability to pay, has both historical and modern relevance. Some of the thrust of housing reform has been against high rent for sub-standard housing. When the economy grows and develops, there are changes in social and political attitudes to what constitutes standard housing and satisfactory urban environments. Affluence and social and political sophistication have widened housing aspirations towards environmentally-related amenities.

The foregoing leads us to accept the mixed roles of the market and government in modern democratic societies, a combination which raises questions on the more specific roles of the private and public sectors and their relationship. Our preliminary examination of the allocational and distributional issues places some analytical perspectives on the merits of market and governmental initiatives in housing. Also raised is the question of whether the advantages of the two parts of housing resources might combine and blend. In continental Europe this is being attempted in new rental and subsidisation policies which create a *para-market* instrument. This is a blended market subsidy achieving tighter control in public expenditure and greater selectivity in placing assistance with groups in housing need. This is fully discussed in Chapter 4.

THE POLICY CONTEXT

In summary, the policy-related issues in modern housing are:

- The widespread aspirations for self-fulfilment; a matter connected to housing choice, tenure, housing history and housing theory.

- The endemic problem of low-income access to housing, presently more complex because of social change, urbanisation and outdated policies in subsidisation, resourcing and organisation.

- The requirement for better general relationships among housing, urban and social policies.

- The need for an overhaul of housing finance to produce better co-ordination, thus enabling households to pursue their aspirations for self-fulfilment.

- The need to adjust to, and learn from the consequences of the severe inflation in the 1970s.

To provide a basis for understanding these issues and developing policies to deal with them, this study will concentrate a good deal of its attention on the following questions:

1. What are the most suitable forms of providing housing
    assistance?   To what extent can social income be
    relied upon to ensure an adequate standard of accommodation?
    How much social housing should be built and organised among
    government, non-profit housing associations, and private
    enterprise?

2. How effective and well-directed are existing programmes of
    housing assistance?   What are their effects upon the
    distribution of income and wealth?

3. How could housing policies be better co-ordinated with
    environmental and social development policies, and with
    the provision of infrastructure?

4. What institutional arrangements and organisation are
    appropriate for administering comprehensiveness in
    housing?   What is the role of localisation, regionalisation,
    and centralisation in housing?   What is the role of
    the community, and private enterprise?   What methods
    of consultation should be adopted?

These questions can be illuminated by historical, comparative and
analytical search, to end up with a study featuring policy-relevant
issues within a modern interpretation of housing.

APPROACH AND SCOPE

This work is a combination of historical, comparative and analytical
studies.   The purpose is not to give comprehensive treatment to each,
nor to each country discussed.   Rather, they are used selectively for
interpretative and policy-related purposes.   Besides the discussion of
housing the method also allows some more general comparison of the
different societies and their adaptation and inventiveness to social
and economic change.   Some perform better than others.   It will be
easy for readers to decide where performance is better.   The author
has formed his own judgements, which have an implicit relevance
throughout the writing, and are introduced deliberately.

The study looks selectively at housing policy developments in Britain,
Australia, West Germany, The Netherlands, Norway, Sweden and the United
States.   Britain is taken as the benchmark for comparative evaluation.
This collection represents three federal countries - Australia, West
Germany and the United States.   West German federalism contrasts with
Australian and American patterns, with very definite implications for
housing reform.   Britain and Australia have been linked in the
Commonwealth, and housing ideas have flowed from the former to the
latter, which has experienced urban problems and reforms which will be
educationally useful for other places.   Continental Europeans are more
aware of ideas and policies in the English-speaking world than vice-
versa.   This is unfortunate because European democracies generally
have more progressive housing policies.   Sweden, Norway and The
Netherlands are renowned for well-developed welfare state policies.
The United States is comparatively *laissez faire*, but with a depth of

technical and analytical research on some key policy issues. Britain,
Australia and the United States have some interesting differences in the
way they have developed public housing, and the other countries offer
major contrasts with these in the way they have given expression to
social goals in housing policy. Britain has been a major source of
ideas in town planning, and Sweden has a reputation for its practical
expression of land development policies. Norway shows direct,
uncomplicated and relatively less bureaucratic approaches to housing
finance and administration, which give it policies that are probably
the most effective among the modern democracies.

It was asserted above that housing policies in modern democratic
societies require a simultaneous solution to problems of social equity,
programming, differentiated finance for production and consumption, and
an urban and regional network with complex relationships between
housing and other physical, social and economic services. The statement is not intended to lure anyone into thinking that harmony can be
achieved among all these requirements. There will be conflicts. The
various parts are connected to other elements, themselves experiencing
social, economic and political change. Essentially, the statement is
presented to indicate the scope of this study, and of modern housing
policy.

NOTES

[1] D.V.Donnison, *The Government of Housing*, Penguin, Harmondsworth,
1967.
[2] In the United States, public housing programmes have been
controlled by severe means tests, access being restricted to some of
the poorest classes. In Britain and Australia, the intent (and
sometimes the controls) has been to provide public housing to the
working classes, but the programmes have been less rigid. By contrast
Norway and Sweden provide assistances aimed at meeting general
community housing as well as the special needs of the aged, the
handicapped and so on.
[3] This comparison between 'private' and 'public' aspects of housing
has some ambiguity in the purest economic sense. In fact, the
'private' aspects of housing are influenced by legislation and
regulations which write social considerations into building standards
(see Chapter 3). The comparison is nevertheless useful for getting
some preliminary conceptualisation of housing.
[4] Richardson uses an 'environmental' preference or 'behavioural'
theory to explain variations in house prices and the factors which
enter into locational choice. See H.W.Richardson, J.Vipond, and
R.A.Furbey, 'Determinants of Urban House Prices', *Urban Studies*, June
1974, pp.189-99.
[5] Wilkinson uses factor analysis to extract the component mix of
services and benefits which are obtained from housing. See
R.K.Wilkinson, 'House Prices and the Measurement of Externalities',
Economic Journal, March 1973, pp.72-86.
[6] This conceptualisation of housing can be extended to examine
issues involved in housing choice and in formulating public policy in
urban renewal and environmental planning. See M.Whitbread and H.Bird,
'Rent, Surplus and the Evaluation of Urban Environments', *Regional
Studies*, Vol.7, 1973, pp.193-223.
[7] Localisation, regionalisation and centralisation are processes of

developing public policy and administration at various levels of government. This is discussed more fully in Chapter 9.

[8] See R.K.Wilkinson, 'Economic Aspects of Low-Income Housing Policy in the Urban Economy', *International Journal of Social Economics*, Vol.2, 1975, pp.74-81.
[9] This topic is discussed more fully in a different context in Chapter 3.
[10] In most democracies, the effective demand for upper-income housing is stimulated by tax and subsidy incentives. This point is taken up in later chapters. Though they are not discussed by Wilkinson, there are some circumstances in which housing in low-income areas can yield higher returns than upper-income housing. Again, we can accept Wilkinson's arguments so far as the assumptions on which they are based are actually present in modern housing sub-markets.
[11] M.Castells, 'Is There an Urban Sociology?', and 'Theory and Ideology in Urban Sociology', in G.V.Pickvance (ed), *Urban Sociology: Critical Essays*, Tavistock, London, 1976.
[12] D.Jackson, *Poverty*, MacMillan, London, 1972.
[13] J.G.Head, *Public Goods and Public Welfare*, Duke University Press, Durham, North Carolina, 1974.
[14] Scottish Development Department, *Housing and Social Work: A Joint Approach*, (Morris), HMSO, Edinburgh, 1975.
[15] Central Policy Review Staff, *A Joint Framework for Social Policies*, HMSO, London, 1975.
[16] Department of the Environment, *Inner Area Studies*, HMSO, London, 1977
[17] *Race Relations and Housing*, Cmnd. 6232, HMSO, London, 1975.
[18] M.Broady, *Planning for People*, Bedford Square Press, London, 1968.
[19] H.J.Gans, *People and Plans*, Penguin, Harmondsworth, 1972.
[20] Ministry of Housing and Local Government, *The Needs of New Communities*, HMSO, London, 1967.
[21] See B.Glastonbury, *Homeless Near a Thousand Homes*, George Allen and Unwin, London, 1971, and J.Greve, *Homeless in London*, Scottish Academic Press, Edinburgh, 1971.
[22] G.Hallett, *Housing and Land Policies in West Germany and Britain*, MacMillan, London, 1977.
[23] A.Murie, P.Niner and C.Watson, *Housing Policy and the Housing System*, George Allen and Unwin, London, 1976.
[24] Historically, deflation has had significant policy impacts in housing. Governments have been dragged into housing by the partial collapse of housing and housing finance markets, by social agitation on crowding and worsening conditions in the slums, and by widespread foreclosures on mortgages. The discussions in Chapter 5 give more historical details of these circumstances.
[25] More detail is given in: *Housing Policy: A Consultative Document*, Cmnd. 6851, HMSO, London, 1977 and G.A.Hughes, *Inflation and Housing* The Housing Research Foundation, London, 1974.
[26] This topic is discussed in greater detail by: G.Bethune, *Urban Home-ownership in Australia*, unpublished PhD thesis, Australian National University, 1977.
[27] See Housing Policy: A Consultative Document, *op. cit.* (1977).
[28] See Housing Policy: A Consultative Document, *op. cit.* (1977).
[29] M.L.Isler, *Thinking About Housing: A Policy Research Agenda*, Urban Institute, Washington D.C., 1970.
[30] As we shall see, most modern housing is subsidised in one way or another. This point is taken up in Chapter 4.
[31] The term *social cost* is being used imprecisely in social science

literature.   In this book, a social cost means that there is an adverse
economic externality present (see the earlier discussion) which can, in
principle, be costed and accounted.   In practice, it is not always
easy to do this.

REFERENCES (SELECTED)

Donnison, D.V., *The Government of Housing*, Penguin, Harmondsworth, 1967.

Harvey, D., *Social Justice and the City*, Arnold, London, 1973.

Head, J.G., *Public Goods and the Public Sector*, Duke University Press,
    Durham, North Carolina, 1974.

Jackson, D., *Poverty*, MacMillan, London, 1972.

Murie, A., Niner, P., and Watson, C., *Housing Policy and the Housing
    System*, George Allen and Unwin, London, 1976.

Whitbread, M., and Bird, H., 'Rent, Surplus and the Evaluation of Urban
    Environments', *Regional Studies*, Vol.7, 1973, pp.193-223.

Wilkinson, R.K., 'House Prices and the Measurement of Externalities',
    Economic Journal, March 1973, pp.72-86.

2 Housing policy, economic theory, social theory and political theory

This and the two following chapters reflect upon the general welfare purposes of housing policy, and our ways of thinking about them. This chapter is about social and economic theory and housing. The next is about past and present issues in social housing policy. Chapter 4 then outlines the development of a modern 'social economics of housing'.

We begin with the relationship between housing policy and the more general first-order principles in economic, social and political theories. Most modern discussion on housing policies implicitly makes theoretical assumptions about society. Some of the more interesting and creative policy developments have emerged from periods, places and situations where pragmatic urgencies provoked explicit theoretical reasoning in a general ferment of ideas. The discussions here will look at some of these situations. The chapter examines the general issues in historical context, reviews general theory and its relationship to housing type, tenure and town planning practice, and introduces ideas of equity and equality - two concepts which feature strongly in modern policy development.

UTILITARIANISM AND RICARDIAN ECONOMICS

The first period of housing reform in industrial Britain was linked to Utilitarian political theory and Ricardian economics. Many of the theoretical ideas which influenced housing policies can be approached by referring to Edwin Chadwick's role. In his early career, Chadwick (1800-1890) had been associated with Jeremy Bentham (1748-1821), the author and advocate of Utilitarianism, which had a reformist thrust. It was directed to a calculus of balancing 'pain' and 'pleasure' at the margin, and viewed government as a means of fulfilling human needs. In its application to government and the social order, Utilitarianism sought institutional arrangements whereby the 'greatest good was enjoyed by the greatest number'. Chadwick applied Utilitarian principles to Poor Law reform and to the reform of housing and urban administration.

Some features of Utilitarianism are close to the development of economic thought, which later adopted utility as a basis for explaining the derivation of economic value. Also, the notion of balancing pain and pleasure at the margin was relevant to considerations of marginal analysis, economic efficiency and cost-benefit comparisons. The formal development of economic cost-benefit analysis was not accomplished until 1940-1970, but given Chadwick's commitment to Utilitarianism, it is not surprising that he applied a general cost-benefit apparatus to housing and public health reforms in 1828-1854. In his *Report on the Sanitary Condition of the Labouring Population of Great Britain* (1842), Chadwick used this to argue that to reduce sickness and premature death resulting from insanitary housing, would confer benefits to society in terms of humanitarianism and greater economic productivity.

19

Chadwick synthesised Utilitarianism with some elements of Ricardian economics. Ricardo (1772-1823) was acknowledged as the leading or most relevant economist of his age, as a result of his professional contributions and his conclusions, which fitted the aspirations of the new class of industrial capitalists. Ricardian economics supported private enterprise industrial capitalism against the inheritance of landed wealth. The historically significant clash of classes in the first half of the nineteenth century was between industrial 'free trade' capital and the 'protected' landed wealth owned by the rural aristocracy. A generation later (with some overlap), social writers discovered other class-based significance in Ricardo's writings.

Ricardo used conceptual categories of 'land', 'labour', and 'capital' to explain economic value, the economic distribution of income and the course of long-term economic development. Under Adam Smith's influence, some parts of Ricardo's writing emphasised harmony, equilibrium and mutual consistencies between sectors of the economy which, if left to the market (*laissez faire*), would yield optimal dividends. Other parts of his writings emphasise class conflict and inherent contradictions in capitalism. However, the historical course of British society mainly selected the harmony, equilibrium and *laissez faire* characteristics of Ricardian economics. [1] By integrating Ricardian economics with Utilitarianism, Chadwick influenced the pattern of development in social, housing and urban policies (this is detailed further in Chapter 3).

Chadwick's approach to housing and urban policies was restricted to solving the disease or sanitary problem. He saw no need to use public funds to relieve overcrowding and high rents in working-class housing of rapidly growing industrial cities. Chadwick reasoned that any disease attributable to insanitary housing and filthy environments was a source of social stress and social costs. Society could reap substantial dividends by devising a public financial and administrative solution to the sanitation problem. Disease was a major cause of insecurity among the industrialised working class. Life itself was at risk; there was also the economic threat of sickness causing people to fall out of work. In another form, the economic benefits to society of improved sanitation, would be capitalised into the values of urban housing. The costs of the improvements (drains and sewers) could be met from a tax on property.

However, Chadwick excluded other possibilities for improving the housing of the working class and rejected any notion that improved housing standards could, or should, be provided by public subsidy or by limited-profit 'model dwelling companies'. Two of Chadwick's contemporaries in social reform, Ashley and Southward Smith, founded the Society for the Improvement of the Conditions of the Labouring Classes, a 'model dwelling company' based on the idea that philanthropic motivations might attract capital to be used to construct low-rental standard housing. Chadwick was invited to assist with the development of the Society, but refused to have anything to do with an idea which implied that rents and returns should be out of line with Ricardian principles.

Ricardian themes have endured in housing policies. The Ricardian argument viewed expenditure on housing as forgone industrial or commercial investment. The latter was justified only when the return exceeded the rate of interest reflecting the cost of borrowing. The more visible nature of the return from these latter forms of investment induced a bias against 'non-productive' investment in social housing. However, as we shall see, (in Chapter 3) it can be argued that economics has inadequately accounted for productivity in housing. The way these returns are accounted in economic theory, depends on how economics defines its concepts and unites them in theoretical explanation.

Utilitarianism has left a deep influence in modern democratic societies. It is a goal-based theory dependent upon the calculation of individual self-interests to derive the greatest margin between inconveniences (costs or disutilities) and benefits (satisfactions, hedonistic happiness, economic product). Its principal author, Bentham, used it to advocate radical reform, but he set it apart from the more moral characteristics of some social contract and natural law theories which were dominant in pre-industrial society. Economic theorists had adopted the amoral characteristic of Utilitarianism and combined it with notions of harmony and equilibrium in natural law theory. As Myrdal has shown [2], this has led mainstream economic theorists to project Utilitarianism from early industrial to twentieth-century society, and in the process to absorb some dilemmas and some distortions in the relationship of economics to ethics and to policy. The basic problem with Utilitarianism as political and economic doctrine is that it tends to empty out ethics, social rights and conflicts of interest. In a sense, the development of housing policy as a welfare state right limits Utilitarianism, although Chadwick did not see it this way. Others did, including Conservative idealists such as Lord Shaftesbury, T.H. Green and other advocates of moral liberalism, and the intellectual authors of theoretical Social Democracy.

CONSERVATIVE IDEALISM

Conservative idealists contributed ideas and some useful practices in housing reform, and these can be identified in the life and career of Ashley (1801-1885) who succeeded to the title Earl of Shaftesbury in 1851 and became a notable social reformer and parliamentarian. Religious evangelism and philanthropy were the motivations for Shaftesbury's activities in educational, industrial and housing reforms. The philanthropic tradition grew in the eighteenth century and took on anti-slavery, temperance and Sunday School causes. It flourished where it could draw upon a humanitarian disposition with access to private fortunes or to the subscriptions from aristocrats and businessmen, and where it had good organisational capability in its leadership. Also, it is important to note that during its period of significant social accomplishments, 1770-1870, neither Socialism nor a morally transformed Liberalism had then matured into social forces which could effectively compete for humanitarian causes in British politics. In early industrial society it was Conservative idealism which provided an ideological alternative to *laissez faire*.

By 1841, Shaftesbury was already familiar with the filth and stench of London's rookeries (i.e., the slums) with their labyrinth of fever-ridden alleys and courts, the living areas of the working class. He had led the Ragged School movement which provided care and education for the waifs and strays who were homeless in the alleys and courts. In 1841, the public health reformer Southward Smith took Shaftesbury into some of London's worst slums in Bethnal Green and Whitechapel.

Shaftesbury then became an advocate of reform in public health and housing. He was involved in the Health of Towns Association which was founded in 1844 to press the cause for legislative action in public health. Along with Chadwick and Southward Smith, Shaftesbury was appointed to the Public Health Board, 1848-1858; the Board was responsible for administering the *Public Health Act*, 1848, Britain's first major national policy initiative in dealing with cholera and typhus which brought death and sickness to industrial towns.

Unlike Chadwick, Shaftesbury was ready to undertake direct involvement in the philanthropic model dwelling companies. In 1842, he took a leadership role in the Labourers' Friend Society which grew in prominence and, in 1844, was re-styled the Society for the Improvement of the Conditions of the Labouring Classes. The Society was concerned with *demonstrating* the feasibility of philanthropy in working-class housing, not with constructing *mass* housing. It was anticipated that once it was shown that healthy, comfortable working-class housing could be organised on the basis of limited profit, then many other benefactors would be attracted to philanthropy in housing. At that time B. Disraeli (1804-1881), A. Cochrane and Lord John Manners were establishing the *Young England* movement (1843) with the idea of changing the class relations in British society. In his novels *Sybil* and *Coningsby* Disraeli described the social plight of the working classes, and he appealed to the aristocracy to get involved in social causes and reform. Shaftesbury's social activities stood out as an example of how humanitarian aristocrats might achieve these aims.

This philanthropic cause among British Conservatives was not general; it had to compete against *laissez faire* interests and philosophies. Some Tory members of the House of Lords owned slum property in London, and Shaftesbury had to use his personal influence to persuade reform. His persuasive role was assisted by a critical press and by some support from public opinion. Over a period of some forty years, Shaftesbury was successful in modifying the *laissez faire* attitudes among Conservatives. In the 1850s, he introduced housing measures in Parliament and argued in favour of stronger public policy roles. These included: giving local government powers to build and manage housing, establishing rehousing plans as a requirement of redevelopment by railway companies and other redevelopers, and encouraging more local government activity in dealing with unfit housing. Although Shaftesbury was successful in getting these measures through Parliament, their effect in administration was very restricted. Shaftesbury's parliamentary colleagues argued that the government's basic role should be limited by *laissez faire* philosophy, but it was proper for government to remove those obstacles which prevented voluntarism and philanthropy from being more effective in housing.

Thirty years later, in the 1880s, Conservative leaders adopted a more positive attitude to government roles in housing. Against a background of increasing agitation in the 1880s, Lord Salisbury argued that philanthropy in housing reform was insufficient and that the government ought to get more deeply involved in providing financial and administrative support for the construction of new housing. However, there is continuity in Conservatism from philanthropy to a (limited) acceptance of welfare state roles. The real discontinuity was that some useful methods of housing practice, and particularly rehabilitation and enterprising housing management, were set outside the new post-1890

policies (see Chapter 5).   This discontinuity is explained by the
dominance of Radical and Social Democratic philosophies in the early
development of the British welfare state.   In other words, after the
1880s it was these other political philosophies which led social reform
causes, and not Conservative philanthropic idealism.

As we mentioned, the Conservative idealism in housing during the 1840-
1890 period was practical as well as theoretical.   Its contribution to
housing practice was substantial, not so much for its quantitative
performance, but rather for its useful ideas.   It was the philanthropic
tradition which developed the idea of rehabilitating older housing and
bringing this housing into a protected low-rent stock.   The idea of
rehabilitation was set out by the Rev. Canon Girdlestone in 1845, used
by the Hastings Cottage Improvement Society, transmitted to Chelsea,
London, and practised by the Rev. R. Burgess who sent an account of its
merits to the Labourers' Friend Society. [3]   Thus, Shaftesbury and the
Society with which he became involved as leader, adopted rehabilitation
methods as well as new construction in demonstrating the philanthropic
cause in housing.   Shaftesbury was always conscious that rehabilitation
was a comparatively good economic proposition.   The idea was also used
by Octavia Hill in her post-1865 activities in low-income housing, and
by the Glasgow Workmen's Dwelling Company (see the later discussions).

Other legacies from Conservative idealism were initially taken up by
benefactors and social activists, and, towards the end of the nineteenth
century, by the emergent town planning and social work professions.
The inspiration of voluntary social workers who got involved with the
slums, especially during the 1870s, was the idea that the barriers
between the middle and working classes should be bridged by combining
personal contact, charity and the example of professionalism.   Clearly,
these ideas were close to those which motivated Shaftesbury and the
leaders of the *Young England* movement.   Some benefactors and people
with broad interests in town planning synthesised philanthropy and
ideas from Owenite 'villages of co-operation' (see the discussion below)
to link social and physical aspects of welfare.   This can be traced
through the history of the town planning profession and it can be
identified in the demonstration examples built by Titus Salt at Saltaire
in 1850, Viscount Leverhulme at Port Sunlight in 1887, and George
Cadbury at Bournville in 1895.   The various strands of this legacy are
discussed more fully in Chapters 3 and 5.

THE TRANSFORMATION OF LIBERALISM

During the second half of the nineteenth century, the *laissez faire* and
Utilitarian emphasis of Liberalism was modified by John Stuart Mill
(1806-1873) and T.H. Green (1836-1882).   Some ideas in the transformed
Liberalism, and particularly those transmitted by Mill, influenced the
development of Social Democrat ideology (see below).   The Social
Democrats and Mill were both attracted to some ideas derived from
Positivism whose author was the Frenchman, Auguste Comte (1795-1857).
Positivists argued that society was prior to the individual, that
scientific and moral forces in history were producing progress, and that
some collectivism (i.e., some use of state power in reforming *laissez
faire*) was inevitable.   The Social Democrats pushed collectivism further
than Mill, but increasingly after 1865 Mill became an advocate not only
of freedom, self-development and moral and intellectual improvement, but

also of government roles in education, factory reform, municipal
enterprise, land tax, subsidised housing and graduated income tax.
Mill [4] supported the radical proposal of the Land Tenure Reform
Association to tax future 'unearned increments' from the increase in
urban land values consequent upon urban growth. He argued that private
property rights in land could be justified in respect to improvements on
land which were the 'fruits of labour', but not on the 'unearned increments' which should be returned to the community. Through his support
for these various government activities, Mill accommodated the Liberal
traditions to Socialism and steered them into housing, urban and social
policy reform.

Drawing upon some ideas from Hegel and other German philosophers,
T.H. Green argued that the state had a moral duty to contribute to
social opportunity and to widen the access to the cultural traditions of
society. Accordingly, Green supported the case for bringing education,
public health, housing and other socially significant goods or services
within the province of the state. By contrast with the Ricardian-
Utilitarian synthesis, he sought a penetrating revision of *laissez faire.*
Essentially, he gave the liberal tradition greater purpose in political
reform and a genuinely moral commitment. Attitudes among some modern
housing reformers reflect a position which is close to Green's. These
reformers tend to be in conflict with those who espouse Ricardian
arguments.

The thrust of the transformed Liberalism was to establish social
rights claims to those goods and services having special significance in
humanitarianism and civilisation. This impact, like the ideas of the
Social Democrats, was reformist rather than revolutionary.

EARLY SOCIALIST THOUGHT

Socialist ideas were developed by a number of nineteenth-century
intellectuals who opposed the profit materialism, the alienation, the
divisiveness, and the social injustice of capitalism. In time
Socialism differentiated, with some of its streams of thought adopting
competing positions on the revolutionary or reformist means of
accomplishing change, and on the amount of state involvement which was
necessary to achieve Socialism. Most of the key sub-themes and
historical differentiations in Socialism have left important and enduring legacies in housing policies and practices.

The idea of *co-operation* - ownership in common, limited profit,
communitarianism - can be traced to the writing of Robert Owen (1772-
1837). This stream of thought, with adaptation and development, has
had major influences on co-operative organisations and on voluntary
self-help in housing, particularly in Scandinavia, West Germany and The
Netherlands. Ideas from Louis Blanc (1811-1882), who advocated a
system of workers enterprises whereby exploitation could be curbed and
then overwhelmed as the system spread throughout society, have also
contributed towards the role of non-profit voluntarism in housing
practice in West Germany and Sweden.

Karl Marx (1818-1883) dubbed Owen and Fourier, 'Utopian Socialists',
and he took a more fundamental position emphasising change according to
the economic laws of society and stating that the socialisation of the

means of production could only follow revolution.   In contrast with
co-operative socialism, Marxists believed in the use of *state* power
(collectivism) to check and revise the results of economic individualism.
Marx clashed with J.H. Proudhon (1809-1865), the intellectual founder of
the Socialist-Anarchists, who also believed that social transition would
be revolutionary.   Proudhon did not favour state collectivism;
instead, he advocated mutualism among workers whereby they would form
associations to provide credit banking, which could be used as a
foundation for eliminating the exploiting and alienating edge in
capitalism.   The differences between Marx and Proudhon were brought
into relevance on housing reform under the pen of Marx's co-theorist,
F. Engels (see below).

In this section we shall examine the ideas and the housing-related
legacies left by the theory of socialist co-operation.   The following
sections will then deal with the Marxist and Social Democratic
inheritances.   First, we examine the ideas and legacies left by Owen
and Fourier.

Owen's ideas developed from an initial interest in 'villages of
co-operation' to a more sophisticated theory of co-operative socialism.
His earlier ideas (*A New View of Society*, 1813) were based upon
philanthropy; that is to say he sought social change on the basis of
support from wealthy benefactors and high-minded leadership from the
enlightened.   Owen's vision of the *new society* took in millennialism
(a perfectly harmonious society), communitarianism and anti-capitalism.
By the late 1820s, Owen was ready to take his anti-capitalism into a
deeper intellectual basis.   Along with the Ricardian Socialists, [5]
he argued that labour was the source of all economic value and he
pressed this point further by concluding that the means of production
should be owned *in common* (i.e., co-ownership) within co-operative
socialism.   This more developed theory had social and political
consequences beyond Owen's demonstration communities, expressed
practically in the village of co-operation at New Lanark and at other
villages in Britain and America.

The practical expression of consumer co-operatives had ante-dated
Owen, but initially Owen was sceptical of creating Socialism
commercially out of trading profits.   However, once Owen had adopted a
labour theory of value, he saw the fuller potential of organised
co-operation and, significantly, he was in contact with the vigorous
London Co-operative Society.   Then in the 1830s, Owen became involved
in the emergent trade union movement where he advocated co-operation,
co-ownership and the elimination of the capitalist mode of production.
In fact, in 1833 the Grand National Guild of Builders was ready to begin
an (abortive) attempt to establish a co-operative self-employment
housing and building enterprise.   As we shall eventually see, there
were important reasons why the later similar initiatives by German,
Swedish and Norwegian trade unions were more successful in socialist
self-help.   Also, consumer (tenant) self-help, which has been
especially significant in Scandinavia, owes its theoretical basis to
Owenite and Fourierist ideas.

Owenite and Fourierist ideas have also influenced housing via the
theory of *environmental determinism* and its impact upon the theory and
practice of the social housing movement and town planning.   Environmental determinists believe that attitudes and social behaviour are

largely influenced by the quality of the physical environment and its
amenities, but some modern sociologists have considered the theory to be
exaggerated and detrimental to urban policy development. [6] Owen and
Fourier gave practical outlines of how the social and economic
environment should express co-operation, education and satisfying work.
They proposed town plans of ideal communities containing about 1,200
people working in farming and manufacturing. The villages of
co-operation, or as Fourier termed his community, the *phalanstery*,
would have communal kitchens, laundries and recreational facilities.
Education and social organisation would emphasise co-operative social
aims and a sense of community rather than individualism. The practical
expressions of communitarian socialism generally failed because the
theoretical basis ignored conflicts of interest, different viewpoints on
how a community should be governed, and it exaggerated the influence of
the environment. Nevertheless, Owenite and Fourierist idealism has
influenced both the Social Democratic political movement and the town
planning profession.

We have seen that Owenite and Fourierist ideas have left two important
legacies in housing, the one influencing self-help voluntarism and the
other the environmental determinism in town planning. The discussions
now turn to a brief review of the further elaboration of these
influences by other theorists and practitioners. First, we look at the
self-help principle in housing finance.

In housing, the practice of mutual self-help was sometimes ahead of
theory. The building society movement in Britain grew out of the
eighteenth-century general self-help movement. [7] Aspirations for
home ownership by better-off workers led to the development of
terminating building societies as specialised extensions of mutuality
and co-operation in the friendly societies. At first, societies
organised housing development as well as finance, but later began to
drop their development roles. In time, the movement departed from its
working-class origins; workers found it difficult to commit themselves
to long-term savings for home ownership when their household budgets
were already hard pressed. The societies also found that they could be
more effective (as financial intermediaries) if they were organised on
the *permanent* basis rather than the terminating basis. These changes
affected the principles of the movement and took away some of its
initial idealism.

A fuller appreciation of the housing-related idealism in building
societies can be ascertained by referring to the German experience,
where the movement appeared later and was designed by intellectuals to
achieve theoretical purposes. V.A. Huber (1800-1869) set out the
principles for creating self-help co-operative housing. Financing
could be mutual and co-operative, and development could emphasise
'garden cities'. This idealism aimed at creating an alternative
to the profitable exploitation by landlords who owned the *mietkasernen*
(i.e., slums). Some of Huber's ideas came from the British building
society movement. F. von Bodelschwingh (1831-1910) was another
intellectual who provided theoretical support for using the home savings
society so workers could achieve home ownership. G. Kropp (1865-1943)
promoted von Bodelschwingh's ideas in a practical way. Similarly, in
Britain T.E. Bowkett devised a special scheme to more purposefully
extend the building society movement to assist the working class, and
R.B. Starr promoted Bowkett's scheme. [8] Starr-Bowkett societies had

a considerable impact in the period 1860-1890 and this form of building society spread to Australia.

The building and home savings societies movement leaves an inheritance of idealism, mutuality and co-operation, an adjustment to changing society, and a role in facilitating home ownership. During the course of its development, the movement has tended to separate the financing and development functions, largely because the risks are different and a complex range of specialist management skills is required. However, modern housing policy development is again emphasising the need for careful linking of the financing and development functions. It is significant that in modern Sweden, where housing policies have probably developed most comprehensively, some parts of the home savings movement have begun to take key initiatives in simultaneously influencing the development function and organising home buyers into a neighbourhood management society. This is discussed further in Chapter 9. Meanwhile, we can note one other point. In the development of housing policies in modern democratic countries it has been necessary for governments to manipulate credit markets and fill in gaps where housing finance markets have collapsed following severe economic recession. Thus, the mutual self-help principle, represented in the building society movement, can hold firm in modern societies only within some key roles from government in pursuing economic stabilisation policies. As we shall see, the co-operative development function also depends for its success on other government roles.

In continental Europe the voluntary social housing movement has been expressed through the co-operative principle, and the non-profit and limited-profit principle (enterprises for public benefit). The terms 'co-operation' and 'public benefit' evoke, in their European context, strong feelings and connotations of social idealism and historical achievement which continue to enthuse key administrators in the voluntary social housing movement. In Germany, V.A. Huber's ideas (see the discussion above) influenced the progress of self-help in housing, also the foundation of the Berlin Building Society (1848), and its affiliated public benefit housing enterprise, the Alexandra Foundation. This revealed a powerful characteristic in European housing - the links between finance, development and a network of specialised affiliated organisations. This characteristic influences the form and enterprise of some modern large co-operative and other limited-profit housing societies.

The self-help example and its idealism grew and spread into the co-operative housing movement. In 1862 Germany's first housing co-operative was founded in Hamburg. It gave expression to the reforming theories advanced by W. Raiffersen (1818-1888) and H. Schultze-Delizsch (1808-1883). However, the movement was retarded by the problem of risk-bearing and the liability of contributors. After 1889 the movement was boosted when government passed a law limiting liability.

Another surge resulted from government financial support; in 1885 the Prussian Government established a Housing Assistance Fund. Gradually State governments (Germany is a federation) expanded their financial involvement in housing. This finance was accessible to co-operatives, public benefit housing enterprises and private developers which complied with conditions on rents and standards. Further initiatives were taken by State governments to expand the role of non-profit housing enterprise. After 1917 they created *heimstatten* (homestead companies) to develop and administer social housing on a wider scale than achieved by small local societies. Unlike Sweden (see below), the German voluntary social housing movement did not develop initially under the dominance of only a few enterprises which operated on a national basis. The key point emerging from German experience (and later repeated in other European countries) was that government finance and organisational initiatives were added to the voluntary housing movement. Enterprise was harnessed to a wider and stronger financial source than possible through members' subscriptions, private savings deposits and localised operations. This feature had long-term historical significance for the voluntary social housing movement, and its importance is heightened in modern policies (see Chapters 5 and 6).

The First World War left housing shortages in Germany followed by severe inflation which disrupted the building industry and stimulated a strong reaction from the trade union movement. In 1919 the building and construction workers set up their own development enterprise, the Association of Building Enterprises (VSB). After 1922, the wider power of the general trade union movement was applied to self-help housing. The German General Labour Unions (ADGE) created a housing development enterprise (DEWOG), to build homes for workers, civil servants and so on. The capital was provided by the unions and co-operative insurance organisations. This developed, and the present-day Neue Heimat - a powerful trade union urban development and housing enterprise - can be historically traced to these early developments.

Germany's voluntary social housing movement was stamped out by Hitler's National Socialist regime in the years 1933-1945. However, after 1945 there were enough idealists ready to repair the damage to these social institutions and to bring continuity to the post-war development of West German society. By 1970, the voluntary social housing movement had constructed one-quarter of West Germany's rental apartments and had also constructed flats and houses for sale. Public housing in the Australian-British-American sense is not significant in West Germany.

The main historical legacy of the Germans' voluntary social housing movement is its institutionalisation of idealism, finance, enterprise, experience in development and government support. Sweden and Norway inherit a similar institutionalisation, but stronger in the co-operative sector of the voluntary housing movement. The co-operative idealism in Sweden and Norway has emphasised shared rights and responsibilities in the formation of income and wealth, non-profit enterprise in contrast to a capitalism which seeks private profit, and democracy in organising the enterprise. Sweden and Norway have gone further than other modern democratic countries in the application of co-operative principles to housing development and tenure. Under what circumstances did it all begin?

In Sweden, in the early 1920s rents rose by more than 20 per cent while wages fell by 30 per cent. In response, working-class tenants took self-help initiatives to form the Swedish Tenants' Savings Bank and Housing Association (HSB), a co-operative which found a durable and effective method of organising housing development within the co-operative principle. The essential requirements to make the co-operative housing principle effective and strong are:

- to achieve continuity of *development* enterprise and managerial skills.

- to overcome the motive of a small group of co-operators to wind up the development operations after each member has satisfied his/her housing needs, and

- to apportion the risks of development and enterprise so that they are acceptable to potential co-operators.

HSB developed an organisational framework meeting these requirements. It splits the developer's role from that of the occupier. The developer concentrates on the construction or the acquisition and rehabilitation of groups of dwellings and assumes the development risks. Hence, the developer is able to accumulate experience in a very complicated business and to use it widely through time and geographically. The occupiers take over the finished housing and organise ongoing estates management. Both the developer and the occupiers are organised as co-operatives and the latter are concurrently members of the development organisation. Where this method is used and supported with adequate resources, successful enterprise is created. On the other hand, where development potential is not thus organised, co-operative housing does not make such an emphatic contribution. HSB has organised itself as a national developer with regionalised branches continually creating occupier co-operatives in groups of houses.

Housing crisis came to Sweden again in 1940 when there was massive unemployment in the building industry. In response, the building trade unions founded the Swedish Co-operative Housing Organisation of Swedish Trade Unions (SR). This general pattern was repeated in Norway; in the 1920s the building unions organised their own corporate enterprise and in 1929 the Oslo Savings and Housing Society (OBOS) was formed as a consumer co-operative. OBOS adopted the effective HSB model of organising and developing co-operative housing. Increased housing vexation occurred in Norway following the destruction of some stock in the Second World War and the cessation of building. Young Left-Wing enthusiasts responded by forming the Young People's Co-operative Housing Society (USBL) which struggled to get access to housing finance, building technology and political recognition.

In each case housing vexation led to the development of self-help co-operative interventions. The initiatives came from the tenants and from organised labour in the building trades. This type of response is a characteristic of people's movements and social traditions in continental Europe. Also, the Conservative political idealism in Norway and Sweden is closer to the values of self-determination and rural agricultural co-operation than the political conservatism of Britain and Australia. In fact, a case can be made out to show that British conservatism is basically collectivist, emphasising hierarchy and central authoritarianism. [9] The traditions in the Social Democratic movements in Britain and Australia add to this tendency towards collectivism.

This review of Owenite legacies in self-help housing indicates the conditions under which the voluntary movements flourish. Drawing upon Olson's modern economic analysis of voluntary group involvements in providing goods or services [10], we can see that co-operative cohesion occurred and developed where: (1) it operated within a supportive legal framework, (2) it was organisationally feasible and without prohibitive administrative costs, and (3) historically, it provided an access to housing which was otherwise unavailable. Co-operation has been more cohesive in European than in British housing. Although since the 1960s there has been a revived interest in the voluntary housing movement in Britain, it makes only a slender contribution to overall housing policies and both the American and Australian movements are attenuated and rather insignificant. The original British movement was diverted to housing finance in the form of building societies, and its original social purposes were re-directed from artisan/working-class self-help to middle-class home ownership. Working-class impulses have had sporadic but not enduring impacts in housing. For example, as was mentioned earlier the 1833 attempt by the Grand National Guild of Builders to establish a co-operative self-employment housing and building enterprise proved abortive. Also, in 1845 under the influence of Fergus O'Connor, the Chartist Land Society was founded, based on the co-operative principle. Its purpose was to provide housing, and land for farming, but the Society was wound up in 1851, although it had developed estates in the South and Midlands of England [11] Later in the nineteenth century the Christian Socialists also failed in their attempt to establish self-help producer co-operatives, and the Co-operative Union has not been able to develop a strong broadly-based impact in housing.

Comparative analysis indicates the reasons for the better progress with voluntarism in housing in *continental Europe*. At the ideological level the collectivist tendencies (i.e., use of state power) in social policy have been less dominant in Scandinavian Conservative and Social Democratic politics. In resourcing and organisation, the West Germans and Scandinavians have successfully harnessed social idealism, finance, administrative experience and development capability to enterprise. As we shall see in later chapters, social goals in European housing are expressed through a financial and administrative framework which is less rigid and separatist than Britain's, with the result that the voluntary housing sector in West Germany, Norway, Sweden and The Netherlands is more competitive and enterprising than the British. In Sweden, the more general role of the co-operative movement is seen as a competitive third sector which informally and unbureaucratically checks the excesses of private enterprise and induces enterprise in public administration. In other words, social goals and enterprise exist simultaneously in all sectors, not as divisive contrasts in separated sectors. Some of these comparative statements will be given further meaning in the discussions on Social Democrat political philosophy, and the modern significance of co-operation in housing will be further discussed in Chapter 9 which deals with organisational issues in housing.

MARXISM

Fortunately, F. Engels (*The Housing Question* published 1872) has left a concise statement of the Marxist view of housing in modern industrialised societies. He attacked the conventional nineteenth-century view of the insecurity of tenure, high rents and shortages in housing, and declared that in organising housing as an investment, private landlords take away (exploit) some value from tenants' productive income and thereby acquire surplus value (unearned). Engels (1820-1895) stated that the 'real' socialist solution (i.e., not the Social Democratic or Utopian approaches) involves an expropriation of existing property rights in land and housing and a socialised re-allocation.

Proudhon (1809-1865), a Socialist-Anarchist, had advocated home ownership for workers, a ban on housing loan interest, a good sanitary inspectorate, co-operative organisation in the building trade and access to credit.   According to Engels, this approach could be only a palliative since it did not correct the problem at the heart of the capital-labour conflict.   He believed the capitalists' philanthropic response to housing problems to be no more than an irrevelant and noble effort on behalf of the health of their workers.   Wealthy housing benefactors might succeed in raising the health status of workers above subsistence, but exploitation in the labour market would lead to a reduction in earnings.   Self-help building societies were regarded as *petty bourgeoisie*, and unrealistic as far as the housing needs of the real workers were concerned.   A real socialist solution would be effective because, according to the Marxist view, it transforms society according to the laws of its own economic development.   By contrast, Proudhonism was seen as an (ineffective) attempt to change society according to prescriptions of justice.   Home ownership, thus, did not adequately reform the capitalist mode of production whereas real socialism would.

The Marxist position can be used by its adherents as a permanent criticism of housing and urban administration in modern democratic society.   Such themes as the speculation and exploitation in urban land and housing have been taken up by modern authors. [12]   These characteristics of urban development, according to Marxists, are seen most conspicuously in commercial developments, but the capitalist problem spills over into housing because housing is viewed as an allied investment of commerce and industry.   Marxist views of urbanisation have attracted some general attention among modern commentators on urban policies.   Generally, although many modern urban specialists do not accept Marxism, a recent trend in interpreting urbanisation has run in favour of explaining its problems by reference to structural economic, social and political conditions in society as a whole. [13]

Although the practical shape of housing policy in the USSR and the Socialist countries of Eastern Europe follows Marxist principles, modern policy issues there reflect similar interests to those in the modern democracies.   These Socialist countries are concerned with such issues as: making subsidies more selective, gearing loans to capacity to repay; establishing a choice among public, co-operative and personal sectors in housing; and reviewing the distribution of costs between the government and individuals. [14]   One interesting aspect of housing policies in the USSR and Eastern Europe is the changing proportions of public, co-operative and personal sectors during the last two decades, and the variations among these countries.   The summary below indicates some of the relevant statistics:

Table 2.1
Comparative Tenure in Some Socialist Countries

	Public housing %		Co-operative housing %		Personal housing %	
	1955	1975	1955	1975	1955	1975
USSR	51	64	0	10	49	26
East Germany	37	45	57	40	6	15
Poland	48	33	10	44	42	23

Source: L. Nemethy, *New Trends in Forms of Tenure in the Socialist Countries of Eastern Europe*, Economic Commission for Europe, 1977.

The changes reflect a combination of influences including policy, urban growth (in urban areas public and co-operative housing dominate). and some pragmatic issues in housing management.   In these countries, the social and political justifications for encouraging the co-operative and personal sectors differ from the type of arguments used in the modern democracies.

In the Socialist countries a general central planning framework is created to shape the circumstances influencing the operation of economic incentives in the decentralised units.   That is to say, pricing and the resourcing of enterprises, including housing, are based upon the idea that incentives should: (1) harmonise the moral and economic considerations to socialism, and (2) make personal interests identical with the social tasks of socialist ideology. [15]   In this context, a co-operative housing sector can be viewed as a set of enterprises which is given specific social tasks within the guidance of the general planning framework.   Thus, Marxists would argue that *private* sectionalism is avoided and the wider society gets the economic and social advantages which flow from some decentralised management and from the mobilisation of some energies in the community.   Co-operation in housing is seen as a way of mobilising decentralised energies and turning them to good social account, especially in estates management. Similarly a personal housing sector operates, but central authority eliminates 'unearned returns' from private renting or trading.   At the more general comparative level, housing in the Socialist countries has low rents/payments (usually less than 10 per cent of income) and less segregation in settlement patterns.   This is achieved with a greater degree of control on private choice than the democracies experience.

SOCIAL DEMOCRATIC IDEALISM

In the mid-nineteenth century Britain was the most advanced industrialised nation, and although *laissez faire* was dominant in social thought and politics, the seeds of Socialism and the new Liberalism had been sown.   By the 1880s, British society was being influenced by reformers who were operating in Radical groups and in the emergent Socialist factions.   Furthermore, under the influence of J.S. Mill and T.H. Green the idea of the welfare state was emerging.   Housing was among those issues which attracted social and political action, and as the theoretical ideas on the welfare state deepened housing became more thoroughly involved with the course of public policy.   The growth and clarification of Social Democratic theory and practice in Britain was built upon: (1) the exigencies of needs in social reform and, (2) the selection and synthesis of ideas from factions and writers who were opposed to *laissez faire*. Advocates for reform included humanistic and religious idealists, and political Radicals. [16]

Collectivist ideas of using state power to achieve social reform were becoming socially and politically significant. Advocates of collectivism were ranged through Radical and Socialist groups (mainly in London), but the differentiation of Socialism into distinguishable Social Democratic, Marxist and other groupings was not clear-cut until after 1900. However, in the 1880s, the London Radicals and the emergent Socialist factions proposed government subsidies in housing, social security provisions, the expansion of education, and municipal enterprise in public utilities. Some of the emergent Socialist leaders took a direct involvement in the anti-slum movement which was strong in London in the 1870s and 1880s. For example, H.H. Campion and R.P.B. Frost who were associated with the Social Democratic Federation (founded as the Democratic Federation in 1881), and Sidney Olivier who was a founder of the Fabian Society (founded in 1884), took active participant interests in London's working-class housing problems.

The theory of Social Democracy was developed by the British *Fabian Society*, founded in 1884. It was through the development of Fabian ideas that Social Democratic idealism was differentiated from Marxism, and the prevailing *ad hoc* collectivism was transformed into a system of political and economic thought. Fabianism stood for peaceful gradual reform through legislation, and for the reduction of economic inequality. It selected ideas from J.S. Mill, T.H. Green and Comte (see earlier discussions), but these were brought into relationship with the reformist and egalitarian thrust of elements in earlier Socialist writing. For Fabians, Socialism meant the coherent integration of society where the alternative, excessive individualism, might lead to disintegration along the lines argued by Comte and his Positivist adherents. The theory of Social Democracy argued for the use of collectivism as the most effective way of achieving egalitarian social reforms. Other groups, including the early co-operative movement and G.D.H. Cole's Guild Socialists, believed that self-help and industrial democracy provided better ways of achieving 'welfare' than the use of 'bureaucratic' state power. The Fabians required an economic theory to underpin their ideas for the welfare state.

The Fabians worked out their economic theory in the period 1884-1889. They synthesised the Ricardian ideas on differential economic rent and the more recent development of marginal analysis which gave integrated explanations of demand, costs, and market pricing. Ricardo (1772-1823) had argued that land was unequally productive owing to inherent differences in soil, aspect and fertility, and this inequality would be reflected in differential rents with the more productive paid the most. The Fabians extended this idea of differential rents to all factors of production and tied these different earnings to price determination in the market. In effect, the payments to most factors reflected amounts above the levels necessary to retain them in their existing employments (i.e., their *transfer earnings*), and these surpluses could be regarded as 'differential rents' which might be appropriate objects of taxation. The proceeds from taxation could be used for welfare state purposes.

The political expression of collectivism also grew in Germany, Norway, Sweden and Australia during the last twenty-five years of the nineteenth century. In Germany, the Social Democrat Party was founded in 1875, and similar parties were founded in Norway in 1887, in Sweden in 1889, and in Australia the Australian Labour Federation was founded in 1890. All of these parties emerged as proponents of Social Democratic (Fabian) political philosophy in the twentieth century. In Britain, various Socialist parties (the Social Democratic Federation, the Independent Labour Party, and the Socialist League) occupied the ground favouring collectivist reform. Eventually, the British Labour Party (founded in 1906) obtained the advantage by linking with the trade union movement, and this link enabled it to become the major British political voice on behalf of Social Democratic policies.

The course of Social Democratic reform and the effectiveness of social policy development has varied among countries. In housing we can identify some key differences. Historically, in Britain the collectivist characteristic has dominated the practice of Social Democratic idealism compared with the competition and blending among self-help co-operation and trade union enterprise in West Germany, Norway and Sweden. This has meant that the British expression of social goals in housing has been historically identified with the development of public housing, whereas in continental Europe social aims have been more flexibly expressed in general financial instruments which are accessible to the voluntary housing movement, to owner occupiers and to private enterprise. The result has been that housing in continental Europe is less rigidly divided into sectors and social aims can be expressed without sacrificing competitive enterprise. In modern times it has become more conspicuous that countries such as West Germany, Sweden and The Netherlands have remained more faithful to Social Democratic theory than Britain. That is to say, the Left in Britain has taken a *regulatory* rather than a *development* approach towards private enterprise. The regulatory approach tends towards bureaucracy and it constrains enterprise and productive possibilites compared with a development approach which can stimulate economic progress and provide productive capacity to build up a strong welfare state. As we shall see, these comparative characteristics emerge conspicuously in housing and urban policy development.

The Social Democratic legacy has been enduring among the modern democracies, but its impacts on housing practice are varied, with some examples of coherence and others somewhat confusing. Some of the confusions centre upon the relative merits of rental and owner-occupier tenure, and upon the (supposed) social benefits of high-density living. In housing administration, Social Democrats have sometimes applied the exaggerations from Owenite environmental determinism, and used the Marxist ripostes against private property to oppose home ownership. These themes and their dilemmas are illustrated in the examples below.

In the first example we look at the views of trade union leaders during the 1880s when Britain held two official enquiries into the housing problem. These views are interesting in their own right and for indicating how working-class opinion on the role of government in housing became more specific and emphatic between 1881 and 1885. In evidence before the Parliamentary *Select Committee on Artizans' and Labourers' Dwellings*, 1881-1882, T.E. Powell of the Machine Rulers' Society acted as spokesman on behalf of the London Trades Council which had appointed a special committee to consider the housing question. Powell's chief concern was with the poor quality of both the private rental housing and the redeveloped tenements built by the Metropolitan Board of Works (i.e., public housing). He also gave an opinion on the desired role of the state in housing policy development. On the quality of housing, Powell's own words are vividly graphic:

> '..... the health of the people cannot safely be longer left to the tender mercies of speculative jerry-builders and greedy rack-renting house farmers*; and laudable, and necessary as private enterprise undoubtedly is, it is more than time that something were done to check that kind of enterprise which gives the people coffin homes, dooms its victims to lives of pain and broken health, fills the dispensaries and hospitals with endless cases of chest disease,* compels grave-diggers to work overtime, and enhances the value of burial grounds on the plea of inordinate demand.'

And on the Metropolitan Board of Works' redevelopments:

> '..... unrelieved by even the most distant pretence of ornament, or anything whatever to please the eye or mind, the cold, cheerless, uninviting appearance of the approaches and staircases, together with the sense of irksome restraint through the conditions and regulations imposed in some of those early examples have assisted largely to engender this feeling of hostility.....'
> 'The individual mechanic cannot be, and will not be, regarded as a unit of a regiment, or of an army, in so far at least as his home life is concerned.' [17]

Powell went on to cite examples of more homely dwellings with sensitive privacies built by the Industrial Dwelling Company (a limited-profit model dwelling company) at the Dover Buildings in the Old Kent Road, near London's dockland. He then proposed that workers be provided with 'home ownership grafted on tenancy' (i.e., shared equity), represented in suburban cottages accessible to commuter railways.

On the question of the role of the state, Powell could not present a detailed and coherent policy, but he set out some points favoured by workers. These points were: (1) ensuring an adequate supply of low-rent dwellings, (2) criticisms against excessive demolition by public authorities, (3) home ownership, (4) central government financial contributions to social housing, (5) the use of private enterprise to achieve satisfactory housing, with government creating the right conditions to make it feasible.

Some of Powell's evidence can be regarded not only as interesting historical attitudes, but also as a prophetic commentary on the subsequent course of housing issues in Britain, and the intelligence which the social economics of housing establishes. First, taking the prophetic view, we see some of the continuing problems of some British public housing through to the modern age. Some housing design and dwelling forms have lacked good architectural imagination, housing

---

* 'House farmers' were real estate middlemen selling tenement rooms in the private market and sometimes demanding 'key' money for the right of access to a scarce resource.
'Chest disease' was tuberculosis.

management has sometimes been bureaucratic and imposing, and a
sensitivity to community and home has sometimes been missing. It has
been all too familiar in popular imagery as well as among well-informed
social critics. This comparative study will show better ways of doing
things. Second, taking the social economics viewpoint, as our
subsequent discussions indicate, Powell's common sense opinions are
fully justified. The key to success in housing policy during the
twentieth century has been in: (1) providing an adequate volume and
quality of low-rent housing whether developed by government or other
developers, (2) avoiding unnecessary demolition and redevelopment,
(3) ensuring an access to home ownership among the working classes and,
(4) using the instruments of government to create an effective
financial and administrative framework. Again, this comparative study
will show that some other countries have done these things better than
Britain.

One of the conspicuous comparative differences between Britain and
continental Europe has been the expression of social goals in housing:
in Britain this was identified with public housing whereas in Europe
the expression was more varied. Powell's evidence can be interpreted
as a case against public housing and favouring alternatives. However,
by 1885, in evidence before the *Royal Commission for Inquiring into
Housing of the Working Classes*, [18] the new spokesman for the London
Trades Council, George Shipton, turned in favour of public housing.
Shipton argued that 'population and economic forces' had outstripped
the endeavours of philanthropy and private enterprise to overcome the
housing problem and, therefore, local government should acquire land
and construct housing. He envisaged (optimistically) that local
government would follow the examples of the model dwelling companies,
and extend them to provide three types of dwelling, one for artisans,
another for labourers and the third for the poorer workers (e.g.,
hawkers). Shipton also noted that many workers aspired to home-
ownership. However, with the advantage of hindsight from modern times
we can say that British public housing and wider housing policies have
been comparatively unprogressive in achieving working-class home-
ownership and in bringing tenants into close relationships with housing
policy and housing management. In Sweden, during the 1920s a very
different Social Democratic legacy was left in housing practice.

The key factors contributing to progress in Swedish housing reform
were the combination of self-help voluntarism, local government policy
and substantial flows of public finance. This occurred in Stockholm.
During 1860-1900 the population of the city trebled and the City
Council began a series of initiatives in housing, ranging through
development regulations, building a garden suburb at Enskede (1903) and
purchasing land for disposal on leasehold terms (1904). Housing
problems continued in the first three decades of the twentieth century,
and were particularly acute during the 1920s. The Council re-organised
its housing agency, the Stockholm City Housing Estate Division, which
adopted a two-part approach to housing policies. One policy thrust
was in providing housing finance and the other in land policy. The
middle classes found that this policy offered a solution to their
housing problems. Garden suburbs were developed on the city leaseholds
with the advantage that the home owners did not need an initial
capital sum for purchasing land.

In 1926 the Social Democrats offered home ownership in garden

36

suburbs to the working classes. The Council launched a scheme of self-build single-family housing backed by loans with easy repayments. The Stockholm City Housing Estate Division sub-divided and serviced the land, organised advisory services and also the production and delivery of components to the building sites, and so on. The future owners took over self-building at weekends and in the summer evenings after work. Eligibility for access to the programme was restricted by income limitations, and the purpose was to turn working-class home ownership into a reality.

The scheme became part of the folklore of housing: these were the 'magic houses', and overseas interest was strong. The scheme was successful for the same reasons as other parts of housing policy (discussed above). 'Magic houses' expressed an idealism and a self-fulfilment purpose within an institutional framework combining suitable finance, administrative commitment, professionalism, and a lot of experience. Now in the 1970s these houses are adding further interest to the folklore of housing policy development (see the discussions in Chapter 7). Unfortunately, this particular Social Democratic legacy receded in Sweden where some more confusing ideas influenced post 1945 housing practice (see below); however, Norwegian Social Democratic policies have adopted the key aspects of 'magic houses' in general policy development. It is in modern Norway where choice is more open on tenure and dwelling type, and where the social goals in housing are broadly equitable in the whole community, and without burdensome bureaucratic entanglements.

Our next example of the Social Democratic legacy in housing shows how social theory, housing theory, and the circumstances of history can produce entangled and confusing mixtures. Taking the rather less useful aspects of these things we identify the following:

1. The ambiguity of some Social Democrats on tenure, and a dominance of the view that home ownership is 'capitalist' and to be discouraged.

2. The inheritance of elements from Owenite environmental determinism *jointly* in the theory of Social Democracy and in the theory and practice of town planning. In practical terms, for our present purposes, this means that some Social Democrats and town planners have believed that high-density living and the provision of community facilities (e.g., laundries and kindergartens) in tenement blocks is the way to create Socialism and a sense of community which they believe is unattainable in owner-occupied single-family dwellings.

3. The use of false, though superficially attractive economic propositions which lead their advocates to argue that low-density living is more costly than high-rise flats. These propositions sometimes ignore the economic evidence, or they rely on narrowly-based selections, and they fail to look at the economics of the *full range* low-rise dwelling forms and varied patterns of low to moderate densities. [19] In modern times these false economic propositions have been given practical expression in a context where (expensive) systems building technology flourished in mass housing and was presented by developers who saw it as *the* solution in overcoming chronic shortages. Consumers and social housing clients had little

choice in the face of acute shortages, but modern professional literature indicates the sociological and economic 'non-sense' which this produced in some housing practice, particularly during the 1960s.

Although Social Democrats were not the only politicians who left a legacy of 'non-sense', our historical examples show that some of them were prone to it. As Headey has shown [20], during the 1940s the Swedes used social democratic economic principles to create a large social housing sector. However, in the period 1950-1975, Swedish Social Democrats succumbed to the errors referred to in point 3, above.

The Social Democratic legacy of confusion began in Vienna in the 1920s with a 'folklore' contribution to housing practice. Vienna in the 1920s has great significance in housing theory and practice in continental Europe. The city lies on the axes which historically divided Europe north and south, east and west. Vienna and Austria as a whole have had considerable historical significance during the past 200 years. Politics, culture, architecture, a surrounding wooded countryside, the way of life and so on attract a diversity of many-sided interests to Vienna. After the First World War, the city became symbolic in housing. An economically backward country had inherited bad housing conditions and the post-First World War inflation made housing, and life, generally difficult. Crowding, high rents and squalid conditions characterised working-class areas. This contrasted sharply with other sources of European interest in Vienna; the art, music, culture and beauty of a city with great traditions.

The Social Democrats controlled city government in Vienna in the period 1919-1934. Drawing upon Fabian principles, the Viennese Social Democrats re-organised city government, created a system of progressive income taxes, and adopted strong initiatives in social welfare, particularly in housing. [21] A solution to the housing problem required cheap land and initiatives in constructing new standard housing. Initially, the city government constructed temporary emergency housing and finished some unfinished private rental housing. Then, in 1923 it launched a vast building programme. Some construction was in the form of four-, five-, and six-storey tenements, around open squares and with communal laundries and kindergartens. Other forms included suburban cottages, but in terms of the locally dominant political ideology the cottagers were thought to make poor Socialists whose lives were too private in comparison with tenement dwellers whose involvements were assumed to be in community activity and politics. As was mentioned above, the ideology included exaggerated elements from Owen's theory of environmental determinism and some loose economic thinking. Nevertheless, the Viennese example attracted a wide European interest which was symbolised in the description that 'Vienna has workers''dwelling palaces'. It was the distinctive break with nineteenth-century housing squalor and the reformist activity of the Social Democrats which created this folklore in housing. The folklore reputation stuck, and other factors were added to it in the post-1945 housing developments in Europe.

In the post-1945 period, housing shortages in continental Europe were acute, but new technology could be applied to create mass project housing. Components could be made in factories and assembled on site. Systems building, and its variants, began to dominate the housing

industry. The new technology spread into continental Europe from
France. The high-density forms were not cheaper than lower-density
forms and as research during the 1960s showed, they had significant
social limitations. However, the technology enabled housing to be
produced in great volume, European governments had designed and
constructed their financial framework to encourage mass construction.
The historical inheritance of social housing theory pointed to examples
such as Vienna with its tenements, neighbourhood amenities and the
(assumed) social advantages of high-density living. The new
technology and the powerful financing instruments would enable modern-
day versions of the Viennese example to be built in all cities. Apart
from environmental determinism, town planners argued that high-density
living had other advantages: it was relatively easy to service by
public transport and supposedly encouraged social interaction and *urban*
life styles. Suburbanisation was not looked on enthusiastically:
indeed some planners and architects despised it. [22] Stockholm's
modern Social Democrats adopted the new technology and the loose ideas
which justified it.

Summarising the points from those confusing aspects of some Social
Democrat legacies we can set down the following conclusions. The
entanglements of Social Democratic theory, town planning theory, tenure
and dwelling type owe much to three factors. First, the inheritance
of Owenite ideas in both Social Democratic thinking and in town
planning. Second, the urgent post-1945 needs to build in volume.
Third, the new building technology and the financial frameworks seemed
to meet the needs of historical theory and pragmatic urgency. However,
by the 1970s all three supports could be analytically and critically
dismantled. Owenite environmental determinism does not produce useful
socialism or good town planning. The European need to build in
volume over long periods has passed. Mass project apartments make no
economic or social sense. Finally under less constraining conditions
and some affluence, consumers are now fulfilling aspirations for their
versions of home ownership. Bringing all the previous social and
economic reasoning together with this review of social theory, there
seems to be no adequate reason why home ownership should not be provided
efficiently and effectively to those who want it. Norwegian policies
show how this can be achieved.

Home ownership (and its cognate forms) does not need to be oversold.
All it needs is something like the Norwegian example. Consumers can
apply for state Housing Bank loans, so can co-operatives and private
enterprise. Choice prevails, and it has produced a varied housing
stock, mass project housing (not much) and a mixture of tenures. Over
75 per cent of the housing has attached gardens, 14 per cent is in
blocks of apartments, home owners absorb 61 per cent of Housing Bank
loans, co-operators 23 per cent and private entrepreneurs 9 per cent.
Comparatively, Norway has had a useful financial framework,
uncomplicated administration and less influence from invalid social
theory. Norwegian theoretical inheritances combine Social Democracy
with an agrarian Conservative self-determination; and its historical
inheritance in housing is the adaptable and individualised timber
homestead, often self-built.

As early as 1916 the Norwegian Labour Party had organised a national
conference to define a Social Democratic housing policy. The outcome
was a set of housing objectives including, support for home ownership,

municipal land acquisition and disposal in leasehold tenure, municipal housing development to relieve acute shortages, support for co-operative housing, and some rent control. By comparison, Social Democrats in other countries had not taken such a comprehensive view of housing, and in Britain the tendencies were running strongly in favour of the public housing approach, and this was instituted into a national programme in 1919 (see Chapter 5). Again, taking another example outside continental Europe, we can refer to Australian policies and the Social Democratic approach there during the first twenty years of the twentieth century. Although State Labour Governments in Australia had taken initiatives in creating home ownership programmes for working-class families, they had no overall housing policy goals. The trade union movement there sought a solution to working-class housing problems through government provision (public housing) rather than by self-help. For example, representing the New South Wales Trades' and Labour Council at a Royal Commission investigating housing, Mrs. K. Dwyer favoured publicly-provided suburban cottages for workers. She strongly criticised tenements associating them with moral degeneration and the destruction of family life. [23] This echoes the views of Powell, the spokesman for London's labour movement in 1881-1882. In the course of subsequent policy development, Australian urban workers did not get high-rise dwelling forms, except sporadically in some cities after 1945, and it was not until after the economic depression of the 1930s that public housing dominated the expression of social goals in housing.

Clearly the theory and practice of Social Democracy in housing has left varied legacies, some more useful than others. Norway stands out as a country where policy development and housing practice has achieved balance and cohesion. Other countries in continental Europe have not adequately sorted out the confusions in attitudes to tenure and dwelling forms. Britain, without a broadly-based people's movement to establish a (socialist) voluntary sector, and with comparatively stronger collectivist tendencies in its Left and Right, [24] has particularised its expression of social goals in the public housing approach. Australia has drawn upon the British inheritance, but with more pragmatism and less social theory. The United States has also been more detached from social theory in the development of its housing policies. All the countries which are featured in this study have been influenced by economic theory, and the discussions now turn to examine the impacts from economic theory.

HOUSING POLICY AND THE DEVELOPMENT OF ECONOMIC THEORY

As noted earlier, the Ricardian inheritance in housing in Britain emphasised harmony, equilibrium and mutual consistencies which, if left to Adam Smith's *laissez faire*, would yield optimal dividends to society. Ricardo's conceptual categories were 'capital', 'labour', and 'land'. Marx and Engels found a class-based significance in Ricardian economics, and used this to create a new theoretical construct with critical socialist purposes. The Marx-Engels viewpoint is a clear departure from the Ricardian inheritance in the modern democracies. For the themes in this study, the essential point about the Marx-Engels approach is that housing and urban problems are symptoms of more basic structural conditions in society. As we shall see, housing vexation and the impetus towards social reform has produced other (less radical) departures from the Ricardian inheritance. Before we look at this, it is important to establish the fuller development of the liberal economic tradition by reviewing the significant contributions made in the second half of the nineteenth century.

It was the authors of neoclassical economics, represented by W.S. Jevons (1832-1882), Leon Walras (1834-1910), Carl Menger (1840-1921) and Alfred Marshall (1842-1924), who created the *theory of value* which lies at the heart of the liberal economic tradition. Although Adam Smith had earlier contributed eloquent expositionary and advocate causes to the virtues of the market system, the theory of value developed by his successor, Ricardo, was based upon labour cost and it was not entirely consistent with market pricing. This inconsistency did not bother Marx who turned his explanations to reveal the exploitation and the surplus values extracted by capitalists.

The neoclassical authors used Utilitarian ideas and the principles of marginalism [25] to produce an integrated theory of value, exchange, income distribution and economic competition. Some of the derived concepts could be used to demonstrate that demand was the satisfaction of wants based upon declining 'marginal utility' as successive increments of a commodity were consumed. Marginalism could also show that the per unit costs of production would rise as successive factors were employed. All of this supports the downward sloping demand curve, the upward sloping supply curve and their intersection - the familiar portrayal of these principles to students entering courses in liberal economic theory. The intersection of supply and demand determines price (exchange value) and this acts as a signalling device for allocating resources to competing uses. Alfred Marshall noted that consumers enjoyed a surplus value (i.e., consumer's surplus) represented by the difference between what they are prepared to pay for the goods they consume and the actual price they pay. As we shall see, Marshallian consumer's surplus concepts are now being used by modern American economists to assess the benefits of social housing programmes.

Neoclassical economics has left various legacies and some reactions. On the one hand it added support to Adam Smith's justifications for competition and *laissez faire*. However, it also contained principles which could be used (controversially) to support the case for progressive incomes tax and ·the development of the welfare state. Some of these elements can be found in Marshall's writing, but A.C. Pigou, his successor at Cambridge University, gave greater emphasis to those welfare state justifications which could be (selectively) found in neoclassical economics. Finally, the neoclassical legacy included the development of *welfare economics*, a branch of study which is aimed at looking at the economy as whole (i.e., in terms of *general* equilibria, not in terms of the parts) and ranking alternative states of the economy for their relative efficiencies. Each of these legacies - the analysis of markets and their implicit justifications, the welfare state orientations, and some varied derivations from welfare economics - has been used in the economics of housing. This gives one source of explanation of why non-Marxist economists perceive and analyse housing variably and contentiously according to their relative commitments to the market economy, to the cause of the welfare state, and to the varied meanings which can be extracted from welfare economics. The following paragraphs outline these varied legacies of liberal economics, but the more substantive discussions of the modern economics of housing can be found in Chapter 4.

As a specialist branch of modern economics, studies of housing are relatively recent, with a build up of the literature from the 1960s. In a subject like economics there are discernable relationships between researchers, their subject matter and the characteristic of those institutions in their society which influences both the subject matter and researchers' perceptions. In housing this has meant that most market-orientated studies have been contributed by Americans whose society is closer to *laissez faire* than Britain or continental Europe. However, to some extent, market conditions influence housing in all the modern democracies, and some countries are encouraging market conditions as a matter of policy reform. Accordingly, the insights contributed by market economists have a broad, but contingent relevance throughout the modern democracies.

The *market* economist will perceive housing as a commodity or a bundle of services which is traded among many buyers and sellers with few restrictions on entering this market. For some economists such as Olsen [26] housing is *homogeneous* whereas others such as Grigsby [27] have emphasised its non-homogeneity and its division into *sub-markets* linked by changing price relativities, but separated by differences in tenure, location, dwelling type and quality. Housing market analysis can be applied to various aspects of housing and to illuminate policy issues. During the 1950s Winnick [28] examined time series data to shed light upon the suburbanisation process, life-cycle factors influencing the demand for dwelling space and dwelling form, and the long-term trend to split the three-generation household into separate smaller households. These processes were the key housing-related interests at that time, and another - the question of racial segregation and the spreading of black living areas into inner urban white living areas - was studied by Rapkin and Grigsby [29]. Before the 1950s, the main (sporadic) interest of market economists was in the consequences of rent control, [30] and this interest has continued to stimulate research into British and European housing. More recently, in the United States during the 1960s, Grigsby [31] and others used market economics to elaborate a theory of *filtering* which argued that if public policy stimulated new construction this would precipitate turnover and a chain of moves in the existing stock, with consequent benefits for low-income groups as their housing sub-market was loosened by this filtering. Filtering is discussed more critically in Chapter 4.

The significant contribution of market analysis in housing is the technical sophistication which it provides, its prognostic value and its incisiveness on some policy issues. For example, the classical case against rent control has had a continual relevance to some housing policies which have been pursued in various countries during the last fifty years or so. The classic case against rent controls is that they form disincentives to new investment in housing, they lead to lower standards of maintenance, they cause slower modernisation, they inhibit mobility and are tantamount to a discriminatory tax on landlords and an arbitrary subsidy to a favoured class of tenants. Some of these arguments can also be used against social housing rent policies which are based upon historical costs, thus arbitrarily resulting in low rents in older dwellings and high rents in new dwellings built under inflationary conditions. The arguments have a definite social welfare thrust because such issues as homelessness in British housing, [32] and vertical and horizontal inequities which exist generally in housing in the modern democracies can be partly attributed to inappropriate rent policies.

The limitations of the market-orientated approach can be found in its narrowly-based conceptions. As we have noted in our discussions on comparative social theory, Utilitarianism tends to omit moral and wider social perspectives which modern Liberalism and Socialism bring into account. Market economics has inherited the Utilitarian legacy and it does not handle questions of distributional equity or welfare state social rights as well as other social theories. Also, comparing it with the other legacies in neoclassical economics, the market orientation tends to ignore or press into insignificance some social costs and benefits which are not always identifiable directly in the price system. Finally, market economics defines its theoretical categories and specifies its relationships in ways which some critics say fails to account for the full 'value' and 'productivity' of housing. This point is taken up in the next chapter.

The *welfare state* legacy from neoclassical economics has developed partly in response -to historical, social and political issues, and partly as a way of articulating a general case for social reform. Firstly, looking at the response to historically relevant issues in housing we note that J.S. Mill and Alfred Marshall supported the cause of public policy interventions in housing. Mill [33] qualified his general support for *laissez faire* by arguing that social and cultural interests were involved in education, in municipal utilities and in the relief of poverty. Accordingly, the state should assist progress in these spheres because otherwise they would be paralysed by discourage- ment in market conditions. Marshall also gave qualified support for egalitarianism and he entered public debates on housing reform during the 1880s. His attitude to the nineteenth-century urban slums is conveyed in these words:

'..... it is undeniable that the housing of the very poorest classes in our homes is destructive both of body and soul, and that with our present knowledge and resources we have neither cause nor excuse for allowing it to continue.....'. [34]

And, in a footnote Marshall gave support to the methods and actions of Lord Shaftesbury and Octavia Hill, the key housing reformers in that period.

It was A.C. Pigou's writing [35] which articulated a more general case for the welfare state. Using marginal utility theory he argued (controversially) that an additional £10 is worth more to a poor family than to the wealthy, and therefore social/economic welfare is increased by taxing the rich and redistributing resources to the poor. Furthermore, Pigou developed the theory of *social* costs and benefits, and used it to argue that the state should implement taxes and subsidies to correct for the failure of the market to account for these non-market interactions. The crux of the social cost/benefit argument is the economic impacts on third parties. Pigou expresses this third party interdependence and the divergence between private and social interests in these words:

'..... Here the essence of the matter is that one person A, in
the course of rendering some service, for which payment is made
to a second person B, incidentially also renders services or
disservices to other persons (not producers of like services),
of such a sort that payment cannot be extracted from the
benefited parties or compensation enforced on behalf of the
injured parties.....'[36]

'..... It will be shown that, in certain cases, self-interest
left to itself does not tend to bring about equality of marginal
net products, and that, therefore, in these cases certain
specific acts of interference with the free play of self-interest
are likely, not to diminish, but to increase the national dividend
.....' [37]

Pigou suggested that the divergences between private and social
interests are widespread, and our earlier introductory discussions
indicated their relevance to housing and urbanisation. Although his
arguments on urbanisation are less developed than modern writers, Pigou
did give specific mention of the externality efficiencies involved in
town planning, and in housing he added in another argument which is
becoming increasingly persuasive in the modern literature. He said
that economic benefits can be created by stimulating the learning of new
tastes through experience. Furthermore, he supported this point by
citing the cases of model dwelling companies and Octavia Hill who had
'made plain superiorities hitherto unrecognised'. [38]

The strength of the Pigovian legacy is that compared with the market
orientations it has width and it makes contact with social theories
which have also influenced the intellectual and theoretical case for the
welfare state. However, the Pigovian approach has its limitations.
Some market economists will argue that the argument for progressive
taxation is only propositional and cannot be unambiguously proven
either in theoretical reasoning or in empirical research. Also, these
same economists will say that social costs and benefits are not always
readily identifiable and they sometimes defy any reasonable efforts to
measure them. Furthermore, the presence of these external costs and
benefits, whilst posing some dilemmas for allocational efficiency, does
not, in itself, provide sufficient grounds for government intervention.
In some cases, it may be more efficient or effective to leave the
externalities uncorrected or to reduce their incidence by voluntary
agreement, because government intervention can be costly. More
significantly, the English-speaking economists did not develop the
Pigovian theory of social costs and benefits to a general 'public goods'
theory. Public goods theory originated among nineteenth-century
Swedish, German and Italian economists [39], and it was not linked to
social cost and benefit theory, and thereby, not fully elaborated until
the 1960s. [40]   Nevertheless, Pigou should be classified as a welfare
state economist who used some rather limited neoclassical theory, but
revealed his egalitarian beliefs, particularly on his later writing. [41]
Modern public goods theory can be regarded as an extension of welfare
economics, a subject to which we shall now turn; and Pigou occupies a
(controversial) place in the history of that subject.

As was mentioned, *welfare economics* attempts to rank the net advantages
and disadvantages of various states of the economic system as a whole.
Pigou's treatment of the subject was dominant until 1932 when it was

attacked by Robbins. [42]   Pigou adapted neoclassical marginalism and value theory to propose that economic welfare increases when society's product was enlarged, providing that low-income groups (whose marginal valuations were assumed to be higher than those of the rich) were not consequently made worse off.   Robbins' attack on Pigou revolved around the normative nature of Pigou's formulation - its interpersonal comparisons of satisfaction, and its assumption that satisfactions could be measured in precise quantities rather than merely ranked in order.   Robbins wanted a more scientific and value free role for economic analysis.   The result was that welfare economics became arid, attenuated and rather irrelevant for policy.   Its technical aspects were drawn to market relevance rather than to social and public sector development.   The principal source for the basic position of 'the new welfare economics' was the neoclassical Italian, Pareto (1848-1923), who had set down conditions for optimality, an outcome whereby, in private exchange, no member of society can be made better off without making another worse off.   Thus conceived, optimality is specified from technical criteria in consumption, production and exchange, and from the value premise that economics should be (almost) value free and 'scientific'.   'Welfare' then becomes a matter of aggregating individual utilities, without any basic concern for the distribution of income or for any 'non-economic' considerations in welfare.   The whole subject became bogged down in hypothetical technical qualifications aimed at modifying the severity of Paretian optimality - 'compensation tests', 'reversal tests' and so on.   In the hands of some economists (e.g., Bergson), welfare economics turned unrealistically towards global alternative ideal states of social, economic and philosophical welfare, never precisely defined, but imagined as abstract 'social welfare functions'.   In some hypothetical way a social welfare function was decreed by superman or superwoman, and the economist was then assumed to apply the appropriate theory and criteria to achieve the goals.

The timing of all this during the 1930s was ironical.   Mass unemployment became a general condition in the democracies, but welfare economics could not be used for policy solutions.   Myrdal [43] had written in 1928 showing exactly how neoclassical economics had improperly divorced political and ethical values from technical considerations, and so taken the subject from its early traditions of being 'political economy'.   However, Myrdal's work was not translated from Swedish to English until 1953, and his ideas remained outside a mainstream which had been influenced by Robbins' plea for a 'scientific' line.   It was during the 1930s that Pigou turned his pen to more general welfare considerations, but his acceptance among economists was rather limited, because the Robbins' scientism dominated.   Writing in 1936, Pigou advocated government roles to correct for social costs, monopoly, a private sector which tended to myopia and consequently ignored intergenerational welfare, economic inequality, and low wages. He said that private and public sector roles must be considered pragmatically, with each case to be argued on its merits.   The final irony was the future change in Robbins' own attitudes to policy and to normative matters in economics, whilst virtually a whole generation of economists adhered to his earlier 1932 views.   Writing in 1954, 1963 and 1978 [44] Robbins suggested that although economics might retain some neutral 'scientific' basis, it was important to give prior consideration to income distribution, to the law of property, to general considerations in public finance, and to a range of social sciences

which also have relevance in public policy.   All of that is good advice
as far as housing is concerned.

In the meantime, from 1932 to the early-1960s, welfare economics, with
its basic Paretian criteria for optimality, was qualified and made less
certain by new theoretical work on monopoly, on 'second best' situations
where the optimum conditions were infeasible, and by increasing
circumspection on the inequality of income distribution.   However, the
subject did not return to Pigou's concepts, but was made more diverse by
the growth and development of *public goods* and *merit goods* theory.
This theory, together with the regenerated interest in social policy in
the 1960s and 1970s, led to a re-invigorated interest in welfare
economics and in the roles for government in education, health, housing
and urban policies.

Public goods theory was developed by Samuelson [45], Musgrave [46]
and Buchanan [47].   The benefits from ordinary market goods are
divisible and can be privatised, but the benefits from public goods are
diffused, indivisible and it is either infeasible or sometimes
uneconomic to take appropriation by pricing.   In circumstances where
the provision of goods can neither be made by the market nor by
voluntary group agreement - and where external benefits are spread
among large numbers, voluntary agreement will be improbable - then a
case for government provision can be established.   (This is further
elaborated in Chapter 7 where the case for government involvement in
land development is discussed.)   Public goods and externality benefits
contain economic and organisational problems which do not occur in
private goods.

Private goods can be traded in markets where the indicators for
consumer preferences, for levels of production and for the use of
resources are overt and determinate.   This in not so clearly the case
with public goods, where benefits are indivisible and external, enabling
individuals to become 'free riders'.   That is to say, it is in their
interests to enjoy the benefits at the cost of others, leading them to
understate their true preferences and thereby avoiding a contribution to
costs.   This is, of course, from an analytical and individualistic
view;   if government makes provisions, then the costs will be covered
from obligatory taxes.   However, government provisions and taxation have
to be economically, or otherwise, justified in some sense.

The economic justifications in modern public finance theory have taken
two courses.   First, in the tradition of the Swede, Wicksell, an
individualistic approach can be adopted.   Wicksell gets rid of the 'free
rider' problem by requiring government provisions to be made
conditionally: (1) one good at a time, (2) simultaneously linking taxes
with provisions, and (3) requiring a unanimity rule for voting.   The
unanimity rule constrains individuals to reveal their preferences, to
bargain and 'trade' the composition of government economic provisions,
or otherwise to forgo the benefits by exclusion from the polity.
Wicksell recognises that unanimity is unrealistic (some modern theorists
have argued that it adds to costs by virtue of individuals adopting a
stubborn hold-out to get their own way), and consequently he reduces the
rule to 'relative unanimity'.   Steiner [48] takes another view.   He
argues that it is political parties, not individuals, which express
preferences for public goods and they propose tax structures.   They
compete for power;   they are in a state of flux in getting support from

loose 'coalitions' of interest; and it is the possibilities for the withdrawal of support by groups and the public at large which constrains and limits proposals for government activity.

The two approaches should not be regarded simply as alternative choices for interpretation; rather they both build up understanding. Wicksell's approach has led to analytical and technical development of public goods theory - its relationships with external social benefits, with joint costs and with the extension of public goods to 'merit goods' theory. (Merit goods were defined in Chapter 1, and the principal authors of this theory are Musgrave [49] and Head [50].) Steiner's approach adds reality to the subject by turning attention towards the real ways in which economics and politics are intertwined. Both approaches have turned this specialist part of welfare economics to 'political economy', thus drawing it away from technical aridity and isolationism.

We can now discern the directions which modern public goods and merit goods theory have taken - directions which are important for intellectualism and for policy in housing. Compared with earlier theory, public finance is now more firmly concerned with egalitarianism, with decentralisation in government, with institutional and organisation-al forms, and with pragmatism on the question of whether individual or social preferences should prevail. Questions of efficiency remain important but there is more circumspection about 'optimality'. As Samuelson, the modern pioneer in public goods theory, has shown [51], although it is possible to specify conditions for optimality in public goods, owing to the indivisibility of benefits and the impossibility of getting appropriations from (differentiated) pricing, it is infeasible to organise optimal efficiency. Add to this the inherent conflicts of interest in public goods provisions (i.e., the incidence of costs and benefits) and contesting views on income distribution, and we find further reasons for seeking 'more' economic welfare rather than taking optimality as our primary quest in public policy analysis.

It has been through the post-1960 development of the theory of public finance that modern economists are now recognising that their subject is not sufficiently equipped to deal with public policy; other knowledge from history, politics and social administration is needed. Also, the respective roles of the private and public sectors should be viewed pragmatically, taking each case on its merits, rather than applying *laissez faire* dogma. In some cases, the external benefits and public goods arguments will be persuasive for government roles, and in others alternative public or private sector provisions may yield important qualitative differences in their results. According to Steiner [52] the way to illuminate these public goods and qualitative factors is to refer them to such questions as: (1) who are the potential beneficiar-ies of government provision? (2) what is the nature of their claim? and (3) what is their best alternative if the claims are rejected? These are clearly important in housing.

Since 1960, various public finance theorists, including Downs [53], Olson [54] and Buchanan [55] have been working in the area at the intersection of economics and politics. Buchanan's work is particularly interesting because he has stayed with and developed this subject throughout the 1960-1980 period; he has set out an alternative theoretical justification for income redistribution compared with

Pigou's Utilitarian basis; and he has been concerned to argue that
precepts of economic individualism lead to the limitation of government
roles, notwithstanding the importance of public goods.

Writing in 1962 Buchanan revived the contract theory of the state, the
kind of social theory which had been used in the period between the
Reformation and the Industrial Revolution as a justification for limiting the inherited absolute power of monarchy.   Classical contract
theory is based upon artificial logical abstraction whereby men and
women are removed from actual society to engage in a pre-society
rational discourse on the constitutional limitations of the state.
Essentially contractarianism is a device for rationalising political
obligation, giving reason and cause why an individual will sacrifice
some freedom to get security, protection, and the opportunity for
development from the state.   The (conceptual) contract expresses
mutuality, limitations on state power, willingness to pay taxes, and
obligations to obey some agreed sorts of laws.   As Gough [56], an
eminent author on social contract theory, has stated, it is those who
have an exaggerated sense of individualism who are led towards the
theory.   Also, the theory has other shortcomings, including its
artificiality and its unhistorical nature, its neglect of factors making
for social cohesion and its logical difficulty in reconciling consent
with obedience.   The theory declined as a significant historical force
at the onset of the Industrial Revolution, but under the pen of Buchanan
and Rawls (see the later discussions) it has been revived in recent
years.

Buchanan's contractarian theory of political economy is based upon his
belief in individualism and his view that the nature of economics
centres around voluntary exchange.   From markets, he extends voluntary
exchange principles to the political sphere.   During the period 1962-
1980, Buchanan has developed the sophistication and scope of his
contractarianism.   In his 1962 writing, Buchanan used his social
contract only to explain and justify the government role in providing
public goods.   At that stage, he was extending Wicksell's work, adding
qualification and elaboration to the unanimity rule.   Like Wicksell,
Buchanan put the questions of property rights and basic income
distribution outside the scope of voting rules and constitutional
agreement.   This was unsatisfactory because *real* political and economic
power is unequal in *real* society, and this is a political issue in *real*
society.   In other words, real society has economic and political
inequality whereas in the fictional society where men and women reason
and agree a social contract, they are assumed to have no preconditional
economic and political power.   The force of real society's inequality
became more obvious in the late-1960s and the early-1970s when the
modern democracies were experiencing various socially- and equality-
motivated reforms.   Public and merit goods areas - education, health,
housing and urban administration - were receiving much intellectual,
social action and political attention.   The reform process was full of
conflicts, contentions and it provoked strong conservative reactions.

Buchanan responded to those circumstances by widening and deepening
his contractarian political economy.   He wanted to account for
egalitarianism, and he felt the need to oppose what he regarded as the
excesses of growing social choice at the expense of individualism.
Accordingly he stuck to individualistic contractarianism, and
incorporated questions of property rights and income distribution.

His modified contractarianism was explained as comprising three stages.
In the first 'preconstitutional' stage men and women were assumed to
discourse on different types of property rights, with their consequent
patterns of income distribution.   At the second 'constitutional' stage,
these men and women were to resolve the constitution, to limit state
power and to decide appropriate voting rules - unanimity, 'relative
unanimity' and others.   Also, they were to understand that over
successive time periods the winners with high incomes may later become
the losers with low incomes.   (Buchanan would not use terms like
winners and losers, because he emphasises mutual gains.)   These
conjectured changes in wealth and income over successive periods might
lead men and women to agree that redistributional powers were admissible
in the polity and in constitutional provisions, but with limitations.
Finally, in a 'postconstitutional' stage, men and women stick to the
constitutional rules, and they can act politically in choosing among
some limited scope alternatives in wealth and income transfers.   This
approach to income and wealth distribution appeals to Buchanan because,
compared with Pigou's approach, he regards his own as 'positive', not
'normative'.   That is to say, Buchanan insists that the inheritance
from Wicksell is based more on economic considerations, rather than on
the imported political content in Pigou's use of Utilitarianism.
(Pigou had argued for redistribution from the basis of his assumption
that the poor had more intense wants to satisfy than the rich.)
However, Buchanan's general and wider purposes were certainly not
apolitical.   He wanted to conserve individualism against what he saw
as the threat of big government.

The political thrust of Buchanan's post-1974 writing is revealed in
the titling of his books: *The Limits of Liberty: Between Anarchy and
Leviathan*, and *Freedom in Constitutional Contract: Perspectives of a
Political Economist*.   These were a conservative intellectual's reaction
to the social reforms of the 1960s and the early-1970s; it was an
argument that the growth of government had reduced personal liberty,
that society was threatened by bureaucracy and that reformist governments
should keep within the bounds of 'constitutional' limitations.
Buchanan thus joins Hayek [57] as a leading intellectual author of the
modern conservatism, a reaction to recent governments' fuller
involvement in social policy development.   These sorts of reaction
have occurred in earlier periods.

During the 1880s, social and political agitation in Britain led to
housing, urban and social reforms.   The conservative intellectual
reactions to the uncontrollable monster 'Leviathan' were written by
Herbert Spencer (1820-1903) under the titles, *The Coming Slavery*, *The
Great Political Superstitution* and *Man Versus the State* [58].   Spencer
approved the conservative reaction to housing reform, written by
Raffalovich who argued that 'housing poverty' was inevitable, and that
government could not have an effective impact on housing which, he said,
should be left to voluntarism and private enterprise.   Generally, we
might acknowledge that in periods of ferment and social reform, the
advocates of reform become over-enthusiastic, and then conservative
reactions in turn become somewhat exaggerated with value-laden titles in
the writings of intellectual proponents of the case against 'Leviathan'.
That is the political nature of things, and we might expect circumspection to re-appear later in the years after the intensity of reform
passes.   Some modern economic theorists in public finance have been
caught up with the political intensities and reactions during periods of

concentrated social reform.

We can now summarise the main general conclusions which emerge from modern welfare economics and public goods theory, pointing our commentary towards welfare state significance:

1. The separation of efficiency and equity can be maintained only for simplistic expositionary purposes. In fact, even at the (merely) technical level, it is impossible to separate out questions of efficiency and equity. At more fundamental levels distributional considerations are obviously important, and even a modern conservative theorist, such as Buchanan, will open up questions about justifications and political resolutions of property rights and the use of political institutions to redistribute income. As for housing, if we take Buchanan's modified contractarianism seriously, with its 'rational' deliberation of property and income distribution, then we might reasonably assume that men and women would want access to various tenures, including home ownership, without hard *laissez faire* impediments.

2. It is not possible to establish a unique social optimum in economics. In the market sector, economists can present Paretian criteria which are used to define a series of optima, each one dependent upon a particular distribution of income and based upon rather restrictive views of what constitutes economics. Once, the realities of monopoly, social costs and benefits and government are admitted into the subject, the notion of optimality becomes limited. The presence of public goods creates further dilemmas, because although conditions for optima can be defined, they cannot be operated in a real pricing system. Governments will be using non-economic considerations and proposing their own values in the provision of public goods and merit goods.

3. Public goods are inherently suffused with general benefits and in their purest theoretical form, when one person consumes them, they are no less available to other consumers. All of this leads to awkward problems of how they should be provided, and how the political system should be organised and structured, in a context where markets are inadequate, and provision involves conflicts of interest and considerable administrative costs. The extension of the public goods case to merit goods, where on grounds of distortions in individual choice, social choice might be substituted, adds more of these sorts of problems.

4. In view of the foregoing, the modern concerns of a welfare or public finance economist include primary significance to income distribution and to the form and organisation of non-market institutions, as well as to economic efficiency. We have clearly seen, as we might have expected, that economic theorists will adopt political and ideological reactions to social change, sometimes incorporating the reactions in their theory and their language.

Welfare and public finance economics has returned to a genuine 'political economy', but in its dominant versions in the modern democracies it is inevitably grounded in liberal economic theory. The subject can offer a variety of good theoretically-based arguments which help to formulate the perspective on problems and to elaborate the

50

broad consequences of policies.   It cannot provide purely scientific
prescriptions on housing and public policy.   However, the general
principles from welfare economics and modern public goods theory can be
used to illuminate housing matters.   This book develops many of its
themes in close association with public goods and merit goods theory,
and with consideration to wealth and income distribution.   In Chapter
3, we discuss housing as property with its tenure-related inequalities.
The public goods and externality aspects of housing are especially
significant in land development policies, and these are elaborated in
Chapter 7.   More generally, housing economists are now drawing upon
some more fertile principles from welfare economics and public goods
theory, using them to argue for equity as well as efficiency in housing
policy.   Some indicative exampling is given in the next paragraph, and
this subject is taken up more elaborately in Chapter 4.

Although welfare economics becomes more eclectic and controversial,
its application to modern policy development in housing widens and
deepens.   For example, during the last decade or so, the modern
democracies have had to confront the prevalence of marked inefficiencies
and inequities in their housing policies.   In fact, it has been public
policies as well as the market which had contributed to these
conspicuous defects.   These problems call for more intellectualism and
theory in housing, not just for technical research.   It is crucial to
know the costs and benefits of housing programmes to consumers, to
social groups and to the wider society.   Since 1970, welfare economists
have drawn upon the legacy of ideas from Alfred Marshall and other
theorists whose contributions were general, rather than specifically for
housing policy development.   One useful breakthrough has been
contributed by De Salvo [59] who uses methods from welfare economics to
get at such questions as: (1) what is the *equivalent income benefit* to
consumers of subsidised housing, (2) how does this income benefit
compare with the cost to society in providing low-priced subsidised
housing, and (3) if the cost to society is greater than the value the
consumers place on the benefits, what are the further sources of benefit
to society to justify the greater cost.   These questions are relevant
to the design and construction of housing allowances, and now that
substantial resources have been poured into research the answers can be
found.   Clearly, welfare economics is becoming more deeply and more
usefully involved in questions of housing policy development.

The development of economic thought contains some reactions against
neoclassical economics, and this has had an impact on housing policy
development.   During the 1870s and 1880s, at the height of agitation
for housing and social reform, some British economists advocated a
branching out from neoclassical traditions towards the *German
institutionalists*.   Institutionalism in economics had dominated German
economic thought in the 1840-1880 period.   Roscher (1817-1894), one of
its principal authors, advocated the use of historical as well as
Ricardian deductive analysis in economic thought.   As agitation for
social reform quickened during the 1870s in Britain, some economists
saw the relevance of historical methods, the advantages of an inter-
disciplinary approach which included philosophy and social discourse,
and some justification for getting humanitarianism into economic
institutions.   W. Smart, the Adam Smith Professor of Political Economy
at Glasgow University, advocated egalitarianism and the synthesis of
economics and social philosophy. [60]   Furthermore, Smart's association
with Glasgow, where housing stress was particularly acute, led to his

involvement with housing policy in that city.

Although Glasgow City Corporation had taken initiatives in the 1870s
to enable its Improvement Trust to construct housing for rental on its
cleared sites, housing stress (bad sanitary conditions, overcrowding
and high rents) continued. Intellectuals., church leaders and civic
groups began to give more attention to housing problems. Smart was
drawn into a church committee [61] which examined the housing question,
and, independently, he developed an economic argument for more
Corporation activity in housing. [62] Other civic initiatives were
taken by the Glasgow Ruskin Society, the Royal Philosophical Society
and some architects. This involvement by the church, by adherents of
Ruskin's aesthetic objections to capitalism and by intellectuals
searching for new ideas against *laissez faire* was representative of the
sort of forces which were generally behind the emergent Radicalism and
Socialism in Britain at that time. Smart's economic ideas in housing
are particularly interesting. Firstly, he reviewed Adam Smith's
contingencies to *laissez faire* and found that a government role could be
justified either when an activity had economies of scale beyond private
enterprise capacity, or when goods had economic externality. Secondly,
he considered the ability-to-pay argument in the theory of public
finance, but found that because municipal finance at that time was
derived from a regressive property tax, the poor, as well as the rich,
would have to pay for any extension of government-assisted social
housing. Furthermore, the provision of social housing would confer a
sectional benefit. Smart stated that in ordinary cases these
considerations would together make a compelling argument against
government provision. However, according to Smart, housing conditions
in Glasgow were exceptional; housing was fever-ridden, demoralising,
and Glasgow's slums were havens for debauchery. He went on to argue
that standard housing would produce social benefits in the form of good
health, quiet at night and a future for children whose lives were
blunted by demoralisation in the slums. Smart concluded that the
Corporation should provide housing for the 'dissolute' poor and housing
for the 'decent' poor could be provided by the new limited-profit
Glasgow Workmen's Dwellings Company which had adopted methods pioneered
by Lord Shaftesbury and Octavia Hill.

Smart's ideas have two sources of interest for economists; firstly,
they contain interesting conceptualisations which have recurred in
modern economic analysis, and secondly they reflect some (limited)
departure from *laissez faire* in housing. The allocational principle
underlying Smart's argument can be identified as a social cost/benefit
case, but some of its targets depended upon an exaggerated belief in
environmental determinism. On the distributional principle, Smart
accepted another popularly misconceived notion in social policy; he
believed that the 'decent' poor could be separated from the 'dissolute'
poor. However, although Smart's ideas contained some weaknesses,
they were significant for their departure from *laissez faire* and their
indication of an alternative to the abstractions and social remoteness
of the neoclassical inheritance in economics. It is in times of social
ferment and agitation for social reform that some economists take up
more interest in history, philosophy and social questions. This is
important because it is not possible to develop subjects like social
administration without the intelligence which economics provides.

Our discussions on the development of liberal economic thought, and

the reactions to it, have emphasised the divisions in the various
legacies and the relative merits of each.   Each branch has something to
contribute to housing policy, and it is difficult to avoid the passing
thought that some synthesis would be appropriate.   Some recently
emerging trends add weight to the need for synthesis.   The introductory
discussions in this study made reference to the need for a co-ordinated
approach to housing subsidies and to the development of *para-market*
instruments in continental Europe, expressing a blending of market and
government allocations in housing.   Also, some post-1970 housing
research in the United States has been concerned with developing a
medium-term predictive economic model in housing which can *simultaneously* show the consequences in housing sub-markets and for public
expenditure when housing policies are revised. [63]   Nevertheless,
much remains to be done in this area.   Subsidisation in modern housing
policies remains riddled with problems of inconsistencies among
objectives, bad rental policies continue, public expenditure is sometimes inadequately controlled, and inequities remain.   Housing-related
equity has emerged during the last decade as a key issue in policy
development, and the concluding section of this chapter examines the
philosophical ideas associated with modern egalitarianism and equity.

EQUITY AND EGALITARIANISM

Equity and egalitarianism are not the same thing, but are related.   A
full discourse on equity would view it from the perspective of needs,
merit and the distribution of economic product through private and
public sector institutions.   Considerations of needs, merit and the
distribution of product through economic institutions are in conflict.
As a practical and an institutional matter in modern mixed economies,
most debates about equity centre around the conflict between needs and
the way society distributes the existing product.   Debates about
egalitarianism are about the same subject matter.   Housing is a prime
candidate for these debates because it is a reflection of inequality in
society; and by its relationship to tenure and changing economic and
urban processes, prevailing inequalities can be compounded, because
asset values increase in line with increases in income, speculation and
improvements in the urban environment.   Furthermore, the equity problem
is given a sharp edge in housing because the patterns of housing-derived
vertical and horizontal inequalities among households tend to be
arbitrary.

    The irony of this is that, after some 70 years of housing reform
achieved mainly under the impact of Green's moral Liberalism and Social
Democratic egalitarianism, the housing derived inequalities have been
increasingly pronounced recently.   For example, in The Netherlands
(more egalitarian than most countries) the inequality in incomes, after
adjustment for taxes and social security, has decreased; but after
allowing for net wealth, it has increased.   Inflation has hoisted the
value of housing and other personal assets, even though structural
economic changes have been removing some of the income advantages in
some professional occupations.

    Broadly, there are four philosophical approaches to equality and
equity claiming relevance to the condition of modern society.   These
are Marxist theory, Utilitarianism, intuitionist theories and contract
theories.   Marxist theory regards such things as equity and equality

as derivatives from the economic foundation of society and its evolutionary laws. Apart from 'dialectical materialism', any commentaries on the concepts would be regarded as class-based assessments and utterly ineffective in achieving real reform, which Marxists believe depends on the economic laws of society and not on prescriptive ideas of social justice.

Some of the earlier discussion centred on interpreting and assessing the Utilitarian legacies in liberal economic theory. Compared with intuitionist and contract theories, Utilitarianism is goal-based (i.e., it is teleological). Essentially, the theory espouses a desired end and sets out the conditions to fulfil this end. For example, hedonistic happiness in society is optimised by designing and constructing social and economic institutions so they produce the maximum increments of 'pleasure' after 'pain' has been subtracted. *Laissez faire* in economic institutions is also advocated because of its allegedly superior performance in adding to the total product. As noted earlier, the problem with Utilitarianism is that it empties moral statements, rights and more overt ways of resolving conflicts of interest.

Intuitionist theories enable moral statements to be accounted. Basically, the intuitionist view of rationality in choosing among social and philosophical values is mainly 'the art of applying, and combining, reconciling, and choosing among general principles in a manner for which complete theoretical explanation (or justification) can never, in principle, be given'. [64] In other words, such values as equality, liberty and authority are frequently in conflict and the trade-off among them has to be weighed, balanced and critically assessed. The intuitionist approach disclaims Marxist 'dialectical materialism', Utilitarian teleology, and the contractual rights-based justifications for particular values. The thrust of the intuitionist approach is towards creating moral and social knowledge by appraising particular situations to find balanced and reasonable solutions. Though the approach is flexible, this advantage is obtained at the cost of staying outside a coherent, consistent and generalising theoretical rationality.

Contract theories tighten the hold of consistency and coherence by setting out their arguments and inferences within axiomatic theories. In earlier discussions on the modern development of the theory of public finance, we have referred to Buchanan's use of contractarian arguments for economic and political justification. Another recent example of a contract theory, but setting out egalitarianism as its basic axiom, is represented by Rawls' theory of social justice, [65] an example of a rights-based theory concentrating its argument (by logical abstraction in a contractual context) [66] on the duty of society to achieve egalitarianism. The advantage is that the argument is focused and concentrated, and values stand out clearly. However, the disadvantage is that the values are produced from unreal situations. When philosophical arguments are pushed hard, some of the 'axioms' are revealed as far-removed from self-evident truths. Nevertheless, Rawls' work is a welcome modern alternative to Utilitarian economic reasoning with its neglect of the basic ethical aspects of public policy.

From these approaches, the position of this study is towards the intuitionist approach. The inclusion of general (i.e., non-dialectical) history and comparative evaluations will particularise the arguments.

Perhaps, much of the analytical discussion in economics (see Chapter 4) will be representative of confronting Utilitarianism with Green's moral liberalism and some Social Democratic egalitarianism. Some of the key housing-related propositions on equity and egalitarianism emerging from this study include:

1. Arbitrary inequalities exist in housing in modern democratic society. This is inequitable because of the arbitrariness and because one important principle of justification for the welfare state is egalitarianism.

2. The inequity is relevant because it acts as a discriminatory barrier against some households achieving self-fulfilment in housing. We know from historical and sociological evidence that self-fulfilment is a strong influence in housing-related motivations, and that housing is important in promoting welfare, particularly for children, the aged and people at social and economic risk.

3. The issues are significant in policy. In recent years, Sweden and The Netherlands accounted tenure-related equity in housing reform. More generally, other European countries have experienced recent housing reforms where attempts have been made to simultaneously account for allocational, distributional and stabilisation objectives. However, the equity-related problems are varied, and the process of reform is far from complete. It should be continued because much is at stake for households still waiting for equity.

4. Some societies are more adaptable to reform than others. Egalitarianism and equity are largely tied up with central government reforms, which are not so easy to achieve in divided and fragmented political systems. However, housing reform also requires more localisation and regionalisation; this may conflict with the need for more egalitarianism. However, some important housing-related economic externalities have implications for egalitarianism; localisation and regionalisation are necessary to attend to these factors (see Chapter 9).

5. Egalitarianism in general often conflicts with freedom and choice. However, in some countries housing choice has been constrained by social theory, professional practice, rigidities in financing, and monopolistic elements in the organisational structures. Choice has sometimes been more apparent than real. In housing, it is possible to design, and construct policies giving more choice and egalitarianism. Once these reforms are accomplished, then egalitarianism and freedom might conflict, but, the Norwegian example shows that egalitarianism, choice and good housing can occur simultaneously.

Quite obviously, these statements mix particularism with general principle, and rely for their support on empiricism, history and a selective analysis. The key terms used in them will be defined and discussed in subsequent chapters. One of the purposes of the study is to arrive, critically, at value statements with policy significance. The statements above are crucial in that context; they are not meant merely as illustrations of how values can be derived from certain methods of study. They point towards a modern social administration of housing.

NOTES

[1] G.Myrdal, *The Political Element in the Development of Economic Theory*, Routledge and Kegan Paul, London, 1953.
[2] G.Myrdal, *Objectivity in Social Research*, Duckworth, London, 1970.
[3] This information was given by W.A.Greenhill MD in evidence to a Select Committee of Parliament: *Report from the Select Committee on Artizans' and Labourers' Dwellings*, Parliamentary Papers, 1882, Minutes of Evidence, paras. 441-2.
[4] See J.S.Mill, *The Right of Property in Land*, Dallow, London, 1873.
[5] The Ricardian Socialists included William Thompson (1775-1833), John Gray (1799-1883), Thomas Hodgskin (1783-1869), and John Francis Bray (1809-1897), who were all contemporaries of Owen. David Ricardo (1772-1823) was acknowledged as the most eminent economist of his age, and he had argued that economic value could be measured in labour units. The Ricardian Socialists went further and said that labour is the *source* of value. Marx subsequently adopted and elaborated the labour theory of value.
[6] See M.Broady, *Planning for People*, Bedford Square Press, London, 1968, and H.J.Gans, *People and Plans*, Penguin, Harmondsworth, 1972.
[7] A detailed history of the British building society movement to 1964 is given by; E.J.Cleary, *The Building Society Movement*, Elek, London, 1965.
[8] For further details, see; Cleary, *op. cit* (1965) pp. 101-15.
[9] A recent review of political conservatism in Britain makes out such a case, see; T.F.Lindsay and M.Harrington, *The Conservative Party 1918-1970*, MacMillan, London, 1974.
[10] M.Olson, *The Logic of Collective Action*, Harvard University Press, Boston, 1962.
[11] The Society organised the acquisition of 50 hectare blocks of land for co-operatively housing and employing 60 cultivators. Shares were bought at £2.50 each, and a parcel of 2,000 shares would buy 50 hectares of land. For a detailed historical account of the Society see; A.M. Hadfield, *The Chartist Land Company*, David and Charles, Newton Abbott, 1970.
[12] See D.Harvey, *Social Justice and The City*, Arnold, London, 1973 and C.G.Pickvance (ed), *Urban Sociology: Critical Essays*, Tavistock, London, 1976.
[13] See the references in Note 12, above, and the contrasting Liberal interpretations by: R.E.Pahl, *Whose City?*, Penguin, Harmondsworth, 1975.
[14] See A.Alecsandrescu, 'Distribution of Housing Costs Between the Public Sector and Individuals', and L.Nemethy, 'New Trends in Forms of Tenure in the Socialist Countries of Eastern Europe', Papers Presented to the Seminar on Housing Policy, Turku, Finland, 4-9 July 1977, Economic Commission for Europe, Committee on Housing, Building and Planning.
[15] These matters are fully discussed by O.Lange, *Papers in Economics and Sociology*, Pergamon, Oxford, 1970.
[16] The development and differentiation of Socialism and Liberalism is dealt with in the following texts: G.Duncan, *Marx and Mill*, Cambridge University Press, London, 1973. R.Harrison, *Before the Socialists: Studies in Labour and Politics 1861-1881*, Routledge and Kegan Paul, London, 1965, G.Lichtheim, *A Short History of Socialism*, Weidenfeld and Nicolson, London, 1970. A.M.McBriar, *Fabian Socialism and English Politics 1884-1918*, Cambridge University Press, Cambridge, 1966. P. Thompson, *Socialists, Liberals and Labour: The Struggle for London 1885-1914*, Routledge and Kegan Paul, London, 1967. W.Wolfe, *From*

Radicalism to Socialism, Yale University Press, New Haven, 1975.

[17] Report from the Select Committee, *op. cit* (1882), Minutes of Evidence, paras. 135-6.

[18] *Report of Her Majesty's Commissioners for Inquiring into Housing of the Working Classes*, Eyre and Spottiswoode, London, 1885.

[19] See C.Pugh, 'Older Residential Areas and the Development of Economic Analysis', in J.C.McMaster and G.R.Webb (eds) *Australian Urban and Regional Economics: A Reader*, Australian and New Zealand Book Co., Sydney, 1976.

[20] B.Headey, *Housing Policy in the Developed Economy*, Croom Helm, London, 1978.

[21] A fuller treatment of Social Democracy in Vienna during the 1920s can be found in: C.O.Hardy and R.R.Kuczynski, *The Housing Program of the City of Vienna*, Brookings, Washington D.C.,1934.

[22] For the intellectual dismantling of the anti-urban attitudes, see H.J.Gans, *The Levittowners*, Penguin, Harmondsworth, 1967.

[23] See *Report of the Royal Commission of Inquiry into the Question of the Housing of Workmen in Europe and America*, Government Printer, Sydney, 1913.

[24] Norwegian Conservatism is based upon self-made homestead farming enterprise whereas British Conservatism has its roots in the aristocratic belief in hierarchy and authority. British Conservatism is discussed by Lindsay and Harrington, *op. cit.* (1974).

[25] Marginalism measures incremental change. For example, the marginal utility yielded by the 'n'th unit of consumption is the total utility of 'n' units, minus the total utility of n-1 units.

[26] E.O.Olsen, 'A Competitive Theory of the Housing Market', *American Economic Review*, September 1969, pp.612-22.

[27] W.G.Grigsby, *Housing Markets and Public Policy*, Philadelphia, University of Philadelphia Press, 1963.

[28] L.Winnick, *American Housing and its Use: the Demand for Shelter Space*, Wiley, New York, 1957.

[29] C.Rapkin and W.G.Grigsby, *The Demand for Housing in Racially Mixed Areas*, University of California Press, Berkeley, 1960.

[30] For a useful set of essays on this subject, see Institute of Economic Affairs, *Verdict on Rent Control*, Institute of Economic Affairs, London, 1976.

[31] Grigsby, *op. cit.* (1963).

[32] See the interpretations by G.Hallett, *Housing and Land Policies in West Germany and Britain*, MacMillan, London, 1977.

[33] J.S.Mill, *Principles of Political Economy*, Ninth Edition, Longmans, London, 1909.

[34] A.Marshall, *Principles of Economics*, Eighth Edition, MacMillan, London, 1930, p.677.

[35] A.C.Pigou, *Wealth and Welfare*, MacMillan, London, 1912, and *The Economics of Welfare*, Fourth Edition, MacMillan, London, 1952.

[36] Pigou, *op. cit.* (1952) p.183.

[37] Pigou, *op. cit.* (1912) p.148.

[38] Pigou, *op. cit.* (1912) p.21-2.

[39] See R.A.Musgrave and A.T.Peacock, *Classics in the Theory of Public Finance*, MacMillan, London, 1958.

[40] J.G.Head, *Public Goods and Public Welfare*, Duke University Press, Durham, North Carolina, 1974.

[41] A.C.Pigou, *Economics in Practice*, MacMillan, London, 1936.

[42] L.Robbins, *An Essay on the Nature and Significance of Economic Science*, MacMillan, London, 1932.

[43] Myrdal, *op. cit.* (1953).

[44] L.Robbins, *The Economist in the Twentieth Century*, MacMillan, London, 1954, *Politics and Economics*, MacMillan, London, 1963 and *The Theory of Economic Policy*, Second Edition, MacMillan, London, 1978.
[45] P.A.Samuelson, 'The Pure Theory of Public Expenditure', 'Diagrammatic Exposition of the Pure Theory of Public Expenditure', 'Aspects of Public Expenditure Theories', and 'Pure Theory of Public Expenditure and Taxation' all reprinted in R.W.Houghton (ed), *Public Finance*, Second Edition, Penguin, Harmondsworth, 1973.
[46] R.A.Musgrave, *The Theory of Public Finance*, McGraw Hill, New York, 1959.
[47] J.M.Buchanan, *The Demand and Supply of Public Goods*, Rand McNally, Chicago, 1968.
[48] P.O.Steiner, 'Public Expenditure Budgeting', in A.S.Blinder (ed), *The Economics of Public Finance*, Brookings, Washington D.C., 1974.
[49] Musgrave, *op. cit.*, (1959).
[50] Head, *op. cit.*, (1974).
[51] For references to Samuelson's work in public finance, see Note 45.
[52] Steiner, *op. cit.*, (1974).
[53] A.Downs, *An Economic Theory of Democracy*, Harper and Row, New York, 1956.
[54] Olson, *op. cit.*, (1962).
[55] J.M.Buchanan and G.Tullock, The Calculus of Consent, University of Michigan, Ann Arbor, 1962, J.M.Buchanan, *The Limits Of Liberty : Between Anarchy and Leviathan*, Chicago University Press, Chicago, 1975, and *Freedom in Constitutional Contract : Perspectives of a Political Economist*, Texas A and M University Press, College Station, 1977.
[56] J.W.Gough, *The Social Contract : A Critical Study of its Development*, Second Edition, Clarendon, Oxford, 1957.
[57] F.A.Hayek, *Law, Legislation and Liberty*, Volume I *Rules and Order*, Routledge and Kegan Paul, London, 1973.
[58] See H.Spencer, *Man Versus the State*, Williams and Norgate, London, 1884, and T.Mackay (ed), *A Plea for Liberty*, John Murray, London, 1891.
This latter text has an Introduction written by H.Spencer and an article on housing by A.Raffalovich.
[59] J.DeSalvo, 'A Methodology for Evaluating Housing Programs', *Journal of Regional Science*, Vol. II, 1971, pp.173-85.
[60] W.Smart, 'The Old Economy and the New', *Fortnightly Review*, Vol. 52, 1891, pp.279-92.
[61] The Presbytery of Glasgow set up a Social Union to report on housing, and published its report as: *Report of the Commission on the Housing of the Poor in Relation to their Social Condition*, James Maclehouse, Glasgow, 1891.
[62] See W.Smart, *The Housing Problem and The Municipality*, Adshead, Glasgow, 1902.
[63] See F. De Leeuw and R.J.Struyk, *The Web of Urban Housing*, Urban Institute, Washington D.C., 1975.
[64] I.Berlin, 'Equality', in W.T.Blackstone (ed), *The Concept of Equality*, Burgess, Minneapolis, 1969.
[65] J.Rawls, *A Theory of Justice*, Oxford University Press, London, 1972 and N.Daniels (ed), *Reading Rawls*, Blackwell, Oxford, 1975.
[66] In contractual theory, rational beings are taken from real society and placed into a simplified set of conditions where a discourse on ultimate values and the nature of society can be discovered. This can be considered as a logical abstraction. Under Rawls' contract theory, rational beings deliberate the terms of a contract which would produce social justice. The contract then defines the rules and principles for

practice in a real society.

REFERENCES (SELECTED)

Berlin, I., 'Equality', in W.T.Blackstone (ed), *The Concept of Equality*, Burgess, Minneapolis, 1969.

Broady, M., *Planning for People*, Bedford Square Press, London, 1968.

Buchanan, J.M., *The Demand and Supply of Public Goods*, Rand McNally, Chicago, 1968.

Cleary, E., *The Building Society Movement*, Elek, London, 1965.

Daniels, N. (ed), *Reading Rawls*, Blackwell, Oxford, 1975.

Dobb, M., *Welfare Economics and the Economics of Socialism: Towards a Commonsense Critique*, Cambridge University Press, Cambridge, 1969.

Duncan, G., *Marx and Mill*, Cambridge University Press, London, 1973.

Gans, H.J., *People and Plans*, Penguin, Harmondsworth, 1972.

Gough, J.W., *The Social Contract: A Critical Study of its Development*, Second Edition, Clarendon, Oxford, 1957.

Harrison, J.F.C., *Robert Owen and the Owenites in Britain and America*, Routledge and Kegan Paul, London, 1969.

Harvey, D., *Social Justice and The City*, Arnold, London, 1973.

Hayek, F.A., *Law, Legislation and Liberty*, Routledge and Kegan Paul, London, 1973.

Lange, O., *Papers in Economics and Sociology*, Pergamon, Oxford, 1970.

Lichtheim, G., *A Short History of Socialism*, Weidenfeld and Nicolson, London, 1970.

Lindsay, T.F. and Harrington, M., *The Conservative Party 1918-1970*, MacMillan, London, 1974.

McBriar, A.M., *Fabian Socialism and English Politics, 1884-1918*, Cambridge University Press, Cambridge, 1966.

Myrdal, G., *The Political Element in the Development of Economic Theory*, Routledge and Kegan Paul, London, 1953.

Pickvance, C.G. (ed), *Urban Sociology: Critical Essays*, Tavistock, London, 1976.

Pigou, A.C., *The Economics of Welfare*, Fourth Edition, MacMillan, London, 1952.

Pigou, A.C., *Economics in Practice*, MacMillan, London, 1936.

Rawls, J., *A Theory of Justice*, Oxford University Press, London, 1972.

Rees, J.C., *Equality*, MacMillan, London, 1971.

Robbins, L., *An Essay on the Nature and Significance of Economic Science*, MacMillan, London, 1932.

Robbins, L., *Politics and Economics*, MacMillan, London, 1963.

Shaw, G.B., (et. al.), *Fabian Essays*, Sixth Edition. George Allen and Unwin, London, 1962.

Simon, W.M., *European Positivism in the Nineteenth Century*, Cornell University Press, Ithaca, 1963.

Smart, W., *The Housing Problem and The Municipality*, Adshead, Glasgow, 1902.

Steiner, P.O., 'Public Expenditure Budgeting' in A.S.Blinder (ed), *The Economics of Public Finance*, Brookings, Washington D.C., 1974.

Winch, D.M., *Analytical Welfare Economics*, Penguin, Harmondsworth, 1971.

Wolfe, W., *From Radicalism to Socialism*, Yale University Press, New Haven, 1975.

ACKNOWLEDGMENTS

The following organisations contributed to my understanding of the voluntary housing movement in continental Europe. In West Germany: Gesamtverband gemeinnutziger Wohnungsunternehmen. In Norway: Norwegian Labour Party; OBOS: USBL. In Sweden: Stockholm City Council; Social Democratic Party; SR.

3   Housing policy and social policy

Modern housing history in democratic societies has some continuing
themes.   But compared with other spheres of social policy, housing has
also experienced discontinuities (interruptions), basic corrections and
substantial amendments.   All of this is essential for understanding
housing as a part of social policy, and it defines one of the purposes
of this chapter.   In the first topic of this chapter we shall draw
upon ideas from the previous chapter on social theory, extend them in
their housing policy context, and examine some selected aspects of
housing policy development.   The second section will review some
important interruptions and corrections to social thought about housing
which have emerged from the research done since 1960.   Third, we return
to an earlier theme to examine policy questions about self-fulfilment
and tenure choice in housing.   Finally, housing policies are set in
their context, in the welfare state, to explore the question of unity in
the development of housing, urban and social policies.

SOCIAL IDEALISM AND SOCIAL ACTION IN HOUSING : THE INHERITANCE

The treatment of this subject will be highly selective, not comprehensive.   Social idealism, social theory and social action have together
influenced the development of housing policies, since the mid-nineteenth
century.   These circumstances have left an inheritance of policies,
ideas and professions.   Because of its early industrial and urban
development the British experience has had wide influence; but there
have, of course, been variations in other countries.

   Chart 3, below, shows schematically the way that social housing and
town planning movements have developed.   They have drawn ideas
eclectically from a variety of sources, some of which were discussed in
the previous chapter.   It will be recalled that the Utopian Socialists
bequeathed the theory of environmental determinism which in a general
way entered town planning and social housing practice.   For example,
in 1849 J.S. Buckingham outlined a proposal to create a utopian city
('Victoria') with an orderly clean environment, community facilities
and so on.   The wider influence of environmental determinism can be
traced through the development of building regulations, theories of
urban obsolescence, slum clearance policies, ideas of residential
social mix and social balance, and the development of new standard low-
rent housing by voluntary housing associations and government.   As we
shall see, the main problem with the idea of environmental determinism
is that it lacks a satisfactory relationship with the economic, social
and political realities of the prevailing society.

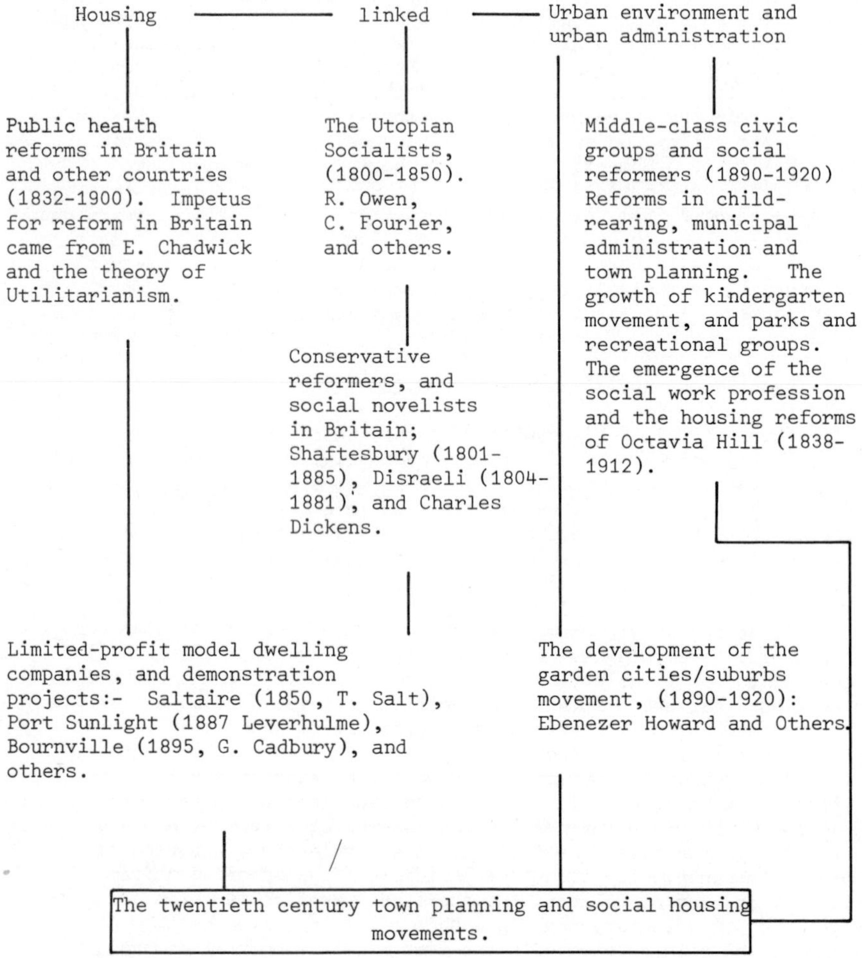

Housing ─────────── linked ─────── Urban environment and
                                                             urban administration

Public health   The Utopian   Middle-class civic
reforms in Britain   Socialists,   groups and social
and other countries   (1800-1850).   reformers (1890-1920)
(1832-1900). Impetus   R. Owen,   Reforms in child-
for reform in Britain   C. Fourier,   rearing, municipal
came from E. Chadwick   and others.   administration and
and the theory of   town planning.   The
Utilitarianism.   growth of kindergarten
                                                    movement, and parks and
                                                    recreational groups.
                           Conservative   The emergence of the
                           reformers, and   social work profession
                           social novelists   and the housing reforms
                           in Britain;   of Octavia Hill (1838-
                           Shaftesbury (1801-   1912).
                           1885), Disraeli (1804-
                           1881), and Charles
                           Dickens.

Limited-profit model dwelling   The development of the
companies, and demonstration   garden cities/suburbs
projects:- Saltaire (1850, T. Salt),   movement, (1890-1920):
Port Sunlight (1887 Leverhulme),   Ebenezer Howard and Others.
Bournville (1895, G. Cadbury), and
others.

                            /

The twentieth century town planning and social housing
                        movements.

CHART 3-1

A Schematic Diagram Showing The Origins Of Town Planning And
Social Housing Movements [1]

The Conservative idealism bequeathed by Lord Shaftesbury and Disraeli also influenced the course of professionalisation in housing and social policies. Some elements in this idealism suggested that more interaction among the classes might be educational, with each learning from the other; working-class aspirations might be raised and the way of life improved; and political radicalism might be staunched. This idealism led to social action in working-class areas (the slums) and ultimately took a course towards housing reform. The idealism and its connections to housing can be traced through personalities, social service and social development responses, and historical circumstances. Again, it influenced housing policy development in such specific things as building regulations, slum clearance, ideas on social mix and the development of standard low-rent housing.

Earlier comments pointed out the exaggerations and the somewhat unrealistic character of the Utopian Socialism. Conservative idealism also has its limitations. The reforming claims of class interaction, personal social services and social development can be exaggerated. Also, some of the assumptions on which the idealism is based, remain outside the influence of systematic knowledge and rigorous testing. These comments do not mean that class interaction, personal social services and social development have no legitimate claims. But they offer rather indirect and less effective routes to reform than other methods. For example, social development might be used in new communities to create leadership, help voluntary organisations and establish contact between people and planners so that the local urban servicing fits their needs better. However, the allocational and distributional problems (e.g., nineteenth-century slums, tenure-related rights to income and wealth), may often require more direct reform in central policy making and revisions to the method of resourcing and financing housing. Often in the nineteenth century, and from time to time in the twentieth, too much has been expected of social development alone; some exaggerated ideas of what it can achieve can still be found in the theory and practice of housing.

Another source of social theory in town planning and social housing has been through the public health movement, which brought together Utilitarian political philosophy, some statistical research on urban housing and social problems, and some moral philosophy via the medical profession. [2] It is interesting to compare the resulting public health philosophy with the ideas of Utopian Socialism and Conservative idealism.

Social ideas about public health tended to be more realistic than Utopian Socialism and Conservative idealism. The public health reforms were also connected more directly with community power and national policy reform. Utilitarianism emphasised 'usefulness', and its reformist aim was to draw public health (and some other things) into public finance and public administration because private enterprise had been ineffective. Housing was insanitary and urban areas were hit by contagious diseases. Chadwick, the key reformer in the years 1830-1854, used the principles of economic externality to show that society would benefit socially and economically by administering proper drainage and sewerage networks, and used social survey data to demonstrate the statistical effects of his case. He was among the first social researchers to combine theory with statistical research. The newly-formed London Statistical Society was also actively developing survey information on housing and urban conditions in this period.

Compared with Utopian Socialism and Conservative idealism, the public health movement was characterised by careful enquiry and useful theory. It thus left a different inheritance. However, though the three had distinguishable characteristics, their historical effects tended to mix and merge. Town planning and social housing are eclectic, and contain some of each influence. The mixture has a historical coherence, but not a rational one. Sometimes the unrealistic idealisms dominate but at other times more rational or practical considerations do. The purpose of this section is to trace some of the changing mixtures.

It can be argued that social thought in town planning and social housing were dominated by unrealistic idealism from about 1850 to 1960. Evidence can be found in a critical assessment of building regulations, theories of urban obsolescence, town planning practice, sociological explanations of urbanisation and so on. During the 1960s some sociologists and economists began to make critical analyses of the theory and practice of town planning. Social scientists during the 1960s and 1970s have drawn upon aims and methods closer to (and now more elaborate than) those used by Chadwick and the earlier contributors to the proceedings of the London Statistical Society. In other words, there has been an historical discontinuity in the development of theory and practice in social housing and town planning. The discontinuities and the corrections might be traced through town planning practices including 'garden cities', new towns, the idea of neighbourhood slum clearance, urban renewal, zoning, master plans and so on. Some of this had also influenced sociological interpretations of urbanisation. For example, in the 1920s the Chicago School of Human Ecology incorporated some environmental determinism into its interpretations.

Another general conclusion which emerges is that the blending of the three nineteenth century tributaries of social thought varies. Ideas for residential social mix seem to owe their origins more to Utopian Socialism and Conservative idealism than to more practical theories, or to an accumulation of systematic knowledge. By contrast, the historical development of building regulations and slum clearance mixes the three sources. But it is not easy to unscramble the three parts to show clearly where practical thought stops and where unrealistic idealism begins. This means that, compared with the development of social security schemes, housing standards do not reflect anything akin to minimum standards of sufficiency; rather they express idealism and some arbitrary economic and administrative controls. Much the same thing could be said about other spheres of social housing and town planning.

Social housing and town planning encompass a wide collection of topics, and our discussions have to be selective and illustrative rather than comprehensive. Aspects of urban renewal, land development and intergovernmental relations will be discussed in subsequent chapters. Here we shall concentrate on ideas about *housing standards*, and the role of *social services* and *social development* in nineteenth-century British housing.

Housing policy development and housing standards

A social and intellectual concern for the right sort of *standards* in

housing has maintained an enduring and strong influence on the theory
and practice of social housing. In recent years, some continental
European countries have made the housing allowance eligibility depend on
people living in dwellings conforming to acceptable standards. Also,
government-assisted housing in Britain and continental Europe is required
to meet specific standards, written into the provisions not only to
control costs and establish administrative criteria for reviewing project
proposals, but more particularly to convey some historical circumstances
and a sense of idealism. The historical circumstances are deeply rooted
in aversions to the nineteenth-century slums and to the vague but widely
held ideal that society would reap very substantial benefits from
providing healthy surroundings, quiet at night, good neighbours and a
future for the children. This kind of thinking influenced the development of building regulations, prescribed minima in social housing
standards and so on.

The first phase of housing reform in industrialised urban societies
centred around public health. In all countries, the general approach
was to set up authorities to supervise buildings to ensure they were
safe and sanitary. These initiatives had obvious justifications; it
was necessary to eliminate contagious diseases and to prevent death or
disability from fire or unstable buildings. Chadwick used an economic
cost-benefit apparatus to show that society would indeed benefit by
eliminating the problems of disease. In some cities, with the worst
problems, sanitary inspectorates were created and local public health
officials appointed. Action in the worst-affected areas went further.
For example, in 1866 the Glasgow City Council created a City Improvement Trust to clear a tract of slums and sell the land for developers
to build standard housing. The aversion to disease, riotous behaviour,
drunkenness and debauchery was so great that the slums had to be
symbolically destroyed, and be replaced with new buildings to demonstrate a new society. The question of standards had obviously gone far
beyond applying just simple technical requirements. The notion of
standards included aesthetics, morals, a dreaded fear of contagious
disease, and a definite desire to avoid political rebellion.

In their day-to-day work, medical officers of health and building
inspectors had to convert the vague scientific [3] and social theories
into operational codes and administrative criteria. A part of the job
involved tracking down stinks and smells and clearing away the nuisances.
Vague and doubtful theoretical precepts were converted into technical
details on plumbing installations, building structure and so on.
Ventilation and light assumed growing technical significance.
Inspectors began to measure relationships between ventilation, cubic
space, rates of change of air, and the consumption of oxygen and the
findings were used to define ceiling heights, room sizes, the position
of windows, and so on. Many of these details have remained without
fundamental revision even though they have not represented basically
valid science. Modern building technology has the potential to produce
dwellings in different and quite adequate ways, but the old ideas still
influence neighbourhood lay-out and the design of houses. Ideas on
road widths, housing lines and neighbourhood recreational areas can be
traced to the age of slums, stinks, and the fear of debauchery in dark
alleys. The legislative landmark of the British public health movement was the *Public Health Act*, 1875, a measure consolidating previous
Acts dealing with sanitation, unfit housing, refuse disposal and model
byelaws on building.

The first phase of housing reform was primarily in public health. But in Britain and some other countries, the housing question after 1870 was about overcrowding, high rents and revelations about urban working-class living conditions. [4] Housing conditions attracted interests which included the 'sensational' press, the serious press, social novelists such as Charles Dickens, poverty researchers such as Booth and Rowntree, voluntary social workers, social and urban reformers, the church and politicians. According to Wohl, in the 1880s 'the agitation was so prolonged and so intense that the housing question became a social issue which no politician could afford to ignore and which no newspaper could neglect'. [5]

Housing standards saw social morality added to the inheritance of thinking on public health. Revelations on crowding and immorality [6] led to the idea that standard housing should have three bedrooms and a living room, this ensuring the conjugal privacy of parents and the separation of older children of the opposite sex. Charities and limited-profit companies were formed to build and promote standard housing. Private benefactors such as George Cadbury and Titus Salt sponsored model housing estates emphasising standards, social mix and social development. Like ideas on public health, those on social morality have had a long term impact on instituted housing practices. The idea of the three-bedroom standard house became so firmly establish-ed that when smaller one- and two-person households began to increase significantly during the 1960s, planners were caught out on overall targets and dwelling types.

The significance of ideas on housing standards in policy development can be traced to the early years of experience in public housing. First, we can refer to the housing policies of the London County Council (LCC - founded in 1888) which attracted widespread attention for its progressive reforming activities. The LCC rejected the idea of using Octavia Hill's methods of rehabilitating older housing for low-income groups because it believed that only in new construction could adequate standards be fulfilled. [7] Furthermore, in the 1890s the LCC disapproved the proposals put forward by the East End Dwelling Company, a limited-profit model dwelling company which operated in London's slum areas and which endeavoured to bring low-cost standard housing within the reach of the lowest paid workers. The LCC was intent upon raising housing standards to its own prescriptions on room sizes, the width of staircases, and the provision of wash-houses. It was probably wrong - in the discussions of urban renewal in Chapter 8, it will be argued that rehabilitation can be a satisfactory way of providing standard housing, and that in some circumstances it is the best policy.

The LCC approach was endorsed in the Report by the Tudor Walters Committee [8] which was used as the basis of the first British central government support for public housing, commenced in 1919. Taking advice from the emergent town planning profession, building technologists, sanitary inspectors, local government housing officers and women's groups involved in tenancy management, the Tudor Walters Committee emphasised the virtues of new construction and the elevation of housing standards through public housing. The Committee thought in terms of the three-bedroom family dwelling with adequate size, a bathroom, play areas for children and neighbourhood lay-out to let in the sun. Furthermore, it discussed whether public housing should have a parlour in addition to the family living room. The provision of a parlour became a key area of

contention in British parliamentary debates during the 1920s.   Like the
LCC, the Tudor Walters Committee took a generally discouraging attitude
to rehabilitation and this attitude dominated public policy despite
contrary evidence provided by Neville Chamberlain's Unhealthy Areas
Committee which reported in 1921. [9]   The cause for raising housing
standards had moved successively from eliminating contagious disease,
then to social morality, and finally towards the extraordinary idea that
adequate standards could be achieved only in new construction.

In this century, ideas on housing standards have also been influenced
by the Swedish functionalist view of housing, which emerged strongly in
the 1930s [10] and by modern attempts to fit housing to a way of life.
Surveys and time and motion studies examined how areas of the dwelling
were used for cooking, laundering and personal hygiene.   The studies
involved blending social and technical information and using it to
extract principles for designing and equipping service areas so they
functioned well.   The early functionalist research was incorporated in
national policy development in the 1940s and 1950s.   Swedish women's
organisations established a Homes' Research Institute, the forerunner
of the National Board for Consumer Policies.   Until the 1960s, the
spirit and scope of research into design and standards was aimed at the
mother and child relationship within the dwelling and at the service
areas of the dwelling.   After 1960, research broadened to examine the
environment, and special needs for such groups as the aged, the
handicapped, students and so on.   Also the greater specialisation in
housing research was reflected in 1960 when the government set up the
Swedish Council for Building Research and the National Swedish Institute
for Building Research.   The Council promotes research generally by
administering the Building Research Fund, [11] and the Institute is in
charge of research and investigational work.

Swedish functionalism has influenced the development of housing
standards in other countries, many now having specialist building
research institutions.   Housing amenities have been researched and the
results are incorporated in criteria for spatial dimension, circulation,
and equipment.   The social content is inextricably bound up with
physical and technical criteria.   Financial criteria are also involved;
governments will support social housing up to limits dictated by their
economic policy and the periodic pressures on public finance.   Once the
standards are 'written' in this complex process, it is impossible to
unscramble the detail of what has been bequeathed by history, or what is
social, technical or financial.   Housing is a complicated social,
economic and technical good.   However, the end results of the instituted standards are not always socially good or economically rational.
Much of the inheritance in housing standards seems to have been dominated by outdated social theory and technical considerations.

Some modern ideas on the development of housing standards are
connected to a 'way of life' approach rather than to public health,
social morality or a rather restricted sort of functionalism.   A
British official enquiry [12] into housing standards emphasised the
relationship between dwelling amenity and the modern way of life.
Standards were recommended to let each member of a household have the
necessary privacy and opportunity to engage in leisure pursuits.   This
approach placed significance on children's play needs and the garden.
Clearly, this is broader in scope than earlier functionalist concerns
with service areas.   The logical conclusion of this approach would

emphasise not just the design of the dwelling but its relationship to shops, schools, adult education, health and social services, transport, recreation, culture and employment. It follows that for family living, a house with a garden is more flexible and offers wider scope than apartments.

Ideas to improve housing **standards** have clearly influenced the historical development of housing policy. Historically they began with causes for eliminating contagious diseases, then took another course to provide conditions for social morality, and in the twentieth century it has been the legacies of Swedish functionalism in the design and the use of dwelling space which have been influential. The overall result is not minimum standards of sufficiency or precisely justified economic and social principles, but rather an unsorted mixture of social idealisms, technical specifications and conventional professional practices. In the themes of this writing, the processes establish the essential complexity of housing and reveal how the 'merit goods' aspects of housing arise. That is to say, social and professional preferences have been substituted for individual preferences in consideration of social benefits; income distributional factors of a special kind meriting some 'in-kind' rather than cash provision have been present in housing; and professional and administrative preferences have been superimposed on those of individuals.

Housing policy, social work and social development

The second specific topic through which we shall trace the development of social thought in housing is in social work and social development, [13] which became significant during the latter half of nineteenth-century British history. Voluntary social work, which had direct relationships with housing reform and a broader interest in working-class urban living conditions, led to the development of the social work profession. The impact of voluntary social work can be traced through the Charity Organisation Society, the Settlement Movement and the work of Octavia Hill. It reflected a social action response, partly based on social ideals, to bridge the gap between the middle and working classes. As already noted, this notion grew from a mid-Victorian Conservative idealism.

The most direct connection between housing, social work, social development and urban conditions was visible in the life and activities of Octavia Hill (1838-1912), [14] who purchased older housing with the intention of improving it and ministering social counsel to her tenants, in whom she took a personal interest. She also trained other women to act as housing visitors. The general principle in her housing activities was to provide good conditions, create self-respect among tenants, and encourage good housekeeping and prompt rent payments. The landlady-tenant relationship was meant to be something *special*; both the landlady and the housewife-tenant were supposed to get satisfaction from the social-educational interaction; the landlady was to provide standard housing, the tenant was expected to care for it and pay the rent. Octavia Hill's housing projects attracted considerable interest in Britain and overseas. The ideas have gained a durable hold in the estates management of twentieth-century social housing, just as the nineteenth's environmental determinism was transmitted into the development of housing standards and slum clearance.

At best, that a landlady should instil improvement in the personal life-styles of tenants amounts to social development; at worst, it amounts to meddling and insufferable intrusion. In twentieth-century social housing practice, the worst aspects of the relationship are compounded when allocation processes dispense 'privileges',and special housing is built for those who cannot afford alternatives. The oppression and stigma are both avoided when public policy provides community housing built by various developers and when society is less class-ridden. Not all of Octavia Hill's inheritance has been socially useful, though her ideas on housing improvement were well ahead of their time. Another inheritance from Octavia Hill and social work has been the role of women in housing. House visiting work has become something of a female career associated wtih housekeeping, family life and so on. Modern social change and feminism are beginning to break this down, in favour of asserting housing rights, tenants' rights and participation rather than dutiful landladying and missionary education.

The Charity Organisation Society (COS) was founded in 1870 to promote social casework principles and to establish professional counselling. Inevitably, the COS voluntary social workers came face to face with bad housing, overcrowding, high rents and so on. In 1873, COS responded by creating a Dwellings of the Poor Committee. By 1874, COS had lost faith in the idea that charitable work alone could provide a solution to housing problems, so it began lobbying for a stronger government role in housing. The Settlement Movement [15] also found that the social development approach to poor neighbourhoods was insufficient. By 1883, Canon S. Barnett, the founder of Settlements, was also advocating a strong government role in housing, and he was influential in founding the East End Dwellings Company in 1884 (referred to above).

These two movements have left a continuing influence. First, the social work profession grew out of them. This profession, along with town planning, has its role on the social side of housing and urban policies. However, it has a continuing interest in the general social sphere whereas town planning, with its greater eclecticism, gives priority to those things which fit changing policies. For example, when society has been concerned about traffic congestion rather than housing, town planning has concentrated on traffic engineering. This stacks the profession with engineers and technologists and leaves it unprepared, except by recourse to its historical idealism, when housing comes into significance. [16] Housing tends to become important during severe economic depressions, post-war reconstruction and when urban administration no longer fits the society's changing needs. Then social workers have been more involved in preparing critical reports on housing and in taking direct action.

This point can be consolidated by further examples. In Australia, in 1944, during debates on post-war reconstruction and development of national housing policies, the Council of Social Services of New South Wales produced an extensive report [17] advocating public housing, re-organisation of urban administration, and regionalisation. These ideas influenced the Commonwealth Housing Commission which reported in 1944. In Britain in 1943, the National Council for Social Services (NCSS) appointed a Community Centre and Associations Survey Group to recommend on future planning for suburban development. The NCSS thought the public housing estates built under the post-1919 programmes lacked social balance and facilities. The outcome of the Survey Group was a report[18] recommending social balance in neighbourhood units for future suburban development. More recently, the NCSS and social workers have been interested in sociological critiques of urban planning, and also in social development. [19] In general, it seems that when social workers produce critical reports on housing and urban policies, this can be interpreted as a warning to politicians and others that something in prevailing policies is wrong.

It should not be surprising that this profession's interest in housing can act as a beacon warning. Social workers are close to social problems and very often housing is in complex cause and effect relationship with these. However, social workers have imported some problems into their housing involvement. Sometimes, they have been the vehicle through which invalid or exaggerated social theory has been incorporated into housing and urban policy. [20] For example, the 1944 report of the Council of Social Services of New South Wales accepted that bad housing produces sexual delinquency among girls. Also, the 1943 NCSS report exaggerated claims that suitable neighbourhood facilities could produce social development. In the 1960s American and other social reformers exaggerated the role of social development and community action in bettering the housing and living conditions of the poor. The social work profession contains some historical inheritance of the 'less elegibility' principle, [21] an emphasis on individuals rather than society, and some ideological conflicts. The profession's pronouncements, therefore, need to be carefully appraised.

SOCIAL RESEARCH : NEW DIRECTIONS

In recent decades, many countries have experienced reform in housing, urban and social policies. Sociologists and economists began critical studies of urban planning. Resident action groups opposed redevelopment and agitated for participation in planning. [22] A new intellectualism in urbanisation exposed the irrelevance and failure of many traditional ideas in social housing and town planning. The agitation among residents was a sign that the theory and practice of urban planning and housing did not fit social and economic conditions of a changing society. Another symptom was that traditional patterns of administrative separatism in government and urban administration [23] no longer suited the tasks at hand. Intellectually, the most significant break-through was the dismantling of the exaggerated claims of environmental determinism.

In the 1920s the Chicago School of Human Ecologists codified metropolitan settlement patterns and explained them in terms of housing conditions. According to this view, the middle classes lived in the suburbs because conditions were better than in the inner suburbs where most of the urban poor lived. In fact, recent economic research [24] shows that, under market conditions, the more affluent live in the suburbs because the land is cheaper there. Consequently these people buy sufficient land to build a larger home and still afford to travel to work. On the other hand, less well-off groups tend to occupy land more densely and live in smaller units closer to work. Poorer people have lived on more expensive land and in relatively more expensive housing in per unit terms. But the less well-off households have economised in the cost and time of getting to work and in their household expenditure on housing. Thus, the explanation of where different income groups live has little to do with the basic quality of the housing and much to do with household incomes and land prices. Other economic aspects of housing choice are concerned with dwelling attributes (form, design, garage space) and amenities (see Chapter 1).

A more direct critique of environmental determinism was made by Broady [25] and Gans, [26] who argued that social aspects of the urban condition could more readily be explained by direct sociological theory and by social structure. In other words, the environment had only limited impact on social attitudes and structure. Once sociological interest in urbanisation had been disconnected from environmental determinism, it was free to fill in the detail of the relationships between social factors and urban planning and to develop new theories. Sociology has taken both courses recently. We now have greater knowledge of neighbourhood interaction, the impact of urban renewal, the consequences of high-rise dwellings, the value of garden space, the significance of amenities and so on. [27] Sociology is also looking at urban planning as a process of allocating income, wealth and opportunity. In this latter development, one branch has taken the title, *the new urban sociology*, and another (previously referred to in Chapter 1) has been directed towards modern Marxist interpretations of housing and the urban condition. [28]

The two new branches represent much better approaches than the environmental determinism and ecological explanations of urban settlement patterns, as represented in the Chicago School and some pre-1960 reactions to that School. However, although the new branches have the advantage of viewing urbanisation in terms of inequalities in property, income and political power, with some consequent emphasis upon how urban 'managers' determine policies and allocate resources, they have not yet really got to grips with bridging sociological and economic theory in housing. The public policy orientation is there, but not with good groundwork in economics, and this is evident in some British sociological analysis of housing sectors, access to different tenures, and the allocation of housing among social and class groups. [29] This work lacks clear-cut definitions of economic costs, benefits and subsidies, and, more significantly, it lacks the realisation that other countries (e.g., Norway) do not have their housing opportunities so rigidly compartmentalised in sectors, or that public housing can be used in more diverse ways than is represented in Britain. Some of these points are taken up in the next section which deals with choice, self-fulfilment and tenure in housing. If we look outside the 'schools' or new 'streams of thought' in urban sociology, we can find a wider diversity of ideas and a more general relevance.

Some recent research has steered a middle course between narrower empirical work and positional theory, and it is opening up important new ideas in housing. This middle course gets closer to the following questions in housing: (1) what are the factors influencing choice?, (2) how do the conventional theoretical precepts influence the allocation of income, wealth and opportunity? To see the point of this 'middle course' in research, we need to understand the respective shortcomings of the too-empirical work and the too-theoretical work.

Much of the empirical research is into housing choice, but it fails to show how conventional theory influences choice. For example, we know from some sociological research that high-rise dwellings inconvenience the mother's supervisory role over young children and create conflicts between their life-styles; [30] but the research does not indicate what sort of social and economic theory has produced these dwellings. At the other extreme is theory of the broad kind which tries to explain how urban processes affect the allocation of income, wealth and opportunity. General theories of this kind come in Marxist, Social-Democratic and Liberal-Democratic forms; they may illuminate large relations between urbanisation and social structure, but they do not offer much-needed re-thinking on specifics like housing, transport, urban services or recreation. Good middle-course research tries to connect its general theories to its practical diagnoses and policies in more constructive ways.

It is clear that housing produces both social and economic satisfactions using economic resources. The important task is to find a theoretical framework, and language, which can deal at one and the same time with the general social aspects *and* the specific economic aspects of the subject, especially because some of the conventional assumptions and methods of economic theory seem to 'fit' housing markets, while others do not. Housing itself allocates income (rental value), wealth (changes in economic value) and opportunities (access to urban services and promoting a way of life); the really interesting question is whether the nature of housing is consonant with the wider allocational processes in society. Some recent ideas from studies by Harvey [31], Whitbread and Bird [32], and Stretton [33] contain interesting and critical perspectives on the questions posed here.

Harvey shows there can be conflict between the social and economic aspirations of residents, and the economic motives of developers, the former being interested in the social characteristics of the suburb and the nearness of housing to shops, work, schools and other amenities. This composition of values is expressed as the 'utility' of housing where this term represents a summary of the attributes giving housing residential value. By contrast, the developer wants profit from sale; or if he is a non-profit entrepreneur the interest is in fulfilling the contract and moving on. The developer has no interest in the utility of housing, only in its exchange value, which is in conflict with 'utility' of housing from residents' perspectives.

Economic theory recognises utility theories of value, exchange theories of value and economic externalities. However, the exchange values are explicit (in financial transactions) whereas utility and externality are not. The economist can meet part of this problem by showing that: (1) in principle, utility value is brought into relationship with exchange value through the observable exchanges in the market, [34] and (2) if feasible, special economic cost-benefit analysis can be used to reveal the 'shadow price' and exchange values implicit in economic externality. [35] Harvey presses the point of conflict between residents and developers. Nevertheless, a developer will consider these things if residents press their wants and if they can turn to alternative developments. [36] In this case, the conflict is resolved through exchange; nevertheless, Harvey correctly exposes the conflict, which highlights the fact that parts of economic theories of value contain problems of conceptualisation, measurement, and application to things like housing. Economics often takes the easier way out, utility and externality explanations being neglected.

72

However, some recent studies in the economics of housing increasingly resort to these concepts, thus tending to bridge the social, physical and economic aspects of housing. In another middle-course study, Whitbread and Bird [37] make externality and utility a more central theme. They are interested in explanations of housing choice, and the environmental/accessibility factors influencing choice, mobility and the cost of housing. Choice is influenced by the cost and value of the dwelling to the household. The cost is its rental value. [38] The value to the household depends on its current and expected housing-related needs, which include access to amenities. Other needs depend on the form and design of the dwelling and whether it enables individuals to fulfil their own home-based activities. [39] Other considerations depend on conditions of tenure and the material interest the household has in the asset value of the house and its management and maintenance.

Clearly, some parts of Whitbread's and Bird's concepts depend on utility and externality values. In particular, Whitbread and Bird would like to know the extent to which utility exceeds cost and what precisely makes up utility value in housing. They appreciate that two general considerations influence utility and cost. First, utility is not static, but it is influenced by changing life-cycle needs (which bridge economic and social considerations) and by continuous urban change. [40] Second, cost (rental value) is also influenced by urban change and by the dynamics of housing markets altering relationships between price and factors such as tenure, location, dwelling type and so on. [41] The basic conceptualisation of housing, together with these matters, link social and economic factors into a coherent whole. They also indicate that it is necessary to get at housing value by moving beyond exchange value. However, like so many economists, Whitbread and Bird cannot find a direct way to measure consumer's surplus, and changes in it (i.e., the difference between cost and utility and its variations). The information can be obtained only indirectly, by surveying mobile households to extract the factors influencing their changes of residence.

Stretton's ideas [42] in this area go further than the other studies we have reviewed. He is not satisfied that economists have analysed housing except within the narrower confines of exchange value, and he remonstrates with them for this. Housing is viewed as the central social and economic asset in the 'domestic sector', which is defined as part of the economy in which capital, resources, time and energy are used for such things as housework, cooking, gardening, hobbies, social meetings, neighbourhood social development and so on. However, this 'productivity' is not marketed, and economists have largely ignored it. Economists recognise a public sector and a private (commercial) sector, they measure the output in these, aggregating it into a GNP. According to Stretton, the omission of the domestic sector leads to an understatement, and a distortion, of economic activity.

The domestic sector has undoubted significance sociologically and historically. Stretton refers to Willmott and Young's sociological study [43] of the changing relationship between work and leisure. This shows that a growing proportion of the goods produced in the private sector are used in the home and that a more affluent society increasingly uses housing for a wider variety of leisure activities. Housing-related activities would also show up significantly in 'use of time' surveys. The broad historical trend towards suburbanisation where more land and housing space is bought now than in the nineteenth century, can be seen as a way of giving scope to housing-related activities.

Stretton uses his ideas of the domestic sector to criticise the allocation of income, wealth and opportunity. The conventional theoretical precepts used to allocate resources to housing do not fit the domestic sector's true productivity, which fails to enter into exchange and which therefore cannot raise finance from its own returns to resource it. Instead, finance has to come from wages and dividends in the private sector, and from subsidisation in the public sector. In short, housing does not get its due.

Stretton pushes his ideas further, and suggests that the relations between the three sectors are reciprocal. The private sector supplies goods to the domestic sector, and the public sector supplies urban services supporting home-based activities. The domestic sector supplies productive labour and useful citizens to the other two sectors. However, for the domestic sector to achieve this, the sort of housing provided must be suitable for promoting diverse home-based activities. [44] This means that, for many households, the most suitable form is a house with an attached garden, because this has greater scope and flexibility. Finally, Stretton sees possibilities for promoting egalitarianism and socialism through housing, because of the scope for co-operative and unalienated work in the domestic sector. [45] By contrast, work in the other sectors is under authority and alienating. Housing egalitarianism shows through providing low-income groups with housing that enables them to use their time as productively as higher income groups.

Clearly, Stretton's theory bridges social and economic factors, and poses critical questions on the allocation of income, wealth, and opportunity in housing. It uses historical and sociological informa- tion as its empirical justification, and redesigns the range of categories and their internal relationships. Accordingly, social research in housing is producing new theory and is creating new moral and logical criticisms of the prevailing patterns. The time lag between this sort of new social knowledge in housing and environmental determinism is about a decade. However, the logical and philosophical distance between the inheritance and succession is great indeed. The past decade of social research in housing marks a distinct discontinuity, and also substantial progress. However, the old and irrelevant idealisms continue to influence ideas in housing standards, urban renewal and so on. The process of correction and redirection is far from complete.

CHOICE AND SELF-FULFILMENT IN HOUSING

The main social motives in housing may be summed up in the broad concept of 'self-fulfilment'. History shows that this is so, and further support for this view of the motives concerned is given by recent sociological research and by the growth of resident and social action groups in the past decade. Self-fulfilment will be expressed in many ways, with specific implications for selection of dwelling type and location. The social factors influencing the selection include class, way of life, and stage in the life cycle. Economic factors are present in terms of the accessibilities to various housing-related amenities,

and the time-distance costs of travel to work.   These factors are
conditioned by income, housing and land costs and by the terms under
which housing finance is provided.   The socio-economic factors combine
to produce regularities in settlement, the pattern depending on the
relationship to housing and land allocation processes. [46]   Self-
fulfilment is thus constrained by the available options of dwelling type,
tenure, location and so on.   This means that the discussion of self-
fulfilment should be coupled with relevant factors influencing choice.

   Historically, there are many examples of how the self-fulfilment
motive has stirred people into social, economic and political action on
housing.   In the late eighteenth century, mutual building societies
were formed spontaneously by British artisans as an extension of the
friendly society movement.   During the 1920s, German building trade
unions and Swedish tenants agitated for more action in housing and set
up self-help enterprises to get on with the job.   In Oslo, in 1946,
young radicals formed the USBL co-operative, working with their own
hands.   USBL struggled, cajoled, negotiated and agitated to get access
to financial institutions, and professional expertise and to win
political recognition.   It was the self-fulfilment motive that built
the houses, when there had previously been no 'roof over the head'.   In
the past 10-15 years, resident and social action groups have sprung up
to oppose urban redevelopment, to get public administration to co-
ordinate its urban policies and to emphasise the social and environmental aspects of housing-related services.

   Some careful sociological work confirms the strength of the self-
fulfilment motive.   Surveys of residents forced to move by urban
renewal show they have grieved for a lost home.   Those most affected
have been poor people, those with low resilience, and those with little
social involvement. [47]   Extensive American social surveys by Rainwater [48] reveal that housing is regarded by its residents as a means
of promoting individual autonomy, a place to re-group energies, and a
refuge and shelter.   Rainwater elaborates how the specific satisfactions in self-fulfilment in the United States [49] vary in relation to
class and tenure.   For low-income renters the home is a haven of
security from the harsh realities of life, whereas for middle-class
home-owners it is a symbol and an elaboration of a life-style.   Gans
[50] has shown that suburban families value their housing for its
privacy, its space and equipment, and its suitability for rearing
children who have important needs for play space in the garden and in
neighbourhood socialisation.   Self-fulfilment in housing has thus been
clarified in recent sociological research.

   For social motives and social theory to become effective, they have to
be *institutionalised*, and there are many ways in which this can be
achieved.   They include the building society movement, public housing,
trade union housing enterprises, government-assisted financing and co-
operatives.   We now need to select an institutionalised form best
symbolising the aim of self-fulfilment and choice in housing.   The
wide-ranging criteria for selection cover the following qualities and
activities;   social theory, self-fulfilment, enterprising administration,
learning and experience in administering a complex process, and access
to resources;   some elements (e.g., enterprise and learning) depend
partly on the wider social, economic and political context.

The co-operative housing movement has institutionalised social theory and self-fulfilment. [51]   In some European countries, the movement is enterprising and experienced, and participates in the government-instituted financial framework.   The institutionalisation of self-fulfilment and choice in housing is illustrated by co-operative housing in Norway.   Some key features of the Norwegian housing context can be briefly set out: the government's banks provide loans and housing allowances; over 75 per cent of new housing is financed through these; in recent years, loans have been taken up as follows - home owners 61 per cent, co-operators 23 per cent, and private entrepreneurs 9 per cent; the co-operatives are stronger in large cities; 75 per cent of new houses have a garden, the rest are apartments; the co-operatives build 70 per cent of their stock as apartments, and have filled a role in that section of the market particularly in the larger cities.

The main features of Norwegian housing are that consumers can choose between taking housing through a co-operative, employing a builder of their own, or approaching a private entrepreneur for housing.   No matter which is selected, the easy-loan system and housing allowances are similarly available through the government's banks.   But if the consumer wants a large house and can afford it, finance can be by private-sector mortgaging.

The co-operative movement claimed attention when, following housing vexation during the 1920s, trade unions and tenants took initiatives to develop non-profit housing.   In 1929, the Oslo Savings and Housing Society (OBOS) was founded as a tenants' co-operative.   It adopted the Swedish HSB model for the development and estates management of housing. [52]   OBOS has been a significant participant in Oslo City Council's housing programmes; the Council is a member of OBOS, and in 1946 transferred some of its housing into co-operative tenure.   In the same year, a group of young radicals formed the USBL co-operative to act more independently of Council and to get more action into housing policies.

The Norwegian co-operative movement has organised its interests on a national scale and the larger societies have been both enterprising and adaptable to social and economic change.   In 1946, the Norwegian National Federation of Housing Societies (NBBL) was founded to promote the co-operative housing movement.   It is closely involved with the wider co-operative housing movement in Sweden, Denmark, West Germany and in other countries.   The European co-operative movement has a dense network of informal and formal professional interaction.   Norway's government has, under the *Housing Societies Act*, 1960, and the *Housing Groups Act*, 1960, given legal protection to co-operators.   In 1976 it prepared an amendment to ensure that individual co-operators had greater participatory rights in the development side of the housing business. Co-operative developers, along with other developers, have had problems of resident participation in planning, despite the fact that members have democratic voting rights to elect delegates and committees.   The individual co-operator is the last one to appear in the planning and development process.   The *development* side of the organisation has to negotiate with local government on land development and housing policy. This part of the operation also assumes the risks of supervising contractors and fulfilling the contract, thus protecting the final consumer from slippages in the complicated processes, and from run-away prices; but the development has to be planned somewhat bureaucratically, and some conflicts can arise from this. The individual co-operator gets the keys to the house *after* the development process is complete and when the housing estate is formed into an *estates management co-operative*. In one Swedish example, an estates management society took legal action against HSB over who was responsible for mending a defective central-heating system.

The co-operative housing movement has recently been influenced by a spate of residents' action and the demands for more participation. For example, at the new USBL's estate at Furuset, Oslo, open meetings were held before planning began. The estate provides a host whose job it is to ensure that social development is realised. Also, the garbage will be collected by boys from a local juvenile reformatory using a horse and cart. This collection is more economic and it is hoped it will achieve a useful social role. As the general concern for housing has broadened from the dwelling to the wider environment, OBOS and other societies have expanded their involvement to include commercial and industrial enterprise, and social development. Thus, the institutionalisation process which began with a mixture of social theory, the need for self-fulfilment and the urgency of getting a 'roof over the head', had adapted to social and economic change.

A co-operative housing organisation (e.g., OBOS) enables members to participate in the following rights. Individual co-operators get a co-owned share in the property. Membership is open regardless of income, political affiliations or religion. Access to housing is achieved from the Society's waiting list, and the waiting time depends on the preference for size and location of dwelling. Membership of the Society confers voting rights and eligibility to candidature for positions in the Society's organisation. Once a member is allocated a house he/she also becomes a member of the estates management co-operative responsible for the house. Members can exchange houses, can transfer membership to a son/daughter or grandparent, and can remain on the waiting list for a house in a particular location. Housing costs are comprised of loan repayments (via the Society to the government's bank) estate management costs, and personal costs on interior maintenance. The Society owns the dwelling, but the member has a legally protected equity share in the property which can be sold to the Society at a value determined by a local government valuation committee.

Self-fulfilment for the individual ends up as a complicated package of rights and responsibilities. However, many social and economic needs are met in this system which is voluntary. Members can also get access to housing outside the Society, so the Society has to be competitive. As life-cycle needs change, a member can change house and location according to preference and the period on the waiting list. The Society is organised democratically, and in the modern world it has had to become more participatory, not just relying upon elections. And, because the Society has to be competitive, it has to be reasonably enterprising and adaptable to social and economic change. In short, co-operative housing organisation in Norway represents the institution-alisation of idealism, self-fulfilment, administrative enterprise and experience, and is integrated into the pattern of community power in politics, finance, industry and public support. It enables individuals and families to express their self-fulfilment in a title to a share in the value of the property.

This institutionalisation is not the epitome of perfection or harmony. Housing is too full of conflict and administrative dilemmas for that. The main point is that social ideals and motivations have to be real, and institutionalised, if they are to be productive and useful. The Norwegian co-operative housing system is a *comparatively* good example of what can be achieved by institutionalisation and a distinctively social means of making property in housing accessible to individuals, some of whom will be from low- and moderate-income groups.

Choice in housing and the development process

Choice of Housing can now be examined at greater depth and can be referred to other factors influencing it. To appreciate the constraints on housing choice, regard has to be paid to the sequence of decisions made by administrators, town planners, architects, accountants, and so on. These 'decision makers' are not always working in a single corporate enterprise, so the degree of co-ordination varies. They will also be responding to some extent to policy, to finance and to existing housing theory. These conditions vary from country to country, few being as cohesively organised as the Norwegian example referred to above.

The sequence of key conditions is as follows: the location and general nature of housing development will be determined by the land development process. In some countries this will be determined by a mixture of *laissez faire* and town planning regulations on zoning, sub-divisional and other regulations. In other countries, (e.g., Sweden and Norway) local government will buy land and use public investment to lead private enterprise to invest. For reasons explained in Chapter 7, different methods of land development produce distinctive settlement patterns, townscapes, urban efficiencies, social *effectiveness* and so on.

Housing types and overall neighbourhood designs will be selected by architects, town planners and administrators. As stated earlier in this chapter, the professional town planning inheritance includes dubious social theory. In some countries, social theory in politics and in town planning have merged to form policy. [53] However, other countries have been influenced less by doubtful town planning theory. Where government finance is involved, housing standards and cost controls will, in many cases, influence the design and specification of dwellings. Private housing will have to conform to building regulations. Again, where there have been acute housing shortages and financial inducements for high volumes have been powerful, particular technologies have been attracted. For example, systems building and its variants has been used for blocks of apartments. These technologies are not usually the most economical or socially effective methods of producing housing.

House producers are better organised than consumers to protect their interests. Industrialists, trade unions, financiers and some professions have depended upon high volume new construction and upon specific technologies. When housing shortages are acute - as they have been in The Netherlands, West Germany, Sweden and other countries - and where barriers of access to alternatives are strong, consumers have little influence on the process. Niskanen [54] discusses the circumstances under which government agencies and their dependent institutions will be in a monopoly relationship with their clients and sponsors. We are to imagine that the sponsors (i.e., politicians) have little knowledge of housing administration. Thus housing agencies can rely on obtaining resources from their sponsors without much critical scrutiny of their demand for funds. These factors, coupled with circumstances of acute shortages referred to above, and with financial barriers and administrative controls on eligibility have applied to the development and allocation of housing in some of the modern democracies. Monopoly control by sponsors and developers, within the pattern described by Niskanen, has constrained housing choice. These circumstances also explain the widespread use of illegal 'key' money deposits in Sweden during the 1960s, as consumers sought to get self-fulfilment in housing under tightly constrained choice. However, once acute housing shortages are overcome and consumers become more affluent, they are able to exercise much more influence over the housing process. This sort of change has been evident in Sweden since 1970 and there is a release of pent-up demand for home ownership and houses with gardens (see the discussions in Chapters 6 and 7).

In summary, housing choice is complicated and depends on a host of conditions, varying from country to country and also by relationship to social and economic change. In some countries, choice has been tightly constrained for most households, whereas in other countries, it has been public housing renters who have suffered most. Even in the more *laissez faire* countries, the relationship between producer and consumer are far more complicated than theoretical economic models of competitive behaviour assume. The foregoing realities of the housing and land allocation process should also be considered by social planners, pre-occupied with such things as social mix, social balance and community studies. The land and housing allocational processes are fundamental in determining the nature of settlement patterns; the rest follows from social structure. The allocational processes are, themselves, determined by social and economic conditions and by land development and housing institutional arrangements. Choice in housing is just as much a function of institutional arrangements, as it is a function of price formation and income.

Self-fulfilment in housing has been a strong social motive; it depends on how institutions perform and on broader social, economic and political issues. Institutions are born out of the stuff of history and they may express a continuous idealism and adapt to change; or they may become bureaucratic and conservative. Even if some of the original idealism fades, institutions can remain enterprising if consumers have choice in housing and developer. Choice has a direct relationship to self-fulfilment. Present social and economic trends indicate that there is more choice in housing for some households. Some of the change has occurred outside policy, but policy seems to be adjusting. Britain has tried to increase choice by developing a co-operative housing sector; but has so far not been really effective. The Social Democrats in West Germany, The Netherlands, and Sweden have recently taken more positive steps towards home ownership. Consumers there are now able to resist mass project apartment dwellings. Choice and self-fulfilment are beginning to enjoy freer rein in some countries, but for new households the economic conditions of inflationary costs, high interest rates and constrained incomes have tightened choice. Some aspects of this, especially in housing systems such as Britain's, are tied in with questions of sectoral divisiveness and tenure.

In Britain and other modern democracies many of the emerging policy issues centre around housing tenure. The importance of tenure is that it is bound up with rights to property, with the distribution of wealth and income, with social divisiveness and with self-fulfilment in housing. Under some housing systems, the price and access barriers which separate tenures act as the means by which some antecedent inequalities in wealth and income are perpetuated and endorsed by consolidation and addition of further inequality. Viewed cross-sectionally at a flashpoint in time, the division of housing into owner-occupier, public rental and private rental tenures gives rise to some arbitrary vertical and horizontal inequities in income. This can be attributed to biases in the tax treatment of housing and to ways in which housing is financed and subsidised. Under other housing systems, where home ownership has been made accessible down the income scale to low- and moderate-income groups, with most finance for mortgaging and housing allowances coming from the saving and the taxes of higher income groups, then home ownership can be regarded as a significant means of reducing inequalities.

Our discussions of housing policy and tenure will be arranged to establish some general perspectives from political ideology and comparative housing experience. Then, referring to income and life-cycle circumstances we shall examine justifications for providing both home ownership and rental tenures. Finally, the discussions will turn to recent issues in British policy, tenure and housing economics. The British housing system is more rigidly divided along tenure lines than the systems elsewhere, and it thereby invites concerns for tenure-related reform.

In all the modern democracies, historical and current realities in housing finance have created biases and barriers to entry which have produced housing inequalities. We can view unregulated private rental tenure as providing insecurity for the poor, and the extent of owner-occupier tenure has often been a function of the development of long-term loans by building societies and/or governments. In the ideological aspects, the centre of interest is the opposing viewpoints of Social Democratic and Conservative traditions, with home ownership opposed or supported as an expression of capitalism and property ownership. However, from a comparative housing perspective, this needs some strong qualification, because the Social Democratic traditions in Norway and Australia have supported home ownership, with greater consistency in Norway. Among Australian States, South Australia has used public housing for varied purposes, including the provision of low-rent stock, establishing opportunities for moderate-income groups to become home owners, and using varied home-ownership programmes for competition with private enterprise housing.

Sometimes the relative proportions of different tenures among countries are interpreted as indices of the 'progressiveness' of their housing policies, some critics favouring rental and others owner-occupier tenure. However, the general position in this study is that the question of progressiveness in housing policy development has to be referred to a much wider set of considerations than tenure. Nevertheless, tenure is a significant issue in housing policies in the modern democracies and in Marxist countries, and it merits some analytical and comparative discussion within the theme of self-fulfilment and equality housing. The relative proportions of different tenures among different countries varies considerably (see below), but these proportions largely reflect historical factors. For example, Australia which has 70 per cent of its housing stock in owner-occupier tenure had relatively well-developed mortgaging instruments in the nineteenth century, and State Labour governments created housing loan programmes for the working classes in the first two decades of this century. By contrast, in the 1940s Swedish Social Democrats reversed their earlier support for working-class home ownership and created a financial and administrative system which strongly supported non-profit rental tenure in national social housing programmes. Countries where rental tenure has dominated, want more home ownership. For example, in Sweden, The Netherlands and West Germany, the Social Democrats who have hitherto been ambiguous on the question of home ownership are now adopting more positive attitudes. The Norwegian Labour Party has, since 1916, favoured home ownership and Norway has organised its general financial and administrative system so that tenure is not a major policy issue. In Britain and Australia, the discussions recur on whether public housing should be rented or sold, and Australia has been more definite (though only sporadically so) on the sale of public housing.

Our major statements on tenure are based on the width of comparative review. [56] For example, in Australia, rents are not regulated, urbanisation is concentrated in major metropolitan areas, and apart from Adelaide and Canberra, the land development processes have been influenced by *laissez faire* more than in Sweden or Norway. The predominant tenure is owner-occupier (some 70 per cent of the stock). In a sense, there is a shortage of rental housing, and though public funds have been used to build about 15 per cent of the housing since 1945, some of this has been sold. Rental housing is not only in relatively short supply; except for public rental housing, rental stock is exposed to market pressures on the land it occupies and to competition from the middle classes who have been buying it up. Under the circumstances, there is a case for expanding public rental tenure, particularly in Sydney and Melbourne, the largest Australian cities.

West Germany, The Netherlands and Sweden offer contrasting examples. None has more than half of its stock in owner-occupier tenure. There have been historical, financial and political impediments against owner-occupier tenure achieving fuller potential. However, conditions are changing. West Germany, The Netherlands and Sweden entered 1970 with some 35 per cent of their stock in owner-occupier tenure, but with important social, economic and political changes and with the phasing out of acute shortages during the 1970s, Sweden and The Netherlands have significantly increased their development of owner-occupied stock. For example, in Sweden in 1970 some 30 per cent of new dwellings were in the house-with-a-garden form, but this proportion rose to 70 per cent in 1976. Most of these dwellings are in owner-occupier tenure. Furthermore, in Stockholm the shortage of houses with gardens and the pent-up demand for them has led to some very high prices.

The ideal situation on tenure choice would be that access to housing finance not be constrained too tightly, and the loans and subsidies be available to developers and individuals on broadly similar terms regardless of which type or tenure of dwelling they want to develop. This is roughly the situation in Norway. By comparison, debates in Britain on

whether public housing should be sold or not, seem narrow.   If an
alternative financial and administrative framework could be imagined and
practised then the tenure issue would move into the background.
Moreover, much of the existing stock in British public and private
housing could be suitably fitted to a general financial envelope (like
Norway's) and the public-private dualism broken down.

The discussions on tenure have shown the extremes and the ideal.   The
extremes (Australia, West Germany and Sweden) need the antidote to their
imbalance;   hence the discussion below will reveal the case for rental
and for owner-occupier tenure.

The analytical case for retaining rental housing has not been fully
appreciated.   It depends on diverse purposes and on long-term perspectives.   Renting is more suitable for individuals and families whose
locational needs are temporary.   For others, rental housing is
appropriate to their way of life.   But there are other more significant
reasons for ensuring that there is an adequate stock of rental housing
in the community.   A brief explanation of life-cycle changes in income
will illustrate an important argument in favour of low-rent or fair-rent
housing.

Figure 3-1 illustrates the general pattern of life-cycle income
changes for many individuals.

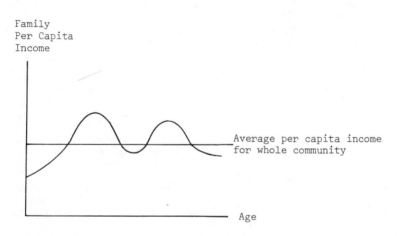

FIGURE 3-1

The Pattern of Life-Cycle Per Capita Income Profiles

The profile demonstrates that life-cycle per capita incomes tend to
fall below the community average in childhood, in the early years of
family formation and in old age.   Because expenditure on housing

absorbs a large proportion of family budgets, it is in these troughs
that many problems of housing access arise. If, during these periods,
the total costs of home-purchase increase at a greater rate than average
earnings, it is likely that most families will need to rent.

For some people, low-cost renting is a temporary need, but for the
poor it is sometimes a long-term need. A stock of low-rent housing
thus serves a basic need for poor families and a transitional need
leading to subsequent home ownership for other families, along with an
assurance of accommodation during their periods of temporary need.

The traditional arguments for home ownership have centred around
creating a stable society, and stimulating more involvement in social
development. Some of this has a quaint ring of nineteenth century
idealism on the virtues of property. In the twentieth century,
property is valued by its owners and they are ready to protect their
interest, but it is scarcely regarded as morally virtuous, except by
some aristocrats. In the more egalitarian countries in continental
Europe, few people would respect the really wealthy; there are more
important things in life than creating private hoards. However, some
property can be part of life's achievement, and for housing this can be
personal, real and full of very human feelings. When the home is
threatened, people are stirred into defensive action. For example,
home owners and others have opposed redevelopment and have agitated for
higher quality urban environments. Far from home ownership creating
stability, it has led to intensive political activity aimed against
bureaucracy and government. Such agitation has cut across traditional
political loyalties and ultimately steered the system into closer
relationship with the community. Housing does get people involved in
social development, especially when there is a threat to the home. The
consequent social development is not always calm and quiet.

Stretton [57] has made an elaborate case for regarding housing as part
of the 'domestic sector' where co-operative inter-personal relationships
are promoted and creative things are done. Inter-personal co-operation
is seen as one element in the socialist tradition. Therefore, home
ownership is viewed as socialist rather than capitalist. The case can
also be supported from the historical-sociological evidence of the
changing relationship between work and leisure, and by 'use-of-time'
surveys. The house, the garden plot, the location of recreational
activities and so on become increasingly important from the social and
(according to Stretton) the economic viewpoint. Self-fulfilment shows
in a variety of ways.

As was mentioned earlier, the tenure-related aspects of income and
wealth distribution have become important in the post-1977 discussions
of policy and economic issues in British housing. This has partly
arisen because the report from the official housing review [58] tended
to avoid thorough inter-sector distributional analysis and did not make
firm proposals to eliminate the basic structural rigidities in sectoral
separatism. The British housing system is one of the most sectorally
divisive among the modern democracies, and any proposals for intra-
sector reforms of finance and consumer pricing raises dilemmas of
unequal and unfair effects in other sectors. Owner-occupiers get
government assistance by virtue of there being no tax on imputed rental
values and no capital gains tax on housing, and those who are repaying
mortgage loans enjoy tax relief on interest payments. Public housing

is not taxed and various special grants, subsidies and loaning arrangements have lowered rents below economic cost. However, the pattern of
rents in public housing combined with the way it has been allocated,
leaves it with much horizontal and vertical inequity. Private rental
housing is taxed, the tenants (unlike owner-occupiers) pay their housing
costs from incomes which are fully taxed, and much of the stock is
subjected to regulated rents.

The modern literature clearly shows the consequent overall vertical
and horizontal inequity. However, it is divided on how subsidies and
costs should be measured, and what policies should be adopted. The
Building Economic Development Committee [59], Stafford [60], and Grey
and his co-authors [61] favour the taxation of imputed rental value in
owner-occupier housing. This follows from principles of inter-sector
equity and the view that housing is an 'investment' rather than a
'consumption' good. That is to say, as an investment good, owner-
occupier housing should be taxed, thus bringing it into equivalence with
the taxed investment income from machines, factories, warehouses and so
on. As we shall see in Chapter 6, Norway, Sweden and The Netherlands
tax the imputed rental value of owner-occupier housing. Leaving owner-
occupier housing untaxed is tantamount to regarding it as a consumption
good; for example, like the use value of cars which is untaxed. Of
course, in some countries the question of whether owner-occupier housing
is taxed or not is determined by political feasibility rather than the
niceties of economic definitions on investment and consumption goods.

For Grey and his co-authors, the taxation of owner-occupier housing
forms one of their several requirements to put all housing sectors on
similar economic bases. In public housing, they would derive the level
of rents from current capital values, to be used as an *analytical* guide,
and to make a break with past practice. Actual rents paid would
depend upon capacity to pay, with the difference between the economic
(analytical) rent and the actual rent being financed by an overt subsidy
from general public finance. Consequently, Grey and his co-authors
would abandon 'pooling' in public housing - a device enabling some
'cross-subsidisation' from older housing built at cheaper historical
financial cost to new higher (inflationary) cost housing. It is a way
of averaging rents and keeping them below market values. According to
Grey and his co-authors, 'pooling' is bad policy because the financial
outlays and rents do not reveal true economic values, economic values
being 'superior' because they act as a management discipline in avoiding
high-cost development (e.g., high rise blocks), they relate the real
values of dwellings to rents, and they break down sectoral separatism
with its vertical and horizontal inequity. By way of contrast, Kilroy
[62] favours 'pooling' and its extension from local and regional
accounting to national accounting. A nationally averaged financial
rent would be used as a benchmark, with some local authorities
contributing surpluses from rental income to the national 'pool', and
others drawing upon those surpluses so that all rents in public housing
could be kept low. For Kilroy, this is equitable because rents are
kept low in a 'social' housing sector, and many owner-occupiers have
advantages from low historical cost outlays. Grey and his co-authors
note that owner-occupiers often change house, and their costs are
thereby connected to current, not historical values. For Grey and his
co-authors, it is current not historical costs which are significant,
and it is more appropriate to examine the housing system as a whole
rather than just public housing.

Grey and his co-authors extend their principle to the private rental sector, where they favour a free market (i.e., deregulation) so that rents reflect long-term costs of building. Then, for general inter-sector equity and to meet the capacity to pay problem, they favour universal housing allowances in accordance with income and needs tests, and rent rebates in public housing, as outlined above. The main purpose of these economic and financial adjustments is to achieve harmonisation of inter-sector subsidies. Grey and his co-authors define 'subsidy' as lower consumer 'prices' of housing, attributable to the overt and implicit nature of government involvement in housing. In other words, it is the difference between what occupiers pay and what they would have to pay if owner-occupier housing was taxed, private sector rents were deregulated and overt subsidies in public housing were withdrawn. Their method of analysis and their favoured policy is to remove all the existing subsidies and then to reform housing finance so that low- and moderate-income families receive housing allowances (or rent rebates if they live in public rental housing) based upon their capacity to pay the full economic costs of housing.

The contrasting positions of Grey with his co-authors and Kilroy revolve around questions of attitude and the way social housing purposes and subsidies are conceived. For Kilroy, it is not a matter of finding an economic current cost or market concept, but one of keeping rents in public housing low. Grey and his co-authors want 'consistency' and a clear association to economic principles, notwithstanding that they also refer the low-income capacity to pay problem to housing allowances and rent rebates. Our comparative review indicates that other alternatives are available. The economic and political dilemmas of tenure-related distribution are reduced when, as in Norway, a mixed public-private mortgaging instrument is: (1) accessible generally and uniformly across tenure lines, (2) housing allowances are accessible to all who qualify by virtue of their income and needs status, again regardless of tenure, and (3) central policy making in housing does not separate into fragmented rental and owner-occupier tenures. The Norwegian method enables government to modify the results of market effects in housing without creating rigidly separatist housing sectors. A case can be properly made for inter-sector equity, but it does not have to rest entirely on market criteria and residual welfare. Norway's alternative is elaborated in Chapters 5 and 6, and its modern development has been dependent upon *co-ordinating* several reforms in housing finance. We add further comment below to show that narrow reform proposals do not in themselves achieve egalitarianism in housing.

Until recently, many housing economists assumed that the taxation of imputed rental value in owner-occupier housing would neutralise tenure choice and lead towards distributional equity. However, Yates [63] has clearly shown that the whole question is rather more complicated. She examines household income and expenditure data, interpreting this in the context of stages in the life-cycle, and relating it to the incidence of actual tax schedules and scales. Although this approach particularises the results to specific situations at defined times - hers were Australia in the late 1960s - it does reveal the significance of life-cycle factors. A tax on imputed rental values of owner-occupier housing can be regressive (i.e., socially unfair) on the aged, and proportional or regressive (i.e., having some unfairness) during the early years of family formation and home ownership, and definitely progressive (i.e., socially fairer) among longer term home owners.

Also, home ownership for low-income groups remains a long-term aspiration which is sometimes fulfilled relatively late in life, compared with middle-income groups. For policy, Yates' findings support simultaneous moves to widen accessibility to home ownership, to establish housing allowances across tenure lines, and to finance housing allowances from the taxation of imputed rental value on owner-occupied housing.

In summary on the tenure-related distribution of wealth and income: An overall view of the tenure issue reveals that four key factors are involved: (1) to strip away old political ideologies and to place the matter on a sounder theoretical and empirical basis, (2) to revise the financial and allocational framework so that some biases are removed and some economic barriers are lowered, (3) to review the distributional question in terms of life-cycle considerations, and (4) to co-ordinate various reforms in housing finance and rent policies, rather than taking an *ad hoc* approach. Some of these issues emerge again as significant themes in the forthcoming chapters on housing economics and housing history. In West Germany, The Netherlands and Sweden attitudes to home ownership are changing. The question of distributional equity has come to the fore in Britain, but policy has not positively responded. Norway has a less acute problem. Australia has no very consistent policy but families there tend to go for home ownership when they can get it. Some progress in neutralising tenure selection will be one indicator of self-fulfilment and choice in housing. It has vital consequences for wealth and income distribution, but it is only one part of choice which, as we have seen, is influenced by many historical, institutional and economic factors.

HOUSING REFORM AND THE WELFARE STATE

Briggs [64] discusses criteria for deciding if a particular activity falls within the province of the welfare state. It does if (1) organised community power is used to modify the market, (2) the intent is to give an income guarantee, (3) the provision of a good or service narrows the range of insecurity, and (4) access to an agreed range of goods and services is given at standards acceptable to society. Clearly, housing falls within the welfare state. Societies have used community power extensively to modify the market in housing. The purpose of housing interventions has been to achieve more equality, to eliminate insecurity and to establish minimum standards. While these purposes have not always been fulfilled, it is on the basis of welfare state criteria that housing policies are often critically assessed.

The welfare state can be interpreted as an historical phenomenon, as an ideological instrument or as a method of institutionalising political conflict. [65] For example, the Marxist views the welfare state as palliative, as a means of continuing capitalism, and as a method of prescribing justice, but not in ways fitting the economic laws of history. Social Democrats see the welfare state as a means to equality and social justice. Another view sees it as a means of creating social rights and citizenship. In real life there is plenty of confusion about aims, and uncertainty about means.

The idea of unity looks simple enough if referred to the co-ordination of housing, urban and social policies. Also, it seems relevant because reform in each area can be substantially explained by reference to social, economic and political circumstances, common to housing, urban and social conditions. Sometimes, the idea of unity has more force because both the social theories used to justify reform and the activist reformers overlap the areas of reform. These are obviously important factors in the question of unity, but do not clinch the issue. What also has to be considered is the degree to which the theoretical precepts underlying the reforms are valid and coherent to the circumstances. If theories are invalid, and do not fit the conditions to which they are applied, unity is weakened. Finally, theory, social motivations, resources and administration have to be institutionalised. Thus the exploration of unity resolves itself into searching out overlapping theories and personalities, and identifying the limitations of theoretical precepts and the degree of co-ordination in administrative institutions.

Co-ordination is particularly important in modern policy development because the *interdependency* between housing and other public policies is growing and becoming more complex. But because of that complexity, co-ordination can be very difficult. As we shall presently see, some advocates of greater co-ordination, scarcely proceed beyond the (implicit) notion that it can be achieved simply by providing more social worker advisers in housing functions. That approach is simplistic because it tends to ignore some crucial questions:-

1. What are the limitations on co-ordination?

2. Is the need for co-ordination created by needlessly fragmented ideas and instruments of policy?

3. What historical and theoretical legacies have left an excessive separatism in welfare state policies and in administration?

Policy all too often creates its own problems. For example, the comparative rigidity of sectoral divisions in British housing, and the general policy instruments which create this rigidity, can be identified as *primary* influences in segregation, and in producing urban social imbalances and inequalities which provoke people to call for better co-ordination. If Britain had better housing policies, the call for co-ordination would be less urgent and co-ordination would be easier to achieve. As an illustration of the general nature of such problems, it is worth tracing the British troubles back to their historical roots.

Nevitt [66] has recently re-stated the need for co-ordination in British housing and social security policies. The modern social security system in Britain evolved from the Beveridge Report, 1942. [67] In deliberating the design for a comprehensive system of social security, Beveridge favoured uniform flat-rate benefits, to be financed from a pool of uniform flat-rate contributions. However, housing costs were a significant item in low-income household budgets, and housing costs varied widely. Growth regions had higher housing costs as short- and medium-term shortages drove up prices, rents and building costs. Within regions, the costs to particular households depended upon whether they occupied rent controlled private housing or public housing; and public housing rents varied according to local policies and the various constraints under which local governments operated their public housing programmes (see Chapter 5). In short, housing costs for working-class and low-income households varied according to regional growth patterns

and the rather arbitrary outcomes of housing policies which had confused
objectives and no effective national policy for public housing rents.
Thus, Beveridge faced a dilemma: he could link social security benefits
to local and regional housing costs which would make social security
administration more complicated; or he could set the issue aside as a
matter to be solved within housing policy, but without great confidence
that it *would* be solved satisfactorily.

In the event, the matter was left as a residual problem in housing
policy and in National Assistance. Thus, housing costs for 'welfare'
families (i.e., those not covered by 'social insurance') were partly
accounted in the rules governing benefits in National Assistance and in
the discretionary judgement of welfare officers. Although, in more
recent times, Britain has broken down the distinction between 'welfare
payments' and 'social insurance', the dilemmas of financing the housing
costs of low-income households have remained, though they are now somewhat changed in significance by the introduction of housing allowances
and 'fair rent' policies (see Chapter 6). Furthermore, Nevitt shows
that the contemporary relevance of co-ordinating housing and social
policies is intensifying and diversifying. Housing establishes rights
of tenure and property ownership which have various effects upon the
economic and social welfare of families and individuals. The changing
social characteristics of modern societies - with their high divorce
rates, with remarrying and with single-parent families - have housing-
related welfare consequences. Thus, in modern societies, the social
aspects of housing and its co-ordination with other policies go deeper
and wider than questions concerning access to subsidies and social
security benefits. A modern social administration of housing is also
bound up with rights to real estate, with sex inequalities and regional
inequalities. Co-ordination will consequently encompass a widening
agenda of issues and administrative needs.

The need for broader and better co-ordination has also been advocated
by official committees. In 1968, the Seebohm Report [68] recommended
that local government should take a wider view of its housing responsibilities. Social service and housing provisions should be co-ordinated
in the care of the elderly, the handicapped, large families, single
parent families and so on. Social workers should be appointed to
housing departments so that services could be extended to those in
housing need and to those with housing-related social needs. Despite
some progress, the Morris Committee was appointed five years later (in
1973) to give more specialised attention to housing and social work.
Its Reports [69] identified the familiar problems of British housing:-

1. The concentration of social problems in certain areas - social
    imbalance, the lack of amenities, unemployment, vandalism and apathy.

2. Homelessness.

3. Inadequate provisions to meet the housing needs of particular groups.

The Morris Committee proposed that better co-ordination between housing and social service functions could improve conditions. Like the
Seebohm Committee, it had much faith in the capacity of social workers
to persuade local government housing managers to deal more helpfully
with the needs of single parent families, battered wives, single persons,
the homeless and itinerants.

As was mentioned earlier, the idea of co-ordination needs to be examined in terms of its limitations and its wider relationship to the policy framework within which the ideals of the welfare state find their expression. From these perspectives we take a more critical view of the work of the Seebohm and the Morris Committees. Neither of these Committees examined those structural conditions in British housing policies which contribute to segregation, homelessness, and divisiveness in administering welfare. Compared with other countries, Britain has concentrated (or, perhaps, confined) its expression of social aims in housing to the public housing idea and to slum living conditions. By contrast, Norway expresses its social aims through more general financial instruments and through all tenure groups (owner-occupiers, co-operators and renters), with the result that social problems less often appear in the form of simultaneous conditions of poverty, inequality and concentrations (geographical and social) in particular housing sectors. In other words, Norwegian social problems are not identifiable as problems of public housing or any other particular housing sector. It is also fairer to say that the Seebohm and Morris recommendations about co-ordination were piecemeal and *ad hoc*. In modern society, the needs for co-ordination, and the case which can be made out for it, extend beyond relationships between housing and social services. The discussions in Chapter 9 explain the more general case, and the way Norway, Sweden and West Germany have undertaken reforms in government and administration, so that co-ordination is exercised more comprehensively and coherently.

Like other things which make claims on economic resources and administrative energies, social work and co-ordination can be costly. Furthermore, the use of cost-effectiveness techniques and other sorts of analyses which can make administration more accountable and purposeful in the selection of priorities, are relatively undeveloped in the administration of social work. Although the 1968 Seebohm Report had the virtue of establishing a case for co-ordination, it did not make the point that 'comprehensiveness' and 'co-ordination' need some clear-cut guiding principles to identify objectives, to monitor performance and to achieve specific effectiveness. In housing, we need to know precisely what social services are justified, and the point where resources are to be cut off and allocated to other ends, or to other ways of achieving welfare in housing. For example, what is the precise form and shape of a useful housing-social service programme covering financial assistance (i.e., subsidies), casework, social development and dispensing information? If we can answer this sort of question we can define the necessary co-ordination more clearly, and we can put some limit to open-ended claims on social services.

Recently, in an extensive American survey of low-income urban housing problems, Grigsby and Rosenburg [70] found that 70 per cent of respondents favoured consumer subsidies only, 15 per cent favoured social services and consumer subsidies together, and for the remaining 15 per cent the 'multi-problem' nature of the circumstances made neither consumer subsidy nor the social service approach entirely satisfactory. The sort of social services which were needed included home locator services, counsel on landlord-tenant relations, budgeting for medical care and aid with transport. This survey was particularly useful in view of the breadth of its view of housing, with investigations into housing standards, stigmatisation and discrimination, neighbourhood amenities, and the rent-income burden. The authors found that *'housing*

poverty' was greater than 'food poverty'. More of this sort of work is
needed to give direction and limitation to the role of social work in
housing and to establish the specific shape co-ordination should take.

Finally, the question of unity and co-ordination among housing, urban
and social policies can be examined in its theoretical and historical
context. The example of the first British reforms in public health and
the relief of poverty serves to show how separatism is created in social
policy development, despite the overt recognition of the need for
co-ordination. Table 3-1 below, summarises the main points of historical and theoretical relevance.

TABLE   3-1

A Summary of Public Health and Poor Law Reform
United Kingdom, 1830-1860

Public Health Reforms[a] Housing & Urban Policies	Poor Law Reforms[a] Social Policies
Background Circumstances	*Background circumstances*
Problems of urban growth and disease were reflected in the demographic and social statistics of the period. Until 1831, death rates per 1,000 of the population showed a steady reduction. However, in 1831-41 this increased from 20.69 to 30.8 in Britain's largest towns. At the same time, Glasgow's population increased by 37%, Manchester's by 47% and Bradford's by 78%. Occupancy rates were increasing in working-class living areas. In parts of Manchester, privies were shared in the ratio of 1 per 215 people. Cholera was the most dreaded disease and was rampant in the middle- and working-class areas in 1831, 1848, 1854 and 1867. Agitation for reform grew.	Prevailing policies of poor law relief were a heavy burden on public expenditure. *Gilbert's Act*, 1872 sanctioned the relief of able-bodied poor outside the workhouse and provided indexed supplements related to the price of bread. In some parishes, the unemployed were allocated to public works or shared among yeoman farmers. The popular view was that these policies placed a burden on ratepayers, demoralised the working class, destroyed the yeomanry, and actually created unemployment and poverty. Out-door relief was also blamed for supporting speculative housing and the creation of bad housing. Agitation for reform grew.

Notes: a The historical details have been derived from S.E. Finer, *The
Life and Times of Sir Edwin Chadwick*, Methuen, London, 1951, M.W. Finn,
(ed), *Chadwick's Report on the Sanitary Condition of the Labouring
Population of Great Britain*, 1842, Edinburgh University Press 1965, R.A.
Lewis, *Edwin Chadwick and the Public Health Movement*, Longmans, London,
1952.

Public Health Reforms
Housing & Urban Policies

Poor Law Reforms
Social Policies

Personalities

Edwin Chadwick was the main source for the cause of reform. His theory (a synthesis of Utilitarianism and Ricardian economics[b]) and his surveys demonstrated that society would obtain substantial benefits from cleansing the slums and installing town-wide networks of drains and sewers. His ideas were supported by medical reformers, Lord Shaftesbury, and by the Health of Towns Association.

Personalities

Edwin Chadwick was the key figure. He advised a Royal Commission investigating the Old Poor Law. When the New Poor Law was created in 1834, Chadwick became Secretary of the Poor Law Commission. He had previously argued that sickness was a major cause of poverty and as Secretary of the Commission, he wanted to spend its funds on cleansing the East End of London to reduce the Commission's net costs. The auditor disallowed this. Chadwick increasingly came into conflict with the unimaginative and conservative, Frankland Lewis, chairman of the Commission. As a result, Chadwick spent more time on public health reform than in administering the New Poor Law.

Theory

Chadwick was an advocate of Utilitarianism; a theory which stated that social and economic institutions were beneficial when they added to human 'happiness' (utility). Since it could be shown that the prevailing system of markets and public administration could not produce efficient and effective public health, new institutional arrangements depending on public finance and public administration had to be created.

The new solutions had second-order effects in public administration and in public health engineering. A new pattern of intergovernmental administration had to be created to ensure reform was achieved. This caused friction and contention between the centre and the localities; and the private sector opposed the loss of some trade (water supplies, garbage

Theory

Poor Law Reform was advocated within three theories. The Malthusians believed that any improved poverty relief would be counter-productive because the means of subsistence would be out-distanced by population growth. Some believed that, if men were given more productive work, the problem would disappear. Chadwick found that the Malthusians were empirically incorrect. He proposed a control device whereby able-bodied poor would get relief only if they were prepared to enter the workhouse. This was the 'less eligibility' principle, and the willingness to enter the workhouse was the test of eligibility. Chadwick's synthesis of Utilitarianism and Ricardian economics was less appropriate to the problem of poverty than to public health.

Notes: b Utilitarian theory and Ricardian economics were discussed in Chapter 2.

collection) to public administration.

The old technology of cesspools
and brick tunnels had to be
replaced with an overall system
of piped water, drains and gravity
flows using principles of
hydraulics. Engineers opposed
the new methods. Chadwick's
solution also depended on a
correct theory of the cause and
spread of disease, and this was
not provided until after public
health and housing reforms had
established their practices.

Chadwick stopped short of expanding the housing supply to
eliminate crowding and to reduce
rents (see discussions in
Chapter 2).

Institutionalisation

The *Public Health Act*, 1848
achieved reform, following
unsuccessful attempts in 1845,
1846 and 1847.   The administration of the Act ran into
conflict with the localities and
private enterprise.   Accordingly
in 1854, the administration of
public health was re-organised.

Institutionalisation

The *Poor Law Amendment Act*, 1834,
gave effect to Chadwick's theories
on 'less eligibility'.   This Act
created the Poor Law Commission.

In effect, though the public health
reforms grew out of society's
concern for poverty they were
administered under separate arrangements.

   The first phase of housing reform had unity in so far as Chadwick and
his theories were used in housing, urban and social reform.   But this
was not enough to create an enduring, theoretical and administrative
unity.   There were various reasons for the splintering of something
which began in a reasonably unified way.

   At the theoretical level, the public health reforms stopped short at
the urban environmental issues and building regulations.   Chadwick
opposed the use of limited-profit philanthropy or public finance to
build new housing; these issues were current at the time, but did not
become significant in public policy until the second phase of housing
reform.   Thus, the theory used to accomplish housing and urban reform
in the first phase limited what could have been achieved in public
policy.   Later, Chadwick's approach to urban and housing reform was
overwhelmed by environmental determinism and Conservative idealisms
emphasising class interaction.   This made reform ideas futile, the most
prominent examples being slum clearance policies.   The mixed theoretical inheritances influenced the second phase of housing reform (see
discussions in Chapter 5) and prevented the development of a coherent
unity among housing, urban and social policies.

Chadwick's theory of poor relief has recently been shown to be irrelevant to the problem in hand. Blaug [71] showed that when Britain reformed its Poor Law, its economy was moving from rural and craft industries to manufacturing. Economies in this state of transformation are characterised by unemployment in the rural and craft sector. Sometimes the full extent of the underemployment is disguised by sharing a surplus of labour among the two sectors. Furthermore, wages were close to subsistence level. The implication was that any increase would make workers healthier, and that means more productive. Under these circumstances, the subsistence allowances paid under the Old Poor Law, and indexed to the price of bread (i.e., subsistence), could be regarded as a welfare state in miniature. Income was brought up to subsistence levels, family allowances were incorporated into its structure, it provided compensation for unemployment, and it developed public works. Thus Blaug shows that Chadwick's determination to re-place these rational principles was inappropriate, except as a method of controlling public expenditure.

The wrong approach to poverty, and the invalid environmental determinism and Conservative idealism in housing and urban policies created barriers against a coherent and logical unity. Other unities such as personal influences and administrative factors cannot be effect-ive unless there is some logical or theoretical unity. In fact, administration was separated rather than unified or co-ordinated. Poor Law programmes and public health were administered separately, to serve distinct problems. Medical officers and engineers dominated public health administration after Chadwick was dismissed from the Central Board of Public Health in 1858. And environmental determinism had an underlying influence in public health. In the poverty relief programme, the harsher practices of the workhouse test were moderated at the turn of the twentieth century and a new system of social security was set up as the basis of a new poverty relief programme. Housing and urban policies were also revised in the first two decades of the new century, but each took its own administrative course (see Chapter 5).

Thus, at the outset of housing, urban and social policy reform, theory, history and administration produced separatism rather than co-ordination and unity. Nevertheless, in periods when there is ferment, agitation for reform, and intellectual criticism of social policy, the case for co-ordination is strongly advocated. Also, poverty studies dating from the pioneering work of Charles Booth and B.S. Rowntree all point to the importance of housing and its costs in the social and economic life of the poor. In fact, as was mentioned above, some modern American studies make the point that *housing poverty* is sometimes more significant than *food poverty* in modern democratic society. Clearly, the idea of co-ordination in social policy development is growing in significance. In Britain, the Central Policy Review Staff has recently reported [72] on the urgent need to get a collective view of priorities, programmes, analysis and prescription in social policy development, including housing. Our discussions have explored the idea of co-ordina-tion with its dilemmas and limitations, and co-ordination enters again into the next chapter where the social economics of housing is reviewed.

NOTES

[1] The origins of the continental European and British town planning

movement are discussed more extensively in L.Benevolo, *The Origins of Modern Town Planning*, Routledge and Kegan Paul, London, 1967.

[2] The detailed history of the British public health movement can be found in S.E.Finer, *The Life and Times of Sir Edwin Chadwick*, Methuen, London, 1951, M.W.Finn (ed) *Chadwick's Report on the Sanitary Condition of the Labouring Population of Great Britain, 1842*, Edinburgh University Press, Edinburgh, 1965, and R.A.Lewis, *Edwin Chadwick and the Public Health Movement*, Longmans, London, 1952.

[3] Even scientific theories were invalid. For example, the knowledge of the cause and spread of disease (its etiology) was undeveloped. In the case of cholera and other contagious diseases, it was thought that the atmosphere was charged with an epidemic influence which became malignant when combined with exhalations from organic decomposition. Knowledge of germs and vibrios was not developed until later in the nineteenth century; for the wrong reasons, sanitary inspectors became intent on eliminating stinks and smells. Also, the technology of sanitary engineering had no scientific foundation until Chadwick and his collaborators began to reform it.

[4] A useful historical account can be found in A.S.Wohl, *The Housing of Artisans and Labourers in Nineteenth Century London, 1815-1914*, unpublished PhD thesis, Brown University, United States, 1966.

[5] Wohl, *op. cit.*, (1966) p.230.

[6] The social conscience of the church and society had been hit by publicity given to overcrowding and incest in working-class areas. Some parts of London housed 30-40 per cent of their families in one- and two-roomed tenement dwellings. See A.S.Wohl, 'The Bitter Cry of Out- cast London', *International Review of Social History*, 1968, pp.189-245.

[7] See London County Council, *The Housing Question in London 1855-1900*, London County Council, London, no date-circa 1900, and London County Council, *Housing of the Working Classes in London, 1889-1912*, London County Council, London, 1913.

[8] *Report of the Committee to Consider Questions of Building Construc- tion in Connection with the Provision of Dwellings for the Working Classes in England and Wales, and Scotland*, (Tudor Walters), HMSO, London, 1918.

[9] *Final Report of the Unhealthy Areas Committee* (Neville Chamberlain), HMSO, London, 1925.

[10] For more historical detail see L.Holm, 'Consumer Research', in Ministry of Housing and Physical Planning, *Swedish Experiences of Self- Building, Co-operation, Consumer Research, Participation*, Ministry of Housing and Physical Planning, Stockholm, 1976.

[11] The Fund receives a government contribution and the proceeds of a special building research levy on buildings.

[12] Ministry of Housing and Local Government, *Homes for Today and Tomorrow*, (Parker Morris), HMSO, London, 1961.

[13] A general history of the emergence and development of social work, though not from a housing perspective, can be found in K.Woodroofe, *From Charity to Social Work*, Routledge and Kegan Paul, London, 1966.

[14] Octavia Hill's grandfather was Southwood-Smith, the public health reformer, who had collaborated with Chadwick. Octavia Hill devoted her life to the educational development of working-class housewives, to housing improvement and to the conservation of parks and common land. Her influence was broad and it included the improvement of the Church of England's housing estates in London, the encouragement of the Settlement Movement, and a friendship with Emma Cons who was manageress of the philanthropic South London Dwellings Company (1878). Octavia Hill's role in housing reform is discussed by Wohl, *op. cit.*, (1966).

[15] The Settlement Movement emphasised community/social development whereas COS was more interested in counselling individuals and families. In the terms of the discussions of this text, the Settlement created externalities in the form of clubrooms, gymnasia, social facilities and neighbourhood social development.

[16] A detailed account of how Australian town planners have asserted a sort of technologism and then been caught short by social economic and political change can be found in L. Sandercock, *Cities for Sale*, Melbourne University Press, Melbourne, 1975.

[17] Housing Policy Committee of the Council of Social Services of New South Wales, *Report on Housing*, Council of Social Services of New South Wales, Sydney, 1944.

[18] National Council for Social Services, *The Size and Structure of a Town*, NCSS, London, 1943.

[19] For example, the NCSS has published M.Broady's sociological critiques of town planning. See M.Broady, *Planning for People*, Bedford Square Press, London, 1968.

[20] The same could be said of some ideas in economics, sociology and so on. However, the real point here is that an organised profession has adopted a role to deliberately influence policy on behalf of its membership and its clients.

[21] This principle was used in the 1834 Poor Law to try to divide the 'deserving' poor from the 'undeserving' poor so poverty relief could be efficient and appropriate. The COS tried to apply the same principle.

[22] Resident action was not new. Working-class tenants in London had organised themselves into the Somers Town Defence League and the Evicted Tenants' Aid Association to oppose railway development in their areas in mid-Victorian times.

[23] Administrative separatism occurs when each level and agency of government pursues its own narrow priority without regard for the corporate situation.

[24] See A.W.Evans, *The Economics of Residential Location*, St. Martin's Press, New York, 1973, and R.F.Muth, *Cities and Housing*, Chicago University Press, Chicago, 1969.

[25] Broady, *op. cit.*, (1968).

[26] H.J.Gans, *People and Plans*, Penguin, Harmondsworth, 1972.

[27] The research confirms economic findings and ranks housing-related amenities thus; proximity to shops, work, public transport, schools, recreational facilities, and entertainment. The ranking is average; it re-orders for such factors as class, stage of life and other circumstances. For example, families with young children rate highly their nearness to parks and schools, while housewives without the use of a private car rate higher the proximity to public transport.

[28] For the new urban sociology branch see R.E.Pahl, *Whose City?*, Penguin, Harmondsworth, 1975, and for the modern Marxist branch see D.Harvey, *Social Justice and The City*, Arnold, London, 1973, and G.V.Pickvance (ed), *Urban Sociology : Critical Essays*, Tavistock, London, 1976.

[29] J.Lambert, C.Paris and R.Blackaby, *Housing Policy and The State*, MacMillan, London, 1978.

[30] See P.Jephcott, *Homes in High Flats*, Oliver and Boyd, Edinburgh, 1971.

[31] Harvey, *op. cit.*, (1973). Some aspects of his study aim at more fundamental theoretical explanations of urban processes; these are not considered in the discussions here.

[32] M.Whitbread and H.Bird, 'Rent Surplus and the Evaluation of Residential Environments', *Regional Studies*, Vol.7, 1973, pp.193-223.

[33] H.Stretton, *Capitalism, Socialism and the Environment*, Cambridge University Press, Cambridge, 1976.
[34] This relationship leaves the consumer with a utility surplus above the exchange value. Whitbread and Bird (see discussion below) use this surplus to discover other things about housing. Utility theory is important in justifying a government role in public utilities (electricity, gas, water, sewerage, public transport and so on) when an exchange or financial criterion produces apparently perverse implications. Some public utilities have direct relations with housing.
[35] Cost-benefit analysis is a specialist and controversial field of economics. It can illuminate the economic aspects of various social policies. My own view is that cost-benefit analysis is easier to apply to some situations (e.g., transport) than to others (e.g., care for the aged). However, it certainly is not as absurd as some critics allege, and is not as bountiful as its strongest enthusiasts claim. Cost-benefit analysis in housing is discussed further in Chapter 4.
[36] I am aware of examples in private suburban development in Australia where developers built shops and other facilities so they could market the estate without tying up capital in unsold houses. For the first few years, the shops were not profitable and other facilities produced no marketed goods or services. The developer does this because consumers can switch their purchasing to other estates, and unprofitable shops and so on can be cross-subsidised from unearned increments on land, which are discussed in Chapter 7.
[37] Whitbread and Bird, *op. cit.*, (1973).
[38] For the owner-occupiers or co-operators, this is an implicit (opportunity cost) value; it is the rent a dwelling would fetch if let on the open market.
[39] Some households will not have many home-based activities compared with others; for them the dwelling is simply a dormitory and a kitchen.
[40] Sociological research had indicated the key importance of social class and stage in the life-cycle as determinants of housing choice. See Gans, *op. cit.*, (1972).
[41] In large urban areas, housing can be regarded as a heterogeneous collection of linked sub-markets, or sub-sections with special characteristics of type, size, condition, social environment, location, tenure and so on. The sub-markets are separated by price, but the relativities alter with changing conditions in urban processes and in the cost of new and old housing. See W.G.Grigsby, *Housing Markets and Public Policy*, University of Philadelphia Press, Philadelphia, 1963.
[42] Stretton, *op. cit.*, (1976).
[43] P.Willmott and M.Young, *The Symmetrical Family*, Penguin, Harmondsworth, 1973.
[44] The statement is made prescriptively because housing and neighbourhoods are largely influenced by professional, administrative and governmental processes rather than by any *straightforward* consumer choice.
[45] One aspect of socialist thought (e.g., Louis Blanc's ideas, 1811-1882) has emphasised the need for co-operation in society and the reform of alienating work. See discussions in Chapter 2.
[46] For example, in large metropolitan areas where most housing is provided by private capital markets and land is allocated under the mixed *laissez faire*-regulatory planning system, (see Chapter 7) the following patterns tend to emerge. Some higher income, small household groups will live in apartments near the centre where the environment is attractive. Poor families and single people sharing accommodation, will live in the inner suburbs at relatively high density on expensive

land. The middle suburbs will be shared by married couples (both working), single people, and middle-class married couples (only the husband working). The outer suburbs will attract middle class families (only the husband working). For useful analytical explanations, see A.W.Evans, *The Economics of Residential Location*, St. Martin's Press, New York, 1973. The general description of settlement patterns as outlined in this Note would need to be qualified where public or social housing is developed on the urban periphery. In this case some low- and moderate-income groups settle in suburbia, but sometimes the housing estates will lack the quality of urban servicing which is available in middle-class suburbs.

[47] See M.Fried, 'Grieving for a Lost Home : Psychological Costs of Relocation', in L.J.Duhl (ed), *The Urban Condition*, Basic Books, New York, 1963.
[48] L.Rainwater, 'Fear and the House Haven in the Lower Class', in J.Bellush and M.Hausknecht, (eds), *Urban Renewal : Politics and Planning*, Doubleday, New York, 1967.
[49] Although class is an important social condition in all societies its character and significance varies. In some of the more egalitarian countries in Europe, way of life factors seem to be gaining ground relative to social class distinctions. Of course, a Marxist would not accept this statement because 'dialectical materialism' makes the class relationship fundamental to the means of production.
[50] H.J.Gans, *The Levittowners*, Penguin, Harmondsworth, 1967.
[51] The key developments in the co-operative housing movement were discussed in Chapter 2; and some of the key organisational aspects of co-operation in housing are discussed in Chapter 9.
[52] The HSB is discussed in Chapter 2. Its essential feature is that the development and the estate management are managed separately, but co-ordinated in membership rights and in their relationship to co-operative principles.
[53] This theme was discussed in Chapter 2.
[54] W.A.Niskanen, *Bureaucracy and Representative Government*, Aldine Atherton, Chicago, 1971.
[55] This section has benefited from exchanges of ideas with J.Kemeny.
[56] Comparative statements on the proportions of different tenures among countries should be interpreted cautiously. For example, regulatory building requirements vary from country to country with higher and costlier standards in West Germany compared with Britain.
[57] Stretton, *op. cit.*, (1976). Stretton's theoretical construct was discussed earlier in this chapter.
[58] See *Housing Policy : A Consultative Document*, Cmnd. 6851, HMSO, London, 1977.
[59] Building Economic Development Committee/National Economic Develop- ment Office, *Housing for All*, National Economic Development Office, HMSO, London, 1977.
[60] D.C.Stafford, *The Economics of Housing Policy*, Croom Helm, London, 1978.
[61] A.Grey, N.P.Hepworth and J.Odling-Smee, *Housing Rents, Costs and Subsidies*, Chartered Institute of Public Finance and Accountancy, London, 1978.
[62] B.Kilroy, *Housing Finance - Organic Reform?*, Labour Economic Finance and Taxation Association, London, 1978.
[63] J.Yates, *The Distributional Impact of Subsidies Arising From the Non-Taxation of Imputed Rent in Australia, 1966-1968*, PSERC Discussion Paper, University of Sheffield, Sheffield, 1979.
[64] A.Briggs, 'The Welfare State in Historical Perspective', *European*

Journal of Sociology, Vol.2, No.2, 1961, pp.221-258.

65   A useful collection of essays on this subject can be found in W.D. Birrell, P.A.R.Hillyard, A.S.Murie and D.J.D.Roche, (eds), *Social Administration*, Penguin, Harmondsworth, 1973.

66   A.A.Nevitt, 'Housing in a Welfare State', *Urban Studies*, Vol.14, No.1, February 1977, pp.33-40.

67   W.Beveridge, *Social Insurance and Allied Services*, HMSO, London, 1942.

68   *Report of the Committee on Local Authority and Allied Personal Social Services*, (Seebohm), HMSO, London, 1968.

69   Scottish Development Department, *Housing and Social Work : A Joint Approach*, Interim Report, HMSO, Edinburgh, 1974 and Final Report (Morris), HMSO, Edinburgh, 1975.

70   W.G.Grigsby and L.Rosenburg, *Urban Housing Policy*, APS Publications, New York, 1975.

71   M.Blaug, 'The Myth of the Old Poor Law and the Making of the New', *Journal of Economic History*, June 1963, pp.151-184, and 'The Poor Law Report Re-examined', *Journal of Economic History*, June 1964, pp.229-245.

72   Central Policy Review Staff, *A Joint Framework for Social Policies*, HMSO, London, 1975.

REFERENCES (SELECTED)

Birrell, W.D., Hillyard, P.A.R., Murie, A.S., and Roche, D.J.D., (eds), *Social Administration*, Penguin, Harmondsworth, 1973.

Blaug, M., 'The Myth of the Old Poor Law and the Making of the New', *Journal of Economic History*, June 1963, pp.151-184 and 'The Poor Law Re-examined', *Journal of Economic History*, June 1964, pp.229-245.

Briggs, A., 'The Welfare State in Historical Perspective', *European Journal of Sociology*, Vol.2, No.2, 1961, pp.221-258.

Broady, M., *Planning for People*, Bedford Square Press, London, 1968.

Evans, A.W., *The Economics of Residential Location*, St. Martin's Press, New York, 1973.

Finer, S.E., *The Life and Times of Sir Edwin Chadwick*, Methuen, London, 1951.

Finn, M.W., (ed), *Chadwick's Report on the Sanitary Condition ot the Labouring Population of Great Britain, 1842*, Edinburgh University Press, Edinburgh, 1965.

Gans, H.J., *People and Plans*, Penguin, Harmondsworth, 1972.

Harvey, D., *Social Justice and The City*, Arnold, London, 1973.

Lewis, R.A., *Edwin Chadwick and the Public Health Movement*, Longmans, London, 1952.

Nevitt, A.A., 'Housing in a Welfare State' *Urban Studies*, Vol.14, No.1, February 1977, pp.33-40.

Niskanen, W.A., *Bureaucracy and Representative Government*, Aldine

Atherton, Chicago, 1971.

Rainwater, L., 'Fear and the House Haven in the Lower Class', in J. Bellush and M. Hausknecht (eds), *Urban Renewal : Politics and Planning*, Doubleday, New York, 1967.

Stretton, H., *Capitalism, Socialism and the Environment*, Cambridge University Press, London, 1976.

Whitbread, M., and Bird, H., 'Rent, Surplus and the Evaluation of Residential Environment', *Regional Studies*, Vol.7, 1973, pp.192-223.

Wohl, A.S., *The Housing of Artisans and Labourers in Nineteenth Century London, 1815-1914*, unpublished PhD thesis, Brown University, United States, 1966.

Woodroofe, K., *From Charity to Social Work*, Routledge and Kegan Paul, London, 1966.

4 Housing policy and social economics

Economic arguments and their relevance to housing appear in every
chapter in this study. We have drawn upon economics to clarify housing
concepts, to give meaning to the history of ideas in housing, and to
explore the relationships between housing and social policies. In
subsequent chapters, economics will be used to re-construct historical
interpretations of housing, to shed light on some key issues in land
development and urban renewal policies, and to evaluate intergovernmental and organisational aspects of housing. Thus, economic
principles enter both as a basis of the general themes of the study and
as specialised contributions in particular topics. The main purpose of
this chapter are: (1) to give a general outline of the scope of the
social economics of housing in a modern policy context, (2) to provide
some support for thematic interpretations in the next two chapters which
deal with housing history, and (3) to reveal clearly the economic
factors which are influencing modern housing reform.

The main themes in this chapter show that what is understood as
'economics' and as 'housing' has been broadened and deepened during the
last decade or so. 'Economics' in public policy topics such as
housing, education, health and urbanisation is bringing a wider *social*
intellectualism into its mainstream currents. This includes aspects of
other subjects such as politics, social administration and sociology.
Also, more attention is being given to the ethical and philosophical
positions on income distribution. 'Housing' is no longer simply understood as 'shelter', but is viewed as a complex interwoven package
covering the characteristics of the dwelling, the neighbourhood, and
accessibility to urban services. The discussions will make some direct
reference to this broadening and deepening interpretation of 'economics'
and 'housing'. These discussions will review the development of knowledge in the social economics of housing around the idea of the 'housing
gap'. The 'housing gap' is the difference between the consumer's cost
of 'standard' housing (expressed in rents or loan repayments) and the
amounts which moderate- and low-income households can reasonably afford
to pay. Clearly, the 'housing gap' is an important concept in discuss-
ing the anti-poverty and the egalitarian aspects of housing.

The 'housing gap' concept can be used to shed light upon historical,
current and comparative policy developments. In this chapter the
alternative approaches to solving the 'housing gap' problem will be
reviewed analytically as policy options. The subsequent chapters on
housing history will place the various policy options in their wider
social and historical context. Those and other chapters will also show
that the idea of the welfare state in housing policy development has to
be drawn more broadly than through the 'housing gap' concept. Welfare
state aims in housing have important connections to locational

---

* An appendix on the technical aspects of housing allowances appears at
  the end of the chapter (pp.137-143).

relationships between employment and housing, to urban land policies, to urban renewal and so on. Nevertheless, for present purposes it will be useful to interpret the development of economic knowledge and policy around the 'housing gap' concept. Thus, the main themes which are stitched together in this chapter are the incorporation of broader social concerns into 'economics', the changing notion of 'housing' and the relationships between policy options and the 'housing gap'.

The discussions in this chapter take up and elaborate some points made in previous discussions. In Chapter 1 we noted that housing and its problems are perceived in various ways according to historical and institutional settings as well as by reference to abstract principles. Although economic literature is seldom interpreted in the broad context of its relationships between history, institutional settings and general abstract principles, this will be the approach adopted here. The discussion is organised to reveal: (1) the development of economic knowledge since about 1960, (2) welfare state issues and policy options arising from the 'housing gap', (3) the ferment and change in policy development during the last decade or so, (4) housing allowances and equity, (5) the economic role of older housing in policy development and (6) the legacy of ideas left by the severe inflation, 1973-1976.

THE MODERN ECONOMICS OF HOUSING AND THE HOUSING GAP

Diversity in economic studies

Economic arguments were used by Chadwick, Lord Shaftesbury, Octavia Hill and other nineteenth-century housing reformers. Also, Alfred Marshall, A.C. Pigou, W. Smart and other theoretical economists contributed ideas to nineteenth-century housing reform. However, only since 1960 has the economics of housing and urbanisation emerged as a subject within the continuous research and teaching programmes of some universities and specialised research institutions. Nevertheless, along with sociology, political science and administrative studies, economics has had a considerable impact upon modern housing policy development. Also, the policy orientation of this interest in housing has influenced the development of ideas in economics. Housing is the sort of subject where crucial insights generally come from putting together intellectual jigsaws over a wide spectrum of subjects, making connecting links, and exploring ideas that seem disconnective. This is also relevant to other areas of public policy including education, health and social policies generally. Economists have taken more specialised interests in all these spheres since 1960. Like their nineteenth-century forerunners, modern economists of housing have found it virtually impossible to isolate the economic aspects of housing completely from its wider relationships with history, social institutions, politics, administration and social processes.

Our discussions will focus mainly upon the welfare state aspects of housing economics. If we identify the 'social economics of housing' with welfare state objectives, the following points become significant. As a part of the welfare state, some housing is produced and allocated so that:-

1. Organised community power is used to modify the market.

2. The 'housing gap' is bridged either by providing low-cost standard housing and/or by using housing allowances.

3. Acting through government, society ensures that some economic assistance is tied to housing, rather than provided simply as general cash assistance.

These conditions influence housing in all modern democratic societies, but the specific ways things are done reveals wide variations among countries. Accordingly, from a comparative perspective, economic issues and discussions tend to be raised in diverse forms. In Sweden, The Netherlands and West Germany modern economic issues have centred around a movement away from deep subsidisation (i.e., from costly, long-term and generally available subsidies) towards more selective targeting and the shifting of some costs from public finance to households. In Britain, it has been the economics of tenure and sectoral separatism which has attracted attention and relevance. In the United States, policy-makers and economists have been interested in housing allowances and their possible impacts upon the costs, rents and supplies in low-income housing sub-markets.

Diversity in economic studies occurs also by virtue of differences in the way 'housing' and 'economics' is conceived. As we saw in Chapter 2, economics has market-orientated, 'welfare economics', welfare state, institutionalist and Marxist inheritances. Furthermore, the development of public goods and merit goods theory during the 1955-1975 period has opened up more non-market economic justifications in economics. In this same period, what we should understand as 'housing' has changed. Housing is now understood in relation to egalitarianism, to poverty, to social development and to locational aspects of urban servicing. Consequently, the social economics of housing has widened into this range of things. Above all, the recent social economics of housing has been closely related to the needs of policy. The whole intellectual enterprise suffers upheavals of doubt and controversy and reconstruction if the main concerns of policy change. There has been such a change from the 1960s to the 1980s. Policy used to be overwhelmingly concerned to improve the supply of housing. But in the 1970s the housing shortages were (largely) overcome; policy must now be concerned with more selective subsidies, better uses and better management of the existing housing stock, questions of tenure and problems of inflation.

Summarising the consequences of the diversity of modern housing economics, we can say the following. First, recent studies need to be discerned for the way in which their authors cognitively perceive housing and their ideological and/or theoretical inclinations. Second, we need to know who will use the studies, politically and administratively, and for what purposes. Third, it is important to know whether the studies establish or lead on to epistemological significance - that is to say, in what ways has new knowledge in housing economics been created. This is especially important in a modern context where knowledge is changing not just by additions within its conventional boundaries, but by the creation of new general and basic principles. Finally, we need to understand the historical and theoretical connections between egalitarian principles and the development of housing policy. The current diversity makes it more difficult to pinpoint a neatly packaged subject termed, 'housing economics', and that is why we need our four-point guide, as set out above, for interpretation and evaluation.

We shall proceed in our interpretation and evaluations by looking at
the housing gap and the controversies surrounding the 'in-kind' and
'cash' approaches to bridging the gap. This will lead into a review of
historical and comparative methods of bridging the housing gap.

*The housing gap and the controversies on the 'in-kind' and cash
approaches to welfare*

When housing is discussed in the context of anti-poverty and egalitarian
objectives, the 'housing gap' becomes a key issue. The 'housing gap'
is the difference between the consumer's cost of standard housing
(expressed in rents or repayment of loans) and the amounts which
moderate- and low-income households can reasonably afford to pay.
Although, the 'housing gap' should not be interpreted simplistically,[1]
social history and social analysis have left some established ideas on
the capacity of low-income groups to pay for housing. Poverty studies
have shown that under historical market conditions, the poor have paid
in the range of 20 to 40 per cent of their income for housing. Also,
the nutritional aspects of poverty studies show that (historically)
where more than 20 per cent of household budgets of the poor have been
spent on housing, standards of nutrition have been lowered to levels
which jeopardise health and welfare. In families, the diet of
married women has been particularly affected by a combination of
'income' and 'housing' poverty. Thus, research in poverty established
that it was reasonable for poor families to pay no more than (about) 20
per cent of their income towards housing. As social and economic
conditions change so do notions of 'poverty'. The 20 per cent of
income standard has become an arbitrary rule-of-thumb in modern society
where it represents a 'relative' standard, rather than a factor affecting diet. Nevertheless, we have found some analytical and welfare
justifications for bridging the 'housing gap'.

We run into problems when these welfare and analytical justifications
are brought into relationship with housing history. Policy-makers have
not always perceived housing problems primarily as the rent-income
burdens of the poor. They have been interested in housing standards
per se, not as criteria for defining the 'housing gap'. As we saw in
Chapter 3, it has been a complicated mixture of social idealism,
technical definitions and administrative prescription which has
influenced the history of housing standards. It has not been
systematic, social and economic analysis which have been used to derive
'minimum' or 'adequate' levels of sufficiency. Although some economic
arguments have been used to show the social costs attributed to
contagious disease and unsafe conditions in 'unfit' housing, it has been
the non-economic considerations which have dominated code prescriptions
in housing standards. The historical legacy has modern policy
relevance. One benchmark in defining the 'housing gap' is in a rather
unsatisfactory and imprecise state. Now that housing allowances have
become prominent in modern policy development, the dilemmas left by the
history of housing standards are conspicuously exposed. One example
of these dilemmas has occurred in the recent large-scale programme of
social and economic research into housing allowances in the United
States. Researchers have used codifications of minimum standards
recommended by professional public health organisations. However, it
has proved difficult to apply these consistently, and researchers have

found that much middle-class housing falls foul of the recommended standards, but with no obvious social cost to the community. [2]

As was mentioned, housing allowances with their requirements for defining 'housing gaps' have become more significant in recent policy development. Historically, the conventional approach to moderate- and low-income programmes has been to use government to subsidise the construction of new standard housing, or to introduce a system of housing credit which stimulates new standard housing development. This is a *production-orientated* approach whereas housing allowances represent a *consumer-orientated* approach. As we shall presently see, changing social and economic conditions have precipitated the growing interest in the use of housing allowances. Nevertheless, economists have sometimes argued the virtues of the *cash* (or voucher) form of subsidy represented in housing allowances as abstractly better than the *in-kind* form of subsidisation in production-orientated approaches. Production subsid- ies have been seen as 'paternalistic' and restricting individual choice, whereas the consumer subsidy approach has been advocated for placing choice within the control of households rather than bureaucrats, professionals and so on. Our discussions below will show that these contrasts are drawn too simplistically and without reference to some of the (partial) in-kind aspects of housing allowances. In the context of welfare state principles it is relevant to look briefly at the relative merits of the cash and in-kind approaches to providing assist ance in housing.

Economists have claimed that consumer subsidies are more effective and selective, they permit more consumer choice, they avoid stigma linked to public housing, and they reduce the heavy transaction costs which are absorbed in public administration. These sorts of claims have been put more deeply and critically in the United States, but they are also used more generally. [3] The major positive influence which housing allowances may contribute to housing policy development is that they can apply a common principle of equity cutting across subsidy relationships to particular social housing programmes. That is to say, the traditional public policies in housing have particularised assistance to specific housing and aggravated some horizontal and vertical inequities. Housing allowances (partially) counteract horizontal and vertical inequities and they can be targeted against the 'housing gap' so that subsidies are more generally accessible to low-income households.

We need to be more circumspect on the other claims made for the superiority of housing allowances. When the question of choice is referred to moderate- and low-income housing, it should be appreciated that such choice is necessarily within sub-markets in the existing (older) stock, or otherwise within overtly subsidised social housing. As our subsequent discussions will show, for moderate- or low-income households which are dependent upon private rental housing, in ordinary circumstances their choices are within limited ranges of the housing stock in terms of quality, age and location. (Such housing may never- theless be adequate and suitable if certain useful policies are pursued.) Furthermore, no conceivable housing allowance which is socially and politically realistic would widen the choice to take in more expensive sub-markets or new unsubsidised housing. In fact, even new subsidised housing is often outside the capacity of the poorest groups to pay. Thus, for low-income groups, housing choice operates within a limited range of options, not as an open-ended invitation.

Some more discernment and circumspection in examining the claims for housing allowances, also shows that they involve substantial administrative costs and they are not completely divorced from the in-kind form of provision. The United States' *Experimental Housing Allowance Program* (EHAP), 1973-1978, has tested the administrative aspects of housing allowances under a variety of circumstances. Administration involves publicising the programme, making contact with the potential beneficiaries, screening applications, verifying incomes and other eligibility conditions, and sometimes providing supportive services. Costs vary according to the methods used and the intensity of administrative effort, but it would be realistic to see administration absorbing some 20 per cent of programme costs. [4]

Compared with production subsidies, housing allowances are related to the income circumstances of households rather than being tied to specific dwellings. In that context, housing allowances are not so definitely an in-kind welfare provision as the production-orientated subsidies. Nevertheless, housing allowances are normally 'earmarked' for use in housing, and not as completely free-use cash grants. In various ways earmarking can influence the direction of housing and non-housing expenditure of eligible households. Eligibility conditions can be written to induce more expenditure on housing by prescribing minimum standards, or by requiring the household to pay for housing certificates, or by relating payments to a percentage-of-rent formula. These varied ways of influencing household expenditure are examined in the Appendix at the end of this chapter. For present purposes, we need to note that earmarking can imply some (partial) in-kind welfare, compared with how low-income households would otherwise spend their incomes in the absence of housing allowances or compared with free-use cash grants. From the point of view of theoretical economics the interesting aspect of housing allowances (and other forms of subsidy) is their relative costs and benefits to households and to society. Under some circumstances, the recipients may value the benefits rather less than the costs to society. In other words, housing allowances need some general social and economic justification to show why society has an interest in altering the housing expenditures of individual households. This point is taken up in subsequent discussions.

Presently, we shall review the case for production-orientated subsidies and producer contributions in housing. At the outset we dismiss the generalised statements from economists who dub the production approach (pejoratively) as 'paternalism', without examination of the relevant theory and evidence. As we have already noted, housing allowances also imply some substitution of private choices by social or collective choices. The case for producer initiatives and subsidisation can be considered by reference to merit goods theory, discussions of qualitative differences in public and private sector provision, the essential complexity of housing, methods of achieving efficiency and lower cost, and the inherent problems with relying solely upon housing allowances. Also, we note at the outset, that policy until the 1960s was to induce high rates of production to overcome chronic shortages, and the production side of the industry could then be used *directly* to achieve policy.

Merit goods theory was introduced in Chapter 1 and placed into its setting in the development of economic thought in Chapter 2. The general principles of merit goods theory can be brought into relevance with several spheres of public policy - health, education, libraries, housing and some sorts of anti-poverty programmes. Merit goods arguments involve critical scrutinies and substitution of individual-based preferences for social preferences. A basis for rejecting consumer sovereignty may exist where: (1) the nature of the good or service is very complicated, (2) individuals' preferences are distorted by the complexity, the lack of knowledge and the externality nature of some of the benefits, and (3) distributional problems of a very special sort are present. Some of the benefits of housing are delayed, indirect and not readily amenable to accurate appraisal by individuals (see Chapter 1). Intra-family distributional matters connected with life-cycle factors are important in housing, especially for dependent women and children (see Chapter 3). Housing is a good which sometimes compounds antecedent inequalities by virtue of its tenure and accessibilities, or otherwise resourced, financed and organised in certain ways, it can redistribute income and wealth (see Chapter 3). As a merit good, the case for public policy and some producer orientation is limited and specific, not general and excluding market and consumer sovereignty completely. All that is claimed is that market and consumer sovereignty arguments should not have absolute dominance in housing provisions.

The merit goods case can be extended to two further related aspects of the housing condition. As a complex good, often resourced and organised under widely varying conditions of accessibility, the costs of search and information gathering are high for consumers. That offers one justification for the provision of housing advisory services. However, even with such services, some significant lack of knowledge will be present among some groups of consumers (see Chapter 1). Also, as we have emphasised in the themes of this piece of writing, the economic and social value of housing depends upon the way neighbourhoods and suburbs are designed, built and resourced. Under market conditions the pressures and constraints sometimes cause important neighbourhood and suburban externalities to be neglected. It is conceivable, though not always guaranteed, that a public provision or some mixed public-private provision under contract or regulation could provide a qualitatively better result than unfettered market provision. Once the possibility is accepted, it then becomes a matter of pragmatically looking at different sorts of market and non-market examples, especially in low-income housing, to ascertain which are the preferred results and the conditions under which they are operated. Some elements from social cost-benefit and cost-effectiveness analyses can be used to give some systematic ranking of qualities.

Further arguments for a producer orientation can be based upon considerations of economic efficiency in the housing and building industry. Organisations can be created to utilise cheap sources of supply and to overcome market inefficiencies. Examples can be cited. In small country towns, the construction industry may be dominated by monopoly and high-cost local operators. A large-scale public development corporation (or a non-profit developer) can break the monopoly by drawing its supplies from wider markets, by sending in pre-made housing, and by widening the range of local options through rehabilitation and other programmes. Or in metropolitan areas, these large-scale operators can buy up land at 'use' values well in advance of development needs and so avoid paying high speculative prices which would later attach to such land. The South Australian Housing Trust (see Chapter 6)

106

has operated these sorts of policies over a period of forty years, and has often been able to produce standard housing more cheaply than private enterprise. Our present argument simply shows that economies can be made from producer initiatives; it is not meant to be a general argument for public housing. As we shall see, governments can take various options in influencing housing production, and they are by no means limited to using the public housing approach.

As another reflection on producer orientations we take account of the reality that moderate- and low-income households will be housed in older rental housing or in subsidised social housing. In both the historical work of Octavia Hill (see Chapter 3) and in modern social-economic analysis [5], it has been shown that the quality of management is the key to success in low-income rental housing. This management involves operating housing so that it is a service simultaneously covering social, physical maintenance, economic and administrative considerations. The ideal service is diverse and professional, delicately avoiding intrusive impositions, but maintaining a workable order in neighbourhoods and providing opportunities for tenant involvement. These management considerations are becoming more significant in both social housing and private rental housing. For economics, this has two main implications. First, housing allowances can be regarded as a support for providing adequate estates management services. Thus, the producers' services and the consumer subsidies reach the same general aims. Second, the whole question of estates management is opened up to economics. Until recently, economics has been primarily concerned with the capital cost of housing and some limited range of questions in rent controls and housing finance. This extension of economics into estates management will deepen its involvement with social and administrative content.

Housing allowances do not, in themselves, solve all the problems in modern housing. Drawing upon evidence from the American EHAP studies [6] we can make two important observations. First, in high-growth regions where low-income sub-markets are tight, housing allowances would swell up demand and drive up short- and medium-term prices. Accordingly, in those conditions, significant portions of the housing allowances would end up as landlord rather than tenant benefits. All of this changes, if production subsidies are co-ordinated with housing allowances so that tight markets are loosened with more medium-term construction. Second, the findings from the EHAP studies reveal that the housing allowance does not provide a common principle of equity, as many economists had previously assumed. Participation rates in housing allowance experiments were low for those whose eligibility depended upon them moving into standard housing. The main reasons for non-participation had very little to do with perception of housing allowances as stigmatising welfare. Rather the explanation centres around relationships among poverty, mobility and how choice in housing is actually made by poor Americans. For many households, in its statistically defined sense, poverty is an intermittent experience. Housing choice is made in a medium-term perspective of up to three years, even for the more mobile households. Mobility has psychological and economic costs.

Clearly, the provision of housing allowances has complex and different economic effects according to the relative looseness and tightness of low-income sub-markets and behavioural restraints upon mobility. In other words, only some low-income households would obtain substantial benefits from the provision of housing allowances, not all low-income

households. Like most production-orientated approaches, housing
allowances actually confer sectional benefits, not universal benefits.
In the United States, opinion among housing economists has turned to
favour a more pluralistic approach, mixing housing allowances, rehabilitation and other non-market interventions. [7] Elsewhere, in
continental Europe, housing allowances have been introduced as a one-
part contribution in an overall set of reforms in housing finance, aimed
at attacking the low-income housing problem (see Chapter 6). Our
discussions now turn to look at social economics in relation to historical and comparative policy options.

The housing gap and policy options

Historically, the 'housing gap' has been conceived and interpreted in
various ways. Only recently has it been as an insufficiency of income
among moderate- and low-income groups, perhaps to be bridged with
housing allowances. Many other meanings have been given to housing
standards, to rent-income burdens and to other aspects of the 'housing
gap'. These include:-

1. People perceive 'excessive' rents in the private rental sector.
    This prompts rent controls. Such policies were pursued in Britain
    and Europe in the period 1914-1970.

2. Housing reformers perceive that the private rental sector cannot
    produce enough standard low-rent housing. This can lead towards
    new standard housing. Public housing emerged in Britain (1870-
    1919), Australia (1912-1940), United States (1937), and sporadically
    in other countries.

3. In the wake of wartime devastation or rapid urbanisation, the
    problem will be understood as one of gross general shortages.
    Policy-makers will be attracted to using mixed public-private
    financial frameworks to induce general (i.e., not just government)
    resources into housing. The access to subsidised and/or easy loan
    terms is designed to attract private enterprise, non-profit
    enterprise, owner-occupier and others. This was pursued in Sweden,
    The Netherlands and West Germany in the period, 1945-1970.

4. The problem can be seen as a shortage or mismanagement of financial
    resources to be attacked by drawing savings from the community and
    using banking instruments to provide long-term easy repayment loans.
    This approach was taken in Norway in the 1890s and followed consis-
    tently through to modern times. It was also used somewhat less
    directly by the United States in the 1930s and in an attenuated way
    by Australia in the 1900-1920 period, with some continuity to modern
    times.

As we shall see in the historical chapters which follow, housing
problems have often been misconceived and policy development has tended
to be *ad hoc*, rather than comprehensive and consistent. In this
present chapter we shall examine some of the perennial causes of
confusion: the economic assumptions and aims of housing policy, and the
dilemmas which have prompted such diverse interpretations of the
'housing gap'.

Before housing was taken up as a specialist and continuous subject for research in the 1960s, some economists had made some sporadic and incisive criticisms of *rent controls.* Rent controls have been used in many of the modern democracies, and their origins can be traced to the First World War when they were used as a price control measure in a period of acute shortages. However, in Britain and in other countries rent controls have tended to remain as significant aspects of housing policies into the 1960s. These controls have been heavily criticised by economists for their long-term consequences. [8] The classic case against them is that they are a disincentive to new investment, they lead to low standards of maintenance, cause slower modernisation, and can be regarded as a discriminatory tax on landlords and an arbitrary subsidy to a favoured class of tenants. Put in another way, where rents are economic and profitable, there will be no long-term shortages, housing will be maintained and priced at levels which reflect consumer demands, and no artificially created disincentives will inhibit mobility and fluidity in the use of the housing stock. Clearly, the theoretical economic case against rent controls is strong. This needs two qualifications. First, incentives for new construction can be created in government subsidies, and in particular Sweden and The Netherlands have stimulated a strong general rental sector by subsidisation. Second, evidence from social and economic surveys shows that the private rental sector operates under a variety of distinctive patterns. The economic issues cover wider opportunities and motivations than as a simple commercial investment. This point is taken up in the discussions on older housing, below.

The *public housing* approach to the 'housing gap' operates differently in Britain, the United States and Australia with significant variations in aims, financing and administration. These present economic commentaries will refer mainly to the dilemmas which arise in the British programme. The direct provision of housing by government appeared as an obvious solution to the insufficiency of private rental housing and its low standards. However, in practice, the 'solution' has raised its own distinctive economic dilemmas. First, the aim to achieve extensive flows of low-cost housing comes into conflict with the periodic need to curb public expenditure. Also, public housing tends to attract ideological contention, the Left regarding it as the uniquely useful way of expressing social goals in housing and the Right checking its growth because it is too distanced from private enterprise. Second, there is a conflict between the impetus to raise standards and to bring housing within the capacity of the poor to pay. In effect, once standards are set, this simultaneously influences costs, rents and practical eligibilities. Third, in practice the housing is not generally accessible, even in the absence of means tests. Cost and rents operate as one constraint. Also, factors influencing mobility make this housing more attractive to younger working-class households, not to the aged and groups at social risk. Fourth, rents are usually set in accordance with historical costs. Rents will vary according to the costs, the subsidy conditions and the housing standards prevailing on particular dates. Through time the public housing stock will grow and housing authorities may be able to 'pool' their consolidated costs and revenues. 'Pooling' enables the authority to cross-subsidise rents in newer housing (built at higher financial costs) from surpluses on older housing. Also, it is possible to achieve some rent rebates so that in a limited way some rents are matched progressively to capacity to pay. However, public housing is not as flexible, as direct and as general as housing allowances in attempting to meet the 'housing gap'

problem.   Thus, public housing, in itself, contains dilemmas of
simultaneously matching rents, subsidies and capacity to pay.   Once
these various economic dilemmas are brought together, it can be seen
that public housing will often fail to fulfil expectations.

Sweden and West Germany have approached the 'housing gap' problem by
*creating deep and general subsidies within a mixed public-private
financial framework.*   This framework is accessible to a variety of
private enterprise and non-profit developers;   that is to say, subsidies
and easy repayment loans are not confined to public housing.   Compared
with the public housing approach, resources are drawn from wider sources
and allocated to a wider range of developers.   Long-term shortages are
overcome and the resultant housing system is less rigid and separation-
ist than the sectoral structure in Britain.   In those respects, the
broader approach fulfils expectations.   Also, the deep subsidies tilt
down the 'consumer price' of housing to ease the 'housing gap' problem.
However, the main economic dilemma is that the deep and general subsidies place heavy burdens upon public expenditure.   If rents/repayments
are tied to historical costs (with the subsidies reducing rents), then
governments cannot ordinarily recapture some of the subsidies from
households which are well able (subsequently) to afford higher costs
from their increasing incomes.   Thus, in the long-run, it is necessary
to move from deep to shallow subsidies, which means making subsidies
more selective, to depart from historical cost renting, and to push some
housing costs from public finance to households.   In themselves, these
revisions would lead to more pressures on the 'housing gap' among some
households.   Thus, the reforms to subsidisation and rents are usually
accompanied by the selective use of housing allowances.   This course of
reform has been taken in Sweden, The Netherlands and West Germany (see
Chapter 6).

The 'housing gap' problem can be met by drawing community savings into
state banks (or other financial intermediaries) and creating *long-term
easy repayment loans*.   The repayments can be designed to achieve levels
lower than the prevailing rents.   Advantages of this method are that it
can be adapted to recapture the 'subsidy', it opens up home ownership to
moderate-income groups, and it does not get deeply entangled in the
economic and political dilemmas associated with the government's *current*
(i.e., not 'capital') revenue and expenditure account.   The 'subsidy' is
not overt, but it exists in the sense that resources are drawn into
housing via the use of government power.   This system can be administered without excessive bureaucracy, and it can be supplemented with
housing allowances.   Norway uses such a system.

All the foregoing options can be classified as overt public policies
with the conspicuous involvement of government as a regulator, or as a
developer, or as a financier with direct impacts on large sections of
the stock.   The fact that government involvement is direct, conspicuous
and related to identifiable sections of the stock, makes this invovement
clearly a welfare state function.   However, welfare state functions in
housing can operate more indirectly, less overtly and through patterns
of involvement which are less conspicuously identifiable in particular
sections of the housing stock.   These patterns have characterised some
of the approaches to social aims in housing in the United States.
During the 1930s, the Federal Government manipulated credit markets to
widen accessibility to home ownership, and in the 1960s it added new
programmes aimed at pushing up rates of new construction so that low-

income housing would be more readily accessible.   More recently,
attention has turned towards using housing allowances and other subsidies within a private market context.   This has meant that policy-makers
needed to have a good knowledge of how housing allowances would be used
by eligible households, and how private markets would respond.
Accordingly, the *Experimental Housing Allowance Program* (EHAP), 1973-
1978, was created to test the feasibility of housing allowances in a
private market context.   The EHAP research has added to knowledge in
the economics of housing and it has shown the opportunities and dilemmas
in approaching the 'housing gap' problem by using housing allowances in
private markets.   In order to get a full appreciation of this recent
American approach to the 'housing gap' problem we need to review some of
the key economic characteristics of private housing markets.   We now
turn to that subject.

*Private housing markets, key economic characteristics of housing
and housing allowances*

The full economics of private housing markets would range over a wide
variety of factors including the structure of the building industry,
interest rates, housing finance and so on.   We shall be primarily
concerned with selecting a few key economic characteristics which need
to be understood by anyone concerned with housing welfare and housing
policy.   For our purposes, three ideas stand out in the post-1960
development of economic analysis.   They are: (1) the *durability* of
housing, (2) the *heterogeneity* of housing and (3) *instability* of demand
for housing and the fluctuations in new production.   These primary
characteristics of housing interact and produce secondary characteristics.   Together, the primary and secondary characteristics distinguish
economic relationships in housing from those in other goods and
services which are marketed.   The paragraphs below define these primary
characteristics and their interactive relationships.

For economists, the *durability* of housing has far wider implications
than is represented physically in the long life of most housing.   It
means that the presence of a large stock of existing housing has a
strong influence on the demand for new construction, on the level of
rents (in uncontrolled sectors), and on the valuation of consumers.
The existing stock can always be dominant in the market where, even in
years of buoyant new construction, this new construction will add no
more than 2 per cent to the total stock.   Existing stock is dominant in
the sense that it is price competitive with the new stock, and its *fixed*
locational attributes offer distinctive choice options compared with new
housing, built mainly in new suburbs.   On the other hand, new housing
offers standards of space and design which are not always available in
older housing.   However, older housing can be modernised and
re-designed within constraints of economic and technical feasibility.
Unlike other 'used goods' which are traded, housing is fixed in location
and some of its economic value is derived from the economic and social
attributes of its wider environment.   These attributes can be altered
by the provision of public services and by the activities of investors
who develop shops, factories and commercial buildings.   Thus durability
is not a static concept in its relevance to housing.   Its main economic
thrust is that it influences overall prices, values and activities in
new building, rehabilitation and so on.   Also, as we shall see, when
durability interacts with other factors it accounts for the relative
sluggishness of rents and prices, despite volatile short-term changes in

111

demand and supply.   This sluggish response is an important secondary
characteristic of housing in private markets.

Heterogeneity adds another key economic perspective to housing.
Housing is differentiated by location, dwelling type, tenure and so on.
It divides into sub-markets where demands can be characteristically
linked to socio-economic class, to stage in the life-cycle and to way-
of-life factors.   The *sub-markets* exhibit price differences, reflecting
the imperfect substitution among dwellings of different types, ages,
tenure and locations.   Again, heterogeneity like durability is not a
static condition.   Price relativities vary through time, reflecting
changes in demand and supply among sub-markets.   Heterogeneity means
that broad aggregative changes in demand and/or supply will be diffused
and have differential impacts in sub-markets.   Thus, it is important to
collect and interpret housing statistics in disaggregated form as well
as in broad aggregates.   All of this has modern policy significance
where new national housing allowance programmes will substantially alter
the demand for low-income housing in private markets.   As we saw in
earlier discussion, the relative tightness and looseness of the relevant
sub-markets will indicate the appropriate policy mixes among housing
allowances, production subsidies and rehabilitation.

Under market conditions, the demand for housing and new construction
is characterised with considerable *instability*.   The instability was
more marked in the nineteenth century when the impact of trade cycles
was more regular and more severe.   However, modern developed economies
still experience some economic fluctuations and these will create
instability in the demand and supply of housing.   Changes in demand
will show up in variable vacancy rates across the course of boom and
recession.   These will be higher in the recession, but they will fall
significantly only when the return to better conditions is regarded as
reasonably certain and secure.   In other words there is some sluggishness in response to changing economic conditions, and more is said about
this below.   Movements in the rate of interest and disturbances in the
flow of funds to financial institutions will also produce instabilities
in demand and supply.   Although these variable economic conditions
influence other goods and services, they are particularly significant in
housing.   In fact, variations in the demand and supply of housing have
widespread influence throughout the economy.   During the 1950-1970
period, housing has tended to absorb about 10 per cent of household
expenditure, it has accounted for some 3 to 5 per cent of national
income, and it has contributed approximately 20 per cent of fixed
capital formation in the modern democracies.   Thus, housing is seen as
both reactive to general economic fluctuations and as deepening and
stimulating them.

As was mentioned above, some housing responses are relatively sluggish
to short-term economic fluctuations.   In designing and operating
subsidy schemes which influence demand and supply conditions in private
markets, it is important to know the lagged effect of housing responses.
For example, if a national programme of housing allowances swells demand
in some sub-markets, policy-makers will want to know how rents and
prices will be altered and when these changes will occur.   Statistical
studies [9] reveal that rents and values react rather sluggishly in the
short-term because households and landlords have good reasons for taking
a medium- or long-term view.   In modern societies, even the more mobile
households tend to hold their housing choices firm for periods of at

least three years. This reduces short-term mobility rates. From the viewpoint of new housing, they have to balance considerations of short-term efficiency with flexibility to medium- and long-term change. The outcome will depend upon a host of factors including the firm's previous experience, its access to cash and the quality of information it can draw upon in making strategic decisions on pricing, organisation and the production process. These factors are fraught with a variety of uncertainties and constraints.

The above observations help to explain why it needs a large and persistent change in vacancy rates to set off significant *general* movements in rents and longer term changes in new production. In fact, at any given time it is important to discern and distinguish short-, medium- and long-term responses in rents, vacancy rates and new construction. Also, it is important to understand the conditions under which existing housing competes with new construction. [10] The forces of competition will bring new and old housing of similar qualities within the same price range. New construction offers middle- and high-income groups the opportunity to achieve spatial and design standards which are not always available in older housing. Normally, the market will provide low-income housing at lower quality and within lower rent and price brackets, but in some circumstances the rents and prices can be higher than new stock. The forces which will push rents and values lower than those on new stock are depreciation and the low income of the consumers. However, if population pressures are strong and dominant, rents and values can be pushed up to levels above new housing. The eventual response in the low-income sector will depend upon a complicated mixture of short-, medium and long-term factors. These patterns are further discussed in their historical setting in the next chapter. Also, more is said on the market relationships between old and new housing in the next section of this chapter, dealing with 'filtration theory'.

These economic principles have crucial relevance in historical interpretations and for modern policy development. Historically, policy-makers (and housing historians) have observed the sluggishness of private enterprise in producing low-income rental housing and they have concluded that government must take direct action in building. However, the commentaries above show that private sector responses should be distinguished in short-, medium- and long-term perspectives. Also, except where population growth is strong and protracted, the private market will supply low-income housing from the existing stock, rather than from new construction. In the past, these economic principles have not been adequately appreciated. Consequently, in their historical development, housing policies have not taken up some useful social and economic opportunities which have been available to governments and within the potential of private enterprise. For modern policy-makers, these opportunities should be recognised and taken up. This means that such things as housing allowances, rehabilitation and estates management enter prominently into policy consideration. We now turn to the economic opportunities and dilemmas associated with the use of housing allowances in private markets.

As we have seen, the housing market can be viewed as a set of sub-markets. Some of these sub-markets provide moderate- and low-income housing. Rents and values vary between sub-markets because housing qualities in respect to dwelling type, dwelling amenity, location and so on are perceived as different and as imperfect substitutes. However, price relativities among sub-markets will change in response to increasing vacancies or over-occupancy. Housing allowances will swell the demand in some sub-markets and, potentially, they can influence changes in housing quality, locational choice and rents. These impacts will vary according to local market conditions. Also, the changes need to be referred differentially to the short-, medium- and long-run periods. In the short-run, say a period of up to three years, housing supply cannot be much changed. However, we also know from earlier discussions that some key changes will be lagged and not appear until the medium-term. In the long-run, say a period of a decade and longer, the markets have time to adjust to change. Thus, the key period in which to explain and isolate changes is the medium-term. Policy-makers will need a medium-term predictive model of housing markets to show the interactive impact of housing allowances, other subsidies and so on with private market responses. The Urban Institute (Washington D.C., United States) has devised such a predictive model [11] and the EHAP research studies have added further knowledge on the interaction of housing allowances, demand, supply and choice in housing markets.

The EHAP and Urban Institute research has already completed sufficient work for us to get some appreciation of the opportunities and dilemmas connected with using housing allowances in interaction with private markets as a means of bridging the 'housing gap'. We shall discuss the policy opportunities and dilemmas first, and some more theoretical issues later. It has already been noted that housing allowances can be used as part of a policy mix including shallow production subsidies and rehabilitation. The particular mix and blend will depend upon local and regional conditions. For example, in tight markets policy-makers can prevent the diversion of benefits from tenants to landlords by judiciously using shallow production subsidies to ease the markets in the medium- and long-term. This means that comprehensiveness in housing has to be achieved not only at the national level, but also at regional and local levels. It is at the local level that housing sub-markets need to be understood and policies designed accordingly.

Like other approaches to the 'housing gap' problem, the use of housing allowances in private markets has some distinctive dilemmas. [12] The dilemmas arise both from the design features of housing allowances, and from the fact that many potentially eligible households do not participate.

Normally, the potential recipients of housing allowances have to fulfil specified eligibility requirements, including the occupation of a dwelling meeting minimum standards. Now, some potential households will be *unconstrained* by this sort of requirement because they already occupy standard housing. We shall term these 'unconstrained households'. However, other households can become participants only if they are prepared to upgrade their housing standards. Although this can be done by rehabilitation, this would require the co-operation of the landlord, and the more direct way of upgrading from the tenant's viewpoint is to move to a suitable house. Thus, if these households are to participate they are *constrained* to modify their housing choices. We shall term these 'constrained households'. Unconstrained households can take the housing allowance without modifying their housing choices. The housing allowance is *easily* accessible to them, but, if they wish, they can upgrade their housing standard. For these households, the main benefit

of a housing allowance is that it enables them to reduce the proportion
of income they spend upon housing; that is to say, it substantially
lowers their rent-income burden. By contrast, the constrained households have to decide whether the cost and effort of upgrading their
housing standards is worthwhile. In the context of the EHAP studies,
the financial inducements to participation were considerable. The EHAP
scheme offered varying payments among different groups to test the
responsiveness to higher financial inducements. Average payments made
amounted to some 50 per cent of average rents; or, put in another way,
the payments represented some 20 per cent of income of the average
potential recipient at enrolment. Despite the considerable financial
inducements, the experiments have shown that the changes in housing
expenditure have been mainly concentrated in a relatively small fraction
of potential beneficiaries.

On average the housing allowances increased housing expenditure among
participants by 10 per cent, and this absorbed some 29 per cent of
housing allowances. However, for the *unconstrained* participants,
expenditure on housing increased by only 2 per cent and this absorbed
only some 9 per cent of the housing allowances. Among the *constrained*
potential beneficiaries, only 33 per cent became participants after one
year. This meant that over 50 per cent of the households who were
offered over $40 per month did not participate in the programme. The
relatively small fraction of *constrained* households which did participate substantially increased their housing expenditure. They increased
their housing expenditures by 39 per cent on average, and this absorbed
some 50 per cent of the housing allowances.

Several points can be taken from these results. First, most recipients were not constrained by the 'housing gap' type of allowance. (A
'percentage-of-rent' type of housing allowance would have been more
constraining - see the Appendix.) Second, the recipients, and
especially the *unconstrained* group, mainly used their allowances to
reduce their rent-income burdens, not to increase their expenditures on
housing. Third, the way housing allowances influence spending patterns
raises theoretical issues on the divergence between the value of the
benefits to the recipients and to the community. This point is taken
up in later discussions. Finally, policy-makers have to look circum-
spectly at the housing allowance approach to bridging the 'housing gap'.
Housing allowances seem to benefit only some categories of those who
experience 'housing poverty'. They do not have any markedly influential effects upon locational mobility. Rehabilitation and other direct
approaches to 'housing poverty' retain their relevance, especially if
the community has an interest in housing standards as well as in rent-
income burdens. Otherwise, some low-income groups would remain in
substandard housing and spend up to 45 per cent of their income on such
housing. 'Housing poverty' is inevitably a problem for the community
with some of it being (surprisingly) beyond solution through housing
allowances alone. Further perspectives will be put on housing allowances in later discussions of (1) policy change during the last decade
and (2) the theoretically relevant issues in the costs and benefits of
welfare state housing programmes.

We may summarise some conclusions about the various approaches to the
'housing gap' problem and the following general statements can be made.
First, a 'social economics of housing' is not confined to studies of
subsidies and overt government policies. A welfare state can design

115

policies based upon interactive relationships between housing markets and various sorts of subsidies. This means that some of the essential economic characteristics of housing and its sub-markets need to be understood. Second, the use of subsidies and rent controls does not produce final solutions. Under some circumstances, rent controls (and regulated 'fair' rents) can dry up investment in housing and produce long-term undermaintenance. This can have effects of shortage, homelessness and segregation in housing (see Chapters 5 and 6). Subsidies can be misdirected, they can confuse the relationships among costs, rents and capacity to pay; and their association with historical cost rents/repayments can aggravate horizontal and vertical inequities. A social economics of housing has to be concerned with these problems, and not confined to making out a case for subsidisation *per se*. Third, the 'housing gap' can lead to various policy prescriptions, but few of those yet experienced are without significant social and economic dilemmas. However, the increasing concern with policy coherence and equity-related issues in housing is producing useful additions to economic knowledge in housing. Both 'economics' and 'housing' are being understood in broader social and political senses than was the case a decade or so ago. Finally, the 'social economics of housing' now occupies a central position in housing policy development. This means that those professions formerly more significant in housing policy development (e.g., social workers, architects, town planners and others) will be able to retain their relevance only with some appreciation of the economics of housing.

POLICY CHANGE : NEW IDEAS AND NEW DIRECTIONS SINCE 1960

As the democratic societies overcame the worst of their post-war housing shortages, they entered a new social and economic phase marked by slower demographic growth, less stable economic conditions, and a diversification of social needs. Housing policies had to adapt to those changes, and so did the sciences on which the policies were based.

In the ensuing ferment of ideas, economists were drawn back to some very basic questions about housing, and the role of government in housing. Why should government intervene at all in the housing business? What are minimum acceptable standards of housing which the community wants to justify? To what extent is egalitarianism a housing-related matter and how much egalitarianism can be achieved *primarily* through employment policies, wages policies, social security and other social policies? Are there better ways of achieving effectiveness and efficiency in the subsidisation of housing? To what extent is the question of *implicit* subsidisation relevant to equity in housing? (Implicit subsidies occur in tax concessions on mortgage interest costs for home owners, and on disregarding imputed rental income among home owners, or taxing it only at low rates.) What is the economic justification for the fact that some recipients of subsidised housing value this subsidy rather less than the community does? The following discussion begins with the inheritance of policies and economic justifications at about 1970, with contrasting patterns in the United States and Europe. Some changes since 1970 are reviewed and evaluated.

The United States : economic justifications in the 1960s

In the 1950-1970 period, new housing construction in the United States accounted for 30.5 million units, some 10 million more dwelling units than new households. Also, the number of units defined as substandard fell from 17 million to 5 million. This improvement in housing was achieved in a policy context which had widened accessibility to home ownership following reforms in housing finance in the 1930s. More impetus especially in the years 1968-1971, was given to increasing the flow of housing to moderate- and low-income groups. The economic rationale for the relevant policies centred around the theory of *filtration*, [13] alternatively termed 'filtering-, 'turnover' or 'chain of moves'. New supplies of housing initiate a chain of moves, which may in theory extend from the top to the bottom of the market as a great many households 'move up one'. The empirical evidence shows that for every 1,000 new dwellings, some 3,500 moves are precipitated and some 9.4 per cent of these occur in sub-markets occupied by the poor. [14]

The economic theory of filtration is roughly as follows: In a time of economic and demographic growth middle- and high-income groups can afford new housing which potentially offers special qualities of design, location and way of life in the suburbs. But, if filtration is to have a significant impact upon housing in general, then the rate of new construction must exceed the rate of demographic growth. This should push prices downwards in relative terms and open up moderate- and low-income access to standard housing. Thus, it is predicted that the reduction in relative prices will not lead to unacceptably low standards of maintenance. Also, where production eases sub-markets down to the bottom of the stock, there should be some way of removing any unwanted (i.e., abandoned) housing without pushing up relative prices and rents at the lowest utilised level. To test these expectations empirically the key variables have to be identified and their expected relationships clearly defined. The key variables are housing prices, housing qualities, the social and economic status of households, and mobility from house to house. They are not all easy to identify and measure, so controversy continues. Economists dispute whether the improvement in housing conditions in the 1950-1970 period was attributable to filtration alone, to 'external' factors such as the growth in incomes alone, or to some combination of the two. Technically it all depends upon whether growth in incomes is perceived as an 'internal' condition of filtration or is regarded as 'external'.

In its welfare implications, filtration theory presents some dilemmas. First, as mentioned earlier, in the context of new social and economic conditions there are more direct ways of dealing with the 'housing gap' problem. Second, the filtration process contains the seeds of its own destruction. If relative prices and values are indeed dragged down by new construction, the competitive edge of existing ('durable') housing will bring a halt to new construction. Demographic growth and income growth are necessary to induce new construction. Third, the process can put housing out of use altogether. It has produced surplus of low-income housing in some cities in the United States. Some stock becomes unwanted, and the condition of the housing is irrelevant if consumers reject the *neighbourhood* for what they see as better alternatives. For these reasons filtration has lost its general relevance as an economic justification for housing policy, but retains importance in explaining the relative looseness/tightness of particular local sub-markets and as an explanation for abandonments. Though the lessons of experience are chiefly American, they may soon have wider significance. European countries are in the process of reforming their policies with the aim of gradually extending the influence of private choice in housing.

Continental Europe and Britain : economic issues in housing and justifications for reform

Although the discussions in this section primarily refer to conditions in Sweden, The Netherlands and West Germany, the economic principles have a wider relevance to circumstances which have occurred sporadically in Britain and the United States. Faced with critical shortages in the post-war period, the European countries used deep and general subsidies to stimulate production by various developers. Subsidised housing was brought within the reach of 70 per cent of the households. Primary emphasis was placed upon rental housing and the subsidised housing was let at historical cost rents. As was previously mentioned in the discussions on the 'housing gap', this aggravated vertical and horizontal inequities and it precluded the government from shifting the burden of subsidy costs from its own budgets to those of households which occupied this housing. The subsidy burdens in public finance grew substantially and eventually forced reforming initiatives by governments of both the Right and the Left. Other economic dilemmas arose from the confusions of objectives in subsidies, rents and capacity to pay. These included under-utilisation of the stock, immobilities, and a general lack of fluidity in the allocation and re-allocation of the stock. By the late-1960s the need for reform was urgent.

In these circumstances, policy-makers could achieve more fluidity and curbs upon public expenditure by withdrawing subsidies and leaving the business to the market. But this would undermine the equity commitments of the welfare state, and might generate significant political opposition. Therefore a more appealing middle-course strategy would involve a set of simultaneous and co-ordinated reforms directed against deep production subsidies, against fixed historical cost rents, in favour of mixing the attributes of a (simulated) market, and in favour of housing allowances. Production subsidies could be reduced by pre-determined degrees, (West Germany), repayments might be geared to an index of costs (Sweden), and rents might be related to an index of costs covering capital and estates management costs (The Netherlands). All of these can be regarded as a means of redistributing some costs from households as taxpayers to households as rent-payers or home purchasers, and as *para-market* instruments blending some simulated attributes of the market with subsidisation. This meant that the costs of housing would increase, but the 'housing gap' could be bridged by introducing or expanding housing allowances. Housing allowances provided a means of matching assistance progressively with needs.

It has been these questions of reforming subsidies, creating para-market instruments and co-ordinating policies in respect to rents, costs and subsidies which have occupied the attention of Dutch, Swedish and West German housing economists. The process of reform and knowledge-building is incomplete. As we shall see in Chapter 6, inflation cut across the Swedish attempt (1968) to reduce burdens on public expenditure by linking repayments of loans to an index of building costs. (Interest rates increased after 1968; these created the larger burdens on costs and they were not index-linked.) Also, the Dutch were forced to re-design their rent policies as inflation overtook the pre-determined scale of increases in successive stages. Following the work of Professor Dr. F. Hartog, rents are now linked to an appropriate index of costs, without pre-determined fixed scaling. West Germany still retains historical cost renting in its social housing, but economists have been elaborating schemes whereby subsidies can be withdrawn from specific dwellings, 'pooled' into a national fund and used in a system of rent rebates which more systematically relates rents to capacity to pay. This would be supplementary to housing allowance programmes, already operating.

Britain falls into neither the American nor the European pattern, but it has features of both patterns. The dominating characteristic of British housing is its sectoral divisiveness. It has the owner-occupier sector where housing is traded and allocated in markets. This means that British housing economists can find some relevance in study-ing private markets, [15] and filtration theory also had some limited significance in policy. Other British economists have turned their attention to the decline of the private rental sector and to explaining the social and economic problems in that sector. This has attracted a modern argument against rent controls and 'fair' rents policies. [16] In an earlier study, Nevitt [17] revealed that the private rental sector was disadvantaged because: (1) public housing was subsidised and it operated as a non-profit venture, (2) owner-occupier housing received tax concessions, and (3) investors in private rental housing could not write off depreciation for tax purposes as investors in commercial and industrial property could. Public housing has been analysed by Bowley [18] who revealed the dilemmas of matching costs and subsidies with capacity to pay. Her criticisms of early policy in public housing have remained valid to modern times. An overall view of British housing by economists interprets the housing system in terms of stratified and segregated sectors. [19] Public policy in Britain has created three sector housing systems, which require distinct methods of analysis and evaluation - as evidenced in this paragraph.

British policy development reflects more complexity and less direct-ness in dealing with the modern 'housing gap' problem than other countries. As we have seen, the United States is developing policy along the lines of using housing allowances (and other subsidies) in interactive relationship with private markets. In Sweden, The Netherlands and West Germany, reforms have proceeded on the basis of co-ordinating a simultaneous revision of policies in rents, subsidies, and matching subsidies with capacity to pay. Housing allowances have been used as one part of these co-ordinated reforms in a context where social and economic changes made reform imperative. By contrast, Britain cannot rely to the same extent on private markets, with or without housing allowances. Moderate- and low-income housing groups are dependent upon public housing and a declining (and rent regulated) private rental sector. Furthermore, the sectoral divisions and the ideological conflicts in British housing have together frustrated any move towards a systematic co-ordination of policies on rents and subsid-ies which might match subsidies to capacities to pay in public and private housing alike. Some British housing economists have examined the question of inter-sector harmonisation (see Chapter 3), but there is an impasse on policy change. Housing allowances are applied only in the private rental sector. The extension of the idea to public housing was accomplished by the Conservatives, 1972-1975, and withdrawn by Labour in 1975. The subsidy burdens in public finance ran out of control in the 1970s and the private rental sector remains incapable of fulfilling its potentially useful and effective economic and social

functions. All of this is further clarified in the next two chapters
where housing history is discussed extensively. Meanwhile we examine
the development of the social economics of housing in relation to
current policy developments. In this field, current American work has
the greatest theoretical interest.

*The costs and benefits of housing welfare, housing allowances, and
equity in housing*

As the end of the housing shortage directs attention back to basic
questions, the whole government role in housing comes into question, and
there is a premium on methods of evaluating the effectiveness of subsidies, allowances, public housing supplies and other interventions.

   Cost-benefit and cost-effectiveness analyses are applied to a wide
range of public activities. The basic idea of these methods is to rank
alternative projects or programmes in terms of 'social' efficiency.
For this purpose, analysts have adopted a broad view of economic and
social impact in such fields as education, health, transportation, urban
renewal, land development, regional planning, housing and other public
policy areas. This type of analysis has some resemblence to private
sector capital budgeting techniques, but it differs in counting wider
ranges of costs and benefits over longer terms in accord with the
thrust towards *social* analysis. Cost-benefit and cost-effectiveness
analyses are characterised by controversies on matters of first principle
and technical details. The controversies of first principle concern
the range of effects to be counted, and the ways of valuing those that
do not have market values. Also, the extent to which income distribution is incorporated into analysis depends upon the purposes of the work
and the predispositions of the analysts. Despite the limitations of
these sorts of analysis, they are nevertheless useful for systematically
revealing the economic and, sometimes, the social implications of
alternative programmes and policies.

   Cost-benefit analysis is distinguished from cost-effectiveness
analysis by the form in which the social 'advantages' flowing from project or programme expenditure are measured. Cost-benefit analysis
measures these 'advantages' in terms of economic returns; the net
benefits (i.e., total benefits less total costs) are aggregated and
expressed as money values. In the case of cost-effectiveness analysis,
however, the 'advantages' are more often expressed as social or non-
monetary indices. Cost-effectiveness analysis can be undertaken
within a general framework of finding the minimum cost of achieving a
specified objective or the maximisation of 'advantages' (measured by
some index) for a given cost. The two types of analysis can be used in
combination where some 'advantages' are difficult to assess in purely
economic terms. Both sorts of analysis have been used recently in
evaluating alternative methods of bridging the 'housing gap'. Cost-
effectiveness analysis is more adaptable to situations where housing
programmes have a variety of objectives which are not all assessable in
monetary terms. On the other hand cost-benefit analysis in housing
does show clear economic relationships; and its results have shown
divergences between the value of subsidies to the recipients and to the
community, divergences which underline the theoretical justifications
for government involvement in housing.

   The application of cost-benefit analysis to housing has its own

distinctive problems.   Downs [20] has indicated that it is not easy to
measure the efficiency and effectiveness of housing because: (1)
housing has *many* objectives, (2) housing subsidies sometimes appear in
mixed forms, and (3) the results in housing depend upon the way
programmes are administered and not just upon the inherent characteristics of subsidies.   On the matter of subsidy, there is an emerging
controversy about the whole question of *whether* housing *gives* or
receives subsidy from the rest of the economy.   On the one hand there
is a sense in which most housing is subsidised, and the argument below
proceeds in those general terms.   But on the other hand there is a
sense in which all housing is penalised.   This view emerges when we
switch attention from the way we tax different kinds of housing income
or different kinds of housing tenure, and give our attention to the way
we tax different land uses.   In commercial and industrial use, the
expenditures on land use are tax-deductible and business enterprises pay
tax only on their profits.   But some residential land uses have to be
paid for wholly or partly out of taxed income.   This makes the
residential use of most urban land and buildings dearer in real terms to
the users than any business use would be.   The essential point can be
viewed from another perspective.   Let us suppose the services of
managing the home and child-rearing are actually compensated with income
payments, and the consequent costs are deducted from that gross income.
This would leave a net income, which might, in principle, then be taxed
at the appropriate rates.   On that basis, the running of business and
housing 'enterprises' would be on similar bases.   If that means the
redefinition of rights to property and income in housing-related
activities, then this should not disturb us as housing economists.
Already, in a variety of ways, we have shown that the social and
economic benefits and costs in housing are very much related to
particular ways property and income rights are instituted in housing.[21]

Returning to the view that most housing is in a sense 'subsidised',
the argument leads in the following direction.   Some implicit
subsidisation occurs through the systems of taxation where concessions
are usually made for owner-occupiers whose mortgage interest costs are
tax deductible, and in some countries the imputed value of rents in this
tenure is untaxed or taxed only at low rates.   Ordinarily, the term
'subsidy' refers to some explicit expenditure of government.   More
appropriately in housing, it should be used to describe any method by
which resources are drawn into housing at levels which could not prevail
under *laissez faire*.   Thus, implicit subsidisation would be included,
and also the effect of manipulations in housing credit to achieve long-
term easy repayment loans in 'privileged' circuits in housing.   However,
for present purposes our discussion is confined to the cost-benefit and
cost-effectiveness analysis of overt government policies.   Also, the
main source of reference is the United States which had a variety of
programme alternatives in the post-1968 period.   This included:
public housing, leased rental of older housing by housing authorities
from private enterprise, rent rebate schemes in association with private
enterprise, and 'below-market-rate-of-interest' (BMRI) subsidies in
home ownership and rental programmes.   Thus, the programmes could,
perhaps, be regarded as alternatives and assessed in terms of their
relative costs and benefits.

· Solomon [22] was the first economist to use cost-effectiveness
analysis to evaluate the efficiency and effectiveness of various government housing programmes.   His criteria for measuring efficiency and

equity were: (1) the maximisation of housing consumption, (2) the equalisation of opportunities for choice in dwelling types, tenure, location and economic/racial mobility, (3) the cheapest way of bridging the 'housing gap' and, (4) the avoidance of vertical and horizontal inequity. Two points should be noted. First, taking up a point from earlier discussions, we should recall that for moderate- and low-income groups the ideals underlying the criteria operate within a limited range, not as absolutes. Also, Solomon's analysis was limited to the United States situation. He would have found that Norwegian policies fulfil his selected criteria better than programmes operated in the United States or many other countries (see Chapters 3 and 6). Second, the economic thrust of Solomon's work was towards a comparative cost analysis, with not much scope for evaluating economic benefits. He found that the leasing of rental housing from private enterprise and the rehabilitation approaches were the more efficient and effective methods of providing low-income housing. Leasing older housing from private enterprise was cheaper than building and letting new housing either built as public housing or as subsidised private rental housing. Rehabilitation was cheaper than new construction. These methods also enabled some (limited) 'scatteration' of social housing in contrast to the concentration in conspicuous projects, often stigmatised as welfare housing. Thus, some anonymity and some choice were achieved under the leasing and rehabilitation approaches. Some further aspects of these results are taken up in the discussions on older housing in this chapter and in Chapters 5, 6 and 8.

Since Solomon pioneered this work, Murray [23], de Salvo [24] and other economists have extended the methods to genuine cost-benefit analyses. This work is significant for opening up wider questions of the economic justification for government involvement in housing, as well as for its statistical findings. These authors examined the costs and benefits of government housing programmes from the viewpoint of recipients and the wider community. Drawing upon theory from welfare economics (see Chapter 2), Murray and de Salvo measure the benefits for the recipients by searching for: the increase in income which could, in lieu of a housing programme, leave the recipient neither better nor worse off than he/she is by participating in the programme. This is the Marshallian-Hicksian 'income equivalent variation', and its technical details are explained in the Appendix at the end of the chapter. The benefits to the general community are perceived in the form of 'social benefits' (i.e., externalities). As we have seen, historically, it was argued that sanitary improvements and building regulations provided social benefits from the reduction of illness from cholera, tuberculosis and so on. The argument was extended to a general theory of environmental determinism covering social morality, quiet at night and other rather general things. This environmental determinism had been exaggerated and in statistical analysis its influence has been found negligible under modern conditions. [25] If the economic benefits from these sorts of environmental determinism cannot be identified and measured, this leaves a dilemma in justifying the economic basis of government activity in housing. This is additionally significant because *in their financial relationships*, the costs of the subsidies exceed the 'income equivalent' benefits to the recipients. Again, the technical demonstration of this is given in the Appendix at the end of this chapter.

The dilemma has led de Salvo to find another basis for justifying

government subsidisation in housing. [26]   Those externalities from the
theory of environmental determinism can be classified as 'production'
externalities because they are derived from the way things are produced.
By contrast, we can also conceive of 'consumption' externalities.   This
arises when persons A and B both obtain private benefits from consuming
a good or service, Y.   However, A, whom we shall assume is the richer
person, also derives benefits from B's consumption of Y.   That is to
say, the consumption of Y has interdependent benefits among consumers
generally in society.   Accordingly society sets minimum standards for
the consumption of Y for all consumers.   This line of reasoning offers
some economic justification for government activity in education, health,
the relief of poverty, and housing.   Thus, we can interpret the
difference between the recipients' valuation of benefits from Y and the
cost of the subsidy to the community, as the minimum value of the
community's benefits.   Non-economists might prefer social, political
and philosophical justifications.   However, non-economists should not
be too disappointed in economics; it is tractable to other justifications within its own terms and it can reveal relative efficiencies and
effectiveness.   The consumption externalities argument in economics
enables economists to approach earmarked housing allowances, public
housing, and other methods of bridging the 'housing gap' with an
'acceptable' theoretical basis of the welfare state.   Put in another
way, 'welfare economics' now contains justifications for welfare state
activity as well as for private enterprise.

The foregoing can be regarded as primarily epistemological and it can
be seen that apart from their welfare state justifications, housing
subsidies and benefits have been conceived rather narrowly. [26]   One
of the emphatic themes of this study is that modern housing needs to be
conceived broadly as a complex and integrated package covering the
economic and social attributes of the neighbourhood and the access to
urban services.   Thus, benefits from housing programmes should be
defined and evaluated accordingly.   This means that new knowledge-
building in the cost-benefit analysis of housing will pursue a broader
range of questions and a richer accounting of benefits.   A new approach
is being formulated in the EHAP research studies.   This aims to classify benefits as: (1) first-order recipients' benefits, (2) locational
benefits and (3) the likelihood of participation in various types of
programmes by different social groups.   This latter factor thus
acknowledges that housing allowances, public housing and so on have
their distinctive patterns of inducement and constraint which vary among
different social groups.   Furthermore, in the past, the access to
programmes and the general patterns of horizontal and vertical inequities have been something of a lottery.   The new research will be aimed
at designing and constructing programmes which are efficient and
effective in bridging the 'housing gap' among target groups.   However,
the 'housing gap' problem is interpreted more widely than rent-income
burdens.   It also covers neighbourhood characteristics, urban public
services, locational factors, and employment and settlement patterns.
The data sources will come from the EHAP research, from Census statistics, and from the Panel Survey of Income Dynamics.   This Panel Survey
has longitudinal data through a period of eight years and covering
statistics on income, employment, housing expenditure, attitudes towards
housing, and comparisons of housing expenditure and food expenditure.

Clearly, the cost-benefit and cost-effectiveness analyses of housing
programmes have been developed to the point where major breakthroughs in

knowledge are about to occur. This approach to analysing and evaluating housing programmes began with an emphasis upon comparative programme cost. However, it was subsequently appreciated that programmes could be administered in various ways, that their definition of benefits needed to be widely drawn to take in housing-related externalities, and that the varied responses to programmes among different social groups need to be accounted. The emphasis began to shift from simplistically ranking programmes on the basis of their relative subsidy costs towards an evaluation of varied responses among recipients. As analysis became more sophisticated in defining and assessing recipient and community benefits the programmes were looked upon as alternative choices for consumers, not just as objects for economic search to find the uniquely least-cost programme. This overtly recognises the many-sided aspects of housing and that questions of efficiency and effectiveness depend upon the ways housing services are administered.

The foregoing discussions on the cost-benefit analysis of housing programmes, together with the earlier discussions on the 'housing gap' enable us to see housing allowances in a broader perspective. Housing allowances have become important as governments sought to make their housing subsidies more selective. The essential feature of housing allowances is that they are related to people rather than to property. They provide cash or vouchers specific to eligible households and with some direction towards housing expenditure. They can be designed for households in any form of tenure; be scaled to increase as needs increase and to decrease as income increases; and be related to rent/instalment levels. The design and construction of housing allowances will vary according to the mix of objectives which are considered relevant so that they are more or less directed towards housing expenditure rather than non-housing expenditure, more or less emphasising tenure-related objectives, and so on. In principle, housing allowances can aim to achieve a common equity principle, and as such, are primarily bearers of equity-related effects, though as we have seen they contain allocational effects which need to be brought into account. That is to say, where housing allowances are operated in unregulated markets, policy-makers must anticipate their influence on rents, values and so on because these effects can counteract the equity purposes. The compelling argument favouring a role for housing allowances in all modern democratic societies is that they provide a more general principle of equity than other forms of subsidy, and are better able to (partially) correct vertical and horizontal inequity.

The extent to which a housing allowance is a provider of additional expenditure on housing depends upon its design and the economic behaviour of recipients. A 'percentage-of-rent' voucher is conditioned to housing expenditure, and from the recipients' viewpoint it is an offer of a grant which has to be matched by some proportional expenditure by the recipients. On the other hand, a housing allowance can be offered as a cash grant which is accessible only on the condition that the recipient occupies housing of some specified standard. This implicitly demands a certain level of expenditure on housing to achieve the specified standards, but it leaves the household free to determine its remaining allocation between housing and non-housing expenditures. The results will depend upon the household's *income and price elasticities of demand* for housing. Elasticity is a term used to denote the proportionate change of expenditure on a good (e.g., housing) consequent upon changes in: (1) price and (2) income. The Appendix at the end of the

chapter elaborates these concepts.   Housing-specific aspects of housing
allowances are to be contrasted with open-choice cash grants in the form
of guaranteed minimum income and negative income tax schemes.   These
schemes do not tie assistance to housing, but leave the choice between
housing and non-housing expenditure unconstrained and entirely in accordance with a household's own income elasticity of demand for housing.   As
we have seen, a recipient of a housing allowance often values its benefits less than its costs to the community.   In any event, a housing allowance will enable a household to reduce its rent-income burden.

Housing allowances need to be co-ordinated with other forms of housing
assistance and with other income-conditioned payments.   We have already
dealt with the advantages of co-ordinating housing allowances with
shallow production subsidies and rehabilitation programmes.   Now we
look at the wider question of more general co-ordination in social policy,
recalling our discussions in Chapter 3 which dealt with the theoretical
and administrative aspects of co-ordinating housing, urban and social
policies.   Problems arise in a context where the argument for income-
conditioned payments have relevance in social security, in welfare food
programmes, and in a variety of social policies.   Housing is not the
only sphere which has accumulated income-conditioned cash/voucher payments within its policy development.   A large proportion of recipient
households would be eligible for several programmes.   Consequently
'welfare' can be more remunerative than 'work' in the more extreme cases,
or for most households as they take up gainful employment and increase
their income they surpass critical thresholds where all their welfare
benefits cut out simultaneously.   In either case there are critical
disincentives to work which statistical analysis has found to be relevant
particularly among young single people and women who head single-parent
families. [27]   These problems can be reduced by some co-ordination
whereby limits are placed upon total participation in income-conditioned
welfare for households and/or sequencing programmes so that their income
value is accounted in administering housing allowances.

Beyond the co-ordination referred to above, income-conditioned welfare
raises a more general economic and administrative dilemma.   Some
policy-makers and economists have argued that housing allowances and
other product/service-specific programmes would be unnecessary if
society provided a more general guaranteed minimum income or negative
income tax scheme.   It is argued that such schemes are cheaper and
offer wider genuine choice to the poor.   However, upon examination it
can be shown that various specific abstract, institutional and
historical arguments can be found to justify product/service-specific
approaches.   This makes it difficult to operate a guaranteed income
maintenance scheme in relation to those that exist and to keep it
within 'reasonable overall costs', usually defined as not exceeding the
current costs of cash welfare programmes.   Thus, it seems that housing
allowances will remain along with other specific income-conditioned
programmes.   Certainly it is not difficult to set out economic,
institutional and other arguments to justify a housing allowance
separately from general income assistance.   All of this adds to the
theoretical and administrative complexity of the welfare state, and
housing allowances have to be assessed and analysed in that wider
complexity.

Housing allowances will stand out in the history of the welfare state.
More sophisticated analytical research and evaluation has gone into

housing allowances than into any other aspect of social policy. Under Sections 501 and 504 of the United States' *Housing and Urban Development Act*, 1970, a thorough and comprehensive programme of research into the housing allowance idea was launched. This took the form of the *Experimental Housing Allowance Program* (EHAP), 1973-1978. Three high-powered social research organisations (the Rand Corporation, Abt Associates and the Urban Institute) have been contracted to comprehensively analyse the economic, social and administrative aspects of housing allowances. The research has been organised in the following way. A *demand experiment* was undertaken by Abt Associates to analyse and evaluate the social and economic responses of households to various types of housing allowances. A *supply experiment* was conducted by the Rand Corporation to assess the impacts of housing allowances upon housing markets. Abt Associates also undertook an *administrative experiment* to test the relative effectiveness and cost of using different methods and organisations to administer housing allowances. Finally, the Urban Institute worked upon *integrated analysis* to fill in gaps in the other three experiments, to generalise the results for national policy development, and to synthesise work from the various research studies. Although the work is not complete, already the build-up of knowledge in housing is considerable, some areas of doubt have been cleared up, and much economic literature of the 1968-1973 period is superseded. Knowledge has been made redundant by knowledge itself. This is a point of general relevance in modern public policy development.

What has been learnt so far? Some results have been discussed earlier. Participation has not fulfilled the theoretical expectations, but for those who have participated the rent-income burdens have been substantially reduced. The effects upon rents and prices vary according to the relative looseness/tightness in local sub-markets, but there were no significant effects in the two experimental sites. Housing allowances have not had any marked inducement effect on mobility. Some social groups (e.g., the aged) are disinclined to leave their existing neighbourhood, but only one-third of all households that did not meet the required housing standards at enrolment became participants after one year. All of this suggests that a variety of social and economic factors influence probable participation among the potentially eligible population. Such factors can be explained in the relationships among mobility, the periodicity of poverty for households, and the conditions influencing housing choice. In other words, 'housing poverty' though related to 'statistical poverty' has its own distinctive features which influence the take-up of housing allowances. In administration, the costs will reach about 20 per cent of the income transfer costs. The use of the media to publicise the programme is more effective than a system of referrals by social service agencies. Generally, housing allowances are feasible. However, in practice they do not provide a common principle of equity, because some groups are more likely to become participants than others. The reasons for this go beyond the relative effectiveness of publicity or any perceived stigmatisation. This re-opens the question of the relative merits of different approaches to bridging the 'housing gap'. Those who are concerned with equity in housing have to look beyond housing allowances.

Equity in housing has to be related to various considerations and perspectives. One key consideration is the tax treatment of owner-occupied housing. Aaron [28] extended the understanding of

subsidisation in the tax system by stating that the imputed rental value
of owner-occupied housing in the United States is untaxed.   In other
countries, for example, The Netherlands, Norway and Sweden, this is
taxed but at a low level, more than offset by the advantages of this
tenure which include repayments of loans fixed mainly in relation to
historical costs, and tax concessions on mortgage interest.   Households
which hold co-operative tenure also enjoy some of these advantages,
though the pattern varies from country to country.   More details on
policies in particular countries are added in later discussions.   The
main point now is that the public finance includes implicit subsidisation and explicit public expenditure subsidies.   From the viewpoint of
the governmental budget, an implicit tax concession has the same effect
as an explicit expenditure.   Both forms of subsidy reduce the
possibilities for using public finance in education, social services,
defence and so on.   From the viewpoint of owner occupiers, the implicit
subsidies increase their allocations to housing where their private
investment returns are highest;   but without subsidy they might have
invested some of the funds elsewhere.

The principles discussed above have distributional as well as
allocational consequences, and bring the whole question of vertical and
horizontal equity into firmer significance.   The earlier references to
equity discussed its relationship with income distribution and historical cost rents/instalments.   Remembering the arguments presented by
Nevitt and Aaron, the question of equity also has to be referred to
tenure-related categories and to tax treatments.   In fact, we can add
to our understanding of the equity issues by listing some of the
relevant comparisons among different categories.   These are:

1. Owner-occupiers, co-operators and renters with society.   Each
    tenure class has an equity relationship with society because it
    exists in society and because subsidisation permeates virtually all
    housing.

2. Newer owner-occupiers/co-operators with older owner-occupiers/
    co-operators.   Because of inflation trends, new housing tends to
    cost more than old housing of a similar standard.   Older housing
    rises in value, but repayments are geared to historical costs.

3. Tenants with landlords.   The relationship depends upon whether
    rents are determined in markets or under legal controls and
    regulations.   Under some forms of rent control, tenants receive
    what is virtually a free gift and landlords receive what amounts to
    a discriminatory tax.   By contrast, in uncontrolled markets, it is
    sometimes possible for tenants to experience very high rents and
    insecurity of tenure.

4. Renters with owner-occupiers/co-operators.   Fiscal subsidisation
    tends to favour owner-occupiers/co-operators.

5. Private sector renters with social housing renters.   The relation-
    ship depends upon the terms of rental policies (see the discussions
    in Chapter 6).   Historically, the social housing renters have had
    rents tied to explicitly subsidised historical costs, or they may
    occupy housing financed from bond-rate borrowing with its current
    rents below market levels.   This result can be effected by *pooling*,
    enabling some 'cross-subsidisation' from older housing built at

cheaper historical cost to newer higher cost housing.   Depending
upon one's social point of view, the consequent low rents are a
subsidy or otherwise they are there because government abstains from
some available rates of profit (see the discussions in Chapter 3).

6.   Renters in new housing with renters in old housing.   See the
     comments under 2 and 5.   More generally, conditions in different
     markets vary considerably (see the discussions on older housing,
     below).

7.   Renters in rapidly growing urban areas with renters in stable-growth
     areas.   The relationship depends upon rental and land development
     policies (see the discussions in Chapters 6 and 7).   Rents in rapid
     growth areas are likely to be high.

8.   Savers with borrowers, and both with financial intermediaries.
     These relationships depend on the distribution of credit risks and
     the design of credit facilities (these are discussed in the section
     on inflation, below).

Such is the complexity of questions of equity and equality in housing.
Inequity is produced through both public policies and private markets.
Some horizontal and vertical inequity in housing is inevitable and it
would be infeasible to eliminate all inequity.   In the recent ferment
of change, equity has become more conspicuous as an issue in policy and
in the development of economic knowledge.   As we shall see in Chapter 6,
policies are beginning to remove some sources of inequity.   Some
countries have introduced (shallow) taxes on capital gains and the
imputed rental value of owner-occupier tenure.   Nevertheless, this
tenure still provides an avenue through which inequalities in income and
wealth are compounded.   It is a form of tenure which is more readily
accessible to middle- and high-income groups.   Norway has moved
furthest in making this tenure accessible to lower income groups.
Other policies which remove some sources of inequity include housing
allowances, dismantling historical cost renting in social housing, and
getting some general coherence into rental policies.   Rents can also be
influenced by the judicious use of shallow production subsidies to
loosen otherwise tight markets in some localities.   The thorniest
remaining problems are associated with the tenure-related inequities,
because under market and investment criteria it is tenure which separ-
ates income groups and then in the duration of a life-cycle the
antecedent inequalities are compounded.   However, as we shall see in
the next two chapters, public policies can influence the degree to which
tenure becomes socially and economically significant.   Meanwhile, our
discussion turns to examine the economic and social role of older
housing in modern policy development.   Some of the most significant
problems of equity are connected with the management and the allocation
of the existing housing stock.

OLDER RENTAL HOUSING

In many modern democracies demographic growth has slowed down and the
severe inflation, 1973-1976, has hit hard.   Housing policies must now
operate in uncertain and unstable economic conditions.   That especially
constrains new construction.   Private home ownership grows when
demographic and economic growth are reasonably steady.   New social

housing tends to be built in similar conditions, when the need for it is evident and the competition for public finance is not tightened by anti-inflationary restraints upon public expenditure. In the 1973-1976 period substantial vacancies occurred in new social housing in Sweden, The Netherlands and West Germany. These dwellings had high rents, reflecting the impact of inflation; and chronic housing shortages had been overcome with the result that the existing stock was price-competitive with new subsidised housing. In the new demographic and economic conditions the existing stock of housing becomes increasingly significant for moderate- and low-income groups. This stock varies in quality and some of it will be outside the economic range of low-income groups. Our discussion will be mainly concerned with the lower end of the existing stock, and especially with the low-income private rental stock.

Social and economic studies of older rental housing in Britain [29] and the United States [30] indicate marked variations in rents, in the economic relations between landlords and tenants, and in the management of the stock. The American economist, Sternlieb, [31] found that older rental housing in Newark was predominantly owned by professional investors from outside the area. They made competitive profits (compared with commercial and industrial investments) by charging high rents and spending low amounts on maintenance. Tenant mobility was high, and neither the landlords nor the tenants had any strong social attachment to the neighbourhood. By contrast, Krohn and Fleming [32] found sub-markets in Montreal where landlords and tenants had strong neighbourhood attachment. Landlords were mainly small-scale 'amateur' operators whose economic relations with their tenants were not dominantly motivated by getting a competitive return on their capital outlays. They tended (implicitly) to trade low rents for reciprocal services by tenants involving some care and maintenance of the property. These 'economic' relationships were complicated by desires for security, long-term involvement and social compatibility. Compared with rental housing in Newark, the landlord-tenant relations represented some features of 'gift' systems in undeveloped economies rather than profit materialism. Other rental markets exhibit various characteristics between these two extremes.

It is important to recognise the variations in rental housing. Policies will be inadequately designed if all landlording is stereotyped as 'exploiting' and 'profiteering'. In modern policy development the essential issues are: (1) how to improve the management of low-income rental housing and, (2) how to finance the costs of housing services (i.e., maintenance, local taxes, utilities, and selected social services). In that context, it seems that policies towards older housing need to be flexible and diverse. Sometimes, the prevailing landlord-tenant relations can be left alone in their administrative aspects. The economic viability can be enhanced with housing subsidies. Where rent controls or low-rent policies exist, better conditions may prevail if controls and regulations are liberalised. In other circumstances (e.g., those like Newark), it would be appropriate to get some better administration and some social intelligence into landlord-tenant relations. This can be achieved along lines developed in Sweden where legislative, financial and administrative instruments have been created to transfer stock from private landlording to co-operative tenure and management. This emphasis upon discernment and differentiation once again points to the need to develop comprehensive-

ness in housing locally as well as nationally.   Uniform national
prescriptions on the regulation and management of older rental housing
are rarely effective.   Older housing requires an administration
covering maintenance, investment in modernisation, rent collection
procedures and proper supervision.   It is an integrative function of
economic, social and administrative elements.   As we have seen, these
aims can be fulfilled in various ways.

The economics of older housing is moving towards new theories of
obsolescence and estates management.   Older theories of environmental
determinism are irrelevant for modern policy development.   The modern
approach should consider the retirement of some stock through abandon-
ment at the end of the 'filtration' process, and the comparative cost of
rehabilitation and redevelopment.   Our earlier discussions described
the 'filtration' process, and we now turn to review the comparative
economics of rehabilitation and redevelopment.

The literature on the comparative costs of redevelopment and
rehabilitation contains some sharp disagreements on the nature of the
problem and the specific treatment of economic variables.   Much of the
literature is about British problems, but the American urban economist,
Schaaf, has made some important contributions.   Schaaf's language is
used in this review.   Rehabilitation began to attract serious attention
in Britain in the 1960s, after a century of virtually unquestioned
belief in redevelopment.   The discussion was conditioned by the nature
of the urban fabric: it was assumed that government would be taking
action mainly in old terraced housing in old industrial towns.   There
was not much hope of spontaneous housing improvement because much of the
relevant housing was in slow-growing towns where it stood densely-packed
in grimy environments with poor amenities.

Needleman [33] was the first economist to develop the principles of
the comparative merits of redevelopment and rehabilitation.   His criterion is:-

Rehabilitate if:

$$C > R + M \; \frac{1 - (1 + i)^{-n}}{i} \; + \; \frac{C}{(1 + i)^n} \tag{1}$$

where:

    C = cost of construction of a new house.
    R = cost of rehabilitation of the old house.
    M = annual savings in maintenance costs with a new
        structure rather than a rehabilitated one.
    n = life of the present structure following rehabilitation.
    i = discount rate.

The test to find the better alternative is dependent upon the
influence of the rate of interest, the future life of the rehabilitated
dwelling, and the difference in running costs.   The relative advantage
of rehabilitation increases the higher the rate of interest, the longer
the expected life of the dwelling after rehabilitation, and the smaller
the difference in annual maintenance costs.

Sigsworth and Wilkinson [34] disputed Needleman's criterion and the
various grounds upon which they believed the rehabilitation policies had

been favoured. They argued that Needleman had ignored the capital value of the existing structure which they believed should have been placed as a charge against rehabilitation.   Also, they argued that rising building costs should be incorporated into the criterion.   These features would together provide the following formulation:-

Rehabilitate if:

$$C > R + B + M \frac{1 - (1+i)^{-n}}{i} \quad + \quad \frac{C(1+Z)}{(1+i)^n} \qquad (2)$$

where for the new terms:

  B = the capital value of the house before investment.
  Z = the annual rate of increase in replacement cost.

Some other differences in the respective approaches of Needleman, and Sigsworth and Wilkinson centred upon the treatment of financing the depreciation of the rehabilitated dwelling.   In fact, the two formulations were based upon the (tacit) assumption that rehabilitation was a way of buying time, perhaps more cheaply, and so the value of the destroyed dwelling was not placed as a charge against redevelopment. To all intents and purposes the older stock was regarded as having no value, save that rehabilitation might extend its life marginally.   In their work on the cost-benefit approach to urban renewal, Mao [35] and Rothenberg [36] had charged the value of the demolished property as a cost of an urban renewal project.   A policy of clearance and redevelopment in effect destroys an asset, whereas rehabilitation adds resources to structures which have some value.   The implication of this view is that rehabilitation is a real alternative to redevelopment and not merely a short stay of execution from the bulldozer blades.

In later work Needleman [37] did not take account of the value of the existing dwelling, but he adapted his criterion so that it could be applied to area analysis and mixed redevelopment-rehabilitation schemes. This reflected the growing practical needs of projects which were usually area-based, not just applicable to individual dwelling units. Some more significant issues were brought into account by Schaaf [38] who took account of rental values of improved housing and other factors which Needleman, and Sigsworth and Wilkinson had ignored.   Schaaf's criterion was:

Rehabilitate if:

$$C > R + M \frac{1 - (1 + i)^{-n}}{i} \quad + \quad \frac{C(1 - nr)}{(1 + i)^n} \quad + D \frac{1 - (1 + i)^{-n}}{i} \qquad (3)$$

where, for the new terms:

  D = difference in the annual rental value of a new
      structure and the rehabilitated dwelling.
  r = the annual rate of depreciation of the new structure.

Schaaf also opened up other issues.   He argued that a renewal authority had a choice among assuming different values for 'C' (the standard of the new house), and 'R' (expenditure upon rehabilitation). The selected level of 'R' would determine both 'M' (the annual difference in maintenance expenses) and 'n' (the future life of the

rehabilitated dwelling). Thus Schaaf proposed a new term 'D' (annual
differences in rental value) in order to reflect the different levels of
amenity between various possibilities in new and rehabilitated dwellings.
It should be noted that the differences in rental income were restricted
to variations in the amenity levels of the structures and in no way
represented rental values from locational or environmental factors.
Modifying this basic formulation Schaaf suggested rehabilitation should
not be regarded as a once and for all time affair, but rather some
future options to increase rehabilitation expenditure or to replace the
dwelling by redevelopment should be considered. Consequently, in
principle, by making assumptions as to the future beyond year 'n', an
optimal decision could be made so that the economic difference between
current redevelopment and various future options to rehabilitate and/or
redevelop could be maximised. This maximising criterion might be
difficult to achieve in practice because it depends upon establishing
values in uncertain and distant futures.

Unlike Needleman, Schaaf was not committed to the view that rehabilitation is simply a means of postponing redevelopment. Accordingly, Schaaf
is led to a different treatment of 'C' in his formulation. Schaaf
introduced the depreciation term 'r' into account so that, in effect, at
the end of the life of the rehabilitated dwelling the owner will have
made provision for replacement up to the value which is just equivalent
to the amount by which the otherwise selected new house would have
depreciated. This places the alternatives on a comparable time basis
with regard to their different amortisation expectations. Schaaf's
whole approach is consistent with a policy context where rehabilitation
was considered a genuine alternative policy in its own right, rather
than a temporary expedient.

Although the economic analyses of redevelopment and rehabilitation are
static and largely ignore externalities, and redistribution, they are,
nevertheless, useful. Much renewal activity is undertaken without any
systematic assessment of the relative merits of rehabilitation and
redevelopment. Such assessments can be useful in revealing economic
reasonableness. [39] This evaluative review of the development of the
literature indicates that rehabilitation is best regarded as a genuine
alternative to redevelopment, and not simply as a temporary expedient.
Housing should be regarded as an asset which is durable providing that
it is well-maintained and modernised from time to time. It is a more
flexible asset than industrial machinery which becomes obsolescent and
exhausted by depreciation. In order that rehabilitation can be used
in moderate- and low-income housing policies it is necessary to bring it
within financing conditions which make it affordable. This is discussed in Chapter 8.

HOUSING FINANCE AND INFLATION

Inflation has various effects on housing. As noted earlier, it can
restrict access to housing, and disturb the relative costs of owner-
occupier and rental tenure. It also affects the costs of housing
services - maintenance, local taxes, utilities, and estates management
costs. In the United States, the Urban Institute has been examining
the medium-term consequences of inflationary trends in relation to
incomes and capacity to pay. [40] Combining a ten-year predictive
housing model with a predictive income model, the Urban Institute has

found that, compared with the 1960s, in the 1970s: (1) housing costs will increase at double their earlier rates and (2) increases in incomes over a decade will fall from 26 to 17 per cent. Thus, rent-income burdens will increase. Housing growth will slow down with more demand for smaller units. Low-income housing problems will intensify. Clearly, inflation has manysided implications in housing welfare. This section will deal chiefly with housing finance. That is only one aspect of the impact of inflation on housing, but it is the aspect of most immediate *economic* concern.

Inflation-induced problems in housing have led to ideas for reforming credit. The low-start or variable mortgaging/credit scheme has attracted attention both as a way of beating some of the inflation-induced problems and of widening access to housing. Figure 4-1, below, illustrates the form of a low-start credit instrument, and compares it with the traditional fixed instalment (*credit foncier*) arrangements.

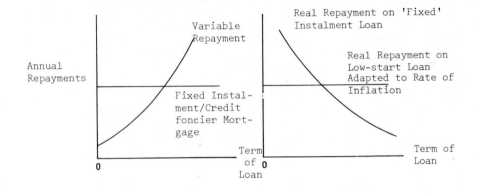

Figure 4-1

The Comparison of Fixed-Instalment and

Variable Credit Instruments

The idea underlying a low-start mortgage is that loan access is eased in the initial years, and then repayments increase by some constant or variable inflation factor, with the total amount being repaid over the cycle of the loan. [41] Figure 4-1 illustrates one possible design for the low-start credit arrangement; many variations exist in the amount of initial repayments, the subsequent scaling of repayments and the duration of the loan. Also, the low-start credit principle can be combined with fixed instalment components in an overall loan.

Economic research has produced both sceptical and optimistic views of low-start credit in the private sector. Revell [42] is concerned that low-start mortgaging disturbs and redistributes the risks borne by savers, borrowers and intermediaries. He starts by sorting out low-start mortgages according to whether the indices (the inflation factors) are related to principal, interest or to both. An index associated only with principal will secure the real value of savings and it is

accordingly equitable to savers.   When the index is connected only to
interest, it will preserve the margin between borrowing and lending
rates, and will partially contain the risks borne by financial intermediaries.   An index geared to both principal and interest is fully
inflation-proofed.   According to Revell, with his scepticism, a low-
start mortgaging arrangement can bring problems of risk and difficulties
in financial management to the intermediaries.   The risks of borrowers'
defaults are raised if future incomes do not keep pace with inflation.
Such risks can materialise if the predetermined index is higher than
actual future inflation or recession.

In the United States, the Federal Home Loan Bank Board has sponsored a
wide range of research studies on alternative mortgage instruments
(AMIs), and has reached far more optimistic conclusions. [43]   These
studies covered a wider range of low-start arrangements, and added in a
'reverse annuity mortgage' whereby an annuity could be paid to an aged
home owner, purchased by a loan which can be secured against accumulated
equity value in property.   Although the opinion on the risk of borrowers' default on low-start mortgages was divided among researchers, even
at the worst they could find no cause for absolute favour for fixed
instalment plans.   The comparative risks of default among fixed
instalment and variable repayment plans were only marginal.   Moreover,
the researchers, though again divided on the precise details, found
that access to home ownership might increase by some 5 per cent.   In
July 1978, in view of the general optimism in the research studies, the
Federal Home Loan Bank Board issued instructions to originate and
purchase AMIs.   The Board anticipates useful social and economic
benefits will eventuate in the counter-inflationary access to finance
among borrowers, and in their choice among instruments to fit their
changing life-cycle needs.   The results will be evident in the market
place during the next few years.

The appropriate strategy for countries which depend for most housing
on private capital markets might be to take the following into account.
First, severe inflation might be regarded as temporary, its worst
excesses being contained or corrected by general stabilisation policies.
Progress on this should afford relief to the allocational, distributional and stabilisation problems.   Second, if the liquid funds of financial
intermediaries grow (caused by high costs cutting out potential
borrowers) they might try experimenting with limited low-start mortgaging schemes.   Third, governments can develop low-start schemes for
housing influenced by direct state-assisted finance.   This might mean
that governments will bear some financial risks within their fiscal
systems.   However, if the financial arrangements were designed and
constructed to achieve equity and selectivity in access, this risk might
be politically acceptable.   Countries with a more dominant role in
housing finance can adopt a more general scheme to try to reconcile the
problems of inflation, equity and access to standard housing.   Sweden
created a general indexed scheme in 1968, but this failed because only
the principal of the loans was indexed and not the interest rates.   It
was interest charges which were most significant in the post-1968 years.
This scheme and the reasons for its failure are discussed in Chapter 7.

Summarising the legacy of ideas for reforming housing finance we can
make the following statements.   Although the proposed schemes improve
accessibility to housing, they marginally increase risks and they
sometimes make assumptions about the future which are incomplete or

unrealistic. It is necessary to consider the implications for financial intermediaries and the managers of funds, as well as the viewpoint of borrowers and savers. Inflation opens up potential conflicts between borrowers, savers and intermediaries. However, proposals for reform re-arrange these conflicts rather than eliminate them. The best solution is to curb inflation and thereby to reduce uncertainties, but if that is not possible the case for reforming mortgage instruments is very strong. Apart from concerns in housing finance, the main longer term problem may become the costs of housing services relative to incomes. These housing service costs will be at least as significant as capital costs in the future and they are more directly relevant to moderate- and low-income housing issues.

CONCLUSIONS

It is only during the last decade or so that the social economics of housing has emerged as a subject for continuous research, teaching and policy relevance. Like other branches of economics, its values and its theory-choices and its policy implications are all controversial. It is especially important to understand what is involved in this entangled relationship between economics as a social science and as a primary contributor to policy development.

  As Rein [44] has pointed out, the social science researcher needs a clear grasp of *the problem* and some clear objectives in order to proceed with analysis and evaluation. But political issues tend to be in a state of flux, with problems and objectives ill-defined, disagreed, and changing. Thus, at the critical preparatory stage, the political process is somewhat confusingly engaged in looking for consensus about acceptable definitions of problems and objectives - a stage at which the political risks of precision would be unbearable. Thus, having regard to the nature of political policy-making, the notion that social scientists can simply solve problems put to them by politicians, *at times when the issues themselves are in a state of flux*, is a myth. The mythical characteristics recede with the passing of time as issues are clarified in the *historical* process, and as knowledge accumulates. This poses dilemmas for researchers. As they contribute to the choice of problems and objectives during times of flux, they are unavoidably entangled and embattled like other politicians. Then intellectual reflection and research have their own time scales, once the work is committed, and life may pass them by as new issues arise in the political world to replace those by which the research was shaped.

  The relations between social science and social policy are important throughout this study. They have been important at critical moments in housing history. Their importance can be illustrated from three examples, all described at length in later chapters.

  First, it will be argued that Britain took the 'wrong' options at a critical point in its housing policy development, with the consequence that future policy options have been severely circumscribed. But at the same time we shall show that British policy was disadvantaged because it was first. Politicians and scientists alike had no theoretical, institutional or comparative examples to which they could refer when faced with urgent and extremely novel policy questions. In something as complex as housing, there are definite advantages in

135

following (in time, not method) the initiatives of others.   The
problems of being the leader and the first are currently experienced in
Sweden (see Chapter 7).

Despite such troubles, the social economics of housing has developed
substantially in its theoretical and its empirical content *because* it
has been brought into close association with policy development.   In
the United States the researchers in the EHAP studies have gone further
than just revealing the technical and empirical issues in formulating
and administering housing allowances.   They have also found it
necessary to consider some basic theoretical issues in explaining the
divergence between private and social/collective valuations of housing
allowances.   Knowledge has become richer and more relevant, with some
interest beyond the housing field from which it originated.   A new
cost-benefit analysis of housing programmes touches upon and contributes
to, the more general matter of the theoretical foundations of the
welfare state.   Similarly in The Netherlands, Professor Dr. F. Hartog
undertook contract research on the problem of subsidisation in housing.
The problem was that subsidies were becoming an increasing burden upon
public expenditure, they were not targeted effectively, but the Dutch
wished to retain housing as a welfare state provision.   Professor
Hartog found a solution which blended the virtues of the market with
egalitarian objectives.   The 'dynamic rent calculation' (i.e., indexing
rents to some relevant current costs) potentially provides a
simultaneous solution to problems of equity, efficiency and adaptability
to uncertain futures.   Taking the American and Dutch work together we
can see that the social economics of housing now has useful systematic
knowledge in: (1) economic justifications for the welfare state, (2)
the social and economic consequences of housing allowances, and (3) the
simultaneous resolution of equity, efficiency and control in public
finance.   There has been theoretical, technical and empirical progress
and it has come from policy-relevant research which has been sponsored
by governments caught up in the confusing *milieu* of policy development
and reform.

It goes without saying that the new branch of economics is imperfect,
controversial, and scarcely beginning its work on large areas of its
subject.   But our review in this chapter has shown that, even in its
infancy, the subject has been able to establish important generalisations
and some useful bases for modern policy-making.   We conclude by
summarising these generalisations and their policy relevance.

The 'new' knowledge is establishing firmer and more varied justifications for the welfare state.   For example, it can be shown that the
conventional controversies on 'in-kind' and 'cash' welfare are based upon
unduly simplistic and general arguments.   In reality, a housing
allowance has some (partial) 'in-kind' characteristics; and it may
expose divergences between private and collective interests which need
to be justified.   More generally, questions of housing-related equity
and egalitarianism are diverse and complicated among owners, renters,
savers, borrowers and so on.   Egalitarian principles also influence
housing via policies in employment, wages and social security.   A
coherent egalitarianism in those policies makes it easier to allocate
and administer housing equitably.   Considerations of equity and
equality raise the question of how 'subsidisation' in housing should be
conceived, defined and administered.   The more significant 'subsidies'
are implicit rather than explicit, and they often compound antecedent

inequalities.

Low-income housing problems have been linked to the economics of subsidies, rents and costs in the past.   This will continue, but in the
future they will become increasingly involved in the qualities of
housing management, and in the allocation and re-allocation of the
existing stock.   The existing stock should not be regarded as an
(absolutely) inferior alternative to new construction.   In appropriate
financial and administrative conditions (see Chapter 7), older housing
can provide useful, and sometimes better, ways of improving the housing
conditions of all groups, including low-income groups.   Properly
managed, rehabilitation can justify itself socially and economically.

Low-income housing problems are also associated with inflation.   In
the long run the significant point is the relativity between rising
costs of housing services and the rate of change in incomes.   In the
short run, the problem is one of adjusting to the severe inflation,
1973-1976.   Experience and research since then have developed a useful
stock of ideas and possibilities for the reform of housing finance, and
other anti-inflationary purposes.

All this useful knowledge and theoretical illumination will be brought
to bear on housing history through the next two chapters.   That was the
point of reversing the conventional order of things, to expound the
theory first and the history afterwards.   It should allow a more
perceptive and critical account of past policies than was possible at
the times when these policies were adopted.

APPENDIX TO CHAPTER 4

Housing allowances and the 'housing gap'

Housing allowances can be designed and used in various ways, but their
one common purpose is for bridging the 'housing gap'.   The 'housing gap'
is the difference between the consumer's cost of *standard* housing and
the amounts which moderate- and low-income households can reasonably
afford to pay.   The social, historical and economic justifications for
defining 'standard' housing and 'reasonable' capacity to pay are
discussed in the Chapter.   This Appendix is provided to show: (1) how
housing allowances can be designed, technically, to bridge the 'housing
gap', (2) the relevance of price and income *elasticities* of demand, and
(3) the divergence between private and social/collective valuations of
housing allowances.

Housing allowances can be 'earmarked' to housing in various ways.
That is to say, eligibility conditions in housing allowances are designed to ensure that recipients spend minimum amounts on housing, or meet
certain minimum housing standards, or match their expenditure on housing
proportionately to subsidy contributions by government.   The technical
and economic explanation for housing allowances thus involves making
comparisons between: (1) housing and non-housing expenditure, (2)
consumer behaviour with and without the housing allowance, (3) differently designed and constructed housing allowances and, (4) alternative ways
of providing assistance.

Figure 4-2, below, shows the effect of an unconditioned social income

grant, without earmarking. It can be understood as a social security
payment, a guaranteed minimum income, or the proceeds from a negative
income tax. This is related to expenditure upon housing and non-
housing.

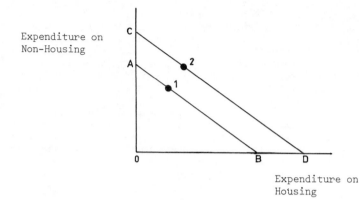

Expenditure on
Non-Housing

Expenditure on
Housing

Figure 4-2

An Unconditional Social Income Payment

Without the social income payment the household can select any
combination of housing and non-housing on the budget line, AB. This
line represents the trade-off possibilities between housing and non-
housing. Any position beneath the line represents worse positions (i.e.
lower economic welfare) than on the line. Positions above the line are
infeasible. This becomes feasible when government provides a social
income payment to supplement the household's other sources of income.
With the social income payment the budget possibilities for the household now lie along line, CD, representing a payment worth AC in non-
housing value and BD in housing value.

Our hypothetical household originally chose the combination of housing
and non-housing goods represented at point 1. This is realistic in the
sense that empirical evidence suggests that low-income groups spend in
the range of 20 to 45 per cent of their income on housing. After the
social income payment is made, the household selects a housing and non-
housing combination represented by point 2. Clearly, the economic
welfare of the household has increased and it can purchase both more
housing services and more non-housing goods. This can be formalised
into the *income elasticity of demand* for housing. The income
elasticity of demand for housing is the result of the ratio of: the
percentage increase in the expenditure on housing (the numerator) and
the percentage increase in income (the denominator) which precipitates
the increases in expenditure. Statistical studies in housing indicate
that the income elasticity of demand for housing is in the range 0.7 to
1.0 but this depends upon how housing is defined and which social group
is the focus of interest. [1] Nevertheless, a value of 1.0 represents
a reasonable approximation for low-income renters, indicating that, say,
a 10 per cent increase in income draws forth an increase in expenditure
on housing by about 10 per cent.

Figure 4-3, below, indicates the influence of a lower relative price
in housing.   It is relevant to households which occupy housing overtly
(or implicitly) subsidised by government, or those that receive a
percentage-of-rent housing allowance (see below).

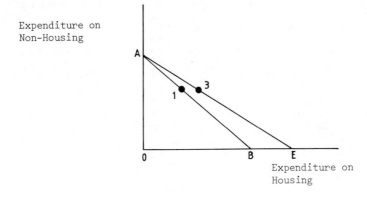

Figure 4-3

A Decrease in the Relative Price of Housing

The decrease in the 'consumer price' of housing (other things unchang-
ed) establishes a new budget line, AE, and the household moves from
point 1 to point 3.   At point 3, the household buys more housing
services and less non-housing services compared with point 1.   The
result represents the net effect of two principles.   First, the lower
price of housing is tantamount to an increase in income - the 'income
effect', which, as we have seen (in Figure 4-2), enables the households
to purchase both more housing and more non-housing.   Second, the 'price
effect' makes the lower-priced good a relative bargain and draws more
expenditure towards it.   Normally, the price effect is stronger than
the income effect, with the consequence that the net result produces
more expenditure on housing and less on non-housing.   The net result
can be formalised as the *price elasticity of demand* for housing.   This
is the ratio of: the percentage increase in the demand for housing (the
numerator) and the percentage decrease in the price of housing (the
denominator), which precipitates the increase in expenditure.
Statistical studies [2] indicate that the price elasticity of demand for
housing is about - 1.0.   This means that as the relative price of
housing either increases or decreases, the amounts which households
spend on housing will remain stable, from this effect alone.   But when
the effect of income elasticities are added to price changes, then
clearly expenditure on housing will react positively with changes in
income.

Housing allowances which are designed and constructed to offer a
percentage-of-rent (i.e., matched with proportionate household
contributions up to some maximum rent) will effectively channel spending
into more housing.   This has affinity with the case in Figure 4-3 above.

Alternative designs in housing allowances provide clear-cut income payments, but apply some constraints on the free-use representations in Figure 4-2. The objective of placing constraints (i.e., earmarking) is to be more positive and directive towards housing expenditure compared with non-housing expenditure. This can be achieved in two ways. First, eligible households can be required to purchase a rent voucher, thus constraining them to yield up some opportunities in non-housing expenditure. Second, access to housing allowances can be made dependent upon occupation of housing meeting minimum standards, and, by implication, minimum costs. In terms of Figure 4-2, this means that if some households want to participate in the programme they have to take up housing expenditure lower down the budget line, CD, than at point 2. Other eligible households may be meeting these requirements before the introduction of housing allowances. For them, the main advantage of housing allowances is that they can substantially reduce the proportion of their income that they spend on housing. In other words, they lower their rent-income burdens. The discussions in the Chapter review the economic behaviour of 'constrained' and 'unconstrained' groups, and their relative responsiveness to housing allowance inducements. That discussion shows that housing allowances are selective in their relative attraction, and that they cannot be regarded simplistically as general mechanistic inducements. 'Housing poverty' and housing choice are more complex than the factors involved in 'income poverty'.

Housing allowances can be defined more precisely in equation form. This is set out below, comparatively, to show 'housing gap' designs and 'percentage-of-rent' designs.

The 'Housing Gap' Formula

$$P = aC^* - bY$$

The housing allowance is based upon the size and the income of the household, and local market (rent) conditions. It pays the difference between a market rent for an appropriate unit and a percentage of the household's adjusted income. (In Britain and Europe, rents are regulated under statute.)

Where:-

P = allowance payment.
C^* = the estimated cost of modest, existing standard housing (related to family size).
Y = net disposable income.

The 'Percentage-of-Rent' Formula

$$P = gR \text{ for } R < \frac{C^*}{a}$$

$$P = C^* \text{ for } R > \frac{C^*}{g}$$

The housing allowance is calculated as a fraction of rent paid by eligible households, and some upper income limit is specified.

R = rent paid by household.
a = a payment level parameter.
b = the rate at which the allowance is reduced as income increases (usually around 0.25).
g = percentage of rent paid by government.

The United States' Experimental Housing Allowance Program (EHAP) used several levels of payment (P) and several rates at which allowances reduce as income increases (b).

We can now demonstrate a crucial theoretical point in government involvements in housing. Some private household choice is *constrained* in various ways; by setting minimum standards or by requiring some payment for a voucher. As we have seen, some potential recipients of housing allowances are constrained to change their pattern of housing and non-housing expenditure by earmarking conditions. In the produc-tion-orientated approach, the constraints are expressed in housing standards, in social-administrative allocation of social housing, and in 'waiting time' for access to cheaper (subsidised) housing. The theoretically interesting point is the comparison between the individ-ual's valuation of housing-related subsidies and the costs and benefits to the wider community. This topic is discussed in a wider context in the Chapter. Here,we are concerned only with showing the divergence between private and social values - these social values being expressed as income payments and/or price reducing subsidies through the governmental process.

In order to establish the private benefits of the subsidy to the (constrained) household, we need to equip ourselves with two additional economic principles. First, we need to look at the consumer's valua-tion of housing and non-housing goods as bundles representing equal value, but containing different combinations of housing and non-housing. In other words, the consumer has a series of bundles which he/she values *indifferently*. These are represented in Figure 4-4, below, as Ii, Iii, and Iiii. The curves take on their characteristic convexity from below, being conditioned by economic and technical factors which need not concern us here. The curves outwards and to the right represent higher levels of economic value than those nearer the origin. The tangency of budget lines and indifference curves indicate the consumer's potential allocations between housing and non-housing.

Our second economic principle is derived from welfare economics. Acknowledging that some sorts of housing allowance (and other sorts of subsidy) constrain some households to spend more on housing than they would in unconstrained conditions, we ask: how much income would we have to give the household, in lieu of the housing allowance, in order that it is neither better nor worse off than with the allowance?   In economic jargon this is the Marshallian-Hicksian *income equivalent variation*. It measures the private value of the housing allowance to the household. In principle, the household is thereby indifferent between the income equivalent variation and the housing allowance. The point of the (hypothetical) exercise is that private valuations diverge from the community's valuation of costs and benefits. This is represented in Figure 4-4, below.

The household's expenditure on housing and non-housing *without* the housing allowance is represented at point 1, the tangency of the budget line, AB, and the indifference curve Ii. A 'constraining' housing allowance requires the household to spend more on housing at some speci-fied minimum if it wishes to participate in the programme. Thus, the allowance is designed so that the household will allocate its expendi-ture on housing and non-housing in a combination represented at point 3. At point 3, the household is on budget line, CD, and its relevant indifference curve at that point is, Iii. Clearly, since the household is on a higher budget line and a higher indifference curve *with* the

housing allowance, it is better off.   But this is not the only
significant aspect of the analysis.

Expenditure on
Non-Housing

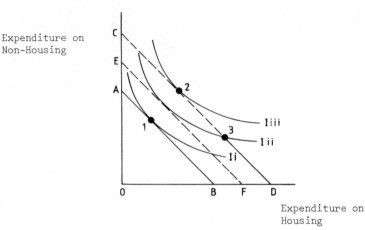

Expenditure on
Housing

Figure 4-4

The Private and Community Costs and Benefits
of Constrained Housing Allowances

The budget line, CD, has a constraint, and on the Figure this is shown
by indicating a section (the broken line section above point 3) which is
not relevant because of the imposition of a constraint to increase
expenditure on housing, compared with point 1.   Had the household been
given an unconstrained choice it would have selected a combination of
housing and non-housing expenditure, represented at point 2.   At point
2 the household is on the same budget line, CE, but on a higher
indifference curve, Iiii, than at point 3.   In terms of the private
valuation of the household, it would be better off in the unconstrained
position at point 2, rather than in the constrained position at point 3.

Now the transfer cost of the housing allowance to society (i.e., its
cash value) is, AC.   However, the constrained household values the
benefit differently.   The amount of income we would (hypothetically)
have to give it in lieu of the allowance so that it is no worse off than
with the allowance is, AE.   That is the 'income equivalent variation',
and we should note that it is determined by taking the indifference
curve, Iii, through point 3 and drawing in its tangency to a budget line,
EF', which is parallel to the original budget line, AB.   Clearly, AE is
worth less than AC, the cost of the allowance to society.   Thus, we
conclude: (1) either society loses because the cost to it is greater
than the benefits to some (constrained) recipients, or (2) society has
some other source of benefits in providing allowances, beyond the private
benefits to some (constrained) recipients.   This raises the important
issue of the justification for housing subsidies - a point discussed in
the Chapter.

We close this Appendix note with a few qualifying comments.   First,

the diagrammatic exposition excludes some costs. The costs of
administering the housing allowances are not brought within the analysis,
and we have every reason to expect these to run at about 20 per cent of
the transfer cost of the subsidy. Second, this analysis excludes
benefits and valuations which are not readily accommodated in the
indifference curve approach.. In particular, we cannot be certain that
all 'externalities' have been accounted. Finally, we should note that
similar sorts of analyses and conclusions can be related to production-
orientated approaches to bridging the 'housing gap'. In both cases
some basic social-political-ceonomic justification has to be reasoned to
show why social (i.e., collectively organised) decisions should override
unconstrained private choice. This study discusses various justifications in this, and in other chapters.

NOTES

[1] The proportions of income which households will spend on housing
will depend on various factors including: temporary life-cycle needs;
long-term probabilities of employment and income prospects; and
prevailing or expected rates of inflation. Not all cases of high
proportionate expenditure on housing should be interpreted as a cause
for social concern, as these circumstances may be transitory.
[2] The dilemmas of applying professional public health standards to
housing allowances have occupied the attention of researchers involved
in the United States' Experimental Housing Allowance Program (EHAP),
1973-1978.
[3] American sources which have advocated housing allowances for these
reasons, include: B.J. Frieden, *Improving Federal Housing Subsidies*,
Joint Center for Urban Studies, Massachusetts Institute of Technology
and Harvard University, Cambridge, Mass., 1971, M.Rein, *Welfare and
Housing*, Joint Center for Urban Studies, Massachusetts Institute of
Technology and Harvard University, Cambridge, Mass., 1972, A.P.Solomon,
Housing the Urban Poor, Massachusetts Institute of Technology Press,
Cambridge, Mass., 1974, and D.Stern, *Housing Allowances : Some Considerations of Efficiency and Equity*, Joint Center for Urban Studies, Massachusetts Institute of Technology and Harvard University, Cambridge,
Mass., 1971. Following the extensive research under EHAP, 1973-1978,
other American economists (see below) have adopted theoretical and
policy positions which are rather more discerning and circumspect on
the relationships between welfare and subsidisation in housing.
[4] Administrative aspects of housing allowances are discussed
substantially, in their American context in W.L.Hamilton, D.W.Budding
and W.L.Holshouser, *Administrative Procedures in a Housing Allowance
Program : The Administrative Agency Experiment*, Abt Associates, Cambridge
Mass., 1977.
[5] The best recent analysis is W.G.Grigsby and L.Rosenburg, *Urban
Housing Policy*, APS Publications, New York, 1975.
[6] See the following publications of Abt Associates, Cambridge, Mass.,
Fourth Annual Report of the Demand Experiment, 1977. S.K.Mayo, *Housing
Allowance Demand Experiment*, *Housing Expenditures and Quality, Part 1,
Report on Housing Expenditures Under a Percent of Rent Housing Allowance*
1977, J.Friedman and S.D.Kennedy, *Housing Allowance Demand Experiment,
Housing Expenditures and Quality, Part 2, Housing Expenditures Under a
Housing Gap Housing Allowance*, 1977.
[7] *The Urban Institute* (Washington D.C., United States) is conducting
research on the policy mix of housing allowances, rehabilitation and

production subsidies under the EHAP studies, 1973-1978. Its role is to integrate research from other contractors in EHAP and to reveal the fuller policy significance of EHAP research.

[8] For a useful set of historical and modern essays on this subject, see Institute of Economic Affairs, *Verdict on Rent Control*, Institute of Economic Affairs, London, 1972.

[9] See F. de Leeuw and N.Ekanen, 'Time Lags in the Rental Housing Market', *Urban Studies*, Vol.10, February 1973, pp.39-68.

[10] For a detailed technical and theoretical explanation of the competition between old and new stock, see F. de Leeuw and R.J.Struyk, *The Web of Urban Housing*, Urban Institute, Washington D.C., 1975.

[11] This model is elaborated in de Leeuw and Struyk, *op. cit.*, (1975).

[12] The ideas in this and the next paragraph were formed in discussions with Stephen D. Kennedy of Abt Associeates Inc., Cambridge, Massachusetts, United States. Abt Associates Inc. has been involved in major social and economic research on the *demand* responses under the EHAP studies.

[13] The key literature on filtration theory is F.S.Kristoff, 'Federal Housing Policies : Subsidised Production, Filtration and Objectives', *Land Economics*, Vol.48, No.4, 1972, pp.309-320 and, Vol.49, No.2, 1973, pp.163-174, E.M.Fisher and L.Winnick, 'A Reformulation of the Filtering Concept', *Journal of Social Issues*, Nos. 1 and 2, 1951. W.G.Grigsby, *Housing Markets and Housing Policy*, University of Philadelphia, Philadelphia, 1963, I.S.Lowry, 'Filtering and Housing Standards : A Conceptual Analysis', *Land Economics*, November 1960, pp.362-370, J.F.Lansing, C.W.Clifton and J.N.Morgan, *New Homes and Poor People*, University of Michigan, Institute of Social Research, Ann Arbor, 1969, and R.V.Ratcliff *Urban Land Economics*, McGraw Hill, New York, 1949.

[14] See Lansing, Clifton and Morgan, *op. cit.*, (1969).

[15] The British writing in housing economics has pursued understanding in private markets, but with wider referencing to overt public policies. For an early example, see L.Needleman, *The Economics of Housing*, Staples Press, London, 1965.

[16] See the critical evaluation of British rental policies, in G.Hallett, *Housing and Land Policies in West Germany and Britain*, MacMillan, London, 1977.

[17] A.A.Nevitt, *Housing, Taxation and Subsidies*, Nelson, London, 1966.

[18] M.Bowley, *Housing and the State, 1919-1944*, George Allen and Unwin, London, 1945.

[19] For the most fully developed example of this approach, see A.Murie, P.Niner and C. Watson, *Housing Policy and the Housing System*, George Allen and Unwin, London, 1976.

[20] A.Downs, *Federal Housing Subsidies : How Are They Working?*, Heath, Lexington, 1973.

[21] Patricia Apps has been developing the theory on which ideas in this paragraph are based, see P.Apps, (1) *Housing Problems and Policies*, Public Policy Research Paper No. 4, School of Architecture, University of Sydney, 1975, (2) *Child Care Policy in the Production-Consumption Economy*, Public Policy Research Paper No.2, School of Architecture, University of Sydney, 1975, and (3) *Government, Housing and Theory*, Paper presented to Housing Economics Conference, Macquarie University, Sydney, 23-25 August, 1978.

[22] A.P.Solomon, *The Cost-Effectiveness of Subsidised Housing*, Joint Center for Urban Studies, Massachusetts Institute of Technology and Harvard University, Cambridge, Mass., 1972, and *op. cit.*, (1974).

[23] M.P.Murray, 'The Distribution of Tenant Benefits in Public Housing', *Econometrica*, Vol.43, No.4, July 1975, pp.771-788. Murray is extending

his work within the EHAP research at Abt Associates Inc.

[24] J.S. de Salvo, 'A Methodology for Evaluating Housing Programs', *Journal of Regional Science*, Vol.11, 1971, pp.173-185, and 'Housing Subsidies : Do We Know What We Are Doing?', *Policy Analysis*, Vol.2, 1976, pp.39-60.

[25] See D.M.Wilner, R.P.Walkley, T.C.Pinkerton and M.Taybeck, *The Housing Environment and Family Life*, John Hopkins, Baltimore, 1962. This study examined the comparative results in child health, education and socialisation from residence in standard public housing and in the slums. Although some better results occurred among those who lived in standard public housing, the comparative differences were of minor and negligible importance.

[26] The ideas in this paragraph were derived from discussions with S.Mayo of Abt Associates Inc. in November 1977.

[27] For a review of this statistical research and for a general discussion of income-conditioned welfare, see H.J.Aaron, *Why is Welfare So Hard to Reform?*, Brookings, Washington, D.C., 1973.

[28] H.J.Aaron, *Shelter Subsidies : Who Benefits from Federal Housing Subsidies?*, Brookings, Washington, D.C., 1972.

[29] The British studies are discussed in their policy context in Chapter 6. The following studies reveal similar contrasts to American studies and they fit the comparative statements presented in the current discussions: (1) J.B.Cullingworth, *Housing in Transition : A Case Study in the City of Lancaster, 1958-1962*, Heinemann, London, 1963, assesses rental housing in a slow-growth small town context, and (2) D.V.Donnison (et. al.), *Housing Since the Rent Act*, Occasional Papers on Social Administration, Bell, London, 1964, reveals some contrasting patterns in metropolitan rental housing in London.

[30] See R.G.Krohn and E.B.Fleming, *The Other Economy and the Urban Housing Problem : A Study of Older Rental Neighbourhoods in Montreal*, Joint Center for Urban Studies, Massachusetts Institute of Technology and Harvard University, Cambridge, Mass., 1972, M.A.Stegman, *Housing Investment in the Inner City : The Dynamics of Decline*, Massachusetts Institute of Technology Press, Cambridge, Mass., 1972, G.Sternlieb, *The Tenement Landlord*, Urban Studies Center, Rutgers University, New Brunswick, 1966.

[31] Sternlieb, *op. cit.*, (1966).

[32] Krohn and Fleming, *op. cit.*, (1972).

[33] L.Needleman, *The Economics of Housing*, Staples, London, 1965.

[34] E.M.Sigsworth and R.K.Wilkinson, 'Rebuilding or Renovation', *Urban Studies*, June 1967, pp.109-121.

[35] J.C.T.Mao, 'Efficiency in Urban Expenditure through Benefit-Cost Analysis', *Journal of the American Institute of Planners*, March 1966, pp.95-107.

[36] J.Rothenburg, *Economic Evaluation of Urban Renewal*, Brookings, Washington, D.C., 1967.

[37] L.Needleman, 'The Comparative Economics of Improvement and New Building', *Urban Studies*, June 1969, pp.196-209.

[38] A.H.Schaaf, 'Economic Feasibility Analysis for Urban Renewal Housing Rehabilitation', *Journal of the American Institute of Planners*, November 1969, pp.399-404.

[39] For example, by using an adaptation of the Schaaf criterion I was able to show that rehabilitation would have been the better alternative compared with a proposed redevelopment scheme in Australia. See C.D. Pugh, 'Older Residential Areas ans the Development of Economic Analysis', in J.C.McMaster and G.R.Webb (eds), *Australian Urban and Regional Economics : A Reader* Australian and New Zealand Book Co., Sydney, 1976.

[40] See D.B.Carlson, *Housing Low-Income Families*, Urban Institute, Washington D.C., 1977.
[41] It is necessary to state that although housing finance is important for access to housing resources, finance itself does not constitute actual housing resources. A sudden flood of housing finance into a fully-employed housing sector would simply escalate the price of housing rather than produce more housing in the short term. Low-start mortgaging would have to be phased and related to resources to avoid this problem.
[42] Organisation for Economic Co-operation and Development (Consultant J.R.S.Revell), *Flexibility in Housing Finance*, OECD, Paris, 1975.
[43] D.M.Kaplan, R.G.Marcis and H.Cassidy, *Alternative Mortgage Instrument Research Study,* Federal Home Loan Bank Board, Washington D.C., 1977.
[44] Martin Rein has been deeply involved in public policy research and evaluation in community development and welfare programmes during the last decade or so. As a result of this intellectual-policy involvement he has been drawn towards epistemological and social explanations of intellectualism in policy development. See M.Rein, (1) *Values, Social Science and Social Policy*, (1973), (2) *The Fact-Value Dilemma*, (1974) and (3) *Policy Research : Belief and Doubt*, (1977), - all published by Joint Center for Urban Studies, Massachusetts Institute of Technology and Harvard University, Cambridge, Mass.; the first two are reprinted with other papers in *Social Science and Public Policy*, Penguin, Harmondsworth, 1976.

NOTES : APPENDIX

[1] For an elaboration of income and price elasticities of demand for housing, see R.F.Muth, *Cities and Housing*, University of Chicago Press, Chicago, 1969, and R.K.Wilkinson, 'The Income Elasticity of Demand for Housing', *Oxford Economic Papers*, Vol.25, No.3, November 1973, pp.361-377
[2] See Muth, *op. cit.*, (1969).

REFERENCE

de Leeuw, F., Leaman, S.H. and Blank, H., *The Design of a Housing Allowance*, Urban Institute, Washington D.C., 1970.

REFERENCES (SELECTED)

Aaron, H.J., *Shelter Subsidies : Who Benefits from Federal Housing Subsidies?*, Brookings, Washington D.C., 1972.

Aaron, J.H., *Why is Welfare So Hard to Reform?* Brookings, Washington D.C. 1973.

Bowley, M., *Housing and the State, 1919-1944*, George Allen and Unwin, London, 1945.

Downs, A., *Federal Housing Subsidies : How Are They Working?*, Heath, Lexington, 1973.

Grigsby, W.G., *Housing Markets and Housing Policy*, University of Philadelphia, Philadelphia, 1963.

Grigsby, W.G. and Rosenburg, L., *Urban Housing Policy*, APS Publications, New York, 1975.

Kristoff, F.S., 'Federal Housing Policies : Subsidised Production, Filtration and Objectives', *Land Economics*, Vol.48, No.4, 1972, pp.309-320, and Vol.49, No.2, 1973.

Institute of Economic Affairs, *Verdict on Rent Control*, Institute of Economic Affairs, London, 1972.

de Leeuw, F., Leaman, SH. and Blank, H., *The Design of a Housing Allowance*, Urban Institute, Washington D.C., 1970.

de Leeuw, F. and Struyk, R.J., *The Web of Urban Housing*, urban Institute, Washington D.C., 1975.

Needleman, L., *The Economics of Housing*, Staples Press, London, 1965.

Organisation for Economic Co-operation and Development, *Flexibility in Housing Finance*, OECD, Paris, 1975.

Solomon, A.P., *Housing the Urban Poor*, Massachusetts Institute of Technology Press, Cambridge, Mass., 1974.

Stegman, M.A., *Housing Investment in the Inner City : The Dynamics of Decline*, Massachusetts Institute of Technology Press, Cambridge, Mass., 1972.

ACKNOWLEDGMENTS

The following housing economists significantly contributed to my understanding of recent and current housing research in the United States: Dr. S. Kennedy and Dr. S. Mayo.

5 The historical development of housing policies in some modern democracies to 1945

Housing policy reform is often retrospectively seen to have responded to vexation arising from housing conditions, and problems affecting the community at large. In the period this chapter reviews, factors influencing the development of housing policy included rapid increases in urban population, two economic depressions and two world wars.

Government influences on housing policy have increased since the mid-nineteenth century. Public health, housing credit markets, town planning, provision of public housing, government support for voluntary non-profit housing associations, subsidy payments, social development and welfare assistance have all been involved in policy. They have evolved from the sources of vexation mentioned above; the early British history of housing in an industrial society is largely an account of vexation and reform, particularly in the 1840s, in 1870-1890 and in 1900-1919.

BRITAIN : THE PERIOD TO 1890

The period 1830-1890 was marked by two phases of vexation and reform; the first, which was discussed in Chapter 3 centred around public health reform in the 1840s, and the second in 1870-1890 was more directly concerned with working-class living conditions - the slums, overcrowding and high rents. These were the times when Liberalism, Socialism and other social theories began to take their modern characteristics. These social theories influenced the development of welfare state policies, including housing policies. There was a parallel growth in the size and scope of government, which allowed practical expression - whether well or ill conceived - of the new social idealism.

Some of the history of housing policy in this period has been well-documented by other authors, [1] but although we shall find their work useful, it does not focus on the main subjects in this study. Thus, it will be necessary to offer some fresh account of British housing history, especially from the perspective of (1) comparative policy development in other countries, and (2) the economics of housing and urbanisation. First, we shall be interested in the variety of policy options which were available and in the reasons why some good ideas were neglected whilst other less useful courses were taken in policy and administration. Second, we recognise that the economic study of housing and urbanisation has only recently blossomed into a specialist subject with critical understanding of its subject matter. Earlier urban historians were not equipped to do much economic analysis; but that analysis is important to an understanding of problems in early housing reform, particularly in the economic and administrative difficulties in slum clearance.

In his interpretation of London's nineteenth-century slums, Dyos writes: 'The slums were the residue left on the market, the last bits and pieces to command a price'. [2] Modern economic studies [3] reveal, that on the contrary, in the circumstances prevailing in London at the time, the crowded slums were the *first* parts of housing to command a price. Housing is divided into sub-markets which can be regarded as imperfect substitutes among consumers concerned with highly specific factors such as quality, type, location and so on. In the period when low income was a mass phenomenon among the working classes, they had to live within walking distance to work, and at affordable rents. *For the household*, economy meant taking less space (i.e., crowding), and where high rents prevailed - as they did in London - the pressures on household budgeting forced crowding. The rents on dilapidated and meanly-built housing were pushed up by the incessant pressures of population growth. These pressures could push slum property values above the cost of building new housing at equivalent space standards, whereas without the population pressures, market pressures would have reduced the value of the most dilapidated housing. Some of the key constraints are relaxed when incomes increase, when the transport technology improves and the time-distance costs of travel in relation to income are lowered, and when social security covers risks of unemployment, sickness, loss of the breadwinner and so on.

Further light is shed on nineteenth-century urban housing conditions by examining the effects of economic boom and slump. In slumps, those households which are hit hardest have to economise further and intensify the crowding into *some* sub-markets. However, *other* housing is left *vacant* with a price below new construction costs and thus acts as a disincentive to new building. New building may occur, but chiefly to cater for higher income groups which are seeking new standards of housing and land space, usually in the suburbs. During economic booms, the proportion of vacancies declines and the incentive for new building recurs; but for working-class housing it was often cheaper to provide this by converting existing housing into smaller units. Housing for conversion became available as higher income groups moved out to the suburbs; any residual working-class demand for housing could then be met by building at low standards in relatively high densities.

The housing problems of rapidly growing nineteenth-century cities can be understood only within those economic interpretations. They shed light upon a multitude of issues which enter policy and administrative experience. For example they can be used to explain: (1) the net economic losses from slum clearance, (2) the vacillations and retreats of private enterprise in building new private rental housing, (3) the continual vexation in finding a satisfactory criterion for compensating owners for expropriation, and (4) the limited capacity of philanthropic model dwelling companies to maintain or expand their activities. These and other issues are taken up in the history, below, but first some of the key social conditions which underlie housing problems are elaborated.

Housing, urbanisation and working class living conditions : 1800-1890

The first phase of housing reform, 1830-1850, had been concerned with problems of disease and urban filth. In the second phase, the key issues were overcrowding in the largest cities, high rents and general urban poverty. No one personality dominated the second phase of reform,

1850-1890, as Chadwick had dominated in the public health reforms. It was influenced more by the existence of established institutions encapsulating earlier theories, idealisms and administrative methods. Urban administration inherited theories of environmental determinism, Chadwick's theoretical resistance to subsidies for working-class housing and some difficulties in centre-local government relations. Outside public administration, philanthropic and other voluntary initiatives were taking place to deal with working-class living conditions. We referred to the housing-related activities of Octavia Hill, the Charity Organisation Society and the Settlement Movement. Another voluntary initiative which will presently be the subject of fuller discussion was the development of the limited-profit model dwelling company movement. These model dwelling companies expressed the Conservative idealism of Lord Shaftesbury and the *Young England Movement*. The British express-ion of social idealism in housing pre-dating public housing.

What sort of social conditions motivated the voluntary initiatives and then the government initiatives in public housing? Wohl [4] puts his finger on the key conditions which led to housing vexation and reform. Looking at London, where the vexation was greatest, its popu-lation increased from 1 million in 1801 to 4 million in 1881, and to 7 million by 1911. In a period of economic growth, average occupancy rates increased from 7.03 per dwelling in 1801 to 7.72 in 1851, and to 8.06 in 1896. The low-income sub-markets (in the slums) experienced very high crowding rates with 9 to 15 persons sharing in tenement rooms and small houses. Rents absorbed 40 per cent of labourers' wages in the worst cases and over 80 per cent of poor families paid more than 20 per cent of their incomes, mainly renting one or two rooms.

The relentless pressure of population growth and high rents were just the statistical aspects of London's slums. These problems and the realities of working-class living conditions had deeper social signifi-cance. Railway companies [5], city improvement trusts and commercial redevelopers were destroying low-income housing; Lord Shaftesbury observed of working-class families '.....their houses were pulled down over their heads'. [6] Although Shaftesbury persuaded Parliament to adopt a Standing Order requiring rehousing provisions in redevelopment planning, this was ignored until after 1885. Protests by the Somers Town Defence League and other tenant groups agitating against redevelopment were ineffective. Apart from the traumas of redevelop-ment, other realities of living conditions in working-class areas aroused the conscience and social action of the church, voluntary social workers and civic groups. It was the Secretary of the London Congregational Union, Andrew Mearns, and his cheap pamphlet *The Bitter Cry of Outcast London* (1883) [7] which had the most powerful impact from among pieces of popular journalism. Mearns' invective was turned graphically against 'rotten and reeking tenements' where 'entire courts are filled with thieves, prostitutes and liberated convicts'. Those courts had 'putrefying carcases of dead cats, or birds, or viler abominations', they were filled with 'poisonous and malodorous gases', and in the crowded tenements 'incest is common'. Thus touching social conscience and the emergent reforming elements in the 1880s, the housing question entered significantly into social and political processes.

The social and economic forces underlying housing problems in the cities were demographic growth, low incomes among the masses, periodic unemployment, the incursions of redevelopment, urban filth and

demoralising environments. As a housing question, it was a problem of
poverty, urban growth, bad housing standards and social development.
As we shall see, housing reforms were not always targeted effectively at
the basic issues, but they attempted to provide solutions to the questions of how to house the working class and whether *laissez faire*
markets could be relied on in housing. The course of housing reform
was protracted, with various impediments - *laissez faire* attitudes to
property, the slow development of a theory for the welfare state, and
difficulties in achieving administrative capacity - delaying the progress. With the advantage of hindsight we can specify the sort of
co-ordinated elements which could have formed good policy development.
Good policies would have encouraged economic growth, provided social
security against poverty, emphasised some public enterprise roles in
land acquisition, and created a financial framework to draw resources
into social housing. Some of these policies were more clearly perceived and administered in other countries, but Britain was taking the
first public policy initiatives in housing. Before reviewing the
legislative landmarks, it is appropriate to look at the mid-nineteenth
century initiatives in philanthropy and limited-profit model dwelling
companies.

Philanthropy and the limited-profit housing enterprise

Compared with voluntary social housing movements in Scandinavia and
West Germany, the British movement grew from Conservative idealism
rather than from Co-operative Socialism, trade union enterprise and
broadly-based people's movements (see Chapter 2). Also, unlike the
German 'homestead' companies or the Swedish 'public benefit' companies,
the British voluntarism in housing development has been largely outside
the mainstream of public policy in housing. (As we shall later see,
modern British policies have been aimed at giving more support for
voluntarism in housing.) In the period 1850-1890 the philanthropic
movement was *the* practical expression of British idealism in housing.
After British local and central governments became committed to public
housing in the period 1880-1919, the voluntary sector dwindled to
nothing, or took on a more restricted charitable role in areas of
specialised social need.

  Tarn [8] and Wohl [9] have written useful histories covering the role
and development of the philanthropic, limited-profit model dwelling
companies. These companies were particularly active in London, but
some had branches in the provincial cities and others operated locally
in rural areas. In the period 1850-1880, some twenty companies were
operating in London. The theoretical basis of these companies
combined a popular preference for voluntary rather than government
activity with Adam Smith's idea that public benefit comes essentially
from private enterprise. That is to say, philanthropy was supported
as a good cause but it was controlled and brought into relationship with
commercial common sense by offering a *limited* profit to shareholders or
benefactors. The movement thrived (sporadically) in its time and
depended for its success on four factors:-

1. Access to finance from benefactors and shareholders attracted to
    good causes.

2. Access to land made available by aristocrats who owned tracts in
    London and by the Metropolitan Board of Works, the housing authority

for London, 1855-1888.

3. Access to low-interest long-term loans (40 year loans at 4 per
    cent interest) from the Public Works Loans Commissioners and
    authorised by the *Labouring Classes Dwellings Acts*, 1866, 1867.

4. General public and political support which was provided whilst
    Conservative idealism held relevance, before the development
    of the theories of Social Democracy and a transformed Liberalism.

The model dwelling companies originated at the height of the agitation
for public health reforms.   Shaftesbury led the *Society for Improving
the Conditions of the Labouring Classes* (1844).   Other large societies
included: the *Metropolitan Association for Improving the Dwellings of
the Industrious Classes* (1841), the *Peabody Trust* (1862), and the
Improved Industrial Dwellings Company (1859).   These two latter
societies gave fresh impetus to the movement which had tended to slow
down during the 1850s. · The Peabody Trust was founded by George Peabody,
an American benefactor who was persuaded by Shaftesbury to direct his
welfare plans to housing.   Sir S. Waterlow, Lord Mayor of London in
1872, provided leadership to the Improved Dwellings Company.   The
companies aimed at building clean, comfortable homes within the
capacity of working classes to pay.   Their critics drew attention to
the fact that they rarely housed the really needy, but concentrated
their attention on those with regular employment in trades or in
better-paid labouring jobs.   Other criticisms were levelled at their
'unfair' competition with private enterprise, their inclination to build
tenements rather than cottages, and their emphasis upon standards, with
some saying the standards were too high and others saying they were too
low.

The movement declined as government activity increased.   Wohl [10]
attributes the failure of the movement to its appearance of failure in
the presence of growing pressures, its inadequate access to funds from
benefactors and its relatively low contribution to the housing stock.
(By 1914, the movement was housing about 100,000 families in London.)
Tarn concluded that the legislative reforms of the 1880s which led to
the development of public housing

> '..... made clear once and for all that the community as
> represented by its elected council and their paid professional
> experts were the most effective as well as the most efficient
> organisation to lay down and carry out a housing policy'. [11]

However, we shall argue that local governments' public housing was
not the only, or the best, policy option available to express social
idealism in housing.   The comparative policy developments in Sweden,
Norway, The Netherlands and West Germany indicate that housing can be
made more enterprising and given wider social expression than has been
evident in British public housing.   It is in continental Europe that
social idealism in housing has been more usefully brought into
relationship with competitive enterprise, the limited-profit idea and
well-designed financial instruments.   Although, the British voluntarism
in housing had the potential to achieve these relationships by careful
reform, this was not realised.   Instead, the British reforms took a
different course and some useful 'voluntary' administrative experience,
and the practice of rehabilitating older housing was lost for the best

152

part of a century, through the formative decades of the British welfare state.

Housing and the Welfare State: The Origins, 1850-1890 [12]

The public health reforms had left a legacy of administrative instruments to encourage the installation of arterial drainage and sewerage systems in urban areas, and to regulate some building standards. But there was still nothing to prevent landlords from letting unfit buildings.

In 1851, Lord Shaftesbury introduced two housing measures with wide-ranging aims into Parliament. Shaftesbury argued persuasively on the humanitarian, the economic and political aspects of housing reform. Drawing upon Chadwick's economic arguments for public health reforms, Shaftesbury explained that although better standard housing implied higher costs, these would be outweighed by the benefits from the lower losses of earnings from sickness. Then, referring to his personal experience in the model dwelling company movement, he elaborated on the healthy and comfortable standards which could be achieved at moderate rents in new and rehabilitated housing. Finally he drew attention to the widespread interest which was being shown by Europeans and Americans who had observed the exhibits of model dwelling companies at the Great Exhibition, 1851.

Explaining that the working class could be classified into 'migratory' and 'stationary' categories for their housing needs, Shaftesbury introduced one measure to deal with common lodging houses, and another to deal with normal family housing. Parliament passed the *The Common Lodging Houses Act*, 1851, and the *Labouring Classes Lodgings Act*, 1851. The first Act required local government to register common lodging houses, to provide inspection and to ensure a well-ordered management. More significantly from the policy development perspective, the second Act gave enabling powers to local government to buy, rent, build and rehabilitate housing. This Act proved premature; it became a dead letter with only Huddersfield showing a passing interest in its provisions. Housing in this idiom was beyond the imagination, the finances and the administrative capacity of local government. Also the measure was permissive, not obligatory. Meanwhile Parliament added to the cause of regulation and inspection by passing the *Nuisances Removals Act*, 1855.

Administrative problems had already begun to frustrate progress in public health reform, with local government jealous of its autonomy and resistant to central regulation and direction. [13]   These problems had been particularly acute in London where the parochial vestries were apathetic to urban and housing reforms, sometimes because the vestrymen and their political supporters made their livings as slum landlords or building contractors. [14]   The reform of local government in London grew into a significant political issue, with deep implications for housing policy development. The first steps in legislative reform were taken in 1855 under the provisions of the *Metropolitan Local Management Act*. This Act created the Metropolitan Board of Works which was comprised of representatives from the City of London and the vestries. The Board had public health and housing powers in London but, as we shall see, its subsequent housing powers were confused by further powers given to the vestries. All the endemic problems of the vestries - parochialism, **apathy** about reform, lack of accountability,

administrative incapacity - continued to retard progress with housing
reform until the London County Council was created in 1888.

Local governments had been generally apathetic to Shaftesbury's
Labouring Classes Lodgings Act, 1851, and it was thought that its
provisions could be made more effective if access to central government
finance was opened.   Accordingly, under the *Labouring Classes Dwellings
Act*, 1866, the Public Works Loans Commissioners were empowered to lend
for working-class housing.   Political opponents favouring *laissez faire*
alleged that this would create an undesirable 'socialism', but in the
event the Act was not used much.   However, the Improved Industrial
Dwellings Company and the Metropolitan Association for Improving the
Dwellings of the Industrious Classes took advantage of the 40-year loans
at 4 per cent interest, borrowing respectively £84,000 and £30,000 [15].
Funds were thus taken up where there was commitment to the housing cause
and experienced administrative capacity.   Local government lacked both,
at that time.

The next legislative initiative in housing reform was taken by T.
McCullogh Torrens, Member for Finsbury, an area with some of the worst
slum conditions in London.   Torrens was committed to housing as social
reform, and to the building societies movement;   he became chairman of
the Building Societies Association in 1869. [16]   In 1866, Torrens
introduced a Private Member's Bill designed to require local government
to enforce the improvement or demolition of unfit dwellings, and to get
more public finance into slum clearance and housing development.
Torrens' Bill was sent to a Select Committee which resisted its
'socialist' provisions, but the government eventually allowed a diluted
version to pass in 1868 as the *Artizans' and Labourers' Dwellings Act*.
The redevelopment proposals of the original 1866 Bill were dropped.
The Act provided that owners were responsible for maintaining dwellings
in *fit* condition, but that if they were negligent then local government
could act.   It could serve notice of intention on neglectful owners;
if they failed to improve or demolish the offending property, local
government could demolish it.   Thus the Act made some inroads into the
principle of *laissez faire* in housing, but it did not provide for very
effective administration.

First in London, the powers were given to the vestries, not the
Metropolitan Board of Works.   The Board had default powers but for
financial and political reasons it was loath to use them.   More
significantly, after 1875 the Board had slum clearance powers under the
Cross Act (see below) which provided for *area* clearance, not the Torrens'
principle which related to *individual* properties.   Thereafter the
London vestries were inclined to set action on housing aside, as a matter
for the Board with its *area* clearance powers.   For its part, the Board
simply thought that the vestries were acting opportunistically to get
out of their housing responsibilities and shift the costs and burdens to
the Board.   Between levels of government, the system was ill-designed.
Similar problems have arisen in London during modern times (see Chapter
9).

Second, the Act made no provision for compensation to owners of
demolished property.   Accordingly, local government was disinclined to
act because of the injustice in the consequences, and also because
closures and demolitions added to housing vexation when there were
already shortages of low-income housing.   Where the claims of justice

to landlords or tenants did not inhibit action, the vested interests of vestrymen and their supporters often did.   Shaftesbury had warned Parliament that these administrative dilemmas, and the failure to enact provisions for redevelopment (as a corollary of clearance), would make the measure somewhat ineffective.   In the event he was right, and in 1879 under the *Artizans' and Labourers' (Extension) Act* the 1868 Act was amended to provide for redevelopment and for compensation.   The Torrens Act had been little used, and housing reformers, the Charity Organisation Society (see Chapter 3) and the Royal College of Physicians agitated for more positive government action.

The Conservative Government, led by Disraeli, passed the *Artizans' Dwellings Act*, 1875 (the 'Cross Act', so-called after the Home Secretary, Richard Cross).   In contrast with the Torrens' Act, the Cross Act depended upon local government taking *initiatives* to purchase land and clear it.   Local government could redevelop the cleared sites only with the Home Secretary's approval, it being assumed that private enterprise and the model dwelling companies would readily take up the opportunities to redevelop.   In London, the powers under this new Act were given to the Metropolitan Board of Works, thus resulting in intergovernmental problems with the vestries in exercising powers under the Torrens and Cross Acts (see above).   Nevertheless, the Board and local governments in Birmingham, Wolverhampton, Liverpool, Norwich, Walsall, Swansea and Nottingham took initiatives under the Cross Act.   Liverpool and Glasgow were involved in clearance and redevelopment schemes under their own special Acts.   The response was significant in view of the complex administrative, financial and political problems involved in urban renewal.   Birmingham, Wolverhampton and Swansea complained of the burden on rates, resulting from net losses on clearance operations. In London the Metropolitan Board of Works soon ran into the complicated dilemmas of slum clearance, including net losses from clearing and selling land.

During the Parliamentary debates, some Members had cautioned Richard Cross of the likely problems in administration.   Members expressed doubts on: (1) whether local authorities would be able to sell the cleared land at reasonable prices, (2) whether the housing aims would conflict with the town improvement purposes of renewal, (3) whether the renewal projects could succeed without subsidies from central government and (4) whether the proposal had sufficient inducement for local government.   Again, Shaftesbury argued that the rehabilitation approach would be cheaper, more effective, and with greater flexibility for gradualism compared with the administratively awkward, expensive and traumatic clearance and redevelopment approach.   His advice was not heeded, and in administration the clearance and redevelopment approach became dominant, though riddled with difficulties.

At the time, each problem was perceived and acted on in an *ad hoc* way with no overall comprehension of the economics of housing and urbanisation.   The net losses on the sale of land were attributed to over-generous compensation provisions, whereas in reality the slums were highly profitable and it was uneconomic to improve them by mass destruction and 'pure' residential redevelopment.   The economics of housing improvement could be made feasible by Octavia Hill's methods (i.e., rehabilitation and good management) or by mixing housing improvement with commercial redevelopment.

155

Joseph Chamberlain successfully used a mixed commercial redevelopment and rehabilitation approach in Birmingham, but he ran into administrative resistance at the central Local Government Board and had to go outside the Cross Act to achieve his intentions. In London, the Metropolitan Board of Works advocated the use of mixed housing and commercial redevelopment, together with a relaxation of the rehousing requirements in the Cross Acts. Rehousing is particularly difficult to administer in clearance and redevelopment schemes because dislocation is inevitable and the higher rents of the redeveloped housing put them outside the economic range of the original residents. Finally, clearance and redevelopment usually involves liaison with a range of landlords, shopkeepers and so on to administer expropriation orders, compensation and (sometimes) relocation. The task is especially difficult if the compensation provisions are loose, unrealistic and unworkable, as they were under the 1875 Act. Compensation in that Act included estimates for future increases in the value of land and property, not just current market value. Under the *Artizans' and Labourers' Dwellings Amendment Act*, 1879, compensation was tied to market value. However, most of the administrative and economic dilemmas remained because bad housing was economically valuable housing, and the general economic conditions of the time accentuated housing stress.

As housing stress heightened, the agitation from housing reformers intensified and politicians were dragged deeper into the dilemmas. The stress came from the incessant population growth in London and the larger cities, and from the long recession that began in 1874. It was this recession which pressed hard on working-class poverty and which removed the incentive for new construction in rental housing, because more crowding left more vacancies, which undermined the profitability of new building. Once the recession disappeared, new construction became profitable and suburbanisation processes began to uncrowd London's inner-urban areas. [17] Working-class housing problems remained, but they can be *partly* regarded as historical legacies. It is important to recognise that housing problems perpetuate themselves historically in more ways than most other social problems do. Given the circumstances of the long recession and the continued growth of urban populations, it is not surprising that the 1880s was the decade when housing agitation, general policy review and stronger legislation were concentrated. These were also the years when Charles Booth was active in his poverty surveys; when the Charity Organisation Society and the idealists in the Settlement Movement were most active; and when the Fabians, the Radicals, and various Socialist factions groped towards a theoretical basis for the welfare state. All of this was significant for the course of housing policy development. Meanwhile local governments in London, Liverpool and Glasgow were face to face with the pragmatic urgencies of some problems in administering clearance and redevelopment. The experience in Glasgow indicates how housing became more deeply a government activity.

Glasgow Corporation began its housing interventions by creating a sanitary inspectorate and suppressing overcrowding. [18] In 1866, the Corporation initiated a slum clearance project in a specific tract of inner-urban land, a City Improvement Trust being created to administer the project. The Trust could clear only as far as private enterprise was prepared to develop, but as the economic recession deepened it experienced difficulty in selling cleared land for redevelopment. This land, with its capital holding charges, was a financial burden on local rates, and this led the Corporation to review Liverpool's use of its local government to redevelop cleared sites in 1869 when it ran into similar difficulties. Thus, the Corporation gave the Trust power to build housing under the *Glasgow Improvement Trust Amendment Act*, 1880. Similar circumstances in London, led the Metropolitan Board of Works to 'write down' the value of land and sell it to the Peabody Trust at a price which made it feasible to build and rent its housing at its standard rents. Thus Liverpool, Glasgow and London were drawn beyond mere clearance to involve themselves with the building of social housing. Lord Shaftesbury had been right in his judgement, and in his general advice on the superiority of rehabilitation and the gradualist approach to urban renewal. He died in 1885, and the nation which had neglected his advice in his lifetime continued to neglect it for eighty years more.

Under public pressure, Gladstone's Liberal Government accepted the need for a general review of the housing question. First it created a Select Committee of Parliament in 1881-82 to review the performance of the Torrens and Cross Acts. Journalists, housing reformers and politicians from all Parties gave more attention to housing and the slums with the result that a Royal Commission was appointed in 1884 with wider terms of reference. All of this stimulated eminent political figures such as the Tory, Lord Salisbury, the Radical, Joseph Chamberlain, and the leading intellectual economist, Alfred Marshall, to write articles on housing. From 1881 to 1885, a spate of ideas and some extensive documentation of practices in housing were offered to the policy-makers. It was a critical moment of choice for British housing policy. [19]

The official enquiries by the Parliamentary Select Committee and the Royal Commission predictably found a series of administrative and economic problems in the existing housing legislation. Redevelopment was uneconomic. Compensation was complicated and difficult to relate to clear principles of justice in the legal or the moral sense. In London, the Metropolitan Board of Works and the vestries had conflicting incoherent policies, and some vestries were apathetic and filled with vested interests ranged against housing reform. Clearance and redevelopment was administratively awkward, it was uncertain and it resulted in protracted delays. Financial constraints held back slum clearance among the few local governing authorities which had shown some enthusiasm. Treasury was insisting upon high interest rates on housing loans whereas local government thought Parliament had intended lower rates. The Local Government Board which supervised local government plans and made recommendations on whether schemes could proceed had behaved with bureaucratic rigidity. Despite all these problems, by 1885 the Metropolitan Board of Works had proceeded with 14 projects under the Cross Acts (1875, 1879). But for the laggard performance of the rest of the nation the Royal Commission blamed failures in administration rather than legislation. In that context it recommended in favour of consolidating housing legislation and hoped that administrative performance would improve as housing came to have social and political significance.

The legislative results of the two enquiries were: (1) the *Artizans' Dwellings Act*, 1882, and (2) the *Housing of the Working Classes Act*, 1885. The 1882 Act was mainly designed to ease the administrative problems of the Metropolitan Board of Works by relaxing the rehousing requirements under the Cross Act (1875), and giving it more flexibility in opening up the courts and alleys in London's slumlands. Lord Salisbury presented the 1885 Bill as 'bi-partisan' and embodying the recommendations from the Royal Commission which contained a wide-ranging representation from the church, politicians from various Parties who had commitments to the housing cause and other eminent persons. The 1885 Act was a measure consolidating the principles of enactments in the period 1851-1882. That is to say, local government could regulate and condemn unfit housing, it could draw up clearance and redevelopment proposals, it could become involved in the construction of working-class housing, and it could administer building regulations. As such, the Act did very little that was new, and it did not really offer any useful policy initiatives. It was not based upon any very consistent social or economic principles. There were plenty of ideas available (see below), but the policy-makers of those years failed to choose their ideas well, or use them inventively.

Some useful experience was available. First, the model dwelling companies had some forty years experience in redevelopment, rehabilitation and administering the limited-profit idea. Given access to land and finance within a general policy framework, they could have expanded their scale of operation. Then in the fullness of time the movement could well have been transformed into something more democratic and representative, transcending its origins in aristocratic philanthropy and Ricardian economics. The movement had commitment and enterprise and it did *not* have a working-class housing monopoly - all of this was good. As we saw in Chapter 2, Powell and Shipton in the London trade union movement had a favourable attitude to some of the housing built by model dwelling companies, and Powell in particular did not see any progress coming from public housing. Sir S. Waterlow, chairman of the Improved Industrial Dwellings Company, favoured a pluralistic approach with emphasis upon developing housing management, building a variety of dwelling types, getting some working-class housing suburbanised, and drawing upon government assistance in acquiring land.

Octavia Hill also gave evidence to the enquiries. She outlined the housing management and rehabilitation aspects of her experience in London's slumland since 1865, and she recommended the key elements of a working-class housing programme:

1. Using housing visitors as social and housing management mediators between tenants and the managing body.

2. Adopting a view of housing management which looks upon house visiting as a way of achieving useful social development and care of the property, not just as rent collection.

3. Making housing accessible to the working classes without restricting eligibilities by means tests.

4. Synthesising and balancing principles of social work, the economic aspects of housing, and good care of the home.

Like the experience of the model dwelling companies, all of this was useful and creative. However, it did need to be harnessed to government roles in finance and access to land, and Octavia Hill was disinclined to accept government roles. She was wrong about that, but (mainly) right about housing management and rehabilitation. In his evidence to the Parliamentary Select Committee, Lord Shaftesbury presented careful arguments and statistics showing the economic superiority of rehabilitation. He also favoured more government support for the limited-profit idea in housing.

If public policy had turned in that direction and made finance and cheap land accessible to the voluntary housing movement, the co-operative movement might have flourished. The best social performers of the day were recommending that course, and so were some leaders of the relevant institutions. Sir Thomas Bassey was urging the Co-operative Wholesale Society to harness building society finance to non-profit working-class housing. In evidence before the Parliamentary Select Committee Benjamin Jones, the general manager of the Society, set out a proposal embracing co-ownership and the mixing of government and private loan finance. Co-ownership would have given participants a share in the equity value of the housing they occupied and security of tenure. On finance, Jones suggested that private borrowing contribute 20 per cent of a total loan, for 22 years at 4 per cent interest. The government should then contribute 80 per cent at 3.5 per cent. The general principle was to link people and resources. This mixture of private and public finance and its linkage with co-ownership, would fit the realities of modern democratic societies admirably. Housing policies in continental Europe have since been developed on the lines recommended by Jones, and they have produced less sectoral rigidity than British policies. Jones had good and feasible ideas. There were also practical exemplars. Since 1869 the Oddfellows Co-operative Building and Investment Company had been making home ownership access-ible to artisans and better-paid labourers. On some 10 per cent deposit, members could buy cottages for about £250. Artisans' wages at that time were about £1.25 weekly, and thus access to home ownership required heroic efforts in saving.

Britain's leading intellectual economist of that period, Alfred Marshall, set out a more general solution to housing stress in rapidly-growing cities. He correctly saw that the key causes of trouble were the pressures from demographic growth, high rents and low wages. Places such as London attracted population growth because industry provided jobs there, and it obtained some economies of agglomeration in big cities. However, this meant that commercial forces were sometimes in conflict with the use of land for housing, and this added to the high cost of inner-urban land. Marshall pointed out that the housing vexation could be relieved by creating new towns which could be built to attract the sort of industry that did not need heavy fixed capital. These new towns could be made accessible to their larger 'parent' towns by planning them in conjunction with the development of railways. Marshall believed the public stimulation of the new towns idea would harmonise public and private interests. From 1898 his ideas were taken up and elaborated by Ebenezer Howard, one of the founders of the twentieth-century town planning movement.

M.G. Mulhall, an economist specialising in finance and investment, suggested that the relief of housing vexation depended upon creating the right sort of financial and administrative framework. Housing needed access to savings, and he proposed that the funds from the Post Office Savings Bank could be allocated to housing. Next, housing needed access to land, and for this Mulhall proposed the creation of statutory development trusts to acquire land, construct housing, and manage property. Thus the Savings Bank funds would be allocated to a Trust Committee which, in its turn, would sponsor development trusts to construct and manage housing. The process could create its own subsidies from commercial leaseholds and it could draw upon some revenue from taxes to keep rents low. This proposal contains the various elements which characterise modern statutory development corporations, new town development corporations and non-profit housing enterprises in continental Europe. Again, we can see that the idea had a useful and creative future, but it did not influence the immediate development of housing policies in Britain.

In Parliament, contrasting ideas came from the Tory, Lord Salisbury, and the Radical, Joseph Chamberlain, a year or two before they joined forces to produce the Unionist alliance. Lord Salisbury argued that housing vexation was caused by the high cost of land and housing, and that philanthropy was insufficient. He advocated a mixed public-private finance solution in the form of loans to model dwelling companies. Also, Salisbury was attracted to various aspects of Marshall's and Mulhall's solutions - the use of the Post Office Savings Bank Funds, and the co-ordinated suburbanisation of industry and housing. Other elements in Salisbury's pluralism included the wider application of Octavia Hill's methods and a wariness against possible inefficient and bureaucratic tendencies in local governments' public housing activities. In contrast, Joseph Chamberlain was opposed to using public finance via private limited-profit enterprise, because he thought local government was more politically accountable than non-representative bodies. Chamberlain also favoured a betterment tax on land so that local government could recoup the costs of improvements from its urban renewal activities - those improvements adding to values in private enterprise and justifying the betterment tax. Finally, Chamberlain could claim a relatively successful practising experience in Birmingham where redevelopment had been mixed with rehabilitation and some of the more sticky economic and administrative problems of urban renewal had been carefully avoided.

In some respects the contrasts between Chamberlain and Salisbury can be viewed as enduring forces in British politics. The Labour Party eventually inherited the Radical tradition. It was committed to Fabian collectivism and its political spokesmen have tended to favour public housing rather than subsidies to private enterprise (non-profit or otherwise) for precisely the same reasons as Chamberlain. Even in modern times with some moderated attitude to the voluntary housing sector, the British Left still favours the pursuit of social goals in housing through local governments' public housing. The Conservatives have inherited the Shaftesbury and Salisbury sense of housing as the home, a place for family and personal aspirations. Their inclinations lead them to give vocal support to the non-profit voluntary sector, but they have not matched their ideals with effective and durable economic and administrative institutions. The problem is that they do not take their ideals of home and family welfare seriously enough, because they favour private full-profit capital in industrial and commercial enterprise. In other words, they do not give their idealism in housing a practical chance, as Shaftesbury tried to do. By default, it was therefore Fabian collectivism which gave its imprint to British housing policy at its most crucial stage of historical evolution. That Fabian collectivism itself took shape in the social ferment of ideas, agitation and reaction to working-class living conditions in the 1880s, and it was first practised by local governments in London and some provincial cities.

The *Local Government Act*, 1888, gave London a democratically and directly elected metropolitan local government, replacing the indirectly elected Metropolitan Board of Works. Fabian theories and programmes began to have a powerful influence in the London County Council (LCC), ensuring progress with public housing and municipal socialism. Although the LCC inherited some strong housing powers from the Board of Works, it wanted a more clear-cut and definite housing authority in London. It made representations to the Government and its wishes were met in the provisions of the *Housing of Working Classes Act*, 1890. Thus in London and in the larger provincial cities the course was set for expanding local governments' public housing. The working class had voting power, local government had housing powers, the Fabians provided a social and economic theory which articulated a case for the welfare state, and their intellectual leaders in London and the leaders of the artisans in the northern industrial towns were committed to public housing. Furthermore, unlike subsequent experience in Scandinavia and Germany, the British expression of Social Democracy did not have broadly-based people's movements or trade union industrial enterprise to blend with collectivism. Social Democratic collectivism in British housing meant that the idealism would be conceived and administered as public housing. And public housing would have to be nourished and protected from its political opponents. From the comparative viewpoint, the results have not been good and other countries have found better ways of expressing Social Democratic idealism in housing.

There were alternatives available in the 1880s. Britain might have selected rehabilitation and housing management along the lines used by Octavia Hill, but it neglected these in favour of clearance, redevelopment and new 'standard' housing. It might have created a mixed public-private financial framework and harnessed it to limited-profit competitive enterprise and to a variety of developers, but philanthropy had been interpreted as inadequate and reforming Radicals and Fabians scorned it as aristocratic and capitalist. Finally, Britain might have used public enterprise to purchase land for urban development generally and to control its freehold and leasehold development. Instead, local government became more concerned to get land for its own public housing, and later to regulate the standards of suburban sub-division. With hindsight it can be said that until the new town initiatives of the 1940s, there was too much bureaucratic enterprise in housing, and not enough in urban land. Most of the creative and useful ideas originated in Britain at the time when housing stress was at its most intense, but other countries were more adept at institutionalising those ideas. Part of the problem arose from the nature of British society and its political institutions, of which more will be said later. But the chief misfortune lay in pioneering the main lines of policy in a hurry under stress, before the development of any very experienced or sophisticated theory of the welfare state.

Housing and the welfare state : the question of subsidies and effective impacts, 1891-1919

The *Housing and Town Planning Act*, 1919, marks the beginning in Britain of the national public housing programme financed by the national government.   This Act followed a period of sporadic public and parliamentary discussions, lasting from 1906, with questions of subsidisation and central-local administrative relationships emerging as the key issues. [20]   Although the question of finance was critical, other factors gave impetus to the more extensive government involvements in housing.   There was a general feeling that private enterprise could not supply sufficient working-class housing.   Housing reformers wanted to make a permanent and decisive improvement in housing standards.   The First World War added some urgent problems and housing shortages.   The war also taught government a great deal about its capacity to ration scarce resources, direct the use of scarce materials, and generally influence the direction of economic development.   The movement for housing reform was well under way before 1914, but the war stimulated general ideas of post-war reconstruction, with housing as a main area of action.

The date was unfortunate, because of the state of opinion on two critical issues.   First, it will be recalled that the theory of environmental determinism and the revulsions against the slums had made the improvement of *housing standards* a significant policy issue.   A complex variety of ideological, technical and administrative factors had taken the ruling ideas of acceptable standards some way beyond rational notions of minimum or 'reasonable' levels of sufficiency.   By 1919 popular opinion, backed up by architects, town planners and sanitary engineers, tended to the view that adequate standards could be achieved only in new construction.   Although, as we shall presently see, the work of Octavia Hill had not been completely forgotten, the rehabilitation methods were widely denigrated as 'slum patching'.   This meant that housing policy development was moving away from economically and socially useful methods of dealing with working-class and low-income housing problems.

A second, and related, misconception concerned the housing role of the private sector.   As was mentioned earlier, housing is best viewed as a set of differentiated sub-markets.   Population pressures can lift the value of old slum housing above the cost of new construction, and act as an inducement to investment in working-class rental housing.   This was the situation before the 1880s when even the building society movement (which primarily served home ownership needs) directed some of its investments into working-class rental housing. [21]   However, with the onset of the long depression, 1874-1894, investment in working-class rental housing was undermined by vacant housing and the depressed economy.   Furthermore, some building societies had over-reached themselves and collapsed, resulting in a general loss of confidence in them and a lower capacity to provide for middle-income home ownership.   As the recession passed, the housing industry revived and was able to increase new construction in the 1900s. [22]   But by then circumstances had changed.   Parts of inner London were uncrowding and losing population, whilst the suburbs were gaining new households.   The private sector was creating suburbia, and this was feasible as trams and railways lowered the time-distance costs of travel in relation to incomes.

Once these processes are understood it becomes clear why those who
were concerned with housing reform did not expect much private investment in new housing for the masses.   The new private housing was going
to young households, usually better-paid workers and the middle classes.
Although these processes might segregate age groups and classes, they
promised to reduce the housing shortages quite effectively.   The
process was beginning in the 1900s with suburbanisation of the middle
classes and some of the working classes.   By 1910, about 10 per cent of
the housing stock was owner-occupied, and this sector was poised for
growth.   With imagination, public policy might have been directed to a
steady extension of the suburban and home-ownership opportunities to
more and more of the working classes.   That direction promised the
least class distinction and sectoral divisiveness.   But as we have seen,
the idea of mixing public and private finance and introducing new
tenures (e.g., co-operative co-ownership) was set aside in favour of
public housing.   During the discussions on post-War reconstruction, the
Building Societies Association revived the idea of mixing public-private
finance, but the Government was committed to public housing.   A better
policy package would have included rehabilitation for working classes in
inner-urban areas and mixed public-private financing for long-term
community (i.e., not 'welfare') housing.   These options were not taken
up, and the history of policy development, below, shows why public
housing dominated.

The early history of public housing in London sheds some light on
issues which persist continuously in British housing history.   As we
saw the London County Council (LCC) took over the housing responsibilities of the Metropolitan Board of Works in 1888, and was successful in
persuading the Government to enlarge these powers in 1890. [23]
Initially, the LCC followed the slum clearance policies of the Board,
but with more vigour.   Although the LCC experienced the sort of
problems which bedevilled the Board in its clearance activities, - the
high cost of land, the rehousing requirements, and the administrative
awkwardness of the process - it had fewer site disposal problems, because it used the sites to build public housing.   Nevertheless, the LCC
felt the economic strains of slum clearance and it sought a liberalisa-
tion of loan conditions by the Treasury.   The Treasury was providing
60-year loans at 2.5 per cent, whereas the LCC wanted the terms altered
to 100 years.   Slum clearance was subsidised from the rates.   The LCC
had rejected the cheaper rehabilitation idea in 1889.

During the 1890s the LCC was concerned that private enterprise was
retreating from building new working-class housing, and that the only
model dwelling company which was active in the slum areas was the East
End Dwelling Company.   Other model dwelling companies had found the
problem of acquiring inner-urban land at affordable costs beyond them.
Moreover the LCC now controlled housing policy in London and it was
imposing higher standards on the East End Dwelling Company, with the
result that the Company's planned projects became uneconomic.   This
meant that the LCC was moving towards a monopoly position in social
housing.   Some of the advantages from competition and enterprise would
be lost as the monopoly deepened.   Also public housing would take its
key characteristics from the constraints of the statutes and the partly
'hidden' policies of the central supervisory body, the Local Government
Board.   In fact, the Local Government Board inherited strongly sanitary

163

rather than social concerns, and it tended to perceive housing standards in strictly physical terms. The LCC and other local governments had to comply with its bureaucratic prescriptions in order to get approval for their projects.

After 1897, the LCC widened its housing activities. First, it began to build suburban rental estates. Eventually, local council housing estates in the suburbs became the dominant form of British public housing. In later history, after the 1930s, they became the object of critical attention by sociologists and social workers for their lack of community and for their working-class homogeneity. These results, of course, reflect the divisiveness and rigid sectoral characteristics of legislative, financial and administrative instruments. However, in the early years of public housing, the involvement with suburban build- ing was regarded as progressive and enterprising. Second, the LCC took up an interest in house sales when the *Small Dwellings (Acquisition) Act* was passed in 1899. This Act empowered local governments to lend 80 per cent of the value of new housing at 4 per cent interest. But the LCC decided this was insufficiently attractive, and instead used Part III of the 1890 *Housing of Working Classes Act*, enabling it to advance 99 per cent of the value of housing. In the event, the *Small Dwellings (Acquisition) Act* did not attract much use, with only some 99 loans being made in Britain in the first two years. Unlike Australia (see the subsequent discussions in this chapter), working-class home ownership was not strong in Britain during this period.

From 1906, rural as well as urban housing problems were troubling policy-makers. The rural problem was that the low wages of agricultural labourers made it impossible for rural local governments to build new public housing within the customers' capacity to pay. This opened the questions of central government subsidies and ways of getting more action from central and local government housing administration. These issues motivated a Private Member's Bill in 1906, the *Housing of the Working Classes Amendment Bill*. However, the Liberal Government resisted the idea of subsidies from public expenditure.

Nationally, argument continued, and the next major initiative came with the *Housing, Town Planning, etc. Act*, of 1909. This Act reflected the influence of the emerging town planning movement and the anxiety that new suburban development might repeat the problems of older slums if inadequately regulated. Accordingly the Act provided for town councils to regulate and plan for new suburban development. However, much of the debating in Parliament centred on problems of rural working-class housing, financing new public housing, and administrative sluggishness in central and local government. The social responsibili- ties had recently been extended to education, children's medical services, and school meals. Local government argued that with its increasing burdens, it could not afford to provide revenue subsidies to working-class housing. Central government was reluctant to finance activity which it could not directly control. As we shall see, there were no easy solutions to these dilemmas.

The impetus for reform grew. During 1912-13, private members introduced Bills aimed at bringing central subsidies into public housing and at overcoming the sluggishness of the Local Government Board. In 1912 Lloyd George created a *Land Enquiry Committee* and this found in favour of: getting more action from the Local Government Board, dealing with the rural housing problem, raising the standards of urban working-class housing, and making local government housing provisions obligatory, not permissive. Then in 1913 the Conservative Party published its panphlet, *The History of Housing Reform*, which advocated more action in housing and the application of state subsidies. Positive reform was imminent, especially when the ruling Liberal Party became committed in 1914. The War years, 1914-1918, were used to plan for post-War reconstruction and the administration of central subsidies. The major assumptions and perceptions of the housing problem had already been drawn before the two major committees dealing with policy development reported. These assumptions were that: (1) housing standards needed to be raised and, (2) private enterprise could not meet working-class housing needs. The die was cast.

The key committees were the Tudor Walters Committee [24] and the Unhealthy Areas Committee. [25] (Other committees dealt with the technical and administrative problems of procuring materials, and supervising building and contracts.) The Tudor Walters Committee was sceptical of rehabilitation and it favoured raising standards by newly constructed housing built to 60-year standards which emphasised health, beauty and convenience. Although the Committee's terms of reference precluded it from considering financial matters, it put that fact on record and suggested that state financial assistance would be necessary in post-War housing policy. On administration, the Committee recommended that the Local Government Board be given a specialist housing department and that it set up regional offices to assist local governments with consultation on surveys, plans and housing management. All of this would be urgently needed in view of wartime disruptions to building and the estimated shortage of 500,000 dwellings. These aspects of the Committee's Report influenced subsequent policy development, but other recommendations were ignored.

Perhaps the most crucial recommendations which were ignored at local policy levels were those on the role of the private sector and on land development. The Tudor Walters Committee emphasised the need to use private enterprise and the voluntary housing movement as well as public housing in the post-War period. It believed that private enterprise would perform adequately if a definite ten-year programme was established. However, the Committee missed two key points. One was that rent controls had been established in 1915 (see the discussions below), and this was inconsistent with long-term private enterprise roles in rental housing. The second omission was that private enterprise roles in rental housing might be induced under a mixed public-private financial framework, with provisions for access by a range of developers. On the land question, the Committee suggested further discussion of the possibilities for local government in acquiring, developing and disposing of land for *general* urban purposes, not just for its own public housing. The Committee should have been more definite and emphatic on the point, especially as the Swedes had already demonstrated the effectiveness of such policies.

The Unhealthy Areas Committee was set up to enquire into slum clearance, redevelopment and rehabilitation, but it did not report until 1921, after the key legislative initiative had been taken in 1919. This time lag reduced the policy impact of the Report. Nevertheless, the Report is significant for its good sense and for the future parliamentary role of Neville Chamberlain, the chairman of the Committee, who became an advocate of rehabilitation. The Committee correctly saw that London's housing problems could not be solved within the LCC's boundaries, but required urban decentralisation. Also, the Committee pointed out the conflicts between relying upon new standard housing as a solution to working-class housing problems and the consequent rental and journey-to-work costs. Arguing that older urban areas have important social values to some working-class families, the Committee stated that:

> '...there is much to be said for the view of the late Miss Octavia Hill that old houses carefully repaired and kept under proper supervision provide as good homes for working-class families as new houses, the rent of which is necessarily so much higher.' [26]

Furthermore, the Committee favoured the purchase of older housing by local government to make the Octavia Hill methods feasible and administratively effective. This policy potential was largely ignored until the mid-1960s, except for sporadic local examples among the voluntary housing sector.

Meanwhile public policy in housing and the introduction of subsidies from central government took their course from the *Housing and Town Planning Act*, 1919. This Act placed a duty on local governments to prepare housing surveys and to ensure adequate housing was built in their areas. It was intended that a seven-year housing drive by government could eliminate shortages, after which private enterprise might be adequate. In the preparatory negotiations with local governments, they were offered central government subsidies of 25 per cent of their net losses. Local government sought a more definite planning criterion and greater inducement. Thus, central government agreed to meet subsidy payments in excess of the product of 0.5 P rate (i.e., amounts above the local revenue obtainable from local rates at the level of 0.5 P rate). This design was criticised because it was open-ended and did not give any incentive for local governments to be economical; in other words public expenditure could not be adequately controlled. Some sections of the Act gave powers for land acquisition, rehabilitation and for the involvement of the voluntary housing movement in social housing. However, none of these provisions was administered to its full potential.

In Parliament, the supporters of housing reform waxed enthusiastic on the commitment to high housing standards, to beauty and economy, and to liberating women from household drudgery and from conditions not conducive to family life. Also, they expected prices to decrease after four years, once the legacy of wartime shortages of materials and high rates of inflation had been overcome. Other parliamentarians were more cautious, warning of bureaucratic sluggishness in public administration, segregation, and the economic necessity to control public expenditure. In short, the great expectations might be cut down in the course of future economic and administrative realities. As we shall presently see, both the enthusiasts and the doubters had some measure of right in the light of subsequent performance. The British public housing programme grew and provided relatively good accommodation for those working-class families that occupied this housing. However, the programme was knocked about by periodic economic restraints, access to it was limited by waiting lists whilst many continued to live in deteriorating older private-rental housing, and it accentuated segregation. Politicians and administrators learned in the fullness of time that it was not possible to do all things at once - to bring in higher standards, to deal with the nineteenth-century legacies of slums, and to get harmony and effectiveness in central-local intergovernmental relations.

Finally in this section, it is appropriate to look briefly and critically at housing policy within the overall development of social and urban policies. From the discussions in Chapter 3 it will be recalled that despite the recognised need for co-ordination in housing, urban and social policies, each had taken separate theoretical and administrative directions during the nineteenth century. Housing and urban policies had adopted some absurdities from theories of environmental determinism, and the New Poor Law (1834) had been based upon some inadequate economic reasoning which 'justified' workhouses as a test of 'less eligibility'. In the period 1890-1919, theoretical and administrative changes occurred in housing, urban and social policies.

Housing took a public housing course, and this sometimes conflicted with urban policy development, as represented in British town planning practice. Town planning in Britain (under the 1909 *Housing, Town Planning, etc. Act*) took a less fertile *regulatory* option rather than the more enterprising and investment-based alternative. That is to say, unlike Sweden, Britain perceived town planning as simply a matter of regulating private developers, whereas an investment-based alternative would have emphasised the acquisition of land, and its development by various enterprises under controlled freeholds and leaseholds (see the discussions in Chapter 7). This meant that housing and town planning were in conflict, with social housing policies moving from regulatory control towards development, and town planning adopting a regulatory thrust.

Following the poverty surveys by Booth and Rowntree, and with the beginnings of the welfare state, the old workhouse system of relieving poverty had out-lived its relevance. The government appointed a Royal Commission to review the old system. [27] The Royal Commission reported in 1909, and the Liberal Government had already taken some initiatives by establishing pensions for the aged in 1908. This Royal Commission had several links with housing-related developments. Its membership included C.S. Loch, Secretary of the Charity Organisation Society, W. Smart, Adam Smith Professor of Political Economy at Glasgow University, Octavia Hill and Beatrice Webb, the Fabian. [28] All of these had contributed to housing, and as a group they had experience in pioneering new practices, developing theoretical and intellectual interpretations, and engaging in social action. However, in the Poor Law reports, housing-related matters entered only peripherally and implicitly. All the commissioners favoured cottage housing for the aged rather than the workhouse. The more progressive Minority Report whose chief advocate was Beatrice Webb recommended the complete abolition of the workhouse system and argued in favour of the home as the right place for family living and the welfare of women and children.

The effects on housing were long term and indirect. They can be seen in the development of social security and income maintenance programmes, and in the recognition that the state has a role in maintaining high

167

levels of employment. It is easier to design and administer a housing
policy in a context of economic growth, high employment and a well-
developed system of social security. These indirect, but very real,
supports reduce financial risks and leave fewer administrative and
allocational problems in operating low-income housing management. As
was mentioned in Chapter 3, the significance of co-ordination in policies,
and particularly in the social aspects of housing, grows rather than
diminishes in modern times. It is appropriate to show the general
historical relationships among housing, urban and social policies.

THE PERIOD 1920-1945

The development of public housing, and dilemmas with subsidies

British public housing has taken its characteristics from its origins
as a *working-class* housing policy, as a means of expressing
egalitarianism, as a reaction to the slums and as a welfare state right.
Public housing in Australia and the United States expressed different
aspirations and intentions. In Australia, public housing is only part
of working-class housing with other parts in separate home ownership
policies. In the United States, public housing has developed as
housing for the poor, not generally for the working classes. Other
countries have found alternative ways of adapting housing policy to
welfare aims, without relying on public housing. It was the *Housing
and Town Planning Act*, 1919, which set the general directions of British
housing policy for a generation or more. This section will be concerned with the consequent economic, administrative and political
dilemmas of British public housing, and with its history to 1945; it
will rely gratefully on work by others, and especially by Bowley, [29]
who has given a really good account of the economic and administrative
dilemmas with subsidised public housing.

In the period under review, the forms of subsidy which central
government used were: (1) specified local government contributions with
the remainder provided by central government, 1919-1923; (2) specified
per dwelling subsidies by central government; and (3) special subsidies
for slum clearance policies after 1930. As noted above the first
initiative by central government, 1919-1923, provided open-ended subsidies with consequent problems in controlling public expenditure. To
correct this defect, new arrangements in 1923 tried to get local
government to share the costs of subsidy on a 50/50 basis. Central
government soon found that the detailed checking of minutiae was a
strain upon administrative resources. Accordingly, a system was
devised whereby the cost-rent was estimated for a hypothetical house,
this was compared with the probable rent and then the central government
set a per unit subsidy (e.g., £6 per dwelling for 20 years) which
covered a proportion of the deficit. Local government was expected to
meet the remainder of the deficit and this was seen as a way of inducing
local economical control, as well as sharing the burden fairly. Loan
finance was obtained on the money and mortgage market, or from public
works loans, depending on policy at the time.

The deeper economic dilemmas of subsidies had more wide-ranging
consequences than in central-local financial relations. These deeper
dilemmas and their consequences arose from the confusion of objectives
among subsidies, rents and costs. Rents of particular houses reflected

the economic conditions at the time they were built - the prevailing
subsidy arrangements, rates of interest, construction costs and so on.
Through time, inflation raised construction costs, and in the economic
depression of the 1930s these and other costs fell.   In the absence of
any general rent policy, public housing tended to be rented out on the
basis of the prevailing historical cost.   However, public housing was
a scarce resource and its allocation was restricted to those families
which met locally administered eligibility conditions.   All of this led
to vertical and horizontal inequity in housing.   That is to say,
relatively low-income groups were living in higher rent housing, and
families in the same income group paid different rents according to
whether they chanced to live in older or new public housing, private
rental housing under rent control provisions or otherwise, and so on.
In the absence of a general housing allowance expressing a common
principle of equity, it was not easy to relate housing costs
progressively to income and needs.   Meanwhile equity considerations
were often contradicted by the need to relate rents to costs.   As
Bowley pointed out, in the 1919-1944 period, policy-makers confused
their objectives and they failed to appreciate the need to work out a
consistent policy relating subsidies to rental policies and costs.   In
fact, generally in that period, the approach to rental policies was *ad
hoc*, unsystematic and inconsistent.   The problems were accentuated by
the enduring rent controls on pre-1914 private housing, first introduced
under the *Rent Control and Mortgage Interest (War Restrictions) Act*,
1915, which froze rents at their pre-War levels.

    The lack of a systematic rental policy had some crucial long-term
consequences.   British housing was separated into three broad sectors:
The owner-occupied, the public rental and the private rental sectors.
The owner-occupied sector grew during this period, the private rental
sector declined and public housing grew.   Cleary [30] shows that the
owner-occupied sector was well supported by the building societies
movement whose advances in mortgages grew from £22.7 million in 1922 to
£140.3 million in 1936.   Several factors accounted for this growth.
First, for some middle-income groups, the period was one of rising
incomes and a shortage of good private rental housing.   Accordingly they
were attracted to home ownership which offered greater security and a
useful investment in an uncertain world.   Second, the building
societies had generally liberalised their loan terms, and in the mid-
1930s a 90 per cent loan on house value was typical.   Also, interest
rates declined after 1924.   Thus, owner-occupied tenure grew from about
10 to 15 per cent of the total stock in 1920 to 31 per cent by 1950.
Some of this growth also reflected the decline of the private rental
sector and the policies which accelerated its decline.

    As was mentioned above, the pre-1914 housing stock came under the
rent control provisions of the 1915 *Rent and Mortgage Interest (War
Restrictions) Act*.   Although subsequent legislation relaxed the controls,
as tenancies became vacant and as some higher value rental houses were
no longer in acute shortage, the pre-1914 stock of working-class housing
remained under statutory rent control. [31]   With the outbreak of the
Second World War, the government again froze all rents, under the *Rent
and Mortgage Interest Restrictions Act*, 1939.   The enduring controls in
the period acted as a disincentive to investment in rental housing.   In
fact, the stock was passing into owner-occupier tenure as more and more
landlords found that their properties were uneconomic.   Rental housing
becomes an attractive investment if expectations are stable, costs are

low, and taxation rules allow depreciation to be written off on similar terms to other investments. In Britain these conditions did not prevail. The rent controls, the political uncertainty about their future, and the relevant cost conditions combined to create a disincentive. In the long term the private rental sector has become identified with pockets of poverty, inner-urban problems, inadequate management and maintenance, and a general incapacity to meet demand in some cities and regions.

In the public housing sector, the policy on rents varied as policymakers dithered between linking rents to costs and to capacity to pay. Under the *Housing and Town Planning Act*, 1919, local governments were advised to have regard to capacity to pay and local amenity, but rents were not linked to definite cost or needs criteria. New subsidy policies were introduced in 1923 and 1924, and in 1924 local governments could charge differential rents within single, specific subsidy programmes. This did not offer much flexibility in meeting needs because the total revenues from specific subsidy programmes had to cover costs, as required in the programmes. Greater flexibility was incorporated into later provisions in 1936. Under the new provisions, local governments could keep consolidated housing accounts and *pool* their revenues and costs, thus enabling some cross-subsidisation from older housing built at cheaper historical cost to newer higher cost housing. However, local governments used this flexibility in various ways and some were constrained by the age composition of their stock and the costs of new construction. Local governments could generally only apply a systematic needs criterion and the progressivity of rents to needs at the expense of ratepayers and some of their tenants. As Bowley points out, central policies were either lacking, or, when proclaimed, they could not be enforced locally. It was not until 1931 that central policy-makers gave a full statement of objectives. These objectives were to set rents appropriate to ordinary working-class housing, and to select tenants according to need. However, as we have seen 'ordinary working-class housing' was rent controlled and set to substantial social and economic problems. Furthermore, during the 1930s the public housing programme became more confined and rigid. Its historical development is outlined below.

Using Bowley's system of classification, the development of housing policy can be divided into: the first experiment, 1919-1923; the second experiment, 1923-1935; and the third experiment in the 1930s. The *Housing and Town Planning Act*, 1919, introduced open-ended central government subsidies. Under inflationary conditions the government feared that it would lose control of public expenditure in housing, and accordingly it limited the programme in 1921. Two years later, the Conservatives' *Housing Act*, 1923, marked the beginning of the *second experiment*.

Neville Chamberlain's 1923 Act provided for a £6 subsidy per dwelling for 20 years. It incorporated design features which would effectively share the costs of subsidies with local government. Also, the Conservatives intended to check the growth of public housing by requiring local government to use private enterprise, except where it could convince the Minister that private enterprise could not fulfil local housing needs. This policy was reversed when Labour came to power in 1924. Under the Wheatley *Housing Act*, 1924, the role of local government public housing was restored, and subsidies were extended to £9 per

dwelling for 40 years, with higher rates for rural housing.   At the
onset of economic recession in 1927, the succeeding Conservative
government reduced the Wheatley programme.   Public housing had a strong
quantitative impact under the two experiments.   In the *first experiment*,
public housing contributed 79 per cent of the new stock, 1919-1923 -
that is, 170,090 dwellings in a total of 213,821.   Then combining this
with the performance under the Chamberlain and Wheatley subsidies, by
1933 some 39 per cent of the total British stock had been built as
public housing and government-subsidised housing.   Furthermore, in the
period 1919-1939, Britain had built over 4 million houses, a substantial
performance which had virtually overcome the acute shortages left by
nineteenth-century demographic and urban pressures.

Turning from quantities to some questions of quality in policy
development, we encounter the ideological and political conflicts which
influenced British housing.   In 1926 Neville Chamberlain, an advocate
of rehabilitation, introduced the *Housing (Rural Workers) Bill*,
subsequently enacted.   It was designed to improve rural working-class
housing conditions by offering government rehabilitation grants and
loans.   The public finance was to be used for installing damp courses,
upgrading roofing, and providing wash-houses and larders, with a limitation to £100 or two-thirds of any cost lower than £100.   The Labour
spokesman, Ramsay McDonald, opposed the measure arguing that public
housing should have priority and that public funds should not be used
to support private landed interests.   The Left was clearly identifying
public housing with ideological purity, and this was sometimes counter-
productive to the pursuit of useful social goals in housing.   Meanwhile
the Conservatives had shown their favour to private enterprise under the
1923 *Housing Act*, with some similar lack of fit between the working
details and the general social aims of their housing policies.

Towards the end of the 1920s, Sir E.D. Simon, Lord Mayor of Manchester
in 1921-22 and experienced in administering public housing, began to
direct public policy towards slum clearance. [32]   During the first
phase of national public housing programmes, the urgencies of shortages
and the easier administration of new development led to an emphasis upon
new suburban development.   However, the anti-slum campaigners pointed
out that the worst housing conditons and the poorer families lived in
the old slums.   A case was made out for improving health and opportunities for children by abolishing the slums.   Simon proposed an intense
ten-year programme to get children out of the slums with supplementary
subsidies linked to family size and to local government rehousing
policies.   Neville Chamberlain's support for rehabilitation was
regarded by Simon as infeasible and ineffective against the legacy of
dilapidation and bad design in nineteenth-century housing.   Thus, the
theory of environmental determinism continued to bedevil the debate.
Simon's campaign was influential in turning policy towards the *third
experiment*.

Labour passed the *Housing Act*, 1930, to give effect to Simon's ideas.
Arthur Greenwood who introduced the Bill argued that better housing
produced better people and that slum clearance would help those in most
need.   He showed that during the 1920s only some 43 slum clearance
projects had been completed.   According to Greenwood the new subsidies
(linked to rehousing and the number of persons relocated) would overcome the administrative impediments.   Neville Chamberlain defended
himself against opponents of rehabilitation.   He hinted that the low

number of dwellings rehabilitated under the *Housing (Rural Workers) Act*, 1926, (2,510 dwellings rehabilitated) was attributable to inexperience in local government housing management.   The COPEC Housing Improvement Society in Birmingham and the St. Pancras Housing Society were operating effective rehabilitation policies.   Slum clearance was pursued concurrently with the Wheatley programmes during the years 1930-1933, but under the Conservatives' general economy measures in the depression, the Wheatley subsidies were repealed in the *Housing (Financial Provisions) Act*, 1933.   Thus, public housing became confined to the relief of slum conditions under the *third experiment*.   The clearance provisions of the 1930 Act were supplemented with measures aimed against overcrowding in the *Housing Act*, 1935.

The main legacies of the 1919-1938 inter-War years were the division of British housing into rigid sectors.   Local governments had responded to subsidies provided by central government and public housing became significant in volume and impact.   It contained some confusions of objectives in linking subsidies to costs and rental policies, and it became the focus of ideological and political conflict.   Meanwhile, the private rental sector was beset with the problems of rent control and the poverty of some who lived in this housing.   It was a declining sector which was not getting any useful or creative attention in public policy.   The opportunities for rehabilitation had been neglected and its social value was generally unrecognised, although the contrasting lack of community identity and the social homogeneity of suburban public housing estates had begun to attract social criticism.   The home ownership sector had expanded rapidly, partly reflecting rising incomes and a preference for security and high standards among those who could afford these things.   However, the growth of this sector also reflected the problems in the private rental sector, and the traumas of slum clearance.   These legacies and sectoral rigidities trouble the country still.

OTHER COUNTRIES

The collection of housing-related problems which emerged in Britain was very similar to those in the other modern democracies.   High rents, anti-slum campaigns, the economic collapse of housing and housing finance markets, rapid urbanisation, and problems in organising and governing large urban areas were common to most nineteenth-century industrial societies.   There was also common ground in the ideas advocated as solutions, including public housing, non-profit and co-operative housing, reform of urban government, slum clearance, interventions in capital markets, garden cities and suburbs, and so on. From the comparative viewpoint the interest lies in the different emphasis and institutionalisation of policies, their varied patterns and the consequences for modern policy needs in housing.   Like other social policies, housing policies tend to mirror the general historical and cultural traditions of societies.   This adds interest to intellectual studies and it provides grounds for critical evaluation and explanation of policy development in any one country.

Britain differs from many of the other modern democracies in several important factors.   It was the first to industrialise, its pre-indus-trial characteristics of aristocracy and regional variation endured longer, and as a pioneer it had to face urgent new urban and housing

problems without benefit of much theory or experience. Perhaps for
that reason its expression of Social Democracy tended - with some Fabian
exceptions - to be untheoretical too, by European standards. Britain
is also a more class-bound society than other modern democracies, and
it seems to many critics to have lost its nineteenth-century flair for
enterprise and competition. However, it has experienced less technological dominance than some European countries, and the sense of home
shows up in much of its housing. Finally, Britain, despite its former
imperialism and status as a world power, presently has far less
internationalism in outlook among its professions and public leaders
than Sweden, West Germany and The Netherlands. This factor also
influences housing policy development; the Europeans have created
dense, informal professional networks among associations, intellectuals
and administrators.

Australia and the United States

Australia and the United States, like Britain, both adopted the public
housing approach to the development of social housing. However, they
have used their public housing in rather more confined ways and some of
their pre-1945 housing policies were aimed at opening up access to home
ownership or at filling in gaps where economic recessions tore holes in
housing and housing capital markets. Although the British building
society movement suffered periodic set-backs from recessions it grew
steadily and had enough resilience to overcome its problems without
strong government involvement in home ownership policies.

Australian [33] involvements with housing capital movements took two
courses. Before and after the turn of the century there were some
traumatic upsets and collapses in the capital market, and a slump in the
bulding society movement. State governments sought to repair the
damage by using their own state-owned Savings Banks to provide housing
loans to moderate- and low-income families. The various programmes
provided under these States' programmes between 1890 and 1920 often
enabled working-class families to buy houses at rates of repayment
below the ruling rates of rents in private rental housing. Even before
the advent of these government initiatives, the proportion of the
housing stock in owner-occupier tenure was high, certainly above 30 per
cent and probably nearer 50 per cent. The government home ownership
programmes were introduced by both Labour and Conservative administrations. Then in 1927-28 at the federal level, the Australian Government
decided to use its own bank to create a national housing loans programme.
This did not develop fully because of the economic depression in the
1930s and the diversion of housing policy development to public housing
and slum clearance. It was Norway (see below) which demonstrated the
full potential for expressing social goals in housing through
government banking systems with the advantages of relatively unbureaucratic administration.

The public housing approach in Australia began abortively in New South
Wales under its *Housing Act*, 1912. This early scheme merits some
attention because it indicates the administrative and political problems
of public housing. The New South Wales Government's intention was to
provide low-cost rental dwellings in competition with the private rental
sector. Accordingly it created a Housing Board to acquire land and to
develop a 'garden suburb' in Sydney. The project began well, with
considerable interest in the demonstration of new town planning

principles, and in the social development activities by community groups. But a sequence of political, administrative and economic problems appeared after 1919 and the Housing Board found itself involved in public scandal and contentions with Government.

A new Government (of the conservative National Party) was elected in 1919 and it wanted to promote sales rather than rental housing. Meanwhile, following the shortages of the First World War, the Housing Board tried to expand its activities, but it ran into shortages of materials, inflationary costs and difficulties in recruiting key professional and technical officers. Some of its dwellings cost more than the prices which it had advertised in its brochures. The Board was then obliged to sell houses below cost with a good deal of private financial anxiety and public political fuss. Worse problems followed when houses on some sites were constructed and sold before filling had properly consolidated. Some of them cracked badly. The Government appointed a Parliamentary Select Committee to enquire into the administration of the Housing Board. Its hearings were bitterly controversial, and in 1924 the Government abolished the Board and terminated the public housing programme.

That failure illustrated some of the general difficulties of building and managing housing under the too close control of politicians. Public housing does demand considerable co-operation among politicians, administrators and community groups if it is to be effective. That tends to mean that, even in the general run of administration, considerable attention is given to containing or avoiding overt conflicts with some consequent loss of enterprise and risk taking.

The States returned to the idea of public housing in the 1930s, and after 1945 their operations were increasingly financed on a national scale by the Commonwealth. As we shall see in the next chapter, the post-1945 public housing programme was not as large as Britain's, and it has been used to extend home ownership as well as to provide working-class rental housing.

The key *United States'* involvements with housing policies began in the 1930s depression when the economic collapse of the building industry, general unemployment and slum living conditions entered national social and political significance. Like Australia, the United States developed policies to fill gaps in housing finance, and to make tentative first steps in public housing. However, the American methods of supporting the expansion of housing finance were more indirect than Australia's, and the use of public housing was more confined as a corollary of slum clearance. These differences can be explained by the deeper commitments to *laissez faire* in the United States and the closer influence of British ideas in Australian society. In a comparative study, American housing policy development in this period is interesting for (1) its different approach to public housing, and (2) its reconstruction of private housing finance to make home ownership more broadly accessible.

Before the Federal Government took policy initiatives during the 1930s, housing finance in the United States had been typically available as 10-year mortgages at high rates of interest and fully repayable at maturity. Therefore, only the relatively rich could afford owner-occupier housing. Following the reforms in the 1930s, housing finance was typically available in the form of 20-year mortgages, fully amortised in the repayments and covering up to 80 per cent of the value of the dwelling. The American approach had been to manipulate the private credit markets towards housing, accomplished by instituting guarantees against borrowers' defaults, introducing a competitive government loan scheme, and operating in the secondary mortgage market to smooth out fluctuations in the flow of funds. This approach has become permanent American housing policy; it is aimed at making private housing choice feasible and effective. By 1976, some 63 per cent of American housing was owner-occupied, most of it financed under the direct or indirect influence of policy initiatives taken during the 1930s.

Policy development during the 1930s took the following course. American Federal Government involvement in housing had begun during the First World War when the US Shipping Board and the US Housing Corporation (set up within the Department of Labor) built 16,000 housing units for war-industry workers. When peace came, following the traditions of *laissez faire*, these were sold to private owners. The economic depression which began in 1929, brought a collapse of credit, and bad housing conditions became a cause for agitation. In 1931 President Hoover called a *Conference on Home Building and Home-Ownership*, which highlighted the financial and employment problems in the housing industry. These developments led to legislation [34] aimed at creating a permanent change in the operation of housing credit. As we have seen, in Britain the building societies movement was widening home ownership at that time and government had no need to create extensive new credit instruments as was necessary in the United States.

The economic depression of the 1930s also led the Federal Government to take initiatives in public housing. The *National Recovery Act*, 1933, established the Public Works Administration (PWA) which began to clear the slums and redevelop the sites with public housing. The PWA was heavily criticised and increasingly it was thought that public housing should be controlled locally. Accordingly, administration was revised under the *Housing Act*, 1937. This public housing programme partly reflected an employment purpose and partly a restricted welfare object- ive as a corollary of slum clearance. In fact, the American public housing programme has remained as a rather restricted residual welfare programme, contributing less than 2 per cent of the total housing stock. As we shall see in the next chapter, public housing in the United States has encountered considerable political and economic difficulties with the result that new methods were used in the 1960s to extend the social goals of housing policy. Unlike Britain, the American public housing programme did not grow into a substantial working-class housing provision, and nor did it follow Australian characteristics, emphasising the housing aspirations of State governments and making contributions to home ownership among the working class.

Norway

In this period, Norway laid the foundations of policies which are possibly the most effective among modern democratic countries. Norwegian policy developments have three main sources of interest in a comparative study. First, Norway has created a framework for housing finance which is less rigid and bureaucratic than those in other countries, but social goals are nevertheless given substantial promin-

175

ence.   Second, as early as 1916, the Norwegian Labour Party had
articulated a coherent housing policy covering varied elements including,
support for home ownership, municipal land acquisition and disposal in
leasehold tenure, municipal housing development to relieve acute
shortages, support for co-operative housing, and security for tenants.
Third, in Oslo, the co-operative and public housing sectors co-existed
in the 1920s and 1930s, but a strong preference for the voluntary sector
emerged with the consequence that public rental housing was transferred
to co-ownership and voluntary housing enterprises.

By 1860, the central government had passed public health legislation
to regulate urban development; and other problems included access to
credit for home ownership - also a problem in rural areas where
homestead farming was a typical way of life.   In 1894, the government
created the Housing Loan Fund to provide housing credit to low-income
families.   This initiative has produced, through successive stages, a
modern housing policy dominated by central government banking.   The
changes occurred by consolidating the role of the central housing banks;
- (1) in 1903 the Workers' Agricultural Property and Housing Bank took
over the functions of the Housing Loan Fund, (2) in 1915, arrangements
were consolidated by bringing them under the National Smallholding and
Housing Bank and, finally (3) in 1946, the government created the Housing Bank, and the Smallholders Bank.

By 1976, the Norwegian central housing banks were providing credit for
over 75 per cent of new housing development.   The Banks operate as
financial and administrative organisations, reviewing applications for
funds and administering the mortgages.   However, the system is
relatively unbureaucratic with such details as designing housing,
contracting and so on left mainly within the customer-developer relationship.   The government's housing programme is now accessible to any
Norwegian, regardless of income, but with limits on the size-standard of
housing which can be permitted; and the allocation of resources to
housing has slotted into a system of national economic and social
planning started in 1946.   The Banks support owner-occupier, co-operative and rental tenure, and the finance is used to build varied dwelling
forms.   In short, the financial and administrative framework is
effective, uncomplicated and comprehensive.

The role of the Norwegian central housing banks has been more easily
defined and developed because Norway had a less complicated and thick-
textured capital market when the first initiatives were first taken by
government.   Other countries had more complex financial and
administrative institutions.   Thus, such effective simplicity has its
explanation in history.   Norway's system of housing finance can be
envied, but it might now be hard to repeat in other countries.

Finally, the pre-1945 period in Norway is significant for the
relationships between the co-operative housing movement and public
housing.   In 1914, the Oslo City Council began a public housing
programme to make more houses available to the working classes.
However, during the housing vexations of the 1920s a self-help housing
movement developed and this culminated in the creation of the Oslo
Savings and Housing Society (OBOS) in 1929.   OBOS adopted the
effective Swedish HSB model of organising and developing co-operative
housing (see Chapter 2).   During the 1940s, some public housing tenants
were dissatisfied with the estates management performance of the City

176

Council.   After protracted negotiations on the settlement of financial
conditions and rights to the title of property, some public housing was
transferred into co-operative tenure and management.   This was
facilitated by City Council representation on the OBOS Board of
Directors; the representation originated in 1935 and reflected the
collaboration in housing policy development and in the professional
aspects of planning and developing housing estates.   As a general
point, it seemed that the voluntary social housing sector more adequately met the self-fulfilment aspirations of the people.   This is not
surprising; social idealism and democratic controls are not so
expressive and close in a system of public administration as in a
voluntary movement which has enterprise and continuity.   The point has
modern relevance, with the growing demand for tenants' rights and
participation in housing management policies.

The Netherlands, West Germany and Sweden

The housing policies of these three countries are interesting for their
use of varied developers, and for the use of a *general* financial
framework to express social goals in housing.   The development of the
German and Swedish co-operative and trade union housing enterprises was
discussed in Chapter 2.   We shall now look at the administrative
frameworks which governments created to support voluntary housing
enterprise and other developers.   These were the means by which these
countries achieved more diversity than those using the British public
housing model.   It has also proved possible in Sweden since 1942, to
develop a strong rental sector expressing social idealism rather than
private profit-seeking.   This Swedish policy development was followed
more generally in West Germany and The Netherlands after the Second
World War period.   The common feature to these countries, for purposes
of comparative housing study, is their use of deep subsidies and
inducements to achieve rapidly-expanding non-state production when it
was necessary to overcome shortages caused by demographic pressure and,
in the case of West Germany and The Netherlands, wartime devastation.
These countries also committed themselves more generally to systems
building technology and mass-project high-rise dwellings in the 1960s
than the other countries featured in this study.   Present trends have
slowed down and sometimes reversed this technological characteristic,
but the modern trends towards comprehensiveness in policy development
give these countries a progressive lead compared with Britain, the
United States and Australia.

  The Netherlands provided the earliest example of a national housing
policy which allocated government financial support through a variety
of developers.   Under the *Housing Act*, 1901, the Dutch started national
policies in slum clearance, town planning and housing.   By 1905, the
central government was advancing housing loans to local government.   A
large proportion of this housing was built by the voluntary housing
sector, which worked with local government in town planning and
performed the role of social housing developers.   The 1901 Act has
been sufficiently flexible for government to inject more public finance
into housing at times of critical shortage.   For example, following the
First World War, subsidisation was extended to the private enterprise
sector to meet urgent needs beyond the capacity of the voluntary sector.
The same principle was used in a far bigger programme after the Second
World War.   By 1975 the ownership of the housing stock was divided:
23 per cent to the voluntary sector, 12 per cent to the municipalities

(i.e., public housing), 38 per cent owner-occupied and 27 per cent private rental. The voluntary sector had also built some of the owner-occupied housing.

In *Germany*, the co-operative housing movement originated in the mid-nineteenth century (see Chapter 2). The movement became more secure after 1889 when the government passed a law limiting liability. However, the principal boost to the movement came from government financial support; in 1895 the Prussian Government established a Housing Assistance Fund. Gradually the State (*Länder*) governments followed the Prussian Government's example. The finance was accessible to co-operatives, public benefit housing enterprises, and private developers who complied with conditions on rents and standards. Government involvements with housing deepened during the First World War when the States expanded the role of non-profit housing enterprise. After 1917, the States created *heimstatten* (homestead companies operating as development corporations) to develop and administer social housing on a wider scale than could be achieved by small local societies. Thus, government initiatives in finance and organisation nourished the development of non-profit housing, and the *heimstatten* represented a method of putting a distance between the cut and thrust of daily politics and the development and management of housing. The Swedes took up this idea in the 1940s. Essentially, enterprise was harnessed to a wider and stronger financial source than would have been possible through members' subscriptions, private savings deposits and localised operations.

German housing experienced economic and administrative dilemmas in the 1920s and 1930s. Like Britain, rent controls cut across investors' confidence in private rental housing, and this lack of confidence was aggravated by the hyper-inflation of the 1920s. Also, the Germans had not worked out a satisfactory method of subsidising social housing, relying upon taxes on existing housing to finance new social housing. Circumstances changed dramatically after the currency reforms of 1948-49. As we shall see in the next chapter, the post-1950 housing policies in West Germany have been effective and this has been facilitated by good general management of the economy.

In *Sweden*, housing vexation in the 1920s and 1940s precipitated the spontaneous emergence of tenants' and trade union co-operatives which have grown into large housing enterprises (see Chapter 2). Like Germany, Sweden has used the resourcing and organisational power of government to support the voluntary housing sector and to create public benefit housing corporations. Following the collapse of private housing and housing finance markets in 1940, the Swedish Social Democrats took decisive action to create a strong community housing policy supported by public finance and non-profit development enterprise. This action was based upon economic ideas developed by Myrdal and Johansson, Social Democrat economists who favoured long-term production targets, low rents and the use of public finance to envigorate local government in developing non-profit housing. [35] The aim was to draw savings into cost-rent housing generally, and this was achieved by creating a mixed public-private financial framework. The public finance component was designed to induce private finance into housing by subsidising the costs of interest and development to the final consumers. (Some of the key details are described in the next chapter which gives a review of the continuity of the system to 1968, and the subsequent

reforms since then.) This investment 'suction' policy was effective
in drawing resources into housing and in meeting the long-term needs
consequent upon high rates of demographic growth and rapid urbanisation.
By 1976, over 75 per cent of the housing stock was owned by non-profit
co-operatives and public benefit enterprises, with the major proportion
held by the local government public benefit companies.

One consequence of this policy was the creation of a strong rental
sector, less beset with the sort of economic and management problems in
Britain's private rental sector. The Swedish rental sector is large
(some 50 per cent of the stock), it accommodates a broader cross-section
of society than the British rental housing, and it provides a greater
security of tenure. In the modern world, similar statements can be
made of the rental sector in West Germany and The Netherlands. However,
as was mentioned in Chapter 3, the owner-occupier sector has been held
back by a central policy framework and by chronic shortages which have
combined to give policy-makers and developers a monopolistic power over
consumers. Since 1971 the bonds of monopoly have been broken by social
and economic change, with the result that important changes are
occurring in housing choice. This point is taken up in the next
chapter and in Chapter 7. Finally, we should recall the point, that
it was in Stockholm during the 1900-1940 period that Social Democrats
demonstrated the creative possibilities for developing community housing
policies on the twin pillars of acquiring cheap land, and bringing
finance and organisational capacity into relation with housing development. Sweden has contributed much to useful ideas and practices in the
modern history of housing.

CONCLUSIONS

At the time when Britain's housing policies moved from concerns with
public health towards housing construction, and the financing and
organising of social housing, it could draw upon a rich variety of ideas
and practices. Limited-profit housing enterprise, rehabilitation and
good housing management had all been demonstrated in ways which
attracted international attention. Some of the most brilliant talents
of nineteenth-century society including Edwin Chadwick, Lord Shaftesbury
and Octavia Hill had been deeply involved in the theory and practice of
housing. During the ferment of the 1880s, Alfred Marshall had contributed good economic reasoning to the housing debates. At the two key
official enquiries in 1881-82 and in 1884-85, many useful proposals came
to the notice of policy-makers. Among the policy options, Britain
might have selected: (1) rehabilitation for older housing, (2) a mixed
public-private financial framework accessible to the voluntary housing
sector, to private enterprise and public benefit companies, (3) a local
government public enterprise role in acquiring land, and (4) an investment inducement design for pulling resources into new construction.
Instead Britain got public housing, administrative vexation with slum
clearance activities and some sectoral rigidities which became more
deeply ingrained with the passing of time.

History took this course for a number of interacting reasons. First,
the full pluralistic set of good policies in finance, land acquisition
and rehabilitation would have placed demands for skills and practices
which public administration was not then fitted to develop. Second,
voluntarism in Britain grew from a Conservative idealism, not from

broadly-based people's movements and socialist inspirations.   As such, British voluntarism became the target for criticism by the emergent Radical and Socialist factions.   As philanthropy waned it took with it useful practices in rehabilitation, housing management, and the sense of home as a place where self-fulfilment and moral virtues could grow. Public housing inherited some of this in an attenuated form and without the personal commitments which inspired Octavia Hill, Lord Shaftesbury, Sir S. Waterlow and others.   Third, the British expressions of Social Democracy and Conservative authority have been more collectivist than their counterparts in Scandinavia.   Finally, British policy-makers had to take urgent action under the pressure of agitation, but before the social and economic theory of the welfare state had been fully and coherently articulated.   The British had to 'muddle through'.   Other countries were allowed more time to think, and they were sometimes less divided or inhibited by the sort of class divisions which existed in British society.

Thus, if we are interested in witnessing the use of creatively mixed public-private financial frameworks, the effective use of non-profit competitive enterprise, the co-ordination of private interests through public enterprise in acquiring land, and the creation of general community housing policies, it is to Norway, The Netherlands, Sweden and West Germany that we should look.   They have selected some useful policy options, and Norway in particular has been very creative. Finally, if we are interested in the rehabilitation idea, we must go into history and examine the work of Octavia Hill and Lord Shaftesbury. It was good work, neglected for generations until it was revived in the United States and Britain.   In Chapter 8 the full potential of rehabilitation will be explored.   Meanwhile in the next chapter we examine the comparative history of housing policy since 1945.

NOTES

[1] For the history of the British public health reforms, see S.E.Finer, *The Life and Times of Sir Edwin Chadwick*, Methuen, London, 1951, M.W.Finn, (ed), *Chadwick's Report on the Sanitary Condition of the Labouring Population of Great Britain*, 1842, Edinburgh University Press, 1965, R.A.Lewis, *Edwin Chadwick and the Public Health Movement*, Longmans, London, 1952.   For the history of the 1850-1890 period, see S.D.Chapman (ed), *History of Working Class Housing*, David and Charles, Newton Abbott, 1971, H.J.Dyos, 'The Slums of Victorian London', *Victorian Studies*, September 1967, pp.5-40, J.N.Tarn, (1) *Five Per Cent Philanthropy*, Cambridge University Press, London, 1973, (2) 'The Peabody Donation Fund: the Role of a Housing Society in the Nineteenth Century', *Victorian Studies*, Vol. 10, 1966, pp.7-38, A.S.Wohl, *The Housing of Artisans and Labourers in Nineteenth Century London*, 1815-1914, unpublished PhD thesis, Brown University, USA, 1966, 'The Bitter Cry of Outcast London', *International Review of Social History*, 1968, pp.189-245, and *The Eternal Slum: Housing and Social Policy in Victorian London*, Arnold, London, 1977.
[2] Dyos, *op. cit.* (1967) p.25.
[3] See F. de Leeuw and R.J.Struyk, *The Web of Urban Housing*, The Urban Institute, Washington D.C., 1975.   R.F.Muth, *Cities and Housing*, University of Chicago Press, Chicago, 1968.   C.Pugh 'Older Urban Residential Areas and the Development of Economic Analysis', in J.C. McMaster and G.R.Webb (eds), *Australian Urban Economics: A Reader*,

Australia and New Zealand Book Company, Sydney, 1976.

[4] Wohl, *op. cit.* (1966) and (1977).

[5] See H.J.Dyos, 'Railways and Housing in Victorian London', *Journal of Transport History*, Vol. 2, No. 1, May 1955, pp.11-21, 90-100.

[6] *Parliamentary Debates, House of Lords*, 1853, Vol. 125, p.403.

[7] A.Mearns, *The Bitter Cry of Outcast London*, Leicester University Press, Leicester, 1970. This publication also contains the housing reform proposals of Lord Salisbury (1883), Joseph Chamberlain (1883), and an evaluative commentary by A.S.Wohl, an eminent housing historian.

[8] Tarn, *op. cit.* (1966 and 1973).

[9] Wohl, *op. cit.* (1966) pp.132-177.

[10] Wohl, *op. cit.* (1966) pp.167-168.

[11] Tarn, *op. cit.* (1973) p.143.

[12] In this section, the themes which are used to explain the evolution of housing policies are adapted from: C.M.Allan, 'The Genesis of British Urban Redevelopment with Special Reference to Glasgow', *Economic History Review*, Vol. 10, 1965, pp.598-613.

[13] See Finer, *op. cit.* (1951) and Lewis, *op. cit.* (1952).

[14] See Wohl, *op. cit.* (1966), pp.180-81, 370.

[15] See Wohl, *op. cit.* (1966), p.137.

[16] For an account of Torrens' activities in the Building Societies Association, see: E.J.Cleary, *The Building Society Movement*, Elek, London, 1965, pp.88, 95, 98.

[17] The details of suburbanisation in London after 1890 can be found in: Wohl, *op. cit.* (1966), pp.414-464.

[18] For an extensive account of Glasgow Corporation's involvement in housing, see J.Butt, 'Working Class Housing in Glasgow, 1851-1914', in Chapman, *op. cit.* (1971). My commentary on housing in Glasgow draws upon Butt's work and on my own research in Glasgow in November 1976.

[19] The key sources of reviews, ideas and practices are: *Report from the Select Committee on Artizans' and Labourers' Dwellings Improvement*, Interim Report, Parliamentary Papers 1881 and Final Report, Parliamentary Papers, 1882. The Minutes of Evidence attached to the Final Report is a better source of ideas and practices than those surveyed by the Royal Commission, cited below. *Report of Her Majesty's Commissioners Inquiring into Housing of the Working Classes*, Eyre and Spottiswoode, London, 1885. A.Mearns, *op. cit.* (1970) with other contemporary articles: Lord Salisbury, 'Labourers' and Artisans' Dwellings', from *The National Review*, November 1883, and Joseph Chamberlain, 'Labourers' and Artisans' Dwellings', also from *The National Review*, November 1883. Alfred Marshall, 'The Housing of the London Poor: Where to House Them', and M.G.Mulhall, 'The Housing of the London Poor: Ways and Means', *Contemporary Review*, February 1884.

[20] These issues and the history of the period are well-covered in three articles, see P.Wilding (1) 'Towards Exchequer Subsidies for Housing', *Social and Economic Administration*, Vol.6, Jan. 1972, pp.3-18. (2) 'The Housing and Town Planning Act 1919: A Study in the Making of a Social Policy', *Journal of Social Policy*, Vol.2, Part 4, October 1973, pp.317-334.   (3) 'The Administrative Aspects of the 1919 Housing Scheme', *Public Administration*, Vol.51, Autumn 1973, pp.307-26.

[21] Cleary, *op. cit.* (1965).

[22] See Wohl, *op. cit.* (1966), pp.414-464.

[23] The early history of the LCC housing activities can be found in: London County Council, *The Housing Question in London, 1855-1900*, London County Council, London, no date - circa 1900, and London County Council, *Housing of the Working Classes in London, 1889-1912*, London County Council, London, 1913.

[24] *Report of the Committee to Consider Questions of Building
Construction in Connection with the Provision of Dwellings for the
Working Classes in England and Wales, and Scotland*, (Tudor Walters),
HMSO, London, 1918.
[25] *Final Report of the Unhealthy Areas Committee*, (Neville Chamberlain), HMSO, London, 1925.
[26] *Final Report of the Unhealthy Areas Committee*, op. cit. (1925), p.9.
[27] *Report of the Royal Commission on the Poor Laws*, HMSO, London,1909.
[28] Beatrice Webb (nee Potter) was active in assisting Charles Booth
with his London poverty surveys after 1887; in assisting with the
management of *Katherine Buildings*, a tenement built by the East End
Dwellings Company; and in Fabian politics.
[29] See M.Bowley, *Housing and the State, 1919-1944*, George Allen and
Unwin, London, 1945.   Other useful texts covering the history of this
period can be found in J.B.Cullingworth, *Housing and Local Government*,
George Allen and Unwin, London, 1966, and J.R.Jarmain, *Housing Subsidies
and Rents*, Stevens, London, 1948.
[30] Cleary, *op. cit.* (1965), pp.184-201.
[31] In 1923 vacant tenancies were decontrolled.   Following the Marley
Committee's Report, the *Rent Restriction Act*, 1933, decontrolled the
more expensive dwellings.   Further decontrol took place under the *Rent
Act*, 1938, again the relaxation of controls being applied to the high-
and moderate-value dwellings.
[32] See Sir E.D.Simon, *How to Abolish the Slums*, Longmans, London,
1929, and *The Anti-Slum Campaign*, Longmans, London, 1933.
[33] A fuller history of Australian housing policies is contained in
C.Pugh, *Intergovernmental Relations and the Development of Australian
Housing Policies*, Centre for Research on Federal Financial Relations,
Australian National University, Canberra, 1976.
[34] The following legislation was passed:

1932	*Emergency Relief and Reconstruction Act*	This set up the Reconstruction Finance Corporation.
1932	*Home Loan Bank Act*	This set up the Federal Home Loan Bank Board, and Federal Home Loan Bank System.
1933	*Banking Act*	This established the Federal Deposit Insurance Corporation.
1933	*Home Owners' Loan Act*	This established the Home Owners' Loan Corporation.
1934	*National Housing Act*	This instituted the Federal Savings and Loan Insurance Corporation, the Federal Housing Administration (FHA), and the Federal National Mortgage Association (FNMA) to operate in the secondary mortgage market and to smooth the flow of funds to the FHA mortgaging operations.

[35] For further discussions of Swedish housing policy development see
B.Heady, *Housing Policy in the Developed Economy*, Croom Helm, London,
1978.

REFERENCES (SELECTED)

Bowley, M., *Housing and the State, 1919-1944*, George Allen and Unwin,
   London, 1945.

Chapman, S.D. (ed), *History of Working Class Housing*, David and Charles, Newton Abbot, 1971.

Cleary, E.J., *The Building Society Movement*, Elek, London, 1965.

de Leeuw, F. and Struyk, R.J., *The Web of Urban Housing*, The Urban Institute, Washington D.C., 1975.

Dyos, H.J., 'The Slums of Victorian London', *Victorian Studies*, September 1967, pp.5-40.

Finer, S.E., *The Life and Times of Edwin Chadwick*, Methuen, London, 1951.

Lewis, R.A., *Edwin Chadwick and the Public Health Movement*, Longmans, London, 1952.

Mearns, A., *The Bitter Cry of Outcast London*, Leicester University Press, Leicester, 1970.

Pugh, C., *Intergovernmental Relations and the Development of Australian Housing Policies*, Centre for Research on Federal Financial Relations, Australian National University, Canberra, 1976.

Tarn, J.N., *Five Per Cent Philanthropy*, Cambridge University Press, London, 1973.

Wilding, P., 'Towards Exchequer Subsidies for Housing', *Social and Economic Administration*, Vol.6, January 1972, pp.3-18.

Wilding, P., 'The Housing and Town Planning Act 1919: A Study in the Making of a Social Policy', *Journal of Social Policy*, Vol.2, Part 4, October 1973, pp.317-334.

Wilding, P., 'The Administrative Aspects of the 1919 Housing Scheme', *Public Administration*, Vol.51, Autumn 1973.

Wohl, A.S., *The Housing of Artisans and Labourers in Nineteenth Century London, 1815-1914*, an unpublished PhD thesis, Brown University, USA, 1966.

ACKNOWLEDGMENTS

The following organisations contributed to my understanding of historical influences in continental European housing. In West Germany: Deutscher Verband fur Wohnungswegesen, Stadtebau und Raumplanung; Gesamtverband gemeinnutziger Wohnungsunternehmen. In The Netherlands: Ministry of Housing and Physical Planning. In Norway, Labour Party; OBOS; USBL. In Sweden: Stockholm City Council; Social Democratic Party; SR.

6　The historical development of housing policies in some modern democracies after 1945

Housing is physically durable and so are its institutions and policies. Organisations, financial institutions, professions and groups in public administration find both narrow and broad reasons for protecting the conventional ways of doing things.　Then, as we have seen, the political Left in Britain has conceived and nurtured public housing as the representation of Social Democracy in housing, and private rental housing has been seen as an undesirable symptom of capitalism.　It was in the 1919-1938 period that British housing developed its major characteristics - the division into the owner-occupier, public housing and private rental sectors.　Other countries also have 'housing sectors', but they are less rigidly drawn than Britain's and they portray ideological causes in more varied ways.　In the post-1945 period, the rigid sectoral divisions have been continued, and in some ways their demarcation lines have been strengthened, although there is some inter-sector mobility, mainly from the private rental to the other two sectors.　The period continues its essential characteristics from the inter-War years, but with some significant attempts to reform housing and give it some new directions during the 1960s.　In 1977 a major official policy review was published, but neither the reviewers nor the Callaghan Labour Government contemplated any very radical departures from conservative continuity in housing.

There is no comprehensive history of policy development since 1945, but nevertheless some specialist authors have made some useful contributions. [1]　The Second World War and its consequences left another legacy of acute shortages;　it was only in the 1970s that attention really turned from 'production targets' to other, more diverse policy aims.　The wartime emergencies were reflected in two legislative responses.　First, in 1938 the *Housing (Emergency Powers) Act* committed the central government to pay the cost of repairs from war damage.　Second, in 1944, the government strengthened its expropriation powers for dealing with devastated areas under the *Housing (Temporary Provisions) Act*, and it committed itself to construct 100,000 prefabricated houses under the *Housing (Temporary Accommodation) Act*.　The war also stimulated general desires for progressive social policies in post-War reconstruction. Some effects on town planning, decentralisation and regionalisation are dealt with in subsequent chapters.　Reflecting the earlier issues in the First World War, policy-makers committed themselves to idealism, to the elevation of housing standards and to the problems of the older housing stock.　In these years of widespread social consciousness, the Conservative Party's *Foundation for Housing* (1944) declared itself in favour of dwelling forms 'domestic in scale and feeling', located in well-serviced urban areas and within the people's ability to pay.　The

Dudley Committee improved the prescribed standards set out in the Tudor Walters recommendations (1918). Finally, the Central Housing Advisory Committee (1945) preferred the replacement of older housing, but also gave some very cautious support to government involvement with rehabilitation.

Labour policies and dilemmas, 1945-1951

Labour was returned to power in 1945 intent upon developing the welfare state. In housing its priorities favoured public housing, a large housing drive to overcome shortages, generous scales of subsidy for local government building, and low rents. During the War, some 200,000 houses had been destroyed and a further 550,000 damaged. Labour's housing policies were contained in the provisions of the *Housing (Financial and Miscellaneous Provisions) Act*, 1946. The main inducement to local government was the annual £22 per dwelling subsidy, extended beyond slum clearance to general building purposes. In the parliamentary debates, the Conservatives stressed the need to avoid segregation, to achieve some home ownership, and to link housing with good town planning. Although the Act incorporated committed purposes and strong egalitarian ideals, it contained all the dilemmas which Bowley [2] had pointed out in her review of public housing in the inter-War years. That is to say, the policies and their subsidy arrangements had confusions of objectives in rent policies, and in the conflict between ability to pay and the need to meet costs. All of this became conspicuous in 1947 when inflationary pressures hit the building industry and this was followed by general economic crisis. The government was forced to curb the programme, and like the original 1919 public housing programme, the expectations were not fulfilled.

These economic problems were compounded with further long-term dilemmas arising from the continued rent controls in the private rental sector. In an incisive study of the comparative policies in West Germany and Britain, Hallett [3] has revealed the bad social and economic consequences of British policies towards the private rental sector. The policies have contributed to homelessness and to the poor quality of large portions of the private rental sector. Rent controls remained in force to 1957, after which controls were removed on higher value housing. In 1965, a system of *rent regulation* replaced the old controls, enabling some increases in rents through conciliation and arbitration procedures. However, as Hallett points out, the regulated rents have generally been uneconomic. Accordingly, the private rental sector has declined rapidly in the period 1945-1977, and some significant issues in British housing history are centred around the problems in this sector.

Labour introduced one more piece of housing legislation before the Conservatives took power in the years 1951-1964. In presenting the *Housing Bill*, 1949, Aneurin Bevan declared that public housing was henceforth to be viewed as 'community housing', not just as a 'working class' housing. However, the continuing realities of the sectoral division of British housing cut across the intent to make public housing 'community housing' in the Norwegian, Swedish, West German and Dutch sense. In these countries, the central financial and administrative framework has been designed to serve wide community housing purposes. The British *Housing Act*, 1949, did not go so far; but it did create a basis for rehabilitation in British policy, and this was some two decades ahead of policy development in continental

Europe. The discussions in Chapter 8 will deal with the more detailed
aspects of rehabilitation policies which have now been accepted by
Labour and Conservative governments.

Conservative Policies, 1951-1964

In 1951 the Conservatives came to power and they were intent upon raising
production targets from 200,000 to 300,000 dwellings per annum, and
switching the priority to the private sector. This meant that home
ownership would be boosted, the private rental sector would not get the
sort of policy development which it merited, and public housing would
follow more confined 'social' purposes. Thus, the Conservatives
switched from their sense of home, their concern about segregation and
their acceptance of egalitarianism in their 1944 pronouncements, to the
idea that the welfare state should be confined, and private enterprise
given freer rein. As we shall presently see, it was a bad policy
mixture with no real recognition of the mutualities involved in
developing the welfare state and private enterprise in concert. The
immediate effect of the new policy was to raise private sales housing
from 12 per cent of the annual construction in 1951 to 36 per cent in
1955. The longer term consequences were to lead to severe social
stresses in London and other areas where both public and private rental
housing were insufficient to meet demands and needs.

The framework for the Conservative policies in the 1950s was described
in the 1953 White Paper, *Houses : The Next Step*. [4] As noted, the
priority was to raise production and to divert resources to owner-
occupier housing. The White Paper accepted the conventional wisdom
that the basic strategy towards older housing should be slum clearance,
but that some housing with 'some years of service' could be rehabilitated. Policy-makers remained unaware that the life of most old housing
could be extended substantially by making good arrears of maintenance
and by modernisation. However, following recommendations from the
Royal Institute of Chartered Surveyors and the Government's specialist
committee, the Girdwood Committee, the Government was prepared to raise
rents on older housing to cover the costs of actual repairs, providing
the (controlled) rents would not otherwise cover these costs. The
Housing Repairs and Rents Act, 1954, gave effect to this policy.

Subsequent Conservative legislation in the 1950s aimed to reduce
subsidies in public housing, to confine public housing to special social
needs, and to decontrol rents. First, the *Housing Subsidies Act*, 1956,
framed new subsidies in such a way as to emphasise a confined slum
clearance purpose in public housing. Furthermore, the Government was
aware that rents in public housing produced vertical and horizontal
inequity and it wanted to constrain local government to charge **'realistic'**
rents. The move towards 'realistic' rents was extended to the private
rental sector under the *Rent Act*, 1957. In presenting this measure,
Enoch Powell argued that its decontrolling provisions (for higher value
housing) would remove the economic inefficiencies and bad social
consequences of rent control. Drawing upon theoretical market economics,
the Conservatives aimed their rent reforms against immobilities, under-
utilisation of accommodation, lack of investment incentive, and
inequities among tenants and between tenants and landlords. This
measure was politically controversial, and it led to a growth of new
housing research studies and more ideological conflict in policy
development (see below).

The Conservative emphasis upon home ownership was consolidated in the *Housing and Home Purchase Act*, 1958, which provided Exchequer advances of £100 million to the building societies movement.   It was intended that these funds should be used for the purchase of pre-1919 housing, thus cutting further into the stock of private rental housing.   In addition, local government home loan programmes were encouraged by providing loans to 95 per cent of the value of housing up to a £2,500 limit.   From the comparative policy viewpoint, it should be noted that these policies consolidated the sectoral divisiveness of British housing. The opportunities to create a mixed public-private financial framework were missed, and the building societies movement was being used to further middle-class home ownership.   In continental Europe, private savings were drawn into relationship with public finance (and subsidies) to create credit instruments which were accessible to public benefit societies, private enterprise and owner-occupiers on broadly similar terms.   In effect, this meant that rental housing could flourish and the sectoral divisions were not so rigid as Britain's.

Some new ideas and modifications entered Conservative housing policies during the 1960s. [5]   Although, the basic policy in public housing was to reduce the burden of subsidies in public expenditure, (then running at £3 million per annum), and to redirect the subsidies to slum clearance, to new towns' housing development, to the relief of crowding and to housing for the aged, the Government was prepared to let general public housing expand in regions where demand was pressing.   In other words, the Government recognised the more urgent needs in some areas and the *regional* differentiation of housing needs.   This issue has grown into greater significance in the mid-1970s, reflecting the general historical insensitivity to the variable regional and local needs in public housing, except that supplementary subsidies have been made for redevelopment and high-density housing.

It was in the early 1960s that the first tentative steps were taken to revive the voluntary housing sector.   These initiatives began with the idea of widening the choice in private (low-rent) housing by providing funds to housing associations to build houses for letting at 'cost rents'. These 'cost rents' were based upon historical costs and were differentiated from rents on new private housing which followed market trends. At that stage Labour was sceptical of expanding the voluntary sector because it believed that public housing expressed greater ideological purity and egalitarianism.   By contrast, the Conservatives placed more significance upon the vertical and horizontal inequities associated with public housing.   However, they did not extend this concern into overall housing policies, and especially into the owner-occupied sector.   In fact, in 1963, the Government abolished Schedule A tax, a tax levied on imputed rental values of owner occupied housing.   During the 1970s this implicit subsidisation of owner-occupier tenure has attracted more and more attention, especially in policy debates about tenure and equity (see Chapter 3).

There were also policy initiatives about older housing.   On the one hand, it was assumed that the need for slum clearance would become more extensive.   Besides destroying unfit housing, it was argued that further large tracts of 'twilight' areas would need redevelopment and environmental improvement.   The Government set a target of building 350,000 dwellings per annum, with some enthusiasm for using systems building techniques to create high-density redevelopment.   Our earlier evaluations, and their fuller substantiation in Chapter 8, point to the economic and social absurdities of this sort of environmental determinism. For a decade it was given a relatively free rein in British public housing and it was responsible for some unfortunate redevelopment in London, Liverpool, Sheffield, Glasgow and other large cities. However, policy-makers were also giving more attention to rehabilitation, and especially to its feasibility in the administration of 'area improvement' schemes, and its possibilities for attracting private investment. The Government was intent upon raising the performance in rehabilitation from 120,000 units per annum to 200,000. The impediments to expansion were the lack of administrative experience in government, and the failure to understand the depth of long-term economic problems in the private rental sector.

The early 1960s can be regarded as a period marking change in housing policies. It was a time of new ideas which had not been tested, a time of making greater endeavours in slum clearance and other policies which had not been effective in the past, and a time when the Conservative bent for private enterprise had recently confined public housing policies to residual social and urban needs. In short, in general the policy mixture was incoherent, but it contained some seeds of useful new directions. For Britain, it was unfortunate that these seeds were scattered into a financial and administrative framework which limited their potential growth and development. Again, it is a problem of structural rigidity. A voluntary housing movement could not prosper in its own self-contained segment of finance and administration. Rehabilitation also needed access to a framework designed to place funds and opportunities in the way of a variety of developers.

The new ideas were incorporated into two pieces of legislation. First, the *Housing Act*, 1961, provided £25 million to housing associations for developing cost-rent housing, including co-operative tenure. Also, the Government restored general subsidies for public housing to those local authorities which were experiencing urgent pressures of demand and need. Second, the *Housing Act*, 1964, strengthened the resolve to develop the voluntary housing sector. This Act set up the *Housing Corporation* to act as a catalyst for channelling building society funds into the voluntary housing movement. The Government allocated £100 million to the Housing Corporation for use in second mortgage loans, the first mortgages coming from the building societies in the form of 40-year loans. Thus, Britain took initiatives to create a mixed public-private financial framework, but confined its application to the voluntary housing sector. Essentially, the Conservatives saw the voluntary housing sector as an alternative to the public housing monopoly in social rental housing. However, this voluntary sector could not grow beyond the limits of government appropriations and the disposition of the Building Societies Association to lend on 40-year terms, rather than on 25-year terms in their regular operations. The 1964 Act also liberalised the conditions on rehabilitation, begun in the 1949 *Housing Act*. However, rehabilitation remained rather sluggish until conditions in housing markets changed and further legislation was passed in the late 1960s. The new Conservative policies added new ideas and programmes, but their overall impact was rather limited. Furthermore, they left a legacy of growing problems to their Labour successors who took office in 1964.

When Labour came to power in 1964 public controversies were raging on
the harassment of tenants in London's private rental housing, and more
social research was being applied to housing. London's housing problems
were under examination and assessment by the Milner Holland Committee,[6]
appointed by the Conservatives in 1963. Housing was growing in social
and political significance, and the combination of intellectual review,
egalitarian dispositions in the community, politicians turning in favour
of reform and the widening relevance of social factors gave the 1960s
some resemblance to the 1880s (see Chapter 5). The process of review
and intensification of housing interest, itself, raised aspirations and
added new concerns to the agenda for reform. At the beginning of the
1960s, the key issues were rent control, the capacity of low-income
groups to pay, homelessness, and the expansion of subsidies in public
housing. In time further concerns were added, including: the adverse
social consequences of slum clearance and high-rise development; the
lack of social planning in new communities; and the wider relationships
between housing and urban/regional development, with some concern for
the rising price of urban land. As in the 1880s the urgency of agitation often led to action (and the political appearance of action) before
the issues had been understood from a sound intellectual and theoretical
basis.

During the early years of the 1960s, the findings and policy thrusts
of the Rowntree Trust Housing Studies [7] (1958-1963) were published.
These studies began with an interest in the consequences of the *Rent Act*,
1957, but they built up general sociological data on the British housing
sectors. The sociological surveys showed that owner-occupied housing
had mainly higher socio-economic groups, public housing had manual workers, and the private rental sector had many aged, unskilled and poorer
groups living in old, substandard housing. Since the partial decontrolling provisions of the 1957 *Rent Act*, the increases in rent were
relatively small in slow-growing moderate-sized towns, but much more
severe in London and areas where employment was rapidly expanding. The
British pattern of private landlording had not changed much since the
1885 Royal Commission reported its findings. It was still dominated by
small-scale operators, lacking professional management, but with some
occasional larger corporate operators. Finally, the research revealed
the general decline of the private rental sector and the patterns of
life-cycle mobility which drew young households towards the owner-occupier and public rental sectors. In short, the 1919-1939 trend towards a
rigid dualism in British housing was continuing. Also, the changing
demographic patterns, and particularly the increasing numbers of smaller
households without children, had not been accounted for by housing
planners.

Again, as in the 1880s, the more vexatious aspects of British housing
problems were revealed in London where the pressures were greatest.
The Milner Holland Committee reported in 1965 that London's pressures on
low-income rental housing arose from the increasing employment in the
region and the decline of the private rental sector. It advised
government to develop regional employment policies, to regionalise
administration, and to reform the economic basis of the private rental
sector. However, as we shall see in Chapter 9, British policies in
regionalisation have been confused and undeveloped compared with those
in Norway, Sweden and West Germany. Also, although Nevitt [8] had

shown the source of economic problems in the private rental sector, subsequent policies were not really aimed at achieving effective results. Nevitt argued that in Britain, private landlords were worse off than *any* other investors. Owner-occupiers got tax cuts based on mortgage interest and untaxed imputed rental income. Owners of industrial and commercial investments could cover the full cost of holding capital, and the tax system also allowed for depreciation. Landlords had none of these advantages, so new investment in rental housing was relatively unprofitable except where capital gains could be obtained. The lower cost public rental housing (i.e., untaxed housing) thus dominated the rental sector, and owner-occupied housing dominated private housing. By contrast, Sweden had drawn investment into non-profit rental housing via a mixed public-private financial framework, and West Germany used the Swedish method, combining it with accelerated depreciation writeoffs against taxation in private rental housing. As we shall see, Britain continued to make investment in private rental housing an unprofitable proposition.

A variety of ideas for policy emerged from the Rowntree Studies and the Milner Holland Report. First, there was concern that public housing with its explicit subsidies was stigmatised as *the subsidised housing sector*, whereas owner-occupier housing received implicit subsidies and the private rental sector suffered disadvantages from being outside any coherent framework for subsidies or tax reliefs. Second, critics noted that British policy development was *ad hoc* rather than comprehensive, and that it was not adequately responding to social and economic change. In continental Europe, policy development was more thoroughly researched. Third, the subsidies to public housing were (as Bowley had noted in 1945) not adequately related to concepts of need or to regional variations in housing problems. Fourth, the private rental sector needed to develop better management practices, to provide security of tenure, and to come within provisions for collaboration between the public and private enterprise sectors. Fifth, the divisions of housing powers under the *London Government Act*, 1963, neither enabled the Greater London Council to achieve a coherent metropolitan policy nor the London Boroughs to achieve wider housing perspectives. (This is discussed in Chapter 9, where better Swedish results are compared.) Finally, it was noted that British housing policies had been excessively influenced by dogmatic ideological conflicts. As we noted in Chapter 5 these patterns were set during the 1880s and built into the institutionalisation of public housing. They have continued to influence the course of policy development during the last decade or so.

Donnison, who had been deeply involved in research and policy during the 1960s, took a more general view of housing and he indicated that Britain was on the verge of passing from a 'social needs' policy towards *comprehensiveness* in housing. [9] The idea of comprehensiveness involved the following features:

1. The government becomes involved in planning housing as a whole, rather than limiting itself to its own social housing sector.

2. Government's involvement in housing widens, and it has to attend to the overall flow of saving into housing development.

3. Housing policy concerns itself with the existing stock as well as new construction.

4. The response to housing problems is related to regionalisation, land development policies and research.

5. Housing policy development depends upon deepening the understanding of poverty and relating social policies to various aspects of: (i) life-cycle poverty, (ii) 'crisis' poverty, (iii) long-term dependency, (iv) regional poverty and (v) inner-urban poverty.

6. Housing has to be understood as a process of community and social development.

Thus, Donnison provided a good general conception of modern housing and its policy relevance. However, progress towards comprehensiveness would be easier in continental Europe which inherited several advantages. Norway, Sweden, The Netherlands and West Germany had been operating *community* housing policies, rather than residual welfare or working-class policies, since the 1940s. They had a more coherent financial and administrative framework in central policies. Finally, these countries had a better prospective performance in economic growth, less social divisiveness and more coherence in managing the economy as a whole. History repeated itself with similarities to the 1880s. Once again the ideas came from British history but they found more fertile soil in other countries.

As was mentioned, British policy-makers acted under political pressures and urgencies. Labour's first step was to reform rental policies in the private sector. Although during the 1964 election campaign Labour had committed itself to repealing the Conservative *Rent Act*, 1957, once in power it decided to steer a middle course between decontrol and full rent control. Under the *Rent Act*, 1965, rents were *regulated* rather than controlled. That is to say, rents were to be determined by a process of conciliation between landlords, tenants and rent officers with provisions for arbitration by tribunals if conciliation failed to produce agreement. Notionally, rent officers and tribunals were to assume a level of rents which would prevail if supply and demand were in balance. As Hallett [10] has pointed out in his recent critical analysis, this criterion was virtually meaningless, except as a way of artificially suppressing increases in rents to economic levels. A better principle would have been to use a rate of return criterion. Alternatively, a more general reform in housing finance along the lines accomplished in Sweden in 1942 would have given the rental sector financial viability and avoided the worst consequences of homelessness - a symptom of insufficient low-rent housing. The 1965 *Rent Act* has formed the basis of modern British policy towards the private rental sector, but this came under review again in 1977-78, following a decade of economic and social failure.

Labour next gave general consideration to other housing problems facing the nation during the 1960s. In two White Papers, [11] published in 1965 and 1966, the Labour Government moved away from a restrictive view of public housing and it began to look at housing more comprehensively. The 1966 statement of policy committed the Government to continuing the support to the voluntary sector and the use of the Housing Corporation to foster rental and co-ownership housing. Also, Labour proposed to offer low-income home owners an 'Option Mortgage' scheme whereby they could choose between tax relief on mortgage interest or a directly subsidised interest which the Government would pay to

building societies.   For those households paying below the standard
rate of income tax, the direct subsidy to the cost of interest was more
beneficial.   The proposal was aimed in a limited way at reducing vertical and tenure-related inequities in housing.   These new Labour
policies were expressed in the *Housing Subsidies Act*, 1967, which was
presented amidst growing agitation in housing.   The television film
Cathy Come Home had graphically shown the plight of young couples unable
to find secure low-rent housing.   *Cathy* moved through a series of evictions, interviews with harassed housing officials, and she stayed sporadically in emergency housing, with the result that her marriage broke
down and she had the problems of rearing her children in a single parent
family.   It was very emotional stuff, making a deep impression on
public opinion in similar ways to Andrew Mearns' 1883 penny pamphlet,
The Bitter Cry of Outcast London.   After eighty years of public policy,
London still had homeless outcasts and much housing stress among its
low-income groups.

The *Housing Act*, 1967, also consolidated Labour's commitment to public
housing.   Subsidies were expanded and related to the cost of borrowing,
with the central government meeting the interest burdens of approved
schemes above the 4 per cent level of interest.   Although the scheme
appeared generous in a period of subsequently rising interest rates, it
led to more detailed central scrutiny of local government housing plans.
As was noted in Chapter 5, the Norwegian pattern of finance and
administration devolved these things to the client-developer relationship with far less cluttering up of central administration.   British
housing administration was becoming more centralist, and the bureaucratic
tendencies would compete for significance with strategic policy making,
research and so on.

Labour's 1965 White Paper [12] represented the first stage in developing a national housing plan whose main concerns were still with the need
to overcome chronic shortages and to eliminate slum conditions.   The
international comparisons with The Netherlands, West Germany and Sweden
showed that these countries were building more houses per 1000 of
population, they were spending more of their national income on housing,
and West Germany and Sweden were spending more of their fixed capital
investment on housing.   The relevant comparisons are set out in Table
4-1, below.

COMPARATIVE HOUSING STATISTICS : BRITAIN, THE NETHERLANDS,
WEST GERMANY AND SWEDEN

	New houses per 1000, population (1964)	Expenditure on housing as a percentage of GNP. (1961-1963)	Expenditure on housing as a percentage of fixed capital formation. (1961-1963)
Sweden	11.4	5.3	23.9
West Germany	9.8	5.6	22.3
The Netherlands	8.3	4.0	16.6
Britain	6.9	3.1	18.8

Source: *The Housing Programme, 1965-1970*, Cmnd. 2838, HMSO, 1965.
          Appendix 14, p.21.

TABLE 4-1

The countries in continental Europe had relatively larger post-1945 shortages to overcome, and so we might expect them to spend relatively more on new construction than Britain, and the statistics reflect this. But more significantly, these European countries were putting about 25 per cent of their GNP into fixed capital formation whereas British investment was sluggish at about 17 per cent. All of this meant that when the more difficult economic climate of the post-1973 period came, Sweden, The Netherlands and West Germany would be better able to weather the storm and to be more circumspect in reforming their welfare policies, including housing policies. Furthermore, the structural design of the financial and administrative instruments was more coherent for meeting the need for comprehensiveness in housing. All of this anticipates some later discussions, but it is relevant to note that some current problems in Britain have their roots in the 1960s, and earlier.

Meanwhile, Labour extended the role of rehabilitation in policies towards older housing by passing the *Housing Act*, 1969. The Act aimed at improving Britain's 'twilight' areas - the inner-urban zones where housing was not unfit, but showed signs of some lack of repair and some unattractive environmental settings. This Act did not fulfil its expectations and the reasons for this are discussed fully in Chapter 8. The Act marks the end of Labour's housing policy developments during the 1960s, and the beginning of a new Conservative approach to housing problems in the period 1970-1974. Labour's intentions in the 1960s had been reformist and towards the priority of the welfare state. However, the Wilson Labour Governments had been beset with balance of payments problems, the devaluation of sterling and deep-seated economic difficulties. Britain could not have a modern and progressive welfare state without a sound economic base. This basis was lacking and the tensions between welfare reforms and the modernisation of the economy have continued to dominate British politics in the 1970s. In housing this has meant that it has been difficult to break the nexus between low wages, uneconomic rents in the private and public sectors, and the clamour for adequate welfare. This was the general background inherited by the Conservatives in 1970.

CONSERVATIVE POLICY AND HOUSING ALLOWANCES, 1970-1974

The Conservatives were intent upon giving housing policies new directions, with an emphasis upon subsidising needy low-income households rather than bricks and mortar. In effect, this meant that they proposed to introduce housing allowances, a device which had been operating in Norway and Sweden for several decades and which the Conservatives advocated in their policy statement, *Fair Deal for Housing*. [13] The familiar arguments favouring the consumer subsidy approach were used : the new subsidies would reduce vertical and horizontal inequity, they would provide a more effective means of closing the 'housing gap' (see Chapter 4), and they would support housing improvement. The housing allowance idea was incorporated into the *Housing Finance Act*, 1972. This Act covered the private rental sector and public housing, where 'fair rents' were to be determined by rent officers using the 1965 *Rent Act* as its basis. Although *Shelter*, formed in 1966 as a voluntary lobby group to agitate against homelessness, favoured the measure, the Labour Party attacked it bitterly. Labour saw the measure as an assault on public housing, as a surreptitious means of making 'profits' from higher rents in public housing and as a threat to workers whose rents

would rise faster than wages.   Ideological dogma was overwhelming
reason, and Labour seemed unaware that their Labour and Social Democrat
counterparts in Norway, Sweden, The Netherlands and West Germany supported the idea of housing allowances and legislated accordingly.

The major design provisions in the British housing allowances included
the following.   Tenants would pay a minimum of 40 per cent of the 'fair
rent' or £1, whichever was the higher.   Then the share of rent costs
varied progressively in accordance with income and a 'needs allowance'.
Larger households had higher 'needs allowances'.   If the 'needs allowance' was higher than adjusted family income, the tenant's rent payments
fall by 25 per cent of the difference between the 'needs allowance' and
income.   On the other hand if the 'needs allowance' was less than
income, rent would be increased by 17 per cent of the difference, up to
the 'fair rent' level.   Clearly the housing allowance subsidies were
co-ordinated with rental policies, but as we have seen, the rental
policies did not give an adequate inducement to the private rental
sector.   In fact, the Francis Committee which reviewed the operation of
the 1965 *Rent Act* supported its economic and administrative principles.
[14]   Thus, the Conservative scheme was vulnerable on two points.
First, Labour was intent upon removing public housing from its provisions,
and in fact did this in 1975.   Second, the Act brought no real solution
to the economic problems of the private sector.   Without housing
allowances, public housing would continue to exhibit confusions and
inequities as a consequence of looseness in defining relationships
between subsidies, rents and capacity to pay.   Local governments would
set rents according to local policies and to the rather arbitrary
circumstances of their capacity to cross-subsidise rents on their new
housing from those on their older stock.   All sorts of vertical,
horizontal and regional inequities would result from this, but the Labour
Party and some local governments preferred this to the Conservative rent
rebates which expressed a common principle of equity in rental housing.

During 1973, the Conservatives published two White Papers [15] dealing
with housing policies.   The most significant change proposed was the
creation of Housing Action Areas (HAAs) which would express concentrated
social planning and housing improvement in the older areas of cities.
This idea was incorporated in the Housing and Planning Bill, 1974, but
Labour was returned to power before it was enacted.   Labour took up the
measure which is discussed more fully in Chapter 8, dealing with urban
renewal.   In their 1973 policy statements, the Conservatives also
committed themselves to giving further support to the voluntary sector,
overcoming homelessness, and encouraging local government to take a more
comprehensive view of their planning for housing.   By 1974, the Heath
Conservative Government was facing crisis in the opposition to its
industrial relations policies and this led to the return of Labour to
office.

LABOUR'S GENERAL POLICY REVIEW, 1974-1977

The Wilson and Callaghan Labour Government was mainly occupied with the
severe post-1973 inflationary pressures, unemployment and balance of
payments problems.   West Germany, The Netherlands and Sweden experienced
similar pressures and responded with tighter controls on public expenditure, including housing subsidies; but they managed to make their
subsidies more selective and to balance equity with efficiency in their

resourcing of housing.   As was mentioned above, these countries were
better able to weather the economic storms of the 1970s because they had
been modernising more extensively through the preceding decades.   In
Britain, Labour at first increased its expenditure on housing subsidies
and these were tending to run out of control.   But it had also
initiated a review of housing finance in 1974 and widened it in 1975 to
a general policy review.   The results were published in 1977. [16]
Thus, Labour's policies in the years 1974-1977 began with some *ad hoc*
reactions to earlier Conservative policy and ended with a wide-ranging
policy review.

   The earlier *ad hoc* reactions followed Labour's historical tendency to
protect and enhance public housing, and to restrict and control the
private rental sector.   First, the *Rent Act*, 1974, extended the 'fair
rents' provisions to unfurnished accommodation and strengthened security
of tenure.   Nothing was done to ensure that there would be an adequate
supply of private rental housing.   Second, under the *Housing Act*, 1974,
the Government increased its support to public housing and adopted the
Conservative idea of creating Housing Action Areas to bring concentrated
social planning and housing improvement to older areas.   This policy
has been overtaken by more comprehensive inner-urban policies, announced
in 1976 and switching the emphasis from environmental improvement to
employment and viable industrial development (see Chapter 8).   Third, in
the *Housing Rents and Subsidies Act*, 1975, Labour achieved its aim of
withdrawing public housing from the 'fair rent' and housing allowances
(rent rebates) provisions introduced by the Conservatives under the
Housing Finance Act, 1972.   In introducing the 1975 Act, A. Crosland
stated its purpose: '.....to cut the throat of the Tory Housing Finance
Act at a stroke'.   Thus, rents and subsidies in public housing were
left without a common principle of equity.   Labour argued weakly that
'fair rents' in public housing were inappropriate, and that local rent
policies in public housing should be within the control of representative local government, rather than resolved by unaccountable rent boards.
Sweden's Social Democrats had found good economic and social reasons for
releasing rents from their bondage to historical costs, and for using
rent tribunals with some tenant representation to determine rents.

   Hallett [17] has shown the inevitable consequences of Labour's
policies.   During the 1970s, expenditure upon public housing subsidies
was rising faster than prices or incomes, and it was not accurately
directed to meet the needs of the poorest.   At constant (indexed)
prices the public housing subsidies cost £525 million in 1971-72 and
they rose to £1,413 million in 1975-76.   The 1977 Green Paper noted
that public housing subsidies and expenditure on housing allowances was
growing over three times faster than investment in new construction in
the period 1969-70 to 1975-76. [18]   All of this can be attributed to
Labour's repeal of the rent rebate provisions covering public housing in
the 1972 *Housing Finance Act*, and its ideological use of public housing
without any systematic linking of rents with costs and subsidies.

   The policy review, 1974-1977, attracted controversy.   It began with
an emphasis upon housing finance, before it was widened to a full policy
review in 1975.   How did the costs of owner-occupier and public housing
compare, and what did they respectively cost the householder and the
government?   The Building Economic Development Committee and the
Department of the Environment found that public housing was relatively
more costly than owner-occupier housing.   Surveys indicated that

consumers' preferences favoured owner-occupier tenure.   Some of the
results of the reports were leaked to the Conservative Party and the
press, and the Labour administration was accused of withholding them
because their recommendations were unwelcome. [19]   The Green Paper
eventually argued that the results on comparative costs among housing
sectors depend upon the way costs are defined, and there is no abstractly
neutral way of doing this exercise.   Nevertheless, public policies
towards the private rental sector have failed and public housing
continues to be characterised by problems of cost, incoherence in rents
and inequities to tenants.   As a sequel to the Building Economic
Committee's review, when its report was published in 1977 [20] reference
was made to the political problems of getting agreement in the tenure-
related policy recommendations.   Cullingworth, a British housing
intellectual, assisted the Committee in sorting out the problem.   The
Committee's report accordingly discussed the taxation of imputed rental
value in owner-occupier housing, the benefits of an economically based
private rental sector, and linking public housing rents to cost
indicators and capacity to pay.

Labour's general policy review had advice from some of Britain's most
eminent intellectuals on the economics and social administration of
housing. [21]   But the Green Paper was careful to point out that the
policy statements were the Government's and not those of individuals who
worked on the review.   The review is a generally cautious and conservative document.   It points out that Britain now has an excess of
dwellings over households, and it is time for priorities to shift from
new construction to rehabilitation and the management of the existing
stock.   The Government has shown an interest in encouraging tenant
participation in the management of public housing, and the use of
co-ownership and co-operative tenure.   The review notes that the
private rental sector has diminished from 52 per cent of the total stock
in 1951 to 15 per cent in 1976.   Many of the prevailing problems of
poverty, bad housing standards and homelessness can be associated with
conditions in this sector.   The Government proposed a more specialised
review of this sector and the consequences of the Rent Acts.

Over all, the review and the Labour government's conclusions from it
were very conservative.   A few new directions were considered - the
expansion of housing allowances, relating rents and repayments to
(indexed) current values, and redirecting public housing subsidies more
selectively and equitably.   But the general intent of the report was to
maintain the prevailing conditions.   In favour of maintaining the
status quo it was argued that people make their housing choices on the
basis of long-term considerations of costs, housing options and employment prospects.   Thus, increasing the burdens of costs by relating them
to (indexed) current values, or drastically altering rents in existing
public rental housing to make subsidies here more selective, might
disrupt established expectations, and further reduce investment in
housing.   The review did accept that rents in public housing should
move in relation to medium-term changes in money incomes, but its broad
purpose was to conserve the *status quo* with its structural and sectoral
rigidities.

As we saw in Chapter 3, Grey and his co-authors, [22] Kilroy [23] and
other housing economists have reacted to the Green Paper, particularly
on the question of tenure-related distribution of income and wealth.
They discuss the subject with a purpose for getting structural reform

whereas the Green Paper argues mainly for the continuation of the prevailing housing system. Issues such as the taxation of imputed rental value in owner-occupier tenure and the general harmonisation of subsidies intersectorally are receiving much intellectual discussion, but not much in the way of policy reform (see the discussions in Chapter 3).

All of this shows that it is not easy to make structural alterations in housing finance and administration. In Britain, the structural conditions were laid down in the first and second phases of housing reform - in the 1880s and then in 1919 when central government contributed subsidies to public housing. As we have noted, some more useful and more flexible ways of doing things were available as options in the 1880s. It rather seems that if the wrong options were chosen in history, they later become sanctified by recourse to the argument that key changes will upset 'normal expectations'. It is a bad argument which is not acceptable to the Norwegians, the Swedes, the Dutch and the West Germans. They have changed their distribution of costs between households and governments, they have made their subsidies more selective and they have brought public expenditure under closer control without sacrificing essential social goals. These aims are not completely outside the scope of British policy commitments; but the development of British policy has all too often been characterised by *ad hoc* change, narrow social aims, protective ideological defences and great rigidities. The final irony is that the building societies began as self-help socialism, but Labour has never learned how to use their potential in modern society. Although the Building Societies Association proposed a mixed public-private finance solution during the First World War, no political party (and each of the three has had opportunity) has taken the idea seriously. It is possible to see public housing - now standing at 30 per cent of the total stock - as a generous contribution to social policy and as an expression of egalitarianism. However, if we examine the right places and histories in other modern democracies we shall find better ways of expressing social aims in housing, including better ways of administering public housing. With the election of the Thatcher Conservative Government in 1979, the main housing policy issues are likely to revolve around the sale of public housing. Ideological divisiveness continues to dominate British housing policies.

OTHER COUNTRIES

The Second World War reconstructed housing policy in many modern democracies. The Netherlands and West Germany faced the devastation and disruption of the Second World War. Post-war policy gave priority to industrial development and to increasing economic productivity. About 5 per cent of national income was allocated to housing production. Although Sweden had no war damage it entered a period of rapid urbanisation and high economic growth. In fact, during the 1960s, the Swedes found it necessary to produce more housing per 1000 of population than either West Germany or The Netherlands. Norway had some problems of post-War reconstruction, and like the other European countries it maintained levels of spending on housing which absorbed some 5 per cent of national income. In Australia, the central government (i.e., the 'Australian Government') became more deeply involved in housing, and it used Commonwealth-State Housing Agreements (CSHAs) to finance public housing and some home ownership. The United States widened its public policy involvements in housing and urban policies, with an early commitment to urban renewal (see Chapter 8), and some diversification of moderate- and low-income housing policies later in the 1960s.

Modern democratic countries face a number of common problems in housing, some of which have featured in our discussions of British policy development. They include the following:

1. Public policy involvements in housing have generally added to vertical and horizontal inequities. As social and political awareness of this has grown, policy-makers have tried to reform their subsidies to make them more selective. Housing allowances have been used to achieve those aims, along with some redesigning of production subsidies so that some costs are 're-captured' from payments by households and some subsidies phased down. Sweden, The Netherlands and West Germany have pursued these sorts of reforms since the mid-1960s.

2. The severe inflation of 1973-1976 added other reasons for reforming subsidies and housing policies. On the one hand it has been necessary to ensure that housing remains affordable, but on the other the pressures to introduce a tighter control on public expenditure have mounted. This has accelerated the process of reform in subsidisation (referred to above), and led to innovation in matching repayments with life-cycle income prospects. Again, it has been the continental European countries which have made most progress in inventiveness, adaptation and balancing economic efficiency and equity.

3. Aspirations for high-quality urban servicing have grown, thus drawing housing policy development closer to urban and social policies. These matters are discussed more fully in Chapters 7, 8 and 9 which deal with land development policies, urban renewal, and the government and organisation of housing.

One significant aspect of these modern policy issues is that they have rushed in one upon the other in a comparatively short period of time. It is this 'congestion' of demands which makes a comparative study highly relevant for understanding modern policy development. The complexity and suddenness of these modern issues identifies the capacity of countries to adapt and reveals the conditions under which useful policies evolve.

Australia [24]

Although public housing has contributed only some 15 per cent of post-1945 housing in Australia, from the comparative perspective it is the aims, financing and organisation of this programme which provide the focus of interest. The distinguishing features of Australian public housing compared with patterns in Britain and the United States are:

1. It is based upon formal agreements between the Australian Government and the States (Commonwealth-State Housing Agreements - CSHAs), and it is operated jointly by the two levels of government.

2. The basic financing instrument is a low-interest 53-year loan from the Australian Government, repayable by the States. Apart from a

temporary change in policy in the years 1971-1973 and some special
programmes for the aged, Aboriginals and other groups, the design of
finance for public housing has avoided direct subsidies from *current*
public expenditure. Thus, the States' housing authorities are
generally expected to be financially viable within the Australian
Government's funding without overt subsidisation from States'
governments.

3. In the States, public housing is administered by State-wide housing
    authorities which are organised as statutory commissions or trusts.
    Thus, compared with public housing in the United States or Britain,
    the organisation is less fragmented and less conditioned by local
    government. Furthermore, the corporate form of a commission or
    trust, gives housing authorities the potential to operate as
    statutory development corporations. As we shall see, South Austra-
    lia has taken full advantage of this wide-ranging potential.

4. The States each use their housing authorities to fulfil State
    government priorities with the result that public housing is used in
    varied ways. For example, in South Australia public housing is
    co-ordinated with government policies in urban and industrial
    development. In Queensland, Tasmania and Western Australia both
    the Labor and the Liberal-National Country Party (i.e., 'Conserva-
    tive') governments have used public housing as a means of expanding
    home ownership. However, sometimes when Labor has held power in
    the Australian Government, some limitations have been placed on the
    extent to which CSHA funds can be used for home ownership. In
    Victoria, the government used public housing as a vehicle for its
    inner-urban clearance and redevelopment policies during the 1960s.
    The New South Wales government used public housing for residual
    welfare during the 1960s.

5. All States have used some CSHA funds for home ownership under both
    Labor and 'Conservative' governments. In fact, since 1955 the
    CSHAs have made provisions for the allocation of funds to home
    ownership through co-operative building societies and the States'
    housing authorities. Taking an overall look at Australian housing,
    compared with Britain and some European countries, owner-occupier
    tenure has had a priority. This tenure reached 73 per cent of the
    total stock in the 1960s, dropping to 66 per cent now that rental
    flats are more popular among young people and other households
    without children. Although most of the growth of home ownership
    has occurred through the building societies and savings banks, some
    support has also been provided via public housing and government
    loans policies.

   In summary, compared with public housing in Britain and the United
States, the Australian expression of public housing has followed more
diverse purposes, it has larger scale organisation, its use of the
statutory corporation gives it some insulation from day-to-day politics,
its relationship to public finance is in the form of capital loans
rather than explicit subsidies from current expenditure, and it has some
direct association with home ownership as well as with rental tenure.
In common with public housing elsewhere, recent intellectual criticisms
centre upon the location and segregation of public housing, questions of
horizontal and vertical inequities, the relative merits of housing
allowances and production subsidies, and the wider involvement of tenants

in housing management.

Under the favourable political and historical conditions prevailing in
South Australia, policy-makers and housing managers have been able to
achieve wider purposes in housing and land development than British or
American local government.   In 1936, the South Australian Government
created the *South Australian Housing Trust* to build low-income housing.
However, the Trust operated within a policy, financial and administrative
framework which co-ordinated housing and industrial development.   Both
'Conservative' and Labor governments have ensured that the Trust has had
sufficient powers and enough differentiated finance to operate as a full
urban development corporation.   This has enabled the Trust to act as a
key participant in operating flexibly as a corporate enterprise involved
as a developer, a financier and an advisor in industry, commerce, retailing and housing.   In housing, the Trust has operated a variety of
programmes covering low-income rental, sales, and rehabilitation
programmes.   Following wider national social policy reforms in the
1970s, the Trust has become more deeply involved in its socially-related
housing involvements, including; housing for the physically and mentally
handicapped, women's shelters, urban Aboriginal housing and other social
programmes.

The Trust has looked upon its land acquisition programme as serving
full urban purposes, and not just low- and moderate-income housing.
Land has been purchased well in advance of development needs in order to
eliminate the high cost of private speculative trading.   As development
proceeds, the Trust has released some land under controlled freeholds
(by encumbrances on covenants), some under profit-sharing agreements
with private enterprise, and some under leaseholds with subsequent
options to purchase.   All of this has meant that the 'unearned increments' in land development processes have been captured by the Trust and
used to cross-subsidise social housing and community development from
values on industrial and commercial land.

The South Australian methods of financing and administering public
housing are akin to those used by British new town development corporations and local government in Sweden.   They also reflect something of
the characteristic of the Swedish and West German non-profit housing
enterprises; HSB, SR, and Neue Heimat (see Chapter 2).   In effect,
the example indicates some loss of opportunities in British local
governments' public housing.   This British expression of public housing
has been more confined and restricted to working-class housing and slum
clearance.   Furthermore, it has lacked the sense of enterprise and
flexibility that is potentially in the statutory development corporation
as an instrument for administering social (and other) housing functions.
The South Australian example could be followed in other places, but it
will be taken up only where housing, urban and social development
functions are broadly conceived and given bi-partisan political support.
South Australian political leaders have understood that the welfare of
the community in its broadest sense embraces economic development, social
planning and affordable housing in both owner-occupier and rental tenure.
Many British migrant families have experienced the advantages of this
broad conception of economic and social welfare.   The South Australian
housing policies and the broad community welfare basis from which they
spring are exceptional in Australian society - the other States' housing
resources have been used in more limited and conventional ways.

United States

American housing policy development since 1945 has three points of
comparative interest. First, the public housing programme has been
relatively small and full of economic, political and administrative
problems. Second, as disenchantment with the public housing grew
during the 1960s, new Federal Government involvements with social housing
created diverse programmes, avoiding the older 'public housing' image.
However, these new programmes also ran up against political, economic
and administrative difficulties. Finally, after 1968, American intellectuals and policy-makers were attracted to housing allowances as a
cheaper and more effective *alternative* means of subsidising low-income
groups. Other countries, and especially those in continental Europe,
conceived and administered housing allowances in combination with
production subsidies. Instead of developing a national programme of
housing allowances, the Americans launched costly and comprehensive
social and economic research studies to assess the financial, administrative and economic impacts of this form of subsidy. During the process
of research it has been found that it would be feasible to administer a
national housing allowance programme, but that the fuller potential of
welfare in housing requires a more pluralistic approach, including the
selective use of production subsidies and some direct interventions.
Also, the recent political tendencies indicate that the welfare aspects
of housing are more widely appreciated and supported than in the 1937-
1968 period. This means that current housing debates in the United
States have centred on the means of providing government assistance and
how programmes should be shaped, rather than on the principle of breach-
ing *laissez faire* in housing.

The American public housing programme is comparatively small-scale with
no more than 2 per cent contribution to the total stock of housing.
(In Britain the level is 30 per cent and in Australia the joint
Australian Government-States' programme is 15 per cent of post-1945
housing.) American public housing has developed as a residual welfare
programme with access restricted by severe income eligibility tests.
The original design and construction of the financial arrangements
broadly provided for rents to cover operating expenses, the Federal
Government meeting amortisation payments on housing bonds issued by local
authorities. During the 1960s, estates management costs rose through
inflation and other causes, including vandalism. Some of the social
problems in the estates were leading to economic and administrative
strains.

Some public housing authorities were ready to increase rents but in
some cases the tenants resisted with rent strikes. The Federal
Government's attitude was that if it contributed towards the costs of
estates management, the State welfare authorities might withdraw the
housing grants which they paid to their clients. (Public housing
tenancies in some areas were dominated by welfare clients and low-income
families.) Eventually, in 1969, Senator E. Brook was able to secure
enough support to steer the *Public Housing Law Amendment* through
Congress. Under this, the Federal Government extended its financial
aid to estates management costs, on condition that welfare authorities
continued to pay their housing allowances, even if rents were decreased.

There are grounds for criticism of the American public housing
programme. Housing finance suffers from entanglement in intergovern-

mental and inter-agency relations.   There are problems, common to most
modern democracies, in reconciling capacity to pay rent with estates
management costs and amortisation costs.   Long-term changes in economic
relativities have pushed up estates management costs, and modern housing
estates tend to require more servicing than older ones.   At the more
general policy level, the economic and administrative problems of
managing public housing are easier to deal with when this housing caters
for a wider cross-section of the community and when it is possible to
charge differential rents according to ability to pay.   These
possibilities are present in some European housing, some British local
government housing and in the South Australian Housing Trust.   Viewed
from another perspective, we can say that the idea that public housing
should be limited to the poorest sections of the community - a view
often put among social workers and by some intellectuals - has some
unacceptable economic and social consequences.

American public housing became identified with undesirable social
consequences.   It faced local and central political hostility; it
accentuated segregation; it was highly stigmatised for its 'welfare'
image and its dominant use by blacks in some cities; it was confined to
sites which other users did not want; it had some bureaucratic
tendencies; and it was relatively expensive.   This imagery forced
policy-makers to push public housing into the background and to use
other methods to express social aims in housing.   Accordingly, in the
1961-1968 period, the Federal Government initiated a series of new
experiments in housing policy development, aimed at inner-urban poverty,
increasing the impact of social housing, and expanding production to
achieve national targets.   The urban renewal aspects of the new policies
are dealt with in Chapter 8.   New trends in social housing involved
greater use of the private sector in social housing, some tailoring of
subsidies progressively to need, encompassing moderate-income groups in
social housing schemes, using rehabilitation in social housing programmes,
subsidising home ownership, and introducing rent supplements.   The
financial design of the new programmes frequently involved the use of
periodic payments from *current* public expenditure.   As programmes
expanded after 1968, the burden of subsidies became more conspicuous and
a source of political contention, thus leading to a suspension of
programmes by President Nixon in 1973.   It was the open-ended nature of
these subsidies and the absence of any provision to recapture escalating
costs from payments by households that undermined the political and
economic viability of the new schemes.

The expansion of American social housing outside the scope of public
housing began in 1959 when Section 202 was added to the *Housing Act*,
1949.   It provided low-interest loans so non-profit and limited-profit
housing associations/sponsors could build rental housing for the aged.
In 1961, this principle was extended by Section 221 (d) (3) to sponsors
of low-income rental housing.   The 1961 programme was aimed at households with incomes which were too high to qualify for public housing,
but too low for owner-occupier housing.   Further significant additions
to the *Housing Act*, 1949, were made under the *Housing Act*, 1965.   These
included rent supplements and empowering local housing authorities and
private sponsors to purchase or lease housing for rental to low-income
groups.   The rent supplements were based upon eligible tenants paying
25 per cent of their income towards rent, with the Federal government
making up the difference between 'economic' (i.e., historical cost)
rent and tenants' payments.   After 1965, the Johnson Democratic

Administration made greater commitments to social housing.

In 1967, two presidential commissions - the National Commission on Urban Problems and the Committee on Urban Housing [25] - reported and recommended the expansion of the moderate- and low-income housing programmes. Although its methods for assessing housing needs have since been criticised [26], the Committee on Urban Housing took a national view of housing and saw the need to develop 26 million dwellings in a decade, 6 million of them for low-income households. It was these ideas which set the policy context for Federal government housing policies in the years 1968-1971. First, under the *Housing and Urban Development Act*, 1968, greater impetus was given to the rent supplement programme, and two further Sections (235, 236) were added to the *Housing Act*, 1949. These Sections extended the subsidy payments from current expenditure to support moderate- and low-income housing, and the Section 235 was aimed at supporting subsidised home ownership. Unlike previous experience in American social housing, the 1968 measures were strongly resourced by Congress. Between 1968 and 1971 federally-assisted new housing increased from 11 per cent of housing starts to 21 per cent. Those moderate- and low-income families which obtained their housing through rent supplement and overtly subsidised home ownership schemes were able to reduce their housing costs by 33 per cent, and more.

As was mentioned above, in 1973 President Nixon suspended social housing programmes pending the results of a comprehensive review. What had gone wrong? At the time the new programmes were introduced in the mid-1960s some Democrats had opposed the extension of subsidies to *moderate-income* groups, preferring a more confined anti-poverty welfare purpose along the lines of public housing. On the other hand, some Republicans opposed the general expansion of social housing programmes because of the burden on public expenditure. Congress had been more cautious than President Johnson, but it nevertheless authorised substantial funding, although it limited the acceptable housing standards (and by implications the level of rents) more stringently than the President's proposals. A financial feature which was favoured at the time, was the use of annual subsidies from current expenditure, rather than using the relatively heavy and 'lumpy' capital loans which concentrated the burdens on public expenditure to particular years. In fact, it was the burden of these open-ended subsidies which contributed to the suspension of programmes. The financial forecasts, based on the commitments to the programmes in 1968-1971, indicated that burdens on public expenditure would rise to $7.5 billion by 1978, the date when the 10-year housing drive was due to terminate.

Other problems characterised the post-1968 housing policy developments. Some programmes had been slackly administered, private entrepreneurs had profiteered, and the programmes added to the existing problems of horizontal and vertical inequities. Housing intellectuals revealed the comparatively excessive cost of some programmes, and they favoured more use of rehabilitation methods and a national programme of housing allowances. [27] Advocates of housing allowances claimed that compared with production subsidies, the consumer subsidies were more effective and selective, permit more consumer choice, avoid the stigma linked to public housing, and reduce the heavy intermediary costs which are absorbed in public administration. The arguments on stigma and inter-mediary costs are more deeply relevant to an American situation where public housing has mainly been used to house the poor, but similar arguments have been directed against public housing in Australia and Britain. In the United States, the housing allowance idea sparked off a lively and controversial debate, [28] even before the preliminary results from powerful official research programmes had been published.

Thus, the demise of the 1968 policies can be attributed to a number of factors. First, at the intellectual level, the 'filtration' strategy to solving low-income housing problems (see Chapter 4) had been found to be less effective than other strategies, particularly as social and economic change made the thrust to overcome 'shortages' less significant. Second, at the administrative level, it was found that collaboration with private enterprise required more varied skills in public administration than were available in 1968. It is now appreciated that administrative capacity and skills are necessary in all social housing schemes, including housing allowances. This is having an impact in public housing where the 1970s concerns are with improving the management of tenancies and estates, rather than simply seeking alternative housing programmes. At the political level, some more conservative forces came to power in the early 1970s, but there is a widening support for social housing policies compared with the political hostilities which have characterised social housing programmes in the period 1937-1970. Finally, the United States has experienced the sort of problems with subsidies that have forced reforms in Britain, Sweden, The Netherlands and West Germany. That is to say, open-ended subsidies place heavy burdens upon public expenditure, vertical and horizontal inequities are hardened by public policies and the overall expectations cannot be fulfilled. All of this leaves United States' housing policies in a state of flux, but with considerable attention from officially commissioned research and from policy-makers. Two aspects of the policy developments in the 1970s have comparative interest.

During the 1960s there was a four-fold increase in grant-in-aid expenditure by the Federal government. Matching and other conditional grants were designed to induce State and local governments to extend their activities in housing, urban and social policies. Some problems arose as a result of the distortion of State and local priorities which the matching conditions required, and also in assessing priorities among over 500 grant-in-aid programmes. These rigidities led to reform in favour of consolidating the growing number of narrowly specific programmes into a few broad groups. The reform was facilitated by the *State and Local Fiscal Assistance Act*, 1972, and the *Housing and Community Development Act*, 1974. Under this latter Act, the 1973 suspension of housing programmes was partially lifted and State and local governments had more flexibility in selecting among programmes. Section 8 of the 1974 Act introduced a new policy, enabling housing authorities to provide housing allowances to renters entering into lease contracts with landlords within an officially designated programme. This reflects a wider official interest in housing allowances (see below). From the perspective of a comparative housing policy, it is interesting to note the increasing significance of intergovernmental and organisational issues in housing, a point dealt with more fully in Chapter 9 which surveys recent reforms in Norway, Sweden and West Germany.

The cause for housing allowances was given wider official recognition under the *Housing and Urban Development Act*, 1970. Section 501 of this Act authorised the development of a large programme of social and

economic research to assess the housing allowance idea. The research
is addressed to such questions as: how much would a national housing
allowance programme cost, which are the most effective forms of a
housing allowance, to what extent do consumers improve their housing
standards and/or decrease their cost burdens, how can the allowances
best be administered, and what relationships will allowances have with
housing markets, general welfare assistance and other forms of housing
assistance. Already, the research programme has added significantly to
our understanding of housing and its economics (see Chapter 4). This
is a worthwhile contribution in itself with general relevance in other
countries. With regard to policy development in the United States, the
housing allowance idea has an uncertain future. On the one hand, the
optimists would emphasise its cost advantages, its potential for making
subsidisation more selective, and its feasibility. But pessimists
would argue that the idea has status only as 'an experiment' with no
definite long-term political and administrative commitment. The more
circumspect observers would point out that the evidence from the research
and overseas experience suggests that the housing allowance idea is best
used judiciously and flexibly within a broader framework of other forms
of housing assistance, and a general public policy aimed effectively at
reducing poverty and enhancing the long-term prospects for the national
economy. It is within that context that Norwegian, Swedish, Dutch and
West German housing policies have been developed.

Although it is possible to state that the welfare aspects of housing
have not been so thoroughly developed in the United States as in Britain
or continental Europe, this does not imply that American housing
policies have completely failed. It will be recalled from Chapter 5
that the major thrust of the American housing reforms during the 1930s
was to improve the terms on which owner-occupier housing was provided.
During the period 1950-1970 the number of dwellings built was some
30.5 million, exceeding the number of new households by about 10 million.
Furthermore, the number of substandard units fell from 17 million units
to 5 million in this period. Housing standards had improved considerably for most groups. The contributory factors were: (1) the inducements to produce new housing, (2) the general increase in incomes in the
community and (3) the 'filtering' of some standard housing to moderate-
and low-income families. Nevertheless, the American approach raises
critical issues on the direction of subsidies (especially implicit
subsidies) which went mainly to the middle classes, and on the very bad
housing conditions among the poorest groups.

These questions of equity and effectiveness, are influencing modern
policy review in the United States. Such questions are made more
complex by the realisation that implicit subsidies - tax relief on
mortgage interest costs, untaxed imputed rental income on owner-occupier
housing - are the major forms of subsidisation, amounting to an estimated
annual value of over $11 billion in 1978. [29] Meanwhile, the poorest
groups remain in bad housing, in bad environments and without access to
employment in new suburban factories. But in some cities, older
housing is being abandoned as it filters out of the wanted stock and
without new waves of migrants to occupy it. These were the main
American housing issues of the 1970s.

Norway

The discussions in Chapters 2 and 5 sketched some historical aspects of

policy development in Norwegian housing finance.   Policies have been
based on government central banking facilities.   In 1946 these were
re-organised and expanded.   The Housing Bank and Smallholders' Bank now
finance more than 75 per cent of Norwegian housing.   Individuals,
co-operative societies, and private entrepreneurs can apply for funds,
and the Banks, with local government, control only costs and the size
of the dwelling, not its type.   In 1978, individuals accounted for 61
per cent of Bank-financed dwellings, co-operative societies for 23 per
cent, and private entrepreneurs for 9 per cent.   Over 75 per cent of
the dwellings were houses with gardens and 14 per cent were in apartment
blocks.   Norwegian housing features choice of dwelling type and tenure,
and people prefer houses with gardens and owner-occupier/co-operative
tenure.   Norway is probably the most successful country in promoting
this sort of choice within a financing system dominated by government
roles.

Norway's housing finance reforms have been direct, and with little
complication.   However, the nation has had its colourful periods, such
as 1925-35 and 1945-57 which witnessed housing vexation, agitation in
the community and the expansion of the voluntary housing movement.   In
fact, the re-organisation of the Banks in 1946 was in response to a
contemporary housing vexation - the private mortgage market was able to
lend only 60 per cent of the value of dwellings and access and repayment
was difficult for most households.   There were acute housing shortages,
following war-time devastation and disruption.   In this period, young
radical idealists formed the USBL to act as a co-operative self-help
housing organisation, and to agitate for more government action.
However, in the long-term, Norwegian housing has displayed continuity
and stability, these characteristics being influenced by a lengthy
political dominance by the Labour Party.   In the 1935-1940 and 1945-
1961 periods the Labour Party governed on its own, and in the period
1940-1945 a broad coalition government ruled in exile.   Since 1961,
apart from two relatively brief periods of non-socialist coalition
governments, the Labour Party has remained in power.

It has experienced virtually no dilemmas in pursuing home-ownership
policies within Social Democratic idealism.   As early as 1916, the
Labour Party had committed itself to home ownership, support for the
voluntary housing movement and the elimination of excessive profiteering
in urban land and housing markets.   The Banks have been used to express
financial aspects of home-ownership aims and also the support given to
the co-operative movement.   Early post-War policy emphasised long-term,
easy repayment loans.   This method of finance was supplemented with
overt fiscal subsidies; a 'depreciation grant' expanded government's
financial assistance.   It was anticipated that the grant would be
necessary only as a temporary measure when post-War costs were high.
However, inflation continued.   While these depreciation grants did not
survive, in 1957 a non-interest bearing loan was built on to the basic
long-term loans, themselves repayable over 100 years at 2.5 per cent
interest.   The repayments on the non-interest loan did not start for 10
years.

There was an unintended legacy from the 1945-1960 period; one useful
as far as modern ideas in social planning are concerned.   The Housing
Bank's policy was in that period to provide up to 95 per cent loans on
terraced houses built in blocks of four and only 75 per cent on single-
family homes.   This created a financial inducement to develop terraced

housing, sell three units for owner-occupied tenure and provide the
fourth unit as a rental dwelling. The consequence was to mix tenure
types through new development, rather than producing estates segregated
by tenure and incomes. This offers an example of something which could
be deliberately repeated anywhere as a clear policy. In 1966, the
Government split Housing Bank loans into first and second 'priorities',
to draw more private finance into housing and to combine a private
second mortgage with a Housing Bank first priority loan. This did not
succeed; **lending** continued to come mostly from the Housing Bank, even
though its second priority loan was repayable over only 15 years. This
system operated until 1973 when fundamental revisions were made because
of inflation and problems of low-income access to housing. It is now
appropriate to look at some of the economic aspects of Norwegian housing
finance.

In modern democracies, one of the key economic factors in housing is
to achieve a flow of savings into housing investment. West Germany
approached this problem by inducements and by designing a suitable mixed
public finance-private mortgaging framework. The Swedish approach
combines public finance and private mortgaging. The Dutch finance some
housing entirely from public finance and attract private finance for
other housing by inducement in the form of production subsidies. In
the United States the approach has been more indirect with the object of
turning loaning conditions into a form suitable for financing owner-
occupier housing. Norway collects savings from savings banks which
have been persuaded [30] to purchase government bonds. The proceeds
are paid into the Banks for loaning to the housing sector. Government
has other policies of general economic management. The Norwegian
approach is direct, uncomplicated and effective.

The 1973 reforms aimed to ease repayment burdens in times of severe
inflation, and to expand the consumer subsidies scheme (inherited from
the 1950s) so that the low-income access to housing was easier. By
1972 this Norwegian scheme covered 55,000 households and cost N.Dr. 60
million. However, the Government became concerned because the rents
on new dwellings were absorbing more than a fifth of low-income families'
household budgets. Accordingly, it revised the scheme so those on the
lowest incomes paid no more than 15 per cent of their incomes on housing.
For those with higher incomes, the scale of assistance reduced to cover
20 per cent of housing costs. The scheme was designed to reach those
income groups just below the average. Housing allowances were available
to owner-occupiers, co-operators and renters. By 1978 they covered
112,000 households and cost N.Kr. 289 million.

The design and construction of the new housing allowance system was
co-ordinated with simultaneous revisions to the Banks' loans, where
applicants could choose between gearing repayments to annual average
earnings ('levelling loans') or repaying a ratio of the principal of the
loan ('nominal loans"). Of borrowers, 85 per cent have preferred
levelling loans which carry a 6.5 per cent interest rate, variable at
any time by Government. The repayments are calculated annually, by
relating them to the average Banks' loans in that year, and they are
fixed in relation to 20 per cent of average male blue-collar earnings,
and are assessed independently of interest. The system is essentially
a low-start mortgage with an accumulating debt in the early years,
because repayments then do not cover interest charges. The nominal
loan system has a 6.5 per cent interest rate and its repayments of the

principal are one per cent for the first 10 years and two per cent for the next five. But the Government can change the rates after the first five years, using the criterion that repayments must amortise the loan as quickly as under the levelling loans.

The new system was designed to allow new households access to housing hit by severe inflation. Unlike the 1968 Swedish system (see later discussions) the Norwegian system does not make specific assumptions about the course of future prices, only the general assumption that future trends in average earnings will be sufficient to repay the loan. In an economy already among the wealthiest in the world, and with prospects enhanced by vast oil reserves, the general assumption does not appear to be too risky. Also, the government is assuming the risk, not the private capital market.

The Norwegian system requires a continuous flow of information on prices, incomes, economic problems in housing and so on, and depends on the Government exercising continual discretionary powers on interest rates and loan repayments. For their part, the Banks will consciously need to plan their finance. Clearly, there is a need for significant and continual consultation, and this is provided by a committee of representatives from the Housing Bank, the Ministry of Finance, the Bureau of Statistics and the National Federation of Norwegian Co-opera- tive Housing Societies, which advises the Minister. The Banks are confident that Government will always take a reasonable view of financial considerations, because the committee has a persuasive influence.

The Norwegian financial framework is thus seen to be comparatively uncomplicated, and the historical cost rental problem has not been as significant as in West Germany, The Netherlands and Sweden. Norway achieved reform in just one step in 1973 by simultaneously altering consumer subsidies and the structure of the Banks' loans. This reform co-ordinated the two changes and was aimed at reconciling access to standard housing for low-income groups with inflationary price movements. Housing has occupied a firm place in national, social and economic planning since 1946. The 1973 reforms continue these welfare state objectives in the light of steady and continuous economic growth. Though housing has been heavily subsidised in the easy loaning and the fiscal senses, price movements have not run ahead of wages and general prices. In 1970-1977, blue-collar earnings rose 120 per cent, consumer prices 78 per cent and housing costs 66 per cent. Expenditure on housing has been 5.5 to 4.9 per cent of GNP. Since 1972 housing has declined from 19.2 to 13.2 per cent of gross capital formation, which in the same period has risen from 27.9 to 33.1 per cent of GNP (but it has declined from 37.8 to 35.3 per cent in buildings).

These statistics begin to reveal recent changes in Norway. Invest- ment is expanding generally in a country with good prospects for the future. Economic growth has continued since 1974, whereas it has slowed down in other countries. [31] Growth produces housing problems, particularly in large cities such as Oslo, Bergen, Stavanger, Tromso and Trondheim. Even with a firm foundation in housing finance and land policies, housing shortages and pressure on housing markets appear in the larger, growing urban areas. This has led to payments of premiums [32] and speculation where housing demand presses hardest. These circumstances mostly hit new moderate- and low-income households. The problems originate in urban areas where employment is expanding. It is not easy to overcome them and certainly they need policy interventions beyond housing finance and public land assembly. Urban development in Norwegian cities is spreading rapidly, at low densities. New policies are needed (see the discussions in Chapter 7).

The urban growth problems have occurred within a national framework in which population growth rates have declined. Housing policy needs regionalisation and variety according to local needs. However, in a general context, Norway is, like other countries, entering a period when there will be a switch of emphasis to the existing housing stock. This is another reason why Norwegian housing policies are likely to become more deeply involved with urban and regional planning.

Since Norway has followed a strong long-term policy of egalitarianism, it is appropriate to examine how wealth and imputed incomes in owner-occupier and co-operative tenures are treated in the tax system. Interest payments are tax deductible in both. [33] However, imputed rental value is taxed at 2.5 per cent on 30 per cent of the value of the dwelling. In co-operative housing, the value is fixed not to the market, but to local authority valuations, which are generally some years behind current market values. As previously mentioned, the pressure of demand in some cities has led to unofficial premium 'key money' payments. These payments are untaxed because, officially, they do not happen. The capital tax on non-housing wealth is at the same 2.5 per cent rate, but it covers the full value of assets and not a reduced 30 per cent as in the case of housing. In 1976 taxation on housing became politically controversial, mainly because of the various methods being used to evade it. [34] Generally, the income and wealth advantages in Norway favour owner-occupier and co-operative tenure. However, except in the rapidly growing large cities, home ownership is accessible to moderate- and low-income groups.

As a final perspective on Norwegian housing policies it is relevant to summarise those characteristics which set them apart from those in other countries. Generally, the historical and theoretical contexts in which policies have developed reveal more coherence among objectives and administrative arrangements than other countries. In Norway, housing has more choice in tenure and dwelling type among the broad range of the community than in other countries. Egalitarian ideals have been expressed in a financial and administrative framework which controls essential factors, but remains relatively unbureaucratic. The egalitarian goals have not suppressed the expression of self-fulfilment and individualism in family and personal lives. Housing institutions have been responsive to the needs of social and economic change, and when change is necessary it has been thoroughly discussed and negotiated before it takes its legislative, financial and administrative shape. Although Norway still has housing problems, given the essential diffi-culties in housing policy development - the internal conflicts of objectives, the problems with co-ordination, and the mismatch between expectations and performance - this country has achieved remarkable results. In short, Norway has used its historical opportunities well, with recourse to useful social thoery, self-help, political agitation, and the expression of social idealism dominantly through banking institutions. Norway has been more definite than Britain, Australia and the United States in using private savings for social and community-wide purposes in housing. Put in another way, the Norwegian policy-makers have better understood housing in its historical, social, economic

and political significance than others.   This has continued into the
1970s when housing finance was reformed in response to inflation and
accessibility problems among first-time home buyers and low-income
groups.   The several reforms - expansion of housing allowances, gearing
repayment of loans to income capacity, and the taxation of owner-
occupier rental value - were co-ordinated and harmonised.

Sweden, The Netherlands and West Germany

These countries have had broadly similar contexts in which they have
developed their post-1945 housing policies.   The discussions in Chapter
5 referred to Swedish initiatives during the 1940s and the use of a
mixed public-private financial framework to induce resources into housing
so that high-volume production could be achieved.   The Netherlands and
West Germany have also co-ordinated public and private finance to
produce wide-ranging community housing policies, with an emphasis upon
producing a substantial low-rent sector.   Although, the general thrust
of post-1945 policies follows common themes in these countries, the
variations in economic and administrative instruments which these
countries have used are, themselves, interesting in their own right.
Furthermore, each of these countries began reforms to subsidisation and
housing finance during the late-1960s.   They are of general comparative
interest and reveal some useful ways of balancing considerations of
economic efficiency and equity.

   The aspects of comparative interest which were referred to above can
be placed within the general thematic context of this study.   First, we
have noted British housing history in the period 1919-1939 revealed
problems of confusions among objectives, and difficulties in achieving a
simultaneous coherence in matching subsidies with costs and rental
policies.   These problems also appeared in Sweden, The Netherlands and
West Germany, but their impacts were more intensified because subsidies
were deeper and more general than in British public housing.   On this
basis alone, the need for reform was an imperative in the late-1960s.
However, as the reform process was set under way, those modern policy
issues which are featured in this study - inflation, housing-related
equity and the co-ordination of housing, urban and social policies -
have also been drawn into the process of reform.   Thus, these further
complications add other aspects of comparative interest, and they are
particularly significant for showing how countries with more comprehensively developed policies adjust these policies with social and economic
change.

Sweden [35]

As was discussed in Chapter 2, Swedish housing policies have been designed and developed to express Social Democratic idealism, with the most
significant policy changes occurring in 1942, following the guidelines
advocated by the social economists Myrdal and Johansson.   With the
collapse of the private enterprise involvement in moderate- and low-
income rental housing in 1942, the Social Democratic policy-makers
created a social housing programme to fill the void.   This programme
was based upon a number of crucial conditions: (1) public benefit
enterprises were to be set up to emphasise *non-profit* principles in
community housing, (2) rents were to be affordable within a general
resourcing and administrative framework which drew upon public finance
and public administration, (3) local government was to be co-ordinated

with central government in developing a dominant social housing sector, (4) the social housing sector was to express good standards of design and convenience (see Chapter 3), and (5) housing shortages were to be overcome by establishing medium-term planning targets.   All of that was coherent and useful in terms of the conditions which prevailed in the period 1940-1970 - the need to emphasise increases in production, the use of government to provide community housing with some expression of egalitarianism, and the political will to use housing as a key instrument in Sweden's rapid urbanisation.   These commitments could be linked to the useful inheritances in land policies and co-operative economic enterprise to create a genuine comprehensiveness in housing (see Chapters 2 and 7 for detailed discussions of these other aspects of housing policy development).   During the 1970s, under the impacts of social and economic change - slower demographic growth, less stable economic conditions, and the significance of tenure-related distribution - Swedish housing programmes have experienced problems of adjustment. It is the policy inheritance from 1942 and the changing circumstances during the 1970s which are pursued as the main themes in our account of Swedish housing.

In the early 1960s policy ideas were clear and relatively uncomplicated.   Rapid urbanisation and population growth then pointed to the need to overcome housing shortages.   In 1964, a national target to build one million dwellings in a decade was set, using the well established mixed public finance-private sector financing scheme.   The private sector provided mortgages up to 70 per cent of the value of the dwelling, and the government added to this a second mortgage, arranged to favour non-profit local authority housing enterprises (public benefit enterprises) and the co-operative sector.   Public benefit enterprises received government loans covering 30 per cent of the value of the dwelling, thus completing financial cover to this housing and the co-operatives received 29 per cent.   Owner-occupiers received a loan covering 25 per cent of the value of the dwelling and private enterprise developers 15 per cent.   This financial framework discriminated in favour of certain developers, but still reflected a social ideal.   Also, it still offered scope for competition among developers.   During the 1960s, government-assisted housing comprised 90 per cent of new development, and its major financial attraction was its heavy fiscal subsidisation of interest costs on the private mortgages.

Although Swedish subsidisation in housing included housing allowances (see below), its main thrust in the 1960s was in deep and extensive production subsidies.   This subsidisation induced rapid development, but the system contained all those dilemmas connected with the burdens on future public expenditure, historical cost renting and housing-related inequities.   It was necessary to achieve a tighter control on subsidies, to pull the system away from historical cost renting/repayments, and to alter the distribution of costs between households and public finance.   The first steps in reform were taken in 1968 when the government introduced a 'parity loan' scheme.

The 'parity loan' scheme was aimed at: (1) raising rents/instalments on overtly subsidised housing (both on the existing stock which had outstanding debt and on new construction), (2) shifting some costs from public finance to households, and (3) making subsidies more selective by concentrating aid in the first years of a household's life cycle. This scheme was designed to ease the transition from the earlier scheme;

the repayments over the first year coincided with the levels of rents/
instalments under the previous scheme. Later, rents/instalments would
rise according to the index of building costs. Thus, rents/instalments
were fixed in relation to current values rather than to historical costs.
However, the index was related only to the principal of the loan, not to
interest rates. Interest rates began to rise after 1968 and the
government saw its fiscal burdens escalate because it had to cover the
increases on the private first mortgage at any rate above four per cent.
The debt increased, and there was little chance that the parity loan
scheme would actually remove some of the burdens from public finance.
In 1974, it was abandoned, partly because it had failed to fulfil its
main objective and partly because new policy issues became significant
during the mid-1970s (see below). However, the Swedish system of
housing finance has retained the principle of gearing repayments to life-
cycle earning capacity. Also, the 1968 'parity loan' scheme marks an
important break with historical cost rents/repayments.

The 1968 reforms in production subsidies were accompanied by other
revisions in housing policy. Rental policies towards the private sector
were altered so rents on older housing would reflect their proper value
in relation to the costs of new housing. Since 1957, the Swedes had
been decontrolling rents of older private sector housing, region by
region, as the more acute scarcities were overcome. The *Rent Act*, 1969,
introduced the idea of regulation as a middle course between market and
controlled rents. Under the 1969 Act, tenants and landlords were
required to consult each other and to try to agree on the appropriate
rent. If no agreement was reached, the matter was to be referred, for
arbitration, to a local rent tribunal, on which tenants' groups were
represented. To reach decisions, tribunals took into consideration the
prevailing rents in similar types of dwellings and locations. In 1975,
an amendment was made so that the tribunals referred to the costs of new
dwellings produced by non-profit developers. Thus, the present
principle is to fix rents to relate to non-profit replacement costs
rather than to market values. The general economic principle is that
rental policies were part of a stage by stage reform of housing policies
as a whole. Changes were necessary in private rental housing for
reasons of the overall consistency of rental policies and because the
older rent controls inhibited mobility and caused other economic dilemmas.

Another step was taken in 1969 when housing allowances were given more
attention, Sweden having operated a system of housing allowances for
families since 1935, under which financial assistance was graduated to
income and related to family size. Local government also operated
supplementary systems with some central government support. Following
the 1968 'parity loan' scheme, consumer housing costs increased and the
low historical rents were abolished. Also, the *Rent Act*, 1969, implied
some increases in private sector rents. In these circumstances, the
government decided to improve the take-up rate of housing allowances and
to give them a firmer emphasis in the new system of subsidisation.
Further reform followed in 1974 when housing allowances were extended to
single- and two-person households as well as to families. Thus the
scope and depth of housing allowances were increased.

The failure of the 1968 'parity loan' scheme and its increasing
burden on public expenditure, meant that production subsidies needed
urgent reform. The need for reform coincided with some considerable
economic pressure on public benefit housing enterprises (the local

governments' housing developers) and with an increase in home ownership. The public benefit housing enterprises had built mainly for rental tenure and they were organised in the powerful Swedish Public Benefit Enterprises (SABO) which pressed the issue of tenure-related distribution, arguing that increased production subsidies were necessary to balance the implicit subsidies which owner-occupiers received. Under the *Housing Act*, 1975, the 'parity loan' scheme was abandoned and production subsidies were geared to general interest subsidies. The subsidies were regarded as being better controlled than under the 'parity loan' scheme, and as a compensation for implicit subsidisation to owner-occupiers. Following a general housing policy review in 1974, from 1975 the matter of tenure-related distribution figured prominently in Swedish housing finance and subsidisation.

Implicit subsidisation in the home ownership sector is complex. As interest rates increase, so does the implicit subsidisation to owner-occupiers. In Sweden, the imputed rental value of housing is taxed and so are capital gains on resale. [36] However, these taxes are generally outweighed by tax concessions on mortgage interest payments. These concessions are not limited to certain income ranges and not scaled to equalise the advantage among different income groups. During the 1950s, when interest rates were low, Swedish tax had a neutral effect because concession and liability were approximately equal for many home owners. However, now that interest rates have risen, the tax concession can be more than one tenth of taxable income among typical home buyers. This is causing conflict and controversy. Also, the co-operatives (HSB and SR) want the tax concessions extended to co-operators, but SABO have lobbied to resist this. The controversy has become all the more significant in view of some recent structural social and economic changes in Swedish housing. These changes have enhanced owner-occupier tenure, and the economic factors referred to in this paragraph have decreased its price relative to rental tenure.

Although rental tenure forms a large and strong proportion of Swedish housing, recent social and economic change has led to the growth of owner-occupier tenure. In 1975, 40 per cent of Swedish housing stock was in rental tenure, 10 per cent in co-operative tenure and the rest in owner-occupier tenure. Rental housing is more dominant in the metropolitan areas. Now that the major post-1942 shortages have been overcome and society is more affluent (but population is growing less rapidly), there has been a marked switch in favour of owner-occupier tenure and houses with gardens. [37] In 1971, houses with gardens contributed only 32 per cent of new dwellings, but by 1976 this form contributed about 70 per cent. Construction of rental apartments declined as housing conditions changed. These changes add more political significance to the Swedish controversies on tenure-related subsidisation. However, owner-occupier tenure is likely to grow, since the economic, social and political conditions are conducive. The impact of demographic, social and economic change is likely to push more households towards home ownership. In 1972-76, the Social Democrats were in minority Government and their attitudes towards home ownership became more favourable, despite a strong renter lobby. When the Conservatives won Government in September 1976 some political hindrances to home ownership were reduced. Savings banks are well-organised to promote home ownership [38] even though the waiting time for government-assisted housing in Stockholm is 10 years.

A general perspective on Swedish housing policy shows that the question of finance and subsidisation is far from resolved. By 1975, the problems of controlling public expenditure and taking deliberate account of tenure-related distribution unsettled housing policy development. However, there are other, deeper difficulties. The demographic, social and economic changes were leaving a trail of problems and controversies. The co-existence of excess supply (26,000 vacant new apartments in 1976) and excess demand showed there had been a breakdown in strategic policy making and programming. This situation has also made segregation more conspicuous (see discussions in Chapter 7). Meanwhile, the organisation of the building industry had been geared to the production of mass project housing, but consumers began choosing to live in more personalised places. The changes also show the need to bring the existing housing stock and urban renewal into key significance.

In summary, it can be seen that Sweden has responded to the need to re-structure subsidies and housing finance. Compared with Britain, Sweden has operated a more successful rental sector, it has accepted the need to (partially) link rents/repayments to current values, and it has used a creative mixed public-private financial framework which serves community-wide housing. However, some of the modern issues in housing remain unresolved in policy development. Swedish rental policies still produce horizontal and vertical inequity and other anomalies associated with legacies from historical cost renting and chronic housing shortages. Also, the incoherent entanglements from among Social Democratic idealism, town planning and social housing theory, the 'ideological purity' of rental tenure, and so on, continue to influence policies (see the discussions in Chapter 2). This has been particularly evident in the Social Democrats' devotion to high urban density and their reluctance to embrace owner-occupier tenure as an expression of self-fulfilment for moderate- and low-income families. Thus, owner-occupier housing and dwelling forms with gardens have been regarded as anti-social [39] However, as we have seen, social and economic conditions have turned in favour of owner-occupier tenure and the bonds which policy-makers could use to constrain choice have now loosened as chronic shortages have been overcome (see Chapter 3).

One aspect of change is the growth of double-income families, which can afford to leave the flats and buy bigger houses with all the amenities. Some heroic saving will enable them to get this housing sooner than the 10-year waiting period for the preferred types under the government-assisted metropolitan housing scheme. In some cases, the double-income situation is a response to the barriers making the preferred types a luxury. With reformed financial and land development policies, this type of housing does not have to be a luxury; it is no more costly to produce than apartments, but presently it sells at higher prices because it is in short supply. The heroic saving is not so much a capitalist endeavour as a symptom of the sort of motives which drive people to achieve self-fulfilment. Housing is perhaps the key focus where family aspirations and the double-income expression of social and economic change meet. The recent move towards home ownership has followed spontaneously from social and economic change; it has not been a policy change.

This contrasts with earlier times (the 1920s) when the Social Democrats in Stockholm created the 'magic house' (see Chapter 2). They organised finance, production and land servicing to encourage moderate- and low-

income families to literally build their own homes.   Sweden's neighbour,
Norway, has shown the modern-day inheritance of that policy.   In 1942-
1970, under vexing housing shortages, Sweden turned Social Democracy and
its housing in another direction.   In Sweden's larger cities, the 'magic
house' is now an expensive luxury, but some mass project flats lie
vacant.   These are technically excellent, but housing involves more
than technological sophistication.   The 'magic houses' are humanist,
they work well for young children, for the comings and goings of teen-
agers and their parents, and they are well cared for.   Essentially,
modern Swedish Social Democrats have not been able to articulate a
consistent and coherent policy on home ownership and choice of dwelling
type, and these are crucial weaknesses in an otherwise useful practice
of Social Democrat idealism in housing.

West Germany

The form and structure of West German housing policies have been
dominated by conditions arising after the Second World War.   The major
comparative characteristic is the design of the financial framework
which has ensured a large flow of savings and investment in housing.
Official estimates in 1950 indicated that West Germany was short of six
million dwellings, owing to wartime devastation, migration and a growing
population.   The essential need was for substantial investment.   Under
these circumstances a major government role in housing was inevitable.
In fact, by the 1960s, more than 60 per cent of the new housing was
influenced directly by government assistance.   During the past decade
or so, along with The Netherlands, and Sweden, West Germany has had to
revise subsidisation to control public finance better, and to meet
changing allocational and distributional housing objectives.

  The Government's housing policies have been expressed through the
First Housing Law, 1950, the *Second Housing Law*, 1956, and some recent
amendments of subsidisation and rental policies.   The Housing Laws
defined the basis of government loans and subsidies, and geared the
amount of subsidisation to the income categories of households.   The
aim has been to make government-assisted housing accessible to most
people and some 70 per cent of West German households have been eligible
for access under Housing Law programmes.   However, many households
which are eligible for overtly subsidised housing choose to rent in the
private market.   The West German private rental sector is strong and
economically viable, and the levels of rent are at about the same as
those for new subsidised housing with its more inflated recent costs.
Social housing (i.e., overtly subsidised housing) is administered in two
categories; the 'Primary Way' with lower income eligibilities and
standards, and the 'Secondary Way' with income eligibility set at 140
per cent of 'Primary Way' housing.   This social housing is rented at
historical costs and in recent years this has led to the usual dilemmas
of vertical and horizontal inequity.   This point is discussed further,
below.

  The housing constructed under the Housing Laws has been developed by
non-profit housing associations, co-operatives and private enterprise.
Housing associations have been significant in West German housing; the
country does not have public housing in the sense that is understood in
Australia, the United States and Britain.   Various developers can use
the financial framework which has been designed and constructed to
support general housing needs in the community.   As was mentioned above,

215

in West Germany the private rental sector should be considered alongside
social housing because it offers choices and values which do not set it
expensively or cheaply apart from much of the social housing. Hallett
[40] has shown that private rental housing is available from a variety
of landlord types and in a variety of dwelling forms. Thus, West
Germans can choose to rent a flat, a set of rooms attached to a family
dwelling (usually the landlord's), a new dwelling or an older dwelling.
Choice among landlords ranges from individuals, through non-profit
operators, to corporate private enterprise. The strength of the West
German private rental sector can be attributed to its comparative freedom from rent controls (though since 1971 rents have been regulated -
see below), and the provisions for accelerating the depreciation against
taxable income.

The dominant financial framework in West Germany combines a private
first mortgage, a government (or a private) second mortgage and own
capital. Private and government financing are mixed. First mortgages
come from mortgage banks, savings banks and insurance companies which
can raise capital from the stock exchange through mortgage bonds. This
part of the financing is clearly exposed to private market influences.
First mortgages are typically amortised over 30-35 years. In social
housing, government subsidies have been provided to compensate for high
interest on first mortgages and are a strong force in pulling resources
into housing. The 'Primary Way' subsidies in the first ten years are
currently worth some 36 per cent of construction costs. 'Secondary
Way' subsidies are worth only 40 per cent of 'Primary Way' subsidies and
they reduce at a greater rate. In fact, since 1967 the West German
production subsidies have been designed to reduce at pre-determined
amounts so that housing costs are more closely related to life-cycle
needs and they are less burdensome in public finance. The 1967
changes, like Sweden's 1968 'parity loan' scheme, mark the intensification of new policies so that the financial framework was more selective
and geared to the need to control public expenditure. Originally, the
successful aim of the framework was to create a large volume of new
production. In the period 1950-1974, some 14.2 million units were
built and the 'housing miracle' was fulfilled in 1974 when the existing
stock was in approximate balance with the number of households.

The government encourages housing-specific savings for *eigenheim* and
owner-occupier tenure, through premiums or tax concessions on the
amounts saved. In a system of progressive income taxes, the premiums
are worth more than the tax concessions to those in the lower income
ranges. Notwithstanding this, the savings scheme and *eigenheim* mainly
benefit the middle classes. The first operates through *bausparkassen*
(home savings societies) and involves accumulating 40 per cent of the
value of a loan over a period of seven years. Savers enter a savings
contract with a *bausparkasse*, entitling them to a specified loan when
they have fulfilled their savings obligations after seven years. The
loans are amortised over a relatively short eight to ten year period.
Currently, the value of government subsidies is 25 to 35 per cent of the
annual contractual savings.

Although owner-occupier tenure in West Germany has been rising, it is
still comparatively low at 37 per cent of the total stock. Rental
tenure dominates, for historical and financial reasons. Historically
the main housing choice in large cities has been rented units in
tenement blocks, these being located close to work and public transport.

For workers, this is a major consideration.   The post-Second World War
programme has continued these historical inheritances.   Modern systems-
building technology (and related variants) has enabled developers to
construct mass project housing at high production rates.   Government
policy has assured a large volume of funds to developers, who have been
motivated to bring technology and finance to terms.   Also, like Sweden,
in the first two post-War decades the suppliers of housing, rather than
the consumers, have been able to dominate and constrain choice in a
context of severe shortages.   Town planning theory and practice has
supported mass project housing (see Chapter 2).   Since 1974, consumer
choice has been less constrained, but *eigenheim* costs about six times
average wage-earners' annual income whereas home ownership in Britain,
Australia and the United States is much cheaper in relative terms.
Finally, it will be recalled that rental tenure in West Germany is
enhanced by the relatively generous depreciation allowances in tax law.
Depreciation allowances have been designed and constructed to run over a
32-year period, but with 40 per cent of the investment written off
against tax during the first eight years.   This places housing investment in a relative advantage to commercial and industrial investments.

The introduction of the *Second Housing Law*, 1956, marked the beginning
of the politically difficult and protracted process of revising the
subsidisation and resourcing of housing.   The key objective was to
shift financing from public sources towards a larger influence for
private capital.   The effect can be gauged by the fact that, whereas
43.9 per cent of the finance in the voluntary housing sector's dwellings
was provided by government in 1951, by 1973 the figure was only 13 per
cent.   As part of a more general policy, the Christian Democratic
Governments 1956-1965, wanted to remove general subsidisation and to
restrict the explicit housing subsidies to a narrower special needs
role.   This policy met political resistance in the community and the
Christian Democrats were forced to revise their approach.

The new approach to housing finance was more differentiated and
selective in its impact.   Government's general production subsidies
might be reduced, and also rent controls dismantled, providing that the
financial impact upon new households and low-income groups was cushioned.
This could be achieved by creating new housing allowances and by carefully and gradually removing rent controls.   Under the *Housing Controls
(Removal) Act*, 1960, the Government began to remove the controls on
private rental housing in the non-assisted sector.   Next, the *Housing
Allowance Act*, 1965, provided housing allowances to low-income renters
and owner-occupiers.   The new subsidies were an extension of the
narrower rent rebate scheme used to relieve financial need among low-
income households whose rental housing was decontrolled under the 1960
Act.   Essentially, the 1965 Act introduced a common equity principle to
cover West German low-income renters and owner-occupiers regardless of
what kind of houses they lived in.   These housing allowances were
graduated in relation to income, family size and rent/instalments.   In
1976 the housing allowances contributed some 14 per cent of total overt
housing subsidies, they covered 10 per cent of total households, and
they were designed so that the lowest income families paid no more than
11 per cent of their income to rent/repayments.

The Christian Democrats had regarded the housing allowances as a
politically acceptable way of reducing the cost of production subsidies
to the community.   However, the Social Democrats (in power since 1968)

initially looked upon them as a means of making housing more egalitarian.
[41]. Changing economic circumstances during the 1970s have led the
Social Democrats to take a harder look at housing subsidies.   First,
there have been too many new apartments, with vacancies reaching 350,000
in 1975.   This indicated a need to alter the direction of allocation
and distribution in housing finance.   More specifically, it called into
question the functions of *general* production subsidies and the implications of historical cost rents.   Second, the severe inflation of 1973-
1976, pointed towards getting a firmer control on public expenditure and
cutting back subsidisation which had no current priority or social-
economic justification.   Specifically, this meant that some costs might
be shifted to rents, and the effects could be cushioned by expanding
housing allowances and making production subsidies more selective.

In the circumstances, these aims were attractive to Social Democrats.
However, we need to bring home ownership into account.   The West German
Social Democrats, like other Social Democrats in Europe, have been
ambivalent in deciding whether home ownership expresses anti-socialist
capitalism or is a legitimate self-fulfilment and serves a social
purpose.   Recently, West German Social Democrats have got to grips with
the dilemma.

Three factors have led to a greater interest in home ownership:
attitudes are changing and the Social Democrats are interested in
workers owning capital in industry and in housing; the severe inflation
of 1973-1976 made the Government more conscious that *eigenheim* and owner-
occupier tenure are ways in which some burdens on public expenditure can
be removed; the Social Democrats shared power with the more middle-of-
the-road Free Democrats who more positively favour home ownership.   In
the campaign for the 1976 Federal elections, the Social Democrats,
returned to power with the Free Democrats, came out in support of home
ownership.

All these social, economic and political factors have combined to aid
a revision of housing subsidisation and finance.   Production subsidies
have continued to occupy a key role, but have been designed to reduce by
pre-determined amounts.   This means some future costs are shifted on to
rents/instalments.   Rental policy now expresses regulation rather than
control as the principle.   Legislation passed in 1971 protects tenants
from eviction and exploitive rents, but rent increases can be authorised
to cover increases in estates management and housing improvement costs.
Also, rents are referred to criteria of cost/price among dwellings of
similar type in comparable locations.   Hallett [42] argues that the new
rent policies may undermine the strength of private rental housing in
West Germany and so lead to social and economic problems associated with
shortages in that section of the housing stock.

Generally, West Germany has adapted its system of housing finance and
subsidisation to meet changing social and economic needs, though it is
by no means certain that this has gone far enough.   One key problem is
the historical cost basis of renting/repayments in overtly subsidised
housing with some consequent dilemmas for economic efficiency and
housing-related inequities.   Housing intellectuals in West Germany are
presently examining ways of making the financial and rental arrangements
in these houses more closely and progressively geared to the needs of
households rather than tied to specific houses.   This could be achieved
by a national pooling of revenues and costs, with rents related to the

income of households and their capacity to pay.

Other current ideas in policy development are centred upon rehabilitation, access to home ownership, and making assistance even more selective
to social needs and to new households facing inflationary costs.
Though more positive interest in urban renewal has been shown (see
Chapter 7), it may be necessary to put more resources and finance into
the existing housing stock, rather than into new development.   Also, as
eigenheim and owner-occupier tenure becomes more popular, this will have
significance in housing finance, and social and land development policies.   The full implications of *eigenheim* are not yet fully appreciated.
Nevertheless, on its recent record, West Germany seems to be sufficiently
inventive and adaptive to make further progress in housing policy
development.

Compared with British housing policies, the West Germans have been more
inventive in linking public and private finance, they have developed a
strong rental sector, and housing choice is less constrained by sectoral
divisiveness.   The British have made home ownership more accessible
than the West Germans.   Taking the Swedish and the West German policies
together, compared with British housing their rental sectors are stronger
and they serve wider cross-sections of the community.   In Sweden, the
rental sector has been developed mainly through public financial and
administrative instruments, whereas the West Germans have used both
public instruments and private enterprise.   The West German experience
shows that private rental housing can grow strong in modern conditions
if its rents are left to market forces and investors are allowed to
depreciate their capital on terms which are broadly similar to, or
competitive with, commercial and industrial investments.   These
arrangements induce supply; they meet consumer demands in respect to
standards, and they keep prices at affordable levels.   Then, the
housing allowances enable needy households to get housing within their
capacity to pay.

The Netherlands

Dutch housing policy development since 1945 is often similar to West
German trends.   The Dutch built a financial framework reflecting the
same aims as the West Germans.   It was designed to channel a large
volume of savings and credit into housing investment to overcome an
estimated shortage of 300,000 units as a legacy of war-time devastation
and economic dislocation.   Since 1967, the Dutch have gone through a
politically difficult and protracted process of reforming subsidisation.
Like the West Germans, their aims have been to make subsidies more
selective, to get to grips with the housing-related equity problem, to
introduce more inflation-proofing in housing finance, and to create some
new instruments to push a greater share of costs to households.

The Dutch have succeeded in achieving reform, and their evolving
pattern is more co-ordinated, equitable and differentiated than earlier
systems of finance.   Another similarity with West Germany is in the way
this reform has been achieved.   The process started with a Right-Wing
Cabinet of Christian Democrats and Liberals intending to reduce production subsidies and to confine them to special needs roles.   There was
powerful resistance in the community and the Cabinet learned that
housing was probably the most socially and politically important area of
social policy in modern Dutch society.   Later, in 1973, the Social

Democrats came to power with a tenuous majority, and they had to depend on some middle-road political support. In housing, they ran into problems of co-existing excess demand and excess supply in different sections of the housing stock. Also, in 1973, inflation struck extra hard and Government had to control public expenditure more firmly.

We can deepen our understanding of Dutch housing by examining its differentiation into sectors, as follows. The first broad division is between the *government-assisted* sector and the *free* sector, with the former receiving overt inducement from government loans and overt subsidies. Then, the government-assisted sector divides into *profit* and *non-profit* sectors, with both of these developing owner-occupier and rental housing. The non-profit voluntary sector includes 'housing corporations' which are controlled by legislative requirements as 'accepted institutions'.

Dutch resource planning in housing is comprehensive, providing for total production estimates and allocation to the sectors specified above. In recent years more attention has been given to allocations for rehabilitating older housing, providing for smaller households and for special needs, and widening the access for young adults (i.e., 18-25 year olds). The changing pattern shows adaptation to a changing society, and the rehabilitation of older housing marks the beginning of giving more attention to the existing stock now that the chronic major post-War shortages have been overcome. However, the policy to widen accessibility for young adults has revealed the need to develop some new units for this group, with some current conflict between resourcing for new development and rehabilitation. The addition of housing resource development for younger people, for smaller households and for special needs groups reflects recent demographic change and the impact of social planning ideas in modern housing. Clearly, the Dutch financing, resourcing and planning of its national housing is geared to a changing policy of comprehensive scope.

The differentiation can be further understood with a review in terms of historical and recent policy developments. Historically, the *Housing Act*, 1901, and its subsequent new version in 1962, enabled the central government to direct financial assistance to local governments, which traditionally relied on the voluntary sector as the developer of social housing. After the Second World War, large shortages led policy makers to draw private enterprise into a wide policy of providing housing generally in the community. Private enterprise housing in The Netherlands is undertaken mainly by life-insurance companies, banks and pensions funds acting as financiers and developers. Government (overt) fiscal subsidies are available to private enterprise as well as to local government and the voluntary sector. The overall implications of this mixed enterprise approach can be gauged from the ownership of the stock. By 1975, owner-occupiers owned 88 per cent, voluntary corporations owned 23 per cent, local government owned 12 per cent and private enterprise owned 27 per cent of the stock. Also, it should be borne in mind that during the 1950s over 80 per cent of new Dutch housing was built with at least some overt government assistance.

Dutch housing can be characterised in greater depth by looking at modern tenure choice. The policy is to attempt to neutralise financial biases in tenure. It is notable that production subsidies are available to both rental housing, and to owner-occupier/co-operative

tenure, which in The Netherlands has not been readily accessible to
people of low income simply because these people have found it difficult
to save enough to take up mortgages and meet repayments. (In recent
years, private mortgages have been available at 9 per cent interest over
30 years and inflation has reduced the proportion of the total value
covered.) Government attempted to open up home ownership by creating
for low-income groups a 'protected sphere' mortgage, which receives
larger production subsidies than does the regular programme. In 1976
this programme was planned to produce some 13 per cent of the total new
owner-occupier housing supported by overt subsidies, but the take-up
remained very small and in 1979 the scheme was abolished. Owner-
occupier tenure is also supported by central and local government sharing
the risk of borrowers defaulting on mortgage repayments.

It can be seen that government supports owner-occupier tenure in
various ways. It is particularly notable that production subsidies are
available to both rental and owner-occupier housing. However, the
central government is also aware that owner-occupier housing confers an
asset (wealth) value and an imputed rental value to its owners.
Accordingly, the Dutch have marginally compensated this effect with a
tax of N.Fl 8 per N.Fl 1000 of assessed capital value. Also, owner-
occupiers have to add to their overt income a 'rent value component'
which is taxed. The Dutch argue that, in view of the implicit subsidisation and other assistances to owner-occupier tenure, housing
allowances should be accessible mainly to renters. In the owner-
occupier sector, since 1979 overt fiscal assistance to housing has been
related to the income of households.

The foregoing indicates the Dutch methods of accounting for tenure-
related equity, and the attempts to neutralise tenure choice. However,
research shows that home ownership is more readily taken up by middle-
income groups, and low-income groups tend to rent older housing.
Tenure choice remains related to income level and accessibility.

The Netherlands, like Sweden, has been experiencing some significant
changes in tenure choice as demographic, social and economic change
re-define the constraints within which choice operates. In 1975
Government thought there was no longer an acute overall shortage of housing, economic affluence was general, the number of double-income families
increases and the rate of demographic growth slows down. However, as
was mentioned earlier, the extension of access to young adults put new
demands for additional development. The social and economic changes
have contributed to the growth of owner-occupier tenure from 37 per cent
in 1970 to 40 per cent in 1977. This sector is well-supported by
mortgage instruments, but the rapid changes in demand have led to relatively higher rates of inflation in this sector. Typically, the sort
of family house (with a garden) sought in suburban parts of moderately-
sized towns, costs five times average wage-earners' annual pay. In the
heavily populated Randstad region (the Amsterdam - The Hague - Rotterdam
- Utrecht quadrangle), single-family housing is more expensive.
However, some of the growth of the owner-occupier sector is from existing
housing in the private sector, not from new construction. In 1979 more
than 30,000 rented dwellings were sold to the occupants. In 1971, the
private rental sector accounted for 52.7 per cent of the total stock, but
since then investors have cut back development and some stock has been
sold to owner-occupiers, leaving this sector with less than 48 per cent
of the stock in 1977.

The sectoral changes referred to above indicate the role of two factors: (1) the demographic, social and economic changes in recent years, and (2) the influence of policy changes begun during the late-1960s. These policy changes were aimed at curbing overt subsidies, overcoming the dilemmas of historical cost renting and rent controls, and generally achieving more mobility and fluidity from market and para-market instruments. (A para-market instrument re-arranges the distribution of costs between the public sector and households, with the overall aim of blending some market virtues with social aims expressed in public finance.) Accordingly, government assistance has been made more selectively with some emphasis to shifting some costs from public finance to households, whilst retaining government's involvement for social and egalitarian objectives. For example, like West Germany, The Netherlands scaled its overt subsidies to reduce by pre-determined amounts over a period of 12 years. This meant rents/repayments would cover 40 per cent of costs in the first year of letting/purchase and increase to 100 per cent after 12 years. However, as we shall presently see this marked only the beginning of a stage-by-stage set of co-ordinated reforms.

As was mentioned above, the recent policies began with redesigning subsidies to decrease annually by pre-determined amounts. This shifts future costs on to rents/instalments, and concentrates assistance on new households. The new design was introduced in 1968 by the Christian Democrats, who later formulated a wider policy in 1972 which also included cut-backs in production subsidies (i.e., government loans and overt fiscal subsidies) and greater encouragement to owner-occupier tenure. However, the Dutch regarded their community housing policies as a welfare state right and there was considerable resistance to any clear government withdrawal from general housing. Thus, the Christian Democrats proceeded cautiously, the redesign of production subsidies in 1968 being the first step.

The next step was aimed at rental policies. Since 1968, the central government had been dismantling rent controls as shortages were eliminated. However, the problem of historical rentals on government-assisted housing, with the vertical and horizontal inequities which this produced, brought the question of rental policy into further significance. The Government accordingly passed the *Rent Harmonisation Act*, 1971, to give powers of direction over *all* rents, not just those in the older private stock. The aim was to push up rents on older housing so that they eventually harmonised with levels on new stock. This was a replacement cost concept, not market rent; also it was scaled, not controlled or periodically regulated. The scale was designed to increase rents at four per cent per annum in the early years, and then to double this rate. Harmonisation was not achieved because inflation hit the economy extra hard in 1973, driving up building costs at more than 8 per cent. In any case, the community was becoming restive and critical of the Government's performance in housing.

Consequently, the Government took its next step, acting more directly on housing-related equity. In 1970, a housing allowance scheme was introduced to provide assistance to renters in government-assisted housing. Thus, it can be seen that the conservative Christian Democrats began 1967 with the intent of introducing more *laissez faire* in housing. But, by 1972 after a push-and-pull relationship between the community and the Government, the result was a mixture of para-market institutions (the rental policy and the new design in production subsidies) and housing allowances. A conservative Government and an agitated community had produced more selectivity and co-ordination in housing finance. It seems paradoxical but it is not. The community had enjoyed the private benefits of low-rent housing over several decades, and they were organised in tenants' groups, unions, developers groups and so on. Low-cost housing had a constituency, and 'participatory democracy' had been learned in the aftermath of social agitations against the Vietnam War and the conservatism of society in the 1950s and early-1960s. On the other hand, subsidisation needed reform and conservatism generally led in the right direction. Conservative reform could work provided it was limited and made more selective. History was producing some coherent political economy.

The Social Democrats came to power in 1973, inheriting a useful coherence in recent reforms. They had to keep their policies within the limits of what political moderates would accept. This factor along with other reasons discussed in the West German context made the Social Democrats more inclined to accept home ownership, if still reluctant to embrace it wholeheartedly. They also found two good reasons for continuing the para-market themes started by the Christian Democrats. First, excess supply began to appear as vacancies in some new flats. This accentuated the need to continue reforms in housing finance and rental policies. Also, the Government had to face the prospect of private enterprise withdrawing from constructing new rental housing. Second, the inflation of 1973 hit hard. Subsidisation needed firmer control and more selectivity, and the older housing stock would get more attention as the general need to meet shortages receded. On the other hand, inflation was pushing up the costs facing new households.

The Government met these problems by extending the reform process. In 1975, the housing allowances were extended to all renters, not just those in the government-assisted stock. The levels of subsidy, its scaling to income and its relationship to rent levels were to be reviewed annually. Government was showing its support for the housing needs of low-income renters in particular. By 1976 the scheme, consciously designed to avoid the administrative problems of the West German scheme, was covering 300,000 households, and the take-up rate was comparatively good, being estimated at more than 90 per cent.

Other reforms had an impact on production subsidies and rental policies. Future rents were to incorporate a 'dynamic rent calculation'; that is a formula-based calculation geared to move rents in relation to the costs of construction and estates management. The dynamic rent calculation was proposed by the Right-Wing Christian Democrats in 1972, but introduced by Social Democrats in 1975. This was a final break with historical cost rents on new housing stock. The introduction of the 'dynamic rent calculation'; has wide comparative significance. Compared with policies in Britain, West Germany and Sweden, the Dutch have been more definite in gearing rents to the cost of new construction and housing services. It will be recalled that the discussions in Chapters 1 and 4 referred to the modern needs for bringing the costs of housing services and estates management more directly into rental policies.

The Government also intended to remove anomalies in the rents of old stock, particularly in view of the failure of the 1971 rent harmonisation

scheme.   Under the *Rent Act*, 1978, a new 'rent adaptation system' was
introduced; it was designed for assessing (and increasing) rents on the
existing stock.   Under the provisions of the Act, the rents in some
areas ('unliberated') are regulated and in others ('liberated') there is
market freedom.   The unliberated areas are the large cities and the
Randstad.   In those places, rental housing is classified according to
its type, size, amenity, age and locality, and landlords and tenants are
required to consult each other to fix an appropriate rent.   If agreement cannot be reached, a rent tribunal will assess the dwelling and
determine the rent.   The system has affinities with recent reform in
Sweden.

Altogether, the Dutch have achieved considerable and useful reform in
the past decade.   They still face problems in steering subsidisation in
new directions, particularly towards older stock, as the West Germans do.
More attention needs to be given to strategic policy-making and programming so that combinations of excess supply and excess demand do not recur.
In 1974, the Dutch Social Democrats declared housing to be a 'merit
good'.   This meant that housing was regarded as an important part of
the welfare state.   It was to be accessible to rich and poor, young
(any household with its head over 18 years) and old, and home ownership
was to be accessible to low-income groups.   Dutch housing finance is
differentiated, is aimed at useful social and economic purposes, and is
deliberately related to housing-related equity.

Comprehensiveness in housing has a wider domain than finance.   It
must also include land development policies, dwelling form and urban
servicing, intergovernmental relations and organisation.   As far as
comprehensiveness is concerned, the Dutch have performed better
financially than in other spheres.   Under acutely difficult circumstances they gave heavy emphasis to mass project housing, but others
are sceptical of the suitability of apartments for family living.   The
economic case for mass apartment blocks is suspect.   However, consumers
are at last beginning to reveal their views of how this housing performs
in a time of wider choice, and higher incomes.   These factors have been
influential in greatly reducing the development of high-rise housing.
By 1976, apartment blocks accounted only for some 22 per cent of new
development, and single-family dwelling forms have increased throughout
the 1970s, absorbing some 78 per cent of new development in 1976.

CONCLUSIONS

The British published the results of their general policy review in
1977.   They would stay on their old course, with some intention to
improve relations between housing and social policies, and to encourage
rents in public housing to keep pace with medium-term increases in money
incomes.   Their housing problems still included homelessness, vertical
and horizontal inequities, and confusions on the purpose of subsidies.
In 1975 Labour had withdrawn the general housing allowance system from
public housing and retreated to its traditional belief, first evident in
the 1880s, that public housing is the uniquely useful way of giving
expression to social goals in housing.   This attitude has combined with
the divided structures of housing finance and administration to give its
major comparative characteristic of excessive sectoral rigidity.   Most
of the poverty and other social problems in British housing lie in the
private rental sector.   They lie there because the public sector cannot

cope with them, while the private rental sector has been given a
legislative and financial framework which puts its private aims into
conflict with most of the good social purposes which it succeeds in
serving in many other countries.

In The Netherlands, Sweden and West Germany things are different.
During the 1950-1970 period these economies were modernised economically,
socially and physically.   These societies had a good economic basis to
weather the structural economic crisis of 1973-1976.   They did not
retain old and irrelevant class distinctions which could produce a cage
of constraints to prevent useful change as the economic crisis deepened.
Thus, these countries were able to be adaptive and inventive in housing
reform.   They had strong rental sectors and they had never thought of
social housing policies as concerning the working class alone.   So they
were able to combine public and private finance in community-wide
housing policies, and this fitted the more general structural condition
of modern mixed economies and their evolving patterns.   Each of these
continental European countries had also inherited a basic economic
problem in their housing subsidies.   The overt subsidies were deep and
general, and as 'social' production subsidies they were associated with
historical cost renting/repaying.   These circumstances led to the need
to reduce burdens upon public expenditure, to make assistance more
selective and to break with historical cost renting.   Reform began in
the late-1960s, and the directions taken were endorsed and pushed
further under the recent impact of inflation and a slowing down in
demographic growth.   Thus, the continental European countries responded
more quickly and more coherently to the necessity of reform when inflation struck hard in the 1970s.

Along with Norway, The Netherlands, Sweden and West Germany also
inherit other advantages compared with Britain.   We have seen that the
needs of modern policy development turn in the direction of comprehensiveness.   This comprehensiveness means that housing is planned as a
whole, it is co-ordinated with urban and social policies, it has regard
for various social purposes (community development, the relief of
poverty and special needs groups), and it brings older housing within
policy development.   British policy has had to move towards this comprehensiveness from its comparatively narrow historical traditions in
public housing, whereas the continental European countries inherit a
community-wide policy basis.   The relative advantage of countries such
as Sweden and West Germany is already beginning to show up in recent
policy changes.   For example, although Britain inherits a rehabilitation policy from the 1950s and the West Germans have began rehabilitation
only in 1971, the West German policies are being formulated within a
better financial framework.   The mixed public-private financing and the
use of subsidies which decrease by pre-determined amounts has been found
effective in West German rehabilitation programmes.   This sort of
financing, together with housing allowances, makes projects viable and
modernised housing is affordable to moderate- and low-income groups.
Also, the generous depreciation write-offs against taxable income have
been extended to rehabilitation to get impetus into the new policies.

Other countries have developed policies which are interesting in their
own right, and which point towards effectiveness in the broad social
administration of housing.   The United States has tried alternatives to
public housing in its social housing policies, and recent experiences
leave some useful legacies.   It is from the United States that we can

learn more about the social and economic impact of housing allowances, and ways to re-direct private choices towards welfare housing purposes, but without dependence upon large-scale public administration.\ On the other hand, in Australia, the South Australian Housing Trust provides an example of how public housing can serve broader and more diverse social, economic and urban purposes than those typically found in public housing elsewhere. Finally, we re-state the considerable virtues of Norwegian housing policies. Norwegian housing has useful theoretical, administrative and financial bases. It is relatively unbureaucratic in its organisational characteristics, it offers more open choice in tenure and dwelling type than elsewhere, it balances egalitarianism and self-fulfilment, and it has a community-wide compass without restriction by way of means tests. This housing conforms more closely to ideals of Liberal and Social Democratic theory than any other. Norway has taken its historical opportunities well, and although it has less thick-textured complications than more heavily populated countries, a close examination of modern policy trends shows that these aspire to principles which are practised in Norway.

NOTES

[1] Some of the post-1945 history of British housing can be found in J.B.Cullingworth, *Housing and Local Government*, George Allen and Unwin, London, 1966, D.V.Donnison, *Housing Policy Since the War*, Occasional Papers on Social Administration, Codicote Press, Welwyn, 1960, and *The Government of Housing*, Penguin, Harmondsworth, 1967.
[2] M.Bowley, *Housing and the State, 1919-1944*, George Allen and Unwin, London, 1945.
[3] G.Hallett, *Housing and Land Policies in West Germany and Britain*, MacMillan, London, 1977.
[4] *Houses : The Next Step*, Cmnd. 8996, HMSO, London 1953.
[5] Conservative policies in the 1960s are described in two White Papers *Housing in England and Wales*, Cmnd. 1290, HMSO, London, 1961, and *Housing*, Cmnd. 2050, HMSO, London, 1963.
[6] See *Report of the Committee on Housing in Greater London*, (Milner Holland), Cmnd. 2605, HMSO, London, 1965.
[7] The Rowntree Trust Housing Studies were funded by the Trust and they centred around historical and social survey studies by J.B.Cullingworth and D.V.Donnison. See *Housing Policy Since the War*, Occasional Papers on Social Administration, Codicote Press, Welwyn, 1960, D.V. Donnison (et. al.), *Housing Since the Rent Act*, Occasional Papers on Social Administration, Codicote Press, Welwyn, 1961, D.V.Donnison (et. al.), *Essays on Housing*, Occasional Papers on Social Administration, Bell, London, 1964, J.B.Cullingworth, *Housing in Transition : A Case Study in the City of Lancaster, 1958-1962*, Heinemann, London, 1963, J.B.Cullingworth, *English Housing Trends*, Occasional Papers in Social Administration, Bell, London, 1965.
[8] A.A.Nevitt, *Housing, Taxation and Subsidies*, Nelson, London, 1966.
[9] See D.V.Donnison, *The Government of Housing*, Penguin, Harmondsworth, 1967.
[10] Hallett, *op. cit.*, (1977).
[11] See *The Housing Programme, 1965-1970*, Cmnd. 2838, HMSO, London, 1965, and *Help Towards Home Ownership*, Cmnd. 3163, HMSO, London, 1966.
[12] *The Housing Programme, 1965-1970*, op. cit., (1965).
[13] *Fair Deal for Housing*, Cmnd. 4728, HMSO, London, 1971.
[14] See *Report of the Committee on the Rent Acts*, (Francis), Cmnd. 4609,

HMSO, London, 1971.

[15] See *Widening the Choice : The Next Steps in Housing*, Cmnd. 5280, HMSO, London, 1973, and *Better Homes : The Next Priorities*, Cmnd. 5339, HMSO, London, 1973.

[16] See *Housing Policy : A Consultative Document*, Cmnd. 6851, HMSO, London, 1977.

[17] Hallett, *op. cit.*, (1977), p.57.

[18] Housing Policy : A Consultative Document, *op. cit.*, (1977).

[19] See *The Times*, p.2, 1st March 1977, and p.2, 3rd March 1977.

[20] Building Economic Development Committee/National Economic Development Office, *Housing for All*, National Economic Development Office, HMSO, London, 1977.

[21] J.B.Cullingworth, A.A.Nevitt and R.K.Wilkinson whose work has been cited at various points in this study were used as key resource personnel. Also, C.D.Foster and M.Harloe of the Centre for Environmental Studies advised the working groups which developed ideas in the report.

[22] A.Grey, N.P.Hepworth and J.Odling-Smee, *Housing Rents, Costs and Subsidies*, Chartered Institute of Public Finance and Accountancy, London, 1979.

[23] B.Kilroy, *Housing Finance - Organic Reform?*, Labour Economic Finance and Taxation Association, London, 1978.

[24] For a fuller account of Australian housing policies, see C.Pugh, *Intergovernmental Relations and the Development of Australian Housing Policies*, Centre for Research on Federal Financial Relations, Australian National University, Canberra, 1976.

[25] See *Report of the President's Committee on Urban Housing : A Decent Home*, (Kaiser), Committee on Urban Housing, Washington D.C., 1968.

[26] See E.M.Fisher, *Housing Markets and Congressional Goals*, Praegar, New York, 1975.

[27] The most general and detailed comparative analysis of costs can be found in A.P.Solomon, *Housing the Urban Poor*, Massachusetts Institute of Technology Press, Cambridge, Mass., 1974.

[28] The relative merits of subject subsidies have led to a lively debate in America. The supporters include: B.J.Frieden, *Improving Federal Housing Subsidies*, Joint Center for Urban Studies, Massachusetts Institute of Technology and Harvard University, Cambridge, Mass., 1971. M.Rein, *Welfare and Housing*, Joint Center for Urban Studies, Massachusetts Institute of Technology and Harvard University, Cambridge, Mass., 1972, A.P.Solomon, *Housing the Urban Poor*, Massachusetts Institute of Technology Press, Cambridge, Mass., 1974, and D.Stern, *Housing Allowances : Some Considerations of Efficiency and Equity*, Joint Center for Urban Studies, Massachusetts Institute of Technology and Harvard University, Cambridge, Mass., 1971. The more sceptical include: C. Hartman and D.Keating, 'The Housing Allowance Delusion', *Social Policy*, Jan/Feb 1974, pp.31-37, C.Hartman, *Housing and Social Policy*, Prentice Hall, Englewood Cliffs, 1975. The moderates include: E.J.Howenstine, 'The Changing Roles of Housing Production Subsidies and Consumer Housing Subsidies in European National Housing', *Land Economics*, Feb. 1975, pp.86-94, and R.C.Weaver, 'Housing Allowances', *Land Economics*, August 1975, pp.247-257.

[29] See US Office of Management and Budget, *The Budget of the United States Government, 1978, Special Analyses*, Government Printing Office, Washington D.C., 1975.

[30] The banks co-operate because in earlier times they were threatened with nationalisation.

[31] Norway's growth in 1974-1976 originated mainly from oil-drilling.

[32] Under Norwegian co-operative housing law, prices on re-sold

co-operative housing are fixed in relation to local authority valuations, not market values. The scarcities have induced some unofficial premium payments. In Oslo, this is called 'key money' and it repeats experience with scarcities in London in the 1880s and in Stockholm in the 1960s.
[33] In Sweden, co-operators do not receive this concession. Rental tenure is more significant in Sweden and the producers' and consumers' interests have lobbied the Government to retain equality of treatment between renters and co-operators. Norwegian co-operators have had a tax concession since 1975.
[34] Apart from 'key money' premiums, tax evasions allegedly took such forms as concealing swimming pools indoors where they were less likely to be seen, and so on.
[35] For a fuller historical account of Swedish housing policy, see B.Headey, *Housing Policy in the Developed Economy*, Croom Helm, London, 1978.
[36] The tax on imputed rent is graduated to assessed value. It is two per cent on the first S.Kr. 200,000, four per cent on the next S.Kr. 50,000, eight per cent on the next S.Kr. 100,000 and ten per cent on additional value. Capital gains are taxed at a hundred per cent if the resale occurs within two years and at seventy-five per cent for any resale in the following eight years. The tax is at the marginal rate of income tax (i.e., the gain is added to taxable income).
[37] The impact of slower demographic growth, economic affluence and the success of overcoming earlier housing shortages can be gauged from the following: in 1971, housing contributed 25.7 per cent of gross capital formation whereas by 1975 this had fallen to 20.3 per cent.
[38] The Stockholm Savings Bank is particularly well-organised and promotes home ownership by using the slogan *You Live in a Savings Box*. This is a reference to the tax concessions and the growth in equity value in owner-occupier tenure.
[39] Swedish Social Democrats have alleged that house-with-a-garden forms amounts to capitalism and consumes more energy than flats. This energy-savings argument depends only on housing heating costs, not all housing-related energy costs. The argument also omits consideration of the productivity of different sorts of dwelling forms and the impact of this on the way of life, which itself has implications for the consumption of energy. At present, this argument is altogether too simplistic.
[40] Hallett, *op. cit.*, (1977), pp.14-20.
[41] A detailed account is given by R.Lawson and C. Stevens, 'Housing Allowances in West Germany and France', *Journal of Social Policy*, July 1974, pp.213-234.
[42] Hallett, *op. cit.*,pp.27-33.

REFERENCES (SELECTED)

Bowley, M., *Housing and the State, 1919-1944*, George Allen and Unwin, London, 1945.

Cullingworth, J.B., *Housing in Transition : A Case Study in the City of Lancaster, 1958-1962*, Heinemann, London, 1963.

Cullingworth, J.B., *Housing and Local Government*, George Allen and Unwin, London, 1966.

Donnison, D.V., *Housing Policy Since the War*, Occasional Papers on Social Administration, Codicote Press, Welwyn, 1960.

Donnison, D.V., *The Government of Housing*, Penguin, Harmondsworth, 1967.

Hallett, G., *Housing and Land Policies in West Germany and Britain*, MacMillan, London, 1977.

Nevitt, A.A., *Housing, Taxation and Subsidies*, Nelson, London, 1966.

Pugh, C., *Intergovernmental Relations and the Development of Australian Housing Policies*, Centre for Research on Federal Financial Relations, Australian National University, Canberra, 1976.

Solomon, A., *Housing the Urban Poor*, Massachusetts Institute of Technology Press, Cambridge, Mass., 1974.

ACKNOWLEDGMENTS

Officers of the following organisations contributed to my understanding of housing policy development in continental Europe.   United Nations: Committee on Housing, Building and Planning of the Economic Commission for Europe.   In West Germany: Deutscher Verband fur Wohnungswegesen, Stadtebau and Raumplanung; Neue Heimat; Gesamtverband gemmeinnutziger Wohnungsunternehmen; Federal Ministry for Building and Planning.   In The Netherlands: Ministry of Housing and Physical Planning.   In Norway: Norwegian Federation of Co-operative Housing Societies; Norwegian Housing Bank, Ministry of Local Government and Labour.   In Sweden: Ministry of Housing and Phusical Planning; National Housing Board; National Board of Physical Planning and Building; Stockholm Savings Bank; Co-operative Building Organisation of the Swedish Trade Unions.

The following housing intellectuals have contributed to my understanding of European and United States' policies.   At the RIW-Instituut voor Volkshuisvestingsonderzoek at the Technological University of Delft: Prof. Dr. H. Priemus, H. Westra, F. Ijmkers, and J. van der Schaar.   At the Instituts fur Siedlungs und Wohnungswesen at Wilhelms University, Munster: Prof. Dr. R. Thoss, Dr. P.H. Burberg and U. Bucher-Glorys. At the Institut fur Wohnungsrecht und Wohnungswirtschaft at the University of Koln: Dipl. Kfm. Helga Erle.   At Abt Associates (an institution specialising in social policy research), United States, Dr. S. Mayo.   At Harvard University: Prof. W. Apgar and Prof. K. Colton.

7   Housing policy and land development

This chapter has three main tasks. First, it compares the merits of
development planning and regulatory planning. Broadly speaking,
development planning means achieving urban planning objectives by
direct public investment in urban development; *regulatory* planning
means trying to achieve those objectives by regulating what other
investors do, e.g., by building regulations, zoning ordinances and
prescriptive land-use plans. Second, as a practical illustration of
that issue, the chapter compares the record of Swedish development
planning with that of British regulatory planning. Third, an economic
case is argued for some public acquisition and development of urban
land.

Relations between land and housing policies are complicated, and are
currently growing more so. The particular relevance of this chapter to
housing policy is (at least) threefold. First, many democratic
societies are currently moving from a primary concern with the quantity
of housing towards a greater interest in the quality of the surrounding
urban environment. This is reflected in the growth of resident action
groups, and of broader roles for local governments. Second, in many
countries development planning is gaining support at the expense of
regulatory planning, especially because it promises better co-ordination
of the urban services upon which good housing depends, whereas regulatory planning has too often produced conflicts between plans and
economic possibilities. Third, some countries are seeing an increasing
need for closer co-ordination of their housing, land development and
urban renewal policies, especially in the rehabilitation and management
of their older urban fabric. Sweden is distinguished by the successful
co-ordination of housing policies, land management and pricing,
development planning and regulatory planning; other countries have paid
quite dearly for failing to achieve that sort of co-ordination.
Altogether there need be no apology for including a chapter on land in a
book about housing.

Land has been an interesting and controversial object of social and
economic theory. It does not fit into the conventional arguments which
justify private property. In 1873, John Stuart Mill wrote a tract [1]
supporting the radical proposals of the Land Tenure Reform Association.
Mill can be regarded as a *laissez faire* economist, but he advocated a
tax levy on 'unearned increments' - that is, on those (future) increases
in value which were attributable to general economic and community
development, not to improvements. As justification for the distinction,
Mill argued that improvements were the private 'fruits of one's labour',
but the 'unearned increments' could be regarded as an unjust 'pecuniary
privilege'. In his *Progress and Poverty* (1880), Henry George [2]
advocated a single tax, applying it to 'unearned increments', and thereby he hoped to solve virtually all aspects of 'unjust distribution'.
For Henry George, 'the value of land is the price of monopoly'. Mill
and George influenced emergent Social Democratic and Radical thought and
policy in the late nineteenth century. Apart from this basic economic
and ideological issue, other contentions are prominent in the

development of land policy. - Can land be taxed without acting as a
disincentive to development? Is it possible to disentangle 'unearned
increments' from other things in the price formation? Will the incidence of a tax be shifted on to the final consumer? To what extent
should land, as property, be subject to planning regulations which
affect the interests of its owners and their rights of control? How
should we interpret the economic efficiency and equity aspects of land
development? To what extent is the process of price formation in urban
land a cause for wider social and political concern? [3] These are the
sorts of questions which are taken up in this chapter.

LAND DEVELOPMENT POLICIES AND THE THEORETICAL JUSTIFICATIONS
FOR PUBLIC ENTERPRISE

The theoretical case for public enterprise in land development policies
is many-sided. Some economists have advocated more *laissez faire* in
town planning and land development policies [4]; however, it can be
demonstrated in theory and practice that efficiency, effectiveness and
equity in urban land development requires public enterprise to have a
significant role. The case is derived from the 'public goods' [5]
nature of many benefits and costs in an urban/regional environment, and
from the profiteering which can accompany the private transformation of
land from rural to urban uses. Public goods are so-called because
they have associated economic externalities. In this class of goods,
there are dilemmas in deciding whether private markets, voluntary
agreements or governments can achieve the more efficient and equitable
results. Economic externalities are tied up with the question of
co-ordinating urban investments, and the use of development planning as
a method of co-ordination.

Economic externality, efficiency, equity and development planning

Housing is a good with mixed public and private characteristics. The
private characteristics are enjoyed exclusively by an individual or
household, whereas the public characteristics depend on the physical,
social and economic qualities of the neighbourhood and the wider area.
Goods with public characteristics frequently prevent market choices from
achieving satisfactory efficiencies and equities. At the very least,
the presence of economic externalities opens up the question of
efficiency, equity and the means of exercising choice.

External economic effects occur in both production and consumption.
For example, a commercial vehicle which pollutes the atmosphere, causing
people to incur expenses so they can rid themselves of this social ill,
is representative of a production-based externality. If the pollutants
came from a private vehicle on a tourist trip, they would be representative of a consumption-induced externality. Essentially, the idea of
economic externality stands for the effects of economic activities on
third parties who either win or lose as a result of activities in which
they are not themselves involved.

Urban environments are affected by a vast range of economic externalities. Some, like pollution, are harmful to third parties. Others
are helpful. For example, an individual who builds a sanitary and
fire-proof house benefits the neighbours by lessening the likelihood of
generating disease and fire. A well-serviced urban environment with

attractive shops, kindergartens, good schools, accessible employment, and useful social services, imparts general benefits reflected in the increased value of housing.

The economic significance of these externalities is that compensation is seldom paid for a social cost and it is often impracticable or too costly to appropriate a price for general social benefits. This might suggest that there are too many social costs and far too few benefits. Whether this proves to be the case depends on a number of other factors. For example, the transaction costs of organising a correction of externalities may be greater than the benefits. It is not always easy to enumerate social costs and benefits or to establish all their effects. Although economists have developed a special type of analysis to apply to situations where externalities are prevalent, it has many problems and controversies associated with it. Even if it is possible to reveal valid and useful information on externalities, it is not obvious how society should organise itself to achieve a correction of the problem.

Externalities can be accounted for by governments acting directly or by using taxes and subsidies to internalise social costs and benefits, or by voluntary agreements. As mentioned above, the cost of organising a correction, by any one of these approaches, may outweigh the benefits. However, among the variety of approaches to the problem, some may be cheaper or more effective than others. A discussion of the relative merits of the variants can provide a deeper understanding of economic externality in housing and in its urban/regional setting.

Most economic externalities are by-products of market processes. In principle, it is possible to tax a product so less of it is produced or to subsidise it so more is produced. The market may be manipulated in this way if society is prepared to pay for reducing a social cost or for providing a social benefit. But this approach has three difficulties. First, as mentioned earlier, it is not easy to enumerate costs and benefits, to identify their cause and effect and to trace them to particular victims or beneficiaries. Second, a taxing and subsidy system designed to correct externalities would be highly differentiated and difficult to administer. Third, there is no reason to suppose that a manipulated market would necessarily produce equitable results. Society may not be prepared to pay enough to significantly reduce a social cost inflicted on a group in a particular location, or on a low-income class. Or society may be prepared to reduce a social cost significantly, but by so doing a particular group or a specific region may thereby experience substantial unemployment. Or the **means** of manipulation may be used by particular groups for inequitable purposes.

Another approach to organising a correction of externalities is to rely on voluntary contractual or informal agreements. Coase [6] has advocated this approach. When the victims of a social cost can identify the perpetrators, bargaining is possible. They might find it worthwhile to bribe the perpetrator to alter his/her behaviour or they might attempt to obtain payment from the perpetrator to compensate for the damages. Essentially, what is involved is a trade-off, the result depending on the relative values society places on the two activities. These relative values are expressed through the market and the bargaining can be initiated by either party. This approach produces a useful insight into the problem of economic externalities. Coase's position depends on seeing how society values and judges the respective activities.

The voluntary agreement approach assumes there are no significant problems of assessing the externality, or of seeing that the victims and perpetrators are identifiable to each other. We might imagine a situation where there are fewer perpetrators than victims, in which case it will be easier for the perpetrators to organise themselves into a collective bargaining block. As the number of victims increases, it may become impossible for them to organise themselves collectively. Where there are large numbers, each individual may calculate it to his/ her advantage, to remain outside the organised group. An individual might obtain the benefit from the group's bargaining role without incurring the costs of organisation and the inconvenience of administering the bargaining process. However, if each individual calculates in this way, there will be no bargaining. The victims will remain unorganised and the externality uncorrected. This is the outcome of the 'free rider' problem where voluntarism cannot force potential beneficiaries into a group. Thus, where social costs and benefits are so diffused that voluntary organisation is virtually impossible, then government may be regarded as an alternative approach to correct the externalities.

The case for government involvement in attending to housing-related externalities is emerging strongly. Many housing-related externalities are widely diffused.[7] Urban change continually redistributes the incidence of housing-related externalities quite arbitrarily. Neither a manipulated market, nor voluntary agreements can take a systematic view of equity. In reality, the scope for voluntary agreements among private participants is limited. This all points to government involvement in urban planning. However, further examination of economic externality will show that any possible government role is likely to be complicated and controversial.

Government activity in urban planning is likely to be costly. The externalities characterising modern urban environments are many and varied. It is hard to comprehensively assess the effects of pollution, traffic congestion and so on. Also, information on the scale economies and the distributional consequences of different urban services is meagre. The discussions in Chapter 3 showed that much has been done in the name of town planning without a firm grounding in systematic knowledge. Government organisation often produces far less than it wills, and sometimes its production process is founded on an insubstantial view of the problems addressed.

Government activity is costly and complicated for other reasons. There are good reasons to believe that, under some parliamentary systems, many elected representatives are ill-informed and ill-equipped to satisfactorily understand specialist aspects of government. [8] Where some electors and parliamentarians are uninformed, it is possible that some public administrations will produce vague and generalised requests for funds and act as monopolists in relation to their electors. Finally, a commitment to a government role in housing-related externalities adds another element in building a manifesto, which is a wide ranging collection of general intentions attracting a party consensus and aimed at presenting a competitive package to the voters. Thus housing and urban policies become part of the general political trading.

In short, the ultimate decisions are far removed from systematic assessments or from the analytical basis of something like economic externality. This can be costly because too much is spent on some things or because things go unattended by default.

These comments show that there is enough in the nature of government for it to be viewed as more than a simple device to correct economic externalities. Even when government is specifically involved in attending to housing-related externalities, there are likely to be controversial results. Government interventions are likely to produce winners and losers among residents, investors and workers. On grounds of social equity, it is important to achieve distributional objectives. We can conceive of a household's 'urban income', which is derived from cost and benefit accessibilities to jobs, shops, schools, recreation and urban services generally. Government can plan and account for these things in ways which are infeasible for *laissez faire* private enterprise. However, urban and regional policies are seldom formulated systematically. Thus, although economic externalities in the urban environment point to a role for government, this cannot be exercised without controversy and without gaps between theory and practice. Conflicts of interest are deeply entangled in the efficiency and equity aspects of economic externality. These conflicts cross area boundaries, divide residents and producers, and exist as differences among local and wider interests. Furthermore, economic externalities raise questions on the relationships between private and public enterprise. The necessity to achieve a balance between private and social interests is brought into sharper focus as the discussions proceed.

Co-ordination of urban investments and the land development process [9]

Private enterprise investments can be based on formal analyses, assessment of risks and uncertainties, and straightforward entrepreneurial hunches. Seldom are such decisions co-ordinated, because this involves the exchange of information undermining important conditions for competition. Private urban investments (i.e., capital construction in physical urban assets) follow this general unco-ordinated pattern. In fact, owing to the influence of administrative separatism, in many of the modern democracies, public urban investments have also been inadequately co-ordinated. The very nature of the urban sphere and the way it is used by residents and producers shows the need for achieving some area-based co-ordination. Centres for shopping, commercial, cultural and social service functions have to be created. Centring will to some degree occur spontaneously particularly in the central business district. However, the evidence of Australian State capital cities indicates that under *laissez faire* land development at low density, suburban expansion will occur without adequate centring. The use of such regulatory devices as zoning and metropolitan 'development plans' [10] does not always guarantee adequate centring, which confers some external 'pecuniary' benefits upon site operators [11] because large and diverse volumes of trade are attracted to a successful centre. From the viewpoint of residents, good centring can lead to real (i.e., not simply pecuniary) benefits through savings on transport, and of time in shopping. Also, when retailing centres are combined attractively with cultural facilities and social services, they add further convenience and general consumer satisfaction. Clearly, the qualitative results of good centring and the accessibilities which it promotes are significant for effectiveness in housing, and for creating 'urban income' for households.

The theoretical case for a public enterprise role in land acquisition and development should be made out. The practice of co-ordinating urban investment has run ahead of theory, but it has been sporadic rather than general. It is important to make out a theoretical case so that good and useful practice can spread. The reasons for a public enterprise role in land development are not well understood. Neutze [12] has provided a well articulated case for a public sector role in the acquisition and disposal of land for new development. His work arose because the cost of urban land was a problem for private and social housing in Australia's major cities during the 1960s. For example, in 1970 the New South Wales Housing Commission reported that land prices had increased by 128 per cent in 10 years. The result was that, whereas the cost of land was only 11 per cent of the total cost of social housing in 1960, by 1969 it was 20 per cent. The pattern was generally repeated in other modern democracies, except in Norway and Sweden [13] which had strengthened the role of public enterprise in land development during the 1960s. Neutze hinged his explanations of the land-price problem on the increases in value which occurred when land was transformed from rural to urban uses. Unlike other goods, land for new urban development had no real substitutes to break the monopoly elements of its fixed supply characteristic. Thus, in growing urban areas, specially where there was no policy of regional decentralisation, a speculative gain was virtually assured under a land development process depending on regulatory planning devices and *laissez faire* development.

In effect, the regulatory planning devices confined development to certain patches of land. This added to the ease of making speculative gains. However, a public enterprise role in acquiring and disposing of land would undermine speculation. A definite policy commitment to public enterprise was required. It was not sufficient to rely only on powers of expropriation, generally used only for specific planning objectives or for particular types of government-assisted development. Sometimes, expropriation had been based on market values, but this could not prevent speculation. Even when expropriation was related to *use* values, unless an authority was committed to buy land for virtually any kind of urban development and had the necessary finance, once again speculation could occur. In fact, when there has been extended speculative trading in land at the urban periphery, it is difficult to precisely establish use values.

The case for public authorities acquiring and disposing of urban land needs to be pressed further. It can be shown that other approaches to the land-price problem are seldom effective, and that other arguments based on efficiency and equity add further weight for public enterprise in land acquisition. We shall now examine the efficiency and equity issues. Under *laissez faire* development, the transformation from rural to urban uses creates a redistribution of wealth from future buyers and renters to a relatively few owners and developers. In general, this makes the wealthy wealthier. Also, the direction of this wealth transfer is from the younger generation (mainly first-home purchasers and renters) to older people. The equity problem is heightened because the wealth transfer is an unearned increment. Some of the land value increase derives from a situation which has nothing to do with product-ive entrepreneurial decisions, but more with speculation in a fixed supply resource.

Laissez faire development can also produce serious inefficiencies.
In particular, land speculation can lead to an uneven growth of
subdivisional activity out of line with the needs of the building
industry. [14]   This adds to the difficulty of organising and programming urban development.   The causal chain of events leading to the
mismatch of needs is as follows: speculation drives the price of land
up and subdividers overreact by supplying a large volume of serviced
land in the next period, and it takes several years for the over-
supplied land to be absorbed.   However, the supply dwindles and the
price is driven up again.   The result is a series of upward price
rises.   At each interval, prices may hold in anticipation of future
upward movements.   Speculation achieves a self-fulfilling prophecy
when demand again exceeds supply.   In short, speculative behaviour
interacts with the lengthy lead time to move prices upwards in a series
of staggered jumps, but if demand falls, the speculative bubble will
burst and the price of land will decrease.   Clearly, there are better
ways of doing things, but Neutze [15] has shown that traditional public
policy approaches to the land-price problem have been ineffective.
They have included forms of taxes or betterment levies [16] on
unimproved urban land values.   These approaches cannot forestall
speculation because a large portion of the levies or taxes can be
passed on to the final purchasers.   This arises because new urban
land is virtually a no-substitute good.   Capital gains taxes on land
also have problems.   If a tax is levied after development has occurred
it can still be shifted to the final purchaser and the developer still
obtains an unearned increment.   On the other hand, if the tax is levied
at the pre-development stage, the developer has no incentive to defer
development to obtain a speculative gain.   However, a tax which is
levied before an income is realised is unpopular.   All this leads
Neutze to the conclusion that, in the case of new development, public
enterprise can best capture the unearned increment by acquiring and
disposing of enough land to have an impact on all new land prices.

As mentioned earlier, the sort of solutions which Neutze has proposed
have been applied only sporadically.   In Sweden and Norway, the
practice is well-established, and in South Australia, this policy has
operated in various ways at various times, on large and small scale,
since the Second World War.   Elsewhere, the practice tends to be
confined to new towns or an occasional continental European city with
a long period of Social Democratic political dominance (e.g.,
Amsterdam).   Two factors have impeded the more widespread use of
public enterprise in acquiring and developing land.   First, *laissez
faire* and other political attitudes have prevented a larger public
enterprise role in land policy.   However, in the case of government-
assisted housing, governments in continental Europe, whether Conservative or Social Democratic, have administered cost controls on land,
materials and other housing costs.   Also, to limit land rights, most
countries have legislated by controls on development and so on.   The
limitations on land and property in industrial societies, began with
public health reform.   The stage has now been reached when some
governments have moved from only regulating land rights towards a more
active development planning role.   The second impediment to achieving
this role is a matter of cognition.   In some places, the reformers are
more concerned with taxing unimproved values and levying betterment
charges.   Neutze has shown that the first priority should be to

236

overcome unearned increments in new development, and as far as possible prevent this ever arising, by using public enterprise in land purchase and disposal.

For all these reasons, public land development is justifiable. But it is far from easy, and is beset with dilemmas, some springing from the nature of government and others from the problems to which land development is addressed. Efficiencies and equities are not easily resolved in complicated patterns of urban interaction. Ultimately, such questions raise the possibility that cities might be organised to achieve overall optimal efficiency. However, recent commentators [17] are sceptical of trying to achieve this. It seems that the efficiency question is best taken up a part at a time and assessed in relationship to other known aspects of urban economics. This is the approach adopted here. The land-price problem and the aim of achieving co-ordination in urban investments have been selected as key issues in modern housing policies. Considerations of equity are even more complicated. In urban environments, considerations of equity are mixed up in conflicts among areas, income groups, residents, investors and producers. These conflicts draw divisions between the groups and divide them internally. Modern welfare economics shows that efficiency and equity are intertwined, and housing is tied to the 'public' goods aspect of an urban/regional area. It is not surprising that modern housing policies become a greater part of political economy, not less. We can now examine how this political economy is proceeding among some of the modern democracies.

TOWN PLANNING PRACTICE IN SOME MODERN DEMOCRATIC SOCIETIES

The foregoing drew attention to the need to co-ordinate urban invest-ments and to attend to urban land-price problems. For professional town planners this means blending regulatory and development planning, with emphasis on the latter. In practice, only in Sweden, Norway and a few other countries has land development proceeded in this way as national policy. In some places only regulatory planning is practised. In others, though the two types exist, they pursue different aims within different programmes. The first purpose of this section is to show how the two types of planning are blended in Swedish practice and related to housing. We will then examine some new problems in Swedish housing and land development policies, and compare British practice. The Norwegians, the Dutch and others tend to look to Sweden for new ideas; and many modern democracies have drawn on British ideas in regulatory planning. [18] Also, Britain has tended to practise regulatory and development planning separately, in distinct programmes.

Sweden [19]

Swedish town planning practice combines regulatory and development planning, which have grown together since the later part of the nineteenth century. From 1965, they have been drawn closer to form a coherent national policy in housing and urban development. Since 1919, in Stockholm, housing policies have been co-ordinated with land policies. At that date, the Stockholm Real Estate Commission was created as the City Council's housing authority. [20] Formerly, outer and inner urban development had been divided between the Agricultural Holding Committee and the Stockholm Finance Commission. Housing vexation occurred after

1918, and led to organisational reforms and, later, to a more active
approach in linking housing and land policy. A number of factors have
combined to contribute towards Sweden's comparatively progressive
performance in linking housing and land policy.

The three main factors are historical, political and housing problems.
Historical traditions in Sweden assert some principles in the *Common
Access Prerogative*, giving the right of access through private farmland
to beaches, rivers, wild berries and so on, providing that such access
does not encroach on the personal privacy of farmers and land-owners.
Also, before the onset of nineteenth-century industrialisation, the
Crown owned most land. In the context of these factors the Swedes tend
to regard modern policies of public enterprise and land regulation as a
return to the historical traditions temporarily altered by the onset of
industrialisation. Housing vexation has also precipitated reforms in
land policy. Acute housing shortages have been experienced in the
1890s, the 1920s and in the period 1941-1970. To deal with these
problems, local government needed access to cheap developable land.
Finally, Sweden has had lengthy political stability and continual
economic growth. Social Democratic Governments were in power for more
than forty years from 1932, and gave steady purpose and continuity to
the extension of government's role in housing and land policies.

The first initiatives in regulatory planning were taken in 1874 when
municipalities were given powers to regulate development. The powers
were widened and strengthened in 1907, 1917 and 1926. Currently the
Building and Planning Act, 1947, provides the basis for modern Swedish
regulatory planning. Local plans are subject to central approval, but
the local authorities have a strong position in Swedish land-use
planning. Local government has a planning monopoly in the sense that
other levels of government and private developers have no rights to
create local physical plans. The local government role in regulatory
planning is strengthened by its activities as a developer in educational
facilities, social service centres, community halls, roads and public
utilities. Also, local governments have established housing corporations, which with other non-profit housing operators, dominate new
housing development. This power enables local government to co-ordinate
urban investment more successfully than local government elsewhere.
Local government influence in planning has increased further since the
1960s when central government provided finance for local government to
buy and sell land.

Stockholm commenced a policy of forward land purchase as early as the
1880s. In this century, this policy has been widened and deepened to
form a national land policy. Central government began its involvement
in 1906 with a land policy designed to curb timber companies and private
corporations from making further encroachment on farming land. Two
years later, powers were given to local government to lease land.
Stockholm has made significant use of this. However, the major
national impacts of land policy have occurred since the 1960s.

In 1968, central government began to provide loans to municipalities
for forward land purchase. Since 1972 local government powers in land
purchasing have been made more effective by altering the basis for
compensation, which before then had been paid at market value. After
1972, it was fixed at the value which prevailed 10 years before the date
of purchase. [21] Since 1968, local government has also had the right

of pre-emption, under which notices of intended land sales have to be sent to the local authority which has the first right of purchase at a negotiated price. [22]   Finally, since 1975, the central government has determined that all new housing it supports financially (it was supporting 85 per cent in 1975) would be built on land acquired by the municipalities. [23]

The Swedish land policy has worked effectively and equitably compared with some other countries.   A recent study [24] showed that of 44 municipalities, the real price of urban land (i.e., the price related to the cost of living) decreased in 25 of them in 1960-1974.   Some of the most spectacular results have occurred in the larger towns and in those with a rapid growth rate.   The unearned increment has virtually been eliminated in Sweden and land prices are no longer significant as social and political issues in new Swedish housing.   Furthermore, regulatory planning with its municipal master plans tends to be transformed into a reality in Sweden because of the support afforded by development planning and land policy.   The blending of regulatory and development planning is evident in housing and in the centring in the metropolitan areas.   For example, since the 1950s much of Stockholm's suburbanisation has been wrapped around new urban centres such as Vallingby (1950s), Tensta (1960s) and Husby (1970s).   The policies described and assessed have been aimed primarily at new development.   However, since 1973 different housing problems have emerged and the existing policies need to be altered and supplemented.

New housing problems in Sweden

In 1976 Sweden had 26,000 vacant new apartments, mainly in new areas of Stockholm, Malmo and Gothenburg.   Simultaneously, some housing which was built in Stockholm during the 1920s was attracting strong demand and high prices.   Also some households had been waiting on savings banks' lists for 10 years so they might get the type of dwelling they wanted. The apparent paradoxes open a variety of complex issues in modern housing policies.   Whereas housing problems in the 1960s were primarily centred around producing enough units to overcome long-term shortages and rapid urbanisation, the 1970s revealed that consumers were resisting some types of housing and making substantial sacrifices to get into the sort of housing they wanted.   The issues which these circumstances illustrate cover such things as the price relativities of old and new housing, choice of dwelling type, social segregation, and the need to reform subsidies and the financial framework.   Some of these have been discussed in detail in other chapters, but it is useful to look now at some of them in the context of co-ordinating land development policies with housing finance, social policy, urban renewal and urban administration.

The vacancies in new apartments can be viewed as symptoms of historical cost renting, inflation and too much production.   Essentially, there are two factors: older units are let at cheaper rents and the worst housing shortages of the 1941-1970 period have been overcome.   Although some progress had been made in reforming suburbanisation, finance and rent policies, the full impact of the new system has yet to develop. Meanwhile, low-income households could begin to exercise choice.   They opted for the older dwelling built at lower historical cost.

Policy-makers in Sweden felt that the vacancies represented more than just symptoms of the post-1942 subsidy system and of the slowing down of population growth. For the Swedes, the vacancies represent a social aversion. They see them as the least desirable places to live, because they represent the bottom of the stock and the recent policy is to provide special funds to improve urban services in these areas. The policy tries to ensure that social segregation does not become too severe.

Segregation is also evident in other sections of the housing stock. The historical commentaries in Chapter 2 drew attention to the Swedish 'magic houses', financed and administered by Stockholm City Council's housing agency, the Stockholm Real Estate Commission. Some were originally accessible only to moderate- and low-income families, and were built on municipal leasehold land, mainly as single family housing. During the 1970s this housing has been much sought after by professional people and two-income households. Some of these households have moved from apartment to apartment and once they have accumulated sufficient savings and settled into a two-income way of life they have been pre-pared to pay high prices for houses with gardens. This housing type was in short supply in metropolitan areas [25] and was being rapidly transferred from lower income households to those with higher incomes. Segregation was beginning to occur in the higher end of the stock as well as at the bottom, which was new housing. Housing 50 years old (self-built, low-cost construction) was preferred by high-income families.

These events have hit the Social Democrats hard. They had 44 years in government [26] and achieved a society more egalitarian than most, with a comparatively well-developed welfare state, but it had some bureaucratic aridities. Segregation has been a socially and political-ly sensitive issue; because there are deep roots in town planning theory and in social democratic thinking favouring high density residential development [27]. Furthermore, the existing legislative, administra-tive and financial rules have been designed and constructed to achieve social purposes in *new* development. They are unsuitable for applica-tion to existing problems. For example, though Stockholm City Council has a pre-emption right on any housing on the market in Stockholm, it cannot act. The high price of the 'magic houses' puts them outside the cost controls written into the existing government-assisted housing programme. Also, any purchasing would not serve a coherent purpose within existing policies, designed to do other things. In fact, during the 1976 election campaign, the Social Democrats were arguing that houses with gardens were anti-social because they used more energy than apartments. [28] The recoil to all this has been to drive some think-ing towards producing more planning regulations and some redevelopment of single family housing areas so that social balance can be achieved.

The new problem is not so far being attacked as inventively as the old land problems were attacked. The land-price problem was overcome by developing more land through extra local government powers and finance. The counterpart in the new situation would be to produce more houses with gardens to break the supply shortage. (Swedish households are already beginning to achieve this spontaneously now that earlier acute shortages have disappeared and family incomes are increasing). Once the supply scarcity of this sort of housing is overcome, the price of magic houses would reflect replacement costs and locational advantage, not just high demand for a *type* of dwelling in short supply. Then the cost conditions on government-assisted housing could be reviewed with the aim of buying some magic houses for low-income groups. The rules on leasehold could be amended so high-value locations are charged a higher rent. [29] In short, some para-market influences should be built into leasing conditions so funds can be accumulated and used to mitigate segretation. These new housing problems need to be confronted with development planning remedies using varied approaches including, housing finance reforms, special social policies to counter segregation, a reformed urban renewal and a more co-ordinated approach among these various policies.

Britain

Ideas and practices in British town planning have had widespread influence in other countries. However, compared with Sweden, Britain has tended to emphasise regulatory planning rather than development planning. Where the latter approach has been used, it has tended to be in particular places for particular purposes, as in the new towns programme since 1946, rather than being practised as a general national policy. Also, land policy in Britain has been tied in with betterment levies and taxes on unimproved values, rather than with efforts to substitute public enterprise for private in the development of new urban land. British town planning is thus more divided and more varied than Swedish. This is especially true of the relationship between housing and land policy. In Sweden, housing policies grew on the twin pillars of finance and cheap developable land. As housing policies widened to cater for general community needs rather than just for a residual social need, Swedish housing and land policies developed wider scope accordingly. By contrast, British public housing programmes have scarcely been conceived or administered as instruments of *general* urban development; and they have suffered a good deal from the unruly behaviour of British land prices.

The town planning movement began with unified ideas of regulatory and development planning. From 1893, Ebenezer Howard (1850-1928) advocated his ideas of garden cities. In 1898 he published them in *Tomorrow: a Peaceful Path to Real Reform*; in 1902 the work was re-published under the more direct title of *Garden Cities of Tomorrow*. Some of Howard's ideas emphasised environmental determinism and orderly development. Others depended on co-ordinating urban investments and influencing unearned increments by using a public benefit enterprise to acquire and dispose of development land. Some private benefactors saw the ideas as encouraging garden suburbs, whereas Howard was more interested in demonstrating a complete new town concept. A more restricted view was that the ideas could be used to regulate new suburban development to avoid future slums. Finally, the attention given to unearned increments might be interpreted as a matter for balancing equity among land-owners who received permission to develop their land and others who were not.

It was the latter two considerations which influenced the aims of the *Housing, Town Planning, etc. Act*, 1909. Local authorities could regulate the standards of new subdivisions and in 1925 and 1932 these powers were extended. This part of public policy sent town planning firmly towards regulatory planning with its plethora of zoning ordinances, master plans and so on. Since the mid-1960s, regulatory planning has become more complex, with master plans broken down into strategic plans, local plans and action area plans. However, the greater separation

241

does not alter the fact that this planning is still regulatory rather than developmental. Howard's more radical ideas about public or co-operative land development joined the good ideas of Shaftesbury and Octavia Hill, in the catalogue of excellent ideas that the British conceived, but did not use.

Another part of the *Housing, Town Planning etc. Act*, 1909, led British town planners to charge betterment levies and to tax unimproved urban land. The attempt to capture these levies has restricted the supply of urban land and increased its price. In 1909, the principle was to levy a 50 per cent betterment charge on those who received development rights and to use this to compensate those who did not receive permission. In 1932, the levy was raised to 75 per cent of betterment. The levies did not prevent trading in land at prices above use value, so it became evident that this approach would not, in the long run, provide cheap land. Accordingly, the government appointed an Expert Committee [30] to review betterment, compensation and the price of land. It recommended that development rights should be vested in the state, which should have powers to expropriate land at use value. Betterment would continue, but as a tax on the assessed value of un-improved urban land. The returns were to be funded and used to compensate land owners for the transfer of development rights to the state.

But the perennial problems continued. Urban land was in short supply because owners had no incentive to sell. Land prices were high because developers were prepared to pay premiums to sell to a market in short supply. The Conservative Party abolished the betterment scheme in 1953, leaving the market sector free to trade at whatever prices could be obtained. But the state continued to expropriate at use value. This was seen among landowners as an inequity and so, in 1959, market value was re-instated as the basis of compensation in expropriation. Subsequently, in 1967, a Labour Government created a Land Commission to acquire and dispose of land for new development and betterment levies were re-introduced.

Though the Land Commission could acquire land, it depended on local government for planning. The division between regulatory and development planning tended to frustrate the potential which the Land Commission would have otherwise realised. A doubt arose on the future of the Land Commission, and in 1970 it was abolished by the Conservative Party. A Labour government resolved its principles in the *Community Land Act*, 1975, and the *Development Land Tax*, 1976; the Conservative opposition promised to repeal these, when opportunity offered. This oscillating approach to policies which above all require continuity if they are to succeed makes sure that neither party makes much real progress with the problem. Even if the land acquisition programme had made headway, British housing and land policies would still be much worse co-ordinated than Sweden's. The British housing sectors are rigidly separated. By contrast, Sweden combines public and private finance and enables any developer to use them.

Some British development under the *New Towns Act*, 1946, and the *Town Development Act*, 1952, aimed at linking housing with other urban investments, and did so convincingly in the new towns. But the potential of this type of development planning was not realised nationally. Regulatory planning tended to dominate the older areas, and this pattern has been repeated in other countries. Another example of the dichotomy between housing and planning occurred in the British regionalisation programme, which started in the 1930s. Following a Royal Commission report [31] in 1940, it was intended that regionalisation should be enlarged. The Commission went further than merely wishing to diversify industry in depressed regions and containing London's growth rate. It recommended the creation of national planning institutions and noted that the existing method of housing development was unsatisfactorily related to employment and social facilities. However, the post-War planning in Britain adopted a divided approach. Regionalisation was seen as a method of helping depressed areas and achieving economic balance, but not really as a way of co-ordinating urban investments and achieving a greater cohesion in administration.[32] The new towns programme was instituted as a method of development planning but with the limited objective of containing the growth of larger cities. Later in the 1960s, the idea of regional balance was joined with the new towns programme when the Central Lancashire Development Corporation was created to blend the two objectives in its area.

For housing to be satisfactorily related to employment, social facilities and other urban investments, a system of regionalised development planning on a national scale should have been created. As we shall see in Chapter 9, planning in Norway, Sweden and West Germany has moved in this direction since 1970, but Britain maintains a pattern dividing regulatory and development planning, with a very limited number of projects which enjoy real developmental planning. Britain has supplied useful ideas in planning, but other countries have created more coherent social and economic institutions to transform ideas into national programmes.

NOTES

[1] J.S.Mill, *The Right of Property in Land*, Dallow, London, 1873.
[2] H.George, *The Complete Works*, Doubleday, New York, 1911.
[3] Some modern economists have regarded urban land prices as a matter for corrective public policy whereas others see it as an exaggerated cause of concern. Much depends upon whether one takes a short-, medium- or long-term view. For a sceptic's view and for more extensive discussion, see G.Hallett, *Housing and Land Policies in West Germany and Britain*, MacMillan, London, 1977.
[4] This approach is strongly put in *Government and The Land*, Institute of Economic Affairs, London, 1974.
[5] In the pure 'public goods' case, any individual can consume the goods without any consequent reduction in amounts available to other consumers. The urban condition is more characterised with *partial* public goods with an areal basis. This means urban public goods are restricted in their areal significance and some loss of benefits occur as they are used up by consumers. Modern public goods theory was introduced in Chapter 2.
[6] R.Coase, 'The Problem of Social Cost', *Journal of Law and Economics*, October, 1960, pp.1-44.
[7] Some externalities are confined to small-scale neighbourhood amenities which can be organised under collective arrangements. Condominiums have this sort of rationality in their legal and economic arrangements. These matters are discussed in Chapter 9.
[8] See the discussions in Chapter 9. The Westminster pattern of government produces less informed parliamentarians than the pattern

prevailing in West Germany, The Netherlands, Norway and Sweden.

[9] These topics have been more extensively analysed by Neutze.   See G.M.Neutze, *Economic Policy and the Size of Cities*, Australian National University, Canberra, 1965, and *The Price of Land and Land Use Planning: Policy Instruments in the Urban Land Market*, Organisation for Economic Co-operation and Development, Paris, 1973.   This section depends heavily on Neutze's work, but there is some elaboration of new ideas in the context of recent experience in housing and land development.

[10] Development plans in Australia have tended to become unrealistic statements of long-term intentions rather than programmes for development.   These plans do not represent examples of development plans in the sense that initiatives have been taken to establish town planning principles by taking a public sector role in land development. In Sweden, urban 'master plans' have become practising realities, because local government has used its powers to acquire land and dispose of it under planning convenants.

[11] Pecuniary externalities are purely *financial* economies rather than resource economies, and express the principle that money spent and received as revenue by one producer would otherwise have been received by another producer in a similar line of commerce.   In contrast to resource economies, they divert resources rather than save them or get more product from them.   In cases where a public authority acquires and then leases the land, it can benefit from good centring as well as the site operators.

[12] Neutze, *op. cit.*, (1973).

[13] In Sweden during 1968-1976, urban land prices decreased;   see subsequent discussions.

[14] This problem is discussed in *Report of the Working Party on the Stabilisation of Land Prices*, South Australian Government Printer, Adelaide, 1973.

[15] Neutze, *op. cit.*, (1973).

[16] The term 'betterment' is used in its modern general sense, relating to unearned increments, rather than to increases in value on specific property arising from neighbourhood improvements.

[17] For useful reviews of urban economics, see H.W.Richardson, *Urban Economics*, Penguin, Harmondsworth, 1971, and *The Economics of Urban Size*, Saxon House, Farnborough, 1973.

[18] This comment refers to instituted practices through legislation and administration, rather than to the professional literature, where ideas have originated in various countries.   However, town planning depends at least as much on statutes and administration as on general ideas.

[19] A fuller account of Swedish land development policies can be found in P.Heimburger, *Land Policy in Sweden*, Ministry of Housing and Physical Planning, Stockholm, 1976.

[20] The discussions in Chapter 2 reviewed the role of the Stockholm Real Estate Commission in providing finance, counselling and other services whereby home ownership schemes were developed on municipal land.

[21] Transitional arrangements were made for 1971-1980, with compensation pegged at 1971 values.

[22] This measure is effective in land, but not in housing.   Properties which local government would like to purchase for social and economic reasons (e.g., to counter segregation) are too expensive and do not conform to the standards prescribed in housing law governing state-assisted housing.   See discussions below.

[23] Most municipal land is sold under encumbrances limiting development rights.   During 1966-1975, about 20 per cent of municipal land was

leased.   Leasing presently offers no planning advantages not available by selling land with encumbrances written into the contract.   Since 1953 leaseholders have had strong rights to something approaching permanent tenure.   Ground rents are revised every 10 years and they are geared to average development costs on newly serviced land, not to market values.   Thus leasing offers no planning or financial advantages to local government.

[24] See R.Svennsson, *Land for Housing Development in the West Coast Region: Analysis of Price Trends Factors Determining Land Prices in Some Sixty Municipalities in Western Sweden*, Swedish Council for Building Research, Stockholm, 1975.

[25] It will be recalled (see Chapter 6) that in 1971, 68 per cent of new housing was built as apartments, but by 1975 only 36 per cent. Swedes were increasingly opting for houses with gardens, and government-assisted housing declined from 89.1 per cent of the new stock in 1971 to 84.5 per cent in 1975.

[26] The Social Democrats lost office in September 1976.

[27] This point was taken up in Chapter 2.

[28] Energy conservation became an election issue in 1976.   The assessment of energy costs in housing was related only to heating costs and neither the full range of energy-related costs (accessibilities and so on) nor the relative productivities of the two types of dwelling were accounted systematically.

[29] The conditions presently provide only for 10-year reviews of the ground rent; these rents are fixed in relation to average new land servicing costs.

[30] *Report of the Expert Committee on Compensation and Betterment*, (Uthwatt), HMSO, London, 1942.

[31] *Report of the Royal Commission of the Distribution of The Industrial Population*, (Barlow), HMSO, London, 1940.

[32] These administrative and organisation aspects of regionalisation are discussed in Chapter 9.

REFERENCES (SELECTED)

Hallett, G., *Housing and Land Policies in West Germany and Britain*, MacMillan, London, 1977.

Heimburger, P., *Land Policy in Sweden*, Ministry of Housing and Physical Planning, Stockholm, 1976.

Institute of Economic Affairs, *Government and The Land*, Institute of Economic Affiars, London, 1974.

Mill, J.S., *The Right of Property in Land*, Dallow, London, 1873.

Neutze, G.M., *Economic Policy and the Size of Cities*, Australian National University, Canberra, 1965.

Neutze, G.M., *The Price of Land and Land Use Planning: Policy Instruments in the Urban Land Market*, Organisation for Economic Co-operation and Development, Paris, 1973.

Peston, M., *Public Goods and the Public Sector*, MacMillan, London, 1972.

Richardson, H.W., *Urban Economics*, Penguin, Harmondsworth, 1971.

8   Housing policy and urban renewal

The ends and means of urban renewal policies in the United States and
Britain are once again in doubt. This follows reforms and new
directions of the 1960s. Since the late 1960s, countries in
continental Europe have taken a more active interest in urban
renewal. Now that many modern democracies have achieved an approximate
balance between the number of dwellings and the number of households,
more significance is being attached to the maintenance and improvement
of older stock. Thus, the current state of urban renewal policies is
that they are growing in political significance, they have experienced
recent reforms not yet fully consolidated in administration, and new
doubts are arising on the theory and practice of urban renewal. These
circumstances tend to produce uncertainties when some new programmes
are being launched rather urgently.

The subject is best understood in an historical way. Social housing
programmes grew out of slum clearance policies, which can be regarded
as a narrower form of urban renewal, [1] and were changed and altered
in the face of problems. For example, it was believed that clearance
was a more effective way of dealing with unfit properties than simply
drawing up building regulations, default notices and condemnation
orders. However, clearance implied more government involvement than
merely issuing regulations. It was then found that private enterprise
and the voluntary housing sector could not always overcome economic
problems in redeveloping sites which public authorities had cleared.
This dragged government deeper into housing; to use sites accumulating
heavy holding charges local housing authorities began constructing
subsidised rental housing on vacant sites. Under pressure of long-term
housing shortages among working class families, governments found their
involvement broadened from replacing cleared housing to adding to the
stock on inner urban cleared land and in the suburbs. Sometimes
suburbia competed with the inner areas for allocations of scarce funds.
In other cases, the need to produce more housing overwhelmed the original objectives of redeveloping bad housing.

Slum clearance and urban renewal have always been difficult to
administer. When property is compulsorily acquired, its owners may
take protracted legal action about their rights or their compensation.
It can be hard to co-ordinate those who take and demolish the
properties, those who must re-organise the physical services, those who
must invest in redevelopment, and those who are supposed to take care
(if any care is being taken) of the displaced population. However
dilapidated the old property is, it is usually expensive enough to buy
to mean that the redevelopment makes financial losses. These problems
have not been clearly understood until comparatively recently. Ideas
of urban obsolescence, and the practice of social housing, have been
based on crude theories of environmental determinism. Bad theory has
led to bad practice and to a variety of administrative problems. These
problems have endured for over a century, but it is only recently that
economic and social research has corrected the excesses of older
theories of urban obsolescence. The corrections have not yet

influenced all spheres of renewal practice, but growing resistance from resident action groups has sometimes blocked traditional ways of doing things.

Modern urban renewal faces a number of challenges. First, it needs to be less destructive socially, economically and physically. A greater use of economic and social analysis would help. Also, master plans which avoid massive redevelopment are to be recommended [2]. Second, renewal policies should be designed and constructed to co-ordinate housing employment, social and cultural facilities. Some of the past destruction was caused by competition for land and resources. In many cases, this can be avoided, and ought to be because there are cheaper and socially better ways of doing things. Third, urban renewal needs a context of support by other economic and social policies. For example, economic growth puts more resources at the disposal of households and various levels of government. Households will normally spend some of their increasing incomes on home improvements; and in the modern context of agitation for improved environments, governments will spend some part of an expanding income on urban improvement. Also, a social policy which tends towards an effective egalitarianism assists in the long term to break up concentrated pockets of bad housing. A regionalised employment policy can also act as a preventive renewal policy; where there are good jobs and high levels of employment, the average quality of the housing stock is improved.

The road to those conclusions has been quite long and difficult for the societies and the professions concerned. We begin by reviewing the history of renewal in the United States and Britain since the Second World War.

THE HISTORICAL PRACTICE OF URBAN RENEWAL

Though European countries cleared and redeveloped some housing, the mainstream of ideas and practice in rehabilitation has, until recently, been in Britain and in the United States. The Europeans have a long-standing interest in urban renewal, but because they have been pre-occupied with housing shortages there has been more talk than action in renewal until recently. On the other hand, the United States has been operating a strong urban renewal programme since 1949, and the British have had some interesting experience with housing rehabilitation from the same year.

The history of renewal since then has been characterised with political vexation and administrative problems. European countries have moved towards a more positive interest in renewal, gaining from American and British experiences earlier. There are signs that Sweden, The Netherlands and West Germany will be able to use the renewal idea more productively than the United States or Britain.

Urban renewal in the United States

The *Housing Act*, 1949, was passed to implement ideas of post-War reconstruction which had emphasised the need to redevelop city infrastructure and to create efficient and effective urban areas. Under provisions in the Act, the Federal Government provided financial assistance to local authorities to meet the net losses of acquiring, clearing and selling sites. Local government took the initiatives, planned and administered projects within the broad provisions of Federal law, and met a small proportion of the net losses. Some local authorities, especially Boston, New Haven, Newark and New York, were more active than others. In operation, the programme became diverted from some of its original objectives.

A set of essentially American experiences superimposed their influences on the historically-based ideas for renewal. During 1940-1959 there was a massive migration of southern blacks to the northern industrial cities, and they settled in the inner urban areas. Their low incomes led them to crowd older sub-standard tenements and some inner-area housing. Simultaneously, the rising incomes among middle-class whites enabled them to move to lower priced land and more spacious new housing in the outer suburban areas. Town planners interpreted this double migratory movement as a chain of 'blight' and 'flight' in a continuous pattern of urban decay. In effect, planners had a strong belief in the idea that bad housing attracted lower income groups, causing the flight of the middle classes. The low per-household expenditure on housing would then, so the theory concluded, result in a continuous deterioration of property, spreading into neighbouring areas. Renewal was thus seen as an imperative to reverse the blight and to apply structural surgery to correct urban obsolescence. These ideas grew out of some older theories developed by the Chicago School of human ecologists[3]. The theory and its extensions are invalid, as discussed in Chapter 3.

During the 1960s, political scientists, sociologists, economists and other social scientists began to criticise the urban renewal programme. Greer [4] provided a more general evaluation than other writers, and with them found that the programme had displaced the poor and brought anguish to the urban blacks. Scarce low-income housing had been destroyed and the programme had diverted resources away from social housing to middle-income housing and commercial enterprise. Urban renewal performance tended to fall well short of its targets, and delays in completing projects added to other problems. According to Greer, the programme was ensnared by constraints it did not produce and could not dissolve.

Under the impact of these criticisms, and mounting resistance from residents, dissatisfaction with the social consequences of renewal increased. This built up and caused a revision of its operation to give a more emphatic social orientation. During the Johnson administration, in the 1960s, the programme was revised to emphasise rehabilitation rather than redevelopment, and the social housing programmes were expanded to include health, social services, employment and educational considerations. These additional programmes, together with a new anti-poverty social development programme, were associated with urban renewal via the *Economic Opportunity Act*, 1964, and the *Model Cities* programme 1965. However, both experienced administrative and political difficulties, which hampered their development. There was a return to more conservative political administration at the Federal level during the 1970s.

Apart from the relatively strong influences of *laissez faire* and the fragmentation of power in American politics, the record in renewal shows that it has been dogged by loose theories, elusive concepts, and unsatisfactory delivery. However, amidst these difficulties, the American experience has also left some useful ideas and some success. The older housing stock began to occupy an increasingly important role in social housing programmes. Recent research shows that, of the methods of providing social housing, the leasing of older housing is the most efficient and effective.[5] It can be leased or purchased by housing authorities for rehabilitation and for renting to low-income groups; it can be scattered throughout an urban area rather than being concentrated in the manner of traditional project housing. In this way, it is possible to reduce segregation. This practice has been used in American social housing policies and it has useful possibilities for application in other countries.

During the 1970s, American experience with urban renewal policies reached a crucial phase. On the one hand, recent research studies have shown that problems in intergovernmental relations and a lack of political will have limited the effectiveness of policies begun in the 1964-1970 period[6]. Political will began to fade in the 1970s as intellectuals and policy makers began to see housing allowances as a means of improving low-income housing and the welfare of low-income groups. However, as the results from economic analyses became evident in 1976, it was clear that the take-up rate of housing allowances would not fulfil expectations and that rehabilitation policies would remain relevant for a *direct* attack on bad housing conditions. On the other hand, all the issues of inner-urban structural problems have been posed anew in the 1970s, and low-income housing problems should not be viewed in isolation, but in relation to employment and access to high standard urban services. In 1977 a Working Group attached to the US Cabinet's Urban and Regional Policy Group, reviewing policy development in urban renewal, argued in favour of opening up employment opportunities in the inner areas, diverting some investment in modern industry from the outlying suburbs and justifying inner-urban subsidisation as a corrective to the prevailing bias in favour of the outer suburbs. Such bias is represented in the public expenditure on urban highways and the implicit subsidisation of home ownership. Thus, urban renewal continues to be significant in housing policy development.

America has also learned a good deal about the administration of renewal. It can be very difficult to co-ordinate the numerous public and private bodies involved in any complicated renewal project. Two renewal entrepreneurs, Danzig in Newark[7] and Logue in Boston[8], were able to overcome these problems of co-ordination and integration. Danzig based his administration on the need to get the collaboration of other participants and to involve experienced professionals in the task. He approached the co-ordination problem by consulting and negotiating with key participants, and only when it was necessary to break a deadlock did he resort to higher political authority. He chose key staff with good reputations in urban administration and ensured that the realities of execution influenced planning. This meant entering detailed discussions with Federal mortgage guarantors, the authorities responsible for approving the projects, and the developers. The details of the project and their objectives were adjusted so a smooth execution was assured. Danzig's organisational structure was flexible to the demands of negotiating, planning and executing renewal. Under a rehabilitation programme residents and businessmen must be included in locally based participation, but in redevelopment, Danzig found it appropriate to negotiate 'behind the scenes' in government

250

agencies. Logue used similar administrative principles in Boston, but with adjustments to account for the different method of achieving renewal. The renewal programme there was mainly concerned with rehabilitation.

American experience during the 1960s reveals renewal as essentially a matter of co-ordination, integration and negotiation. This confirms deeper historical evidence. Renewal is one of the more administratively awkward areas of urban policy. In fact, one modern challenge in policy is to find approaches which avoid some of the administrative complexity. During the 1970s, renewal in the United States faced other difficulties. Now that migration into inner-urban areas has slowed down in some cities, older housing stock is becoming vacant. This poses new problems as indicated in Chapter 4.

The rehabilitation of older housing in Britain

After 1945, Britain's housing policies emphasised new construction. After 1950, new construction and slum clearance came first. Since the 1960s rehabilitation has been added[9]. Rehabilitation policies began in 1949 with grants for owner occupiers and landlords to improve properties, to achieve standards defined by the legislation. The take-up of grants was unimpressive and in 1954, 1955 and 1958 the conditions were liberalised so the programme could grow. Grants were available in two categories. 'Standard' grants, for installing basic amenities (bath/shower, water closet, wash hand-basin, hot and cold water, and food store) were provided 'as of right' to cover half the costs up to a specified maxima. 'Discretionary' grants could be provided by local authorities to cover half the costs of a 12-point standard on the state of repairs, damp, utilities, heating, storing food and storing fuel. 'Standard' grants were applied only to housing with an expected life of over 15 years, discretionary grants for housing with 30 years or more of life.

The programme attracted greater interest during the 1960s. Some reforms were accomplished to improve the organisation and to emphasise community-based schemes rather than individual houses. A system developed in Leeds became the model for reforms incorporated into the *Housing Act*, 1969. Leeds commenced its housing rehabilitation programme in 1957, with attention focused on the old back-to-back terrace housing built in the earliest phases of the industrial revolution. Initially, the authorities issued certificates of disrepair, and notices of intention to condemn property. However, litigation and resistance from owners delayed the programme and strained the city's administrative resources. A new approach was adopted.

The authorities began by making area surveys of housing deficiencies, followed with letters seeking the collaboration of owners in improving the housing. The authority took a liberal attitude to discretionary grants and offered advisory services on housing improvement, and loans to owners to cover their expenditures. In cases where owners were still reluctant, the authority offered to purchase and undertake the rehabilitation on its own account. However, Leeds proceeded with expropriation reluctantly, and only in cases where patches of neglect might jeopardise the overall effectiveness of an area improvement plan.

The features which attracted interest in the Leeds method were the use

251

of persuasion and encouragement rather than regulation and compulsion, and the idea of area improvement rather than treatment on a house-by-house basis. Though the *Housing Act*, 1964, provided for improvement areas, the powers were restricted to rented houses and the administration procedures cumbersome. To achieve a more flexible area improvement programme in which housing and environmental improvement could be co-ordinated, Leeds had to obtain special powers under the *Leeds Corporation Act*, 1966. The method influenced the design of the *Housing Act*, 1969, which expanded the concept of General Improvement Areas (GIAs) and further liberalised grant conditions. Grant levels were raised and their scope was extended to cover the cost of repairs and some of the costs of environmental works.

During the 1960s, housing rehabilitation was seen first as a supplement to national housing programmes, and then partly as an alternative to redevelopment. Rehabilitation is gradually assuming a role as a major component of national housing policies. Until 1963, public policy still accepted redevelopment as the major strategic weapon to deal with unfit, substandard and 'twilight' housing in older suburbs of industrial towns and cities[10]. After 1966, as a result of a succession of official reports[11], research studies[12], and finally, a recognition that new development and redevelopment alone could not fulfil national housing needs, policy began to change.

Rehabilitation had come of age in national housing policy in the *Housing Act*, 1969. It had taken a long time. For example, the limited-profit Glasgow Workmen's Dwelling Company had been operating a successful rehabilitation programme in the 1890s. But nationally, new building and redevelopment took precedence over rehabilitation until the late 1960s. Redevelopment and the use of high-rise apartment blocks fell into disfavour after 1967. The Ministry of Housing and Local Government[13] found sociological and economic reasons for discouraging high-rise housing redevelopment. This increased the future significance of rehabilitation.

The programme under the *Housing Act*, 1969, has encountered dilemmas and problems. In some relatively slow-growing industrial towns demand for improvement was sluggish, but in the metropolitan areas, and particularly in London, it has been strong. By 1972 it was evident that private development companies and middle-class owners were obtaining benefits and capital gains from the public finance provided in the GIA programme. Traditional working-class rental housing in London's inner areas was passing into affluent owner occupation and commercial uses, thus aggravating the housing problems of the low-income groups. The attractiveness of the older housing for private owners and companies arose because the increasing costs of new housing made older property a useful economic option, and the changing dynamics of urban development made inner-urban housing competitive with housing in London's commuter belt. Also, as single and two-person households increased, there was a buoyant demand for old London houses to be converted for multiple occupation, and the original rehabilitation grants were especially generous to conversions.

Whilst London's older housing attracted high rents[14], and speculative eviction and profiteering, older housing in the slow-growing industrial towns generally failed to attract the grants intended for it. Research into the use of improvement grants in the older industrial

towns[15] showed that the housing which attracted rehabilitation
expenditure was only about 30 years old and had relatively good
standards of amenity and space. The expenditure tended to be associated
with middle-income young adults with families. Thus the 1969 programme
had serious troubles. In metropolitan areas, subsidised rehabilitation
encouraged profiteering and added stress to the low-income private
rental market, whereas in low-growth regions the older housing remained
largely unimproved.

In this dilemma, policy could be refashioned to avoid one or other
of the above shortcomings; or some more radical approach could be
sought. The intensity of London's housing stress and public agitation
pulled reform towards the capital's problems. Also, the return of a
Labour Government in 1974 tipped the balance in favour of some reforms
in rent regulations, in landlord-tenant relations, and in framing
rehabilitation programmes to achieve more egalitarian purposes. Local
government sometimes led the way. By 1972 the London Borough of Camden
had placed all its new GIA grant holders under contracts restricting
their rights on tenanting, renting and the termination of tenancies.
These contracts were designed to prevent evictions, harassments of
tenants and speculation. Under the Labour Government's new *Rent Act*,
1974, a firmer protection was given to all tenants.

In the London Borough of Islington, landlords were not responding to
notices seeking housing improvements. Some housing was in multi-
occupation and without baths, hot water, and inside toilets. The
Council abandoned its attempts to get the co-operation of landlords and
began to use powers of expropriation to achieve area improvement and to
retain this housing as low-income housing stock. The *Housing Act*, 1974,
widened the powers of local authorities to use expropriation in the
interests of tenants and for purposes of managing bad housing, and
enabled them to propose Housing Action Areas (HAAs) for the areas of
worst housing conditions. Rehabilitation was to be encouraged with
subsidies, but conditions on the grants prevented an owner from
profiteering, and rents were to be registered for seven years. The HAAs
were viewed as stress areas, identified by bad housing conditions, and
unsatisfactory social conditions, (e.g., high occupancy rates, multiple
occupancies, lots of poor people). The housing stresses in Islington
have also led to policy initiatives in developing tenant participation
in rental housing and the use of co-operative principles in low-income
housing. The Department of the Environment commissioned a study and
report on the subject in 1975, and the Housing Corporation created a
special Co-operative Housing Agency[16].

Though HAAs can be interpreted as a necessary response to housing
conditions in London, the British approach to rehabilitation still
contains many problems. London and its housing-related needs do not
represent the general pattern in Britain[17]. Other problems arise
from organisational issues within the GIA and HAA programmes, and from
the general use of area rather than house-by-house approaches.

Recent knowledge and experience in area rehabilitation suggests the
following methods of administration. Potential GIAs should be reviewed
to assess social, economic and physical information. The administration
of the schemes should be participatory and authorities should maintain
good relations with the community. Project management requires strong
and effective co-ordination. In recent research, Roberts[18] shows that

all these matters pose serious difficulties for local authorities. In a careful study of 75 GIAs declared in 1969-1972, he found that co-ordination was often ill-organised and programmed, and the necessary commitment was sometimes lacking. Furthermore, local authorities had gone outside the intended objectives of the GIA programme by designating areas including villages, urban conservation neighbourhoods and public housing estates. The intention of the programme was to direct central government funds to areas of bad private housing. Some local authorities simply used the GIAs to improve their own housing estates, and this opportunity was attractive for improving private housing areas. Roberts concluded that because the GIA programme was set out only in terms of general guidelines, local authorities distorted its purpose and administered it within methods they understood (rather than by a new-style co-ordination) and to their own advantage.

Deakin[19] commented on further problems which he associated with the GIA and HAA area-based project approaches to rehabilitation. He objected to some effects of 'positive discrimination', especially in the design and administration of the HAAs. Drawing on American experience with this type of programme, Deakin outlined the following problems;

1. The method is costly and difficult to administer.

2. The political will to develop these programmes arises from unrest among the affected population.

3. The resourcing of the programme is marginal and little spreading effect is anticipated.

4. The evasion of applying the policy is widespread and easy.

5. Some new social injustices emerge which offset the gains from positive discrimination.

6. Resentment is generated among the non-beneficiaries.

Some of these problems are closely connected with Roberts' findings and with other experience, the subject of earlier discussions in this chapter. The case against area-based projects aimed at achieving 'positive discrimination' is strong. According to Deakin, special allocations to disadvantaged areas are justified only when: (1) the geographical basis fits the social policy decision, (2) the resourcing is sufficient to be effective or to alter the behaviour of institutions beneficially, and (3) the activity can be conducted without producing stigma.

It is possible that area-based projects are becoming outdated. The approach can be traced to the British *Cross Acts* of 1875 and 1879. The original justification was that bad housing occurred in areas rather than as scattered units in the urban fabric. Though there is some geographical and economic justification for retaining such projects for dealing with bad housing, perhaps the relative significance of the approach could be diminished. This question is examined later at greater depth, but meanwhile it is relevant to say that British experience casts doubt on the use of area-based positive discrimination in urban renewal. This could have wider significance as the European countries develop their own programmes.

Before looking at European approaches, it is worth noting some ideas
of R. McKie.[20] He is sceptical of promoting concurrent renewal in
comprehensively planned areas of 300-500 houses and favours renewal in
smaller pockets, and the principle of gradualism. This differs from
traditional policy emphasising uniform minimum standards in large areas
on the basis that housing has a finite life. McKie emphasises the
point that resources can be added to housing improvement gradually.
For most housing, the life will extend beyond the notional finite norms
adopted by town planners. He says that renewal programmes should be
transformed into environmental and social management tasks with the aim
of strengthening any useful *functions* which older areas serve. For
example, the older inner areas of London provide workers in service
industries; older housing in Peterborough (a medium-sized provincial
town) provides an opportunity for younger couples to get a relatively
cheap home. For McKie, the significant social and economic issues in
renewal are function, household type and mobility, householder's
concepts of environmental deficiencies and the nature of neighbourhood
social interaction.

The British experience repeats some lessons of the United States
renewal programme. The primary needs in renewal are to administer it
coherently, and to develop the right relationships with the community.
Rehabilitation has replaced redevelopment as the most preferred
strategy. British experience suggests that rehabilitation may become,
increasingly, a matter for continuous, low-keyed administration,
rather than a matter for area-based projects involving 'positive
discrimination'. It begins to look as though renewal and rehabilitation
will mature as routine parts of urban administration everywhere,
depending as much on land development policies and general housing
policies as on special urban renewal projects.

Like the United States, Britain has been concerned for a generation
by the tendency of many growth industries to locate away from the
existing centres of industrial population. Nationally, British
industry has shifted south leaving under-employed population in the old
industrial north; within many cities, industry has shifted to the
suburban margins, out of easy reach of the old inner-urban
concentrations of population. These problems cannot be attacked by
housing policy alone, or in most cases by regional industrial policies
alone; they require integrated policies for the rehabilitation and/or
relocation of housing and industry together. Following some
commissioned reports on the troubles of inner urban areas,[21] the
Callaghan Labour Government announced a new inner-urban rehabilitation
and employment programme late in the 1970s.

Urban renewal in other countries

Continental Europe has shown long-standing interest in renewal, but
only since the late 1960s have governments prepared forceful
programmes of action. The mood is towards transforming existing
renewal activities from redevelopment and infrastructure change to
rehabilitating housing. West Germany, The Netherlands, Norway and
Sweden intend to approach renewal with an up-to-date professionalism
in social and economic analyses, participation and administration.
Aspirations in renewal are more diverse and complicated than in the
earlier American and British programmes and Europeans intend to link
renewal policies with broadly-based community housing programmes. In

The Netherlands, Norway and Sweden, there is a definite aim of avoiding
segregation; segregation is viewed in social class and in relation to
household type (family, single and two-person household and so on).
Furthermore, this new interest has coincided with a period when
residents have formed groups to agitate for a better relationship
between housing and the urban environment.

However, while the Europeans begin new programmes with better knowledge and with more socially-orientated objectives, they are also
confronted with the new problems. First some perennial renewal
problems are more significant - for example, to match capacity to pay
with increased rentals. Remembering that, since 1945, housing
programmes have been heavily subsidised, the problem has a more cutting
political edge. Second, one major European housing aim has been to
elevate standards and to ensure that public finance in housing is used
only for high standard development. Renewal requires greater
flexibility in this than does new development. Since the high inflation
of the 1970s governments have been trying harder than usual to curb
public expenditure for anti-inflationary reasons. Policy makers (for
example in Sweden) have had to choose between spreading funds thinly or
achieving higher standards in fewer dwellings. Third, in West Germany,
The Netherlands and Sweden, building technology produces at great volume
by using systems techniques and variants. But renewal requires a more
sensitive and individualised treatment than such systems can provide.
Finally, West Germany, The Netherlands and Sweden have vacant new
apartments but a buoyant demand for other houses. This problem has
repercussions in land development, and social policies, housing finance
and urban renewal.

So far, this chapter has sketched the historical development of
current issues in urban renewal, as the clearest way of showing what the
issues are, and how they have arisen. The following sections offer a
systematic summary of the present state of the art, and its future
prospects.

THE SOCIAL ADMINISTRATION OF MODERN URBAN RENEWAL

The remainder of this chapter is arranged around three general themes:
(1) the administrative complexities of urban renewal need to be reduced,
(2) effective renewal requires development planning as well as
regulatory planning, and (3) renewal needs to issue from coherent
policies of land development, industrial and housing location, housing
rehabilitation, and general urban management.

*The justification for area-based renewal projects and the limitations of
the approach*

Area-based approaches to urban renewal are only one element in overall
rehabilitation policies but they deserve extended discussion owing to
the complications associated with so-called run down or blighted areas.
Blighting processes originate in social, economic and environmental
factors. In many large cities, there have been areas which for decades
languished in decay or blight. Where resources are not used to maintain
housing and its environment, blight can increase and spread. In severe
cases, blight can affect the morale and behaviour of residents and cause
an area to be described as a slum, where there is a high risk to the

physical or emotional well-being of residents.

In favourable circumstances, blighting processes will reverse and run-down areas will regenerate socially and physically. Many metro-politan areas in most modern democracies have some areas which have regenerated spontaneously, and often this is associated with some of the housing stock 'filtering up' to wealthier people, who have been able to rehabilitate the housing stock privately. A conspicuous improvement throughout whole neighbourhoods has eventually been evident. Such circumstances show that blighting is a process, and is reversible. Old and dilapidated areas can become attractive to richer people if they have locational advantages and if other sections of housing stock are less suitable or if their relative cost rises.

On the other hand, some areas which for one reason or another are unfavourable for spontaneous rehabilitation, continue to languish in blight. Things like noise, vibration, dust and similar nuisances will discourage owners from upgrading their properties. In other cases, landlords are deterred from improving properties because of rent regulations or disadvantages in the tax system. A private landlord may thus prefer a public authority to acquire the property at market value so that he can re-invest elsewhere. Finally, where there is an area-based concentration of housing all showing poor maintenance, this in itself often deters an individual owner from undertaking improvements. These reasons cause areas to remain run-down. Residents sometimes have no feasible alternative because they either lack information or face financial and other barriers preventing them from opting for other suitable housing.

Area-based concentrations of under-maintained housing present neighbourhood external costs (i.e., social costs or negative externalities) to residents. These adversely influence the motivations and economic choices of residents. Each property owner in the area will reason that it is a waste to spend anything on improving a dwelling. The neighbourhood detriments would mean that there would be no direct value increase of a single improved house in relation to the expenditure. Its value will be dragged down by the neighbourhood. Consequently, the most likely outcome is that each property owner will be deterred from rehabilitation, with the overall result that the area remains blighted[22]. Even where an individual is prepared to improve a dwelling, it is likely that a lending institution will be cautious about making a loan to be secured on the value of a property in such an area.

These circumstances justify some sort of co-ordinated or collective action. Where there are many owners, it is unlikely that this co-ordination could be achieved by voluntary association. The costs and effort of organising the collective approach would be considerable and any individual would gain most if the neighbours improve their properties whilst he/she does nothing. In this way, an individual could obtain an increase in value from new external benefits without incurring any private cost. Thus, in many cases, the most effective way to achieve co-ordination is to use a public authority to regulate and/or acquire and develop the area. Such action can remove prevailing disincentives and all properties will tend to improve in value beyond the cost of improvements. This offers one clear explanation of why speculation occurs in rehabilitated areas where the demand for housing is strong.

However, the social administration of such area rehabilitation is complicated. We have referred earlier to some of the likely difficulties. It may be hard for public agencies to buy the property they need to 'lead' the rehabilitation, or to do so at prices which do not compel losses. There may be conflicts of interest and opinion among the residents which make it hard to proceed in a participant way, but equally hard to proceed in any high-handed way. It may be thought undesirable to improve the neighbourhood in ways which will take its rents beyond the means of its existing residents. And so on. But in one respect, the work is easier than it was: more is known about it, and the world is more experienced than it used to be. From that experience, it is possible to arrive at a number of statements of principle about the social administration of area rehabilitation.

The first is: public authorities sometimes have to take initiatives to create area improvement. Experience in Britain shows the relative ineffectiveness of simply providing financial loans or grants for individuals to use on their own initiative. Some of the worst housing conditions will remain untouched unless there is active administration of improvement. Meanwhile, grants and loans will be taken by owner occupiers or private landlords whose property is not among the worst. A *general* programme of inducement produces no clear priorities which could be justified on grounds of equity, efficiency or effectiveness. These problems can be controlled by a more active development planning role among the worst sections of the housing stock and by regulations limiting the beneficiaries' rights over tenanting or selling property improved by use of public funds.

The second is: in area rehabilitation, co-ordination of various participants with planning, development, financing, social or political roles in renewal is required. Renewal involves assembling, managing and developing professional skills including architecture, planning, economics, sociology, surveying, engineering and estates management. Plans have to be designed and executed rationally and to a time scale. A 'critical path' method can be used with proper administration and not just as an unadministered guidance chart. Participants will have conflicting priorities. Renewal has to have administrative controls so it is committed and executed rather than simply planned.

The third statement is: there has to be a framework of resident participation. Local social networks can create persuasion and influence spreading throughout neighbourhoods. Where authorities have proceeded without engaging citizen participation, local social networks have spread suspicion, hostility, and sometimes organised resistance. However, unless an area is socially and economically homogeneous, participation is quite likely to expose conflicts of interest about housing improvement, its effect on rents, development priorities in neighbourhood services and traffic management schemes. There can also be conflicts between the neighbourhood concerned, and the neighbouring community. At best, participation will stimulate social development, and will call forth useful ideas on area improvement and some creative planning; but at worst, there are risks of high cost, political impasse and an administrative breakdown. The public authorities must accept the risks and proceed by common sense and patient negotiation. The main thing to remember is that the troubles are likely to grow worse, to the point of stopping rehabilitation altogether, if impatient authorities try to proceed without participation.

The fourth statement is: the policy on standards and amenities should relate flexibly to the existing social and economic realities. Utopianism and uniformity may produce unnecessary and futile conflicts. Some households will be living in obsolescent dwellings with arrears of maintenance because this is appropriate to their preferences and their incomes. As long as these living conditions do not constitute a danger to the physical and mental health of neighbours or produce extreme negative externalities there is no urgent need to force higher standards on residents who do not want them. On the other hand, other residents will want improvements which have been impeded by general neighbourhood drawbacks or by reluctant landlords, and here an intervention to improve standards and amenities has a limited justification. Housing improvement can be matched to a wide range of standards, can occur gradually in stages and should not be regarded as a once-and-for-all matter. Improvement can proceed by persuasion and co-operation except where private landlords have no benefit from renewal, in which case expropriation and investment by public authorities may be necessary.

The fifth statement is: programmes should be designed and constructed to restrict private speculators. Speculative opportunities can lead to rack renting, evictions and general insecurity among low-income tenants or owner occupiers. Suitable conditions on tenanting, rentals and rights of resale can be written into contracts where public funds have been used and this should prevent excessive speculation.

These five principles together suggest that deliberation, consultation and attention to detail are required for effective area rehabilitation. They support a carefully discerned and gradual approach with some anticipation that conflicts of interest will occur in administration and in relationships with the community. From another viewpoint, area rehabilitation under these requirements has costs and risks. Can these problems be avoided?

Reducing administrative complications in housing improvement

Bad housing conditions throughout an area sometimes call for an area-based project approach. But the administrative complexity and high organisational costs of such an approach make it appropriate to question how far the area-based approach is necessary, and whether it has so far been practised only because better strategies were not available. We will now review some ideas which offer to replace the area-based approach. They spring from recently developed concepts of social planning and economic efficiency, and instead of using the traditional language of 'slum' and 'blight' they use such terms as 'arrears of maintenance' and 'improving neighbourhood services'.

The attempt to reduce costs and complexities of rehabilitation can begin by classifying housing with arrears of maintenance into a number of categories, as follows:

1. Odd dwellings with arrears of maintenance, in urban or rural areas, which otherwise have well-maintained housing. This tends to arise when households dependent on pensions, social security[23], or chronic low earnings can no longer afford to maintain dwellings.

2. Groups of single-family houses, terraced housing or tenements
   exhibiting poor maintenance, but in areas where spontaneous
   rehabilitation is rapidly occurring. These circumstances tend to
   occur when middle and double-income families move into areas which
   have been the traditional preserve of low-income groups. The
   housing with poor maintenance remains, either because the transformation of the area is incomplete, or because prices have risen
   too rapidly.

3. Groups of various types of housing (or isolated housing) which have
   poor maintenance, in locations gradually experiencing upgrading.
   This tends to occur where incomes are derived from blue-collar work
   but where employment among residents has been regular over a long
   period. The economic progress of residents allows some expenditure
   on improvement. This pattern is commonest in owner-occupied areas.
   In private rental housing, the incentives for improvement are
   sometimes lacking, especially where rents are regulated and
   landlords get no adequate depreciation allowances against taxable
   income.

4. Areas of housing which have languished in continuing deterioration.
   These will generally be in 'rough' neighbourhoods, or will have
   housing forms not wanted when others are available. This can occur
   in either old or new areas. New areas may be lacking in neighbourhood services, or may consist of mass project housing of low status.

5. Areas which have been influenced adversely by long-term town
   planning classifying them for changed land use. This is known as
   'planning blight'.

Rehabilitation policies can be adapted to each of these five
categories. The odd dwelling inadequately maintained in an area of
otherwise good housing may be bought by a public or non-profit
landlord and perhaps rented to a household in some kind of social need.
This action is simple, and serves a number of social and urban
objectives at once.

In areas where there is an influx of middle-income or double-income
families, a rehabilitation policy should be designed to ensure that some
of the housing remains within reach of low-income families. Loans and
grants, with appropriate conditions to control speculation, could be
provided to low-income owner occupiers. Also, finance could be used to
acquire, improve and transfer the housing to the non-profit sector.
This policy has the double advantage of avoiding excessive segregation
and being relatively simple to administer. Some of the purchasing
can be undertaken shrewdly in anticipation of middle and double-income
incursions, providing that the purchasing authority has a clear idea of
how metropolitan housing markets operate.

A rehabilitation policy for areas experiencing gradual improvement
can be designed to endorse the process and to ensure that some housing
is still accessible to low-income groups. Selective purchasing of
private rental housing with some expenditure on improvement, and then
transfer into the non-profit sector should ensure that the area is
accessible to low-income households. In other ways, the spontaneous
and gradual renewal can be encouraged through advisory services and by
allocating some local authority expenditure to improving neighbourhood

services. Again, the process is relatively simple to administer and can be operated in the background rather than as a conspicuous once-and-for-all project.

The areas which have languished in continuing depression need a more concentrated approach to rehabilitation. They need to be administered along the guidelines discussed earlier. However, the emphasis of such approaches in urban renewal can be scaled down here. Except where the problems are intractable, the area-based project approach should be avoided. It is simpler to use investment finance for *general* acquisition and improvement. As this alternative is increasingly used, the number of localities needing 'action area' approach should diminish.

All the proposals for creating a variety of approaches to rehabilitation require organisation, management and control. However, no worthwhile social or economic purpose is served by adopting administratively difficult strategies when simpler and cheaper ones are available. The simpler approaches outlined very much depend on development planning and require economic and financial resources together with enterprising and skilful administration.

The proposals have some contingencies and they need to be complemented by other policies. The rehabilitation proposals require a land development policy which avoids traumatic changes in land use. This is a matter for planning the form and organisation of towns and cities. Plan forms emphasising transport corridors and a collection of strong centres operate most effectively. Radial cities, with a dominant central business district and extensive suburbanisation around, tend to lead to traumatic changes in some locations, especially at the centre, in the inner suburbs and in high value retailing points in the outer suburbs.

Another consideration in rehabilitation is that employment should be accessible to the rehabilitated housing and that the future job opportunities in the area should be assured. This may mean that employment opportunities need to be planned in terms of new industrial development and also in relation to the economic structure of existing regional industry, commerce and public service. Land use planning and long term economic planning need to be done together, and housing policies should connect to this sort of planning.

Urban renewal may also need links with regional planning policy. Spontaneous rehabilitation depends on secure and growing incomes. It occurs because some part of every income increase is spent on housing. This elasticity of demand varies among social classes. The specific measure depends on what is included in the term 'housing'[24]. However, the main point is that housing improvement is a generally expressed desire in the community and that it will occur as regular incomes are assured and the economy grows. Employment and social policies which support these conditions also improve the tax base and so increase the opportunities to use some public finance for housing improvement. Similarly, a strong basis for local and regional public finance gives governments at this level more opportunity to achieve better neighbourhood servicing. However, processes of urban change can lead to area redistributions of employment (particularly growth sector employments) and to some area redistributions of incomes and wealth. These changes in turn affect local government finance. For these and other reasons, regional policies and some devices to equalise local public finance are necessary to support renewal.

The regional perspective broadens our view of urban renewal, and also shows how the costs of organising it can be trimmed. Modern renewal becomes akin to general urban estates management not in its narrower traditional sense but in a broad sense which includes most aspects of the urban estate owned by public authorities, private enterprise, non-profit groups and other investors. The scope of estates management includes regulating and maintaining the housing stock, improving neighbourhood servicing, mitigating segregation and as far as possible engaging tenants, owner-occupiers, landlords, public authorities, and private investors in the common enterprise. Estates management in this sense has emerging policy significance as older theories and practices in urban renewal have become obsolete and as emphasis switches from new development. This opens up a new domain for economic analysis, social planning and urban administration, and means that new skills will have to be developed in housing management, town planning and in other professions. The works will be no less challenging or interesting than that associated with new development.

Finally, to ensure that new policies of estate management are turned to actual individual and social needs, they should include continuous attention to the pattern of housing opportunities. Passing reference has been made to the significance of housing opportunities in rehabilitation policies. These can be regarded as the choice available to households by cost, tenure rights, dwelling type and location. Together, these and the differentiation within each category provide a chain of choice. For many households choice is reduced to a few options. Choice of dwelling is dictated by accessibility to work, shops, schools and other daily routines. Little is actually known of how various factors balance and compromise when households choose their dwellings,[25] but the factors obviously change through households' life cycles, and with changes in the urban environment. Urban renewal affects the pattern of options in a variety of ways, by changing the physical fabric, the price structure, access to jobs and public services, and so on. Since these effects on housing options may amount to the main social impact of renewal policies, they should be central in the consideration and choice of policies.[26]

The economic evaluation of choice in urban renewal has been mainly concerned with the impact on rents, the elimination of bad neighbourhood influences, and with social benefits assumed to flow from slum clearance.[27] Social considerations have been accounted for so far as the impact on rents is concerned, and also by examining some slum-generated social costs assumed to flow from risks of fire, disease and social stress. However, the accounting of these social costs has been unsatisfactory. So have some other aspects of the economics of urban renewal. For example, a change in land use from low-income housing to commercial development can sometimes be 'justified' by an economic project appraisal. However, these appraisals are often narrowly conceived without reference to various ways of giving form and organisation to urban development. Also, much economic assessment tends to be cross-sectional and the dynamics of urban change limit the usefulness of this sort of analysis.

Economic assessments can nevertheless help policy makers to choose between rehabilitation and redevelopment. Under most relevant circumstances, rehabilitation is the more efficient and effective[28]. The main shortcoming of economic analyses in urban policy making is that no satisfactory way has been found to enumerate social costs and benefits, and the focus has been on the buildings and their earnings and costs rather than on the impact of housing opportunities among tenants and owner occupiers.

Future progress in accounting for externalities can proceed on two fronts. First, we need to know more about the factors to be considered as households make their housing choices. We already know that social and environmental factors enter the assessments and give value to housing. But we do not know how the net result of these is determined. Urban renewal will tend to disturb these choices because of its impact on values and externalities. Accordingly, it can be made more effective if we learn more about what determines revealed preferences. Second, we can find out more about housing externalities by researching how members of households allocate their time and resources in their trips to shops, work, school, health centres, and so on. This research will have reciprocal advantages for planning housing, the social services, transportation, and urban investments of all kinds. Until now, the economic assessment of social costs and benefits has been limited to a short list of physical factors and sociological analysis has been too narrowly focused on low-income access to housing and on 'attitude' surveys. By its connections to the Chicago School of urban ecology, some sociological research has, like economics, imported environmental determinism into its theorising. The present need is to establish how the composition of factors entering revealed preferences under various conditions is determined.

Urban renewal alters housing costs. In modern democratic societies these are shared by renters, landlords, owner-occupiers, and governments. By altering costs and changing the environment, urban renewal also has an impact on other housing opportunities, which include housing in other locations with choice of tenure, type and cost. These should be assessed for their cost, relative ease of possession and other attractions or inconveniences. The value of these assessments is in determining whether renewal will help more people than it constrains or dislocates or hurts. These assessments become increasingly important as many modern democracies find their national housing stock in approximate balance with the number of households. Furthermore, these assessments add useful social content to the urban renewal decision and to the design and construction of policy.

Final reference can be made to some key strategic policy issues. The main emphasis in this chapter has been on conceptualising some new aspects of urban renewal. Along with these issues, it should be decided whether renewal should be made widely accessible to the community and how it should be divided between the private and public sectors. For example, private landlords and owner occupiers could be stimulated to undertake more renewal if taxing systems were designed to permit depreciation allowances at generous levels or even at levels comparable to industrial investments. On the other hand, it might be thought that private rental housing should be transferred to the voluntary housing sector, though in many countries, there is an economic sense in which some private landlording is already low-profit or non-profit.

Other key issues raise questions of how much renewal there should be and just who should obtain the benefits. Modern renewal is many-sided, a function of land development policies, regionalisation and inter-governmental relations. As such it needs some dissociation from its past. A lot of its potential relevance can be found in these other areas. Urban renewal is growing in significance, especially in countries which have overcome their major housing shortages. It may be necessary in these countries to cut subsidisation on general new development and to divert resources to the existing stock.

NOTES

[1] Urban renewal in its widest sense covers all changes in the built environment and their relationship to economic, social and political issues. Most attention is normally paid to overt public renewal policies, which have varied in emphasis and objectives. Slum clearance was more directly associated to housing whereas renewal covers all urban investments.
[2] This is an argument for a multi-centred or linear plan form rather than a radial form which has a single dominant centre. A radial city puts pressure on central and inner areas as it grows and develops.
[3] The original theory can be found in: E.W.Burgess, 'The Growth of the City' in R.E.Park, E.W.Burgess and R.A.McKenzie, *The City*, Chicago University Press, Chicago, 1923.
[4] S.Greer, *Urban Renewal and the American Cities; the Dilemma of Democratic Intervention*. Bobs Merrill, New York, 1965. Other informative reviews include: M.Anderson, *The Federal Bulldozer: a Critical Analysis of Urban Renewal, 1949-1962*, Massachusetts Institute of Technology Press, Cambridge, Mass., 1964. M.Fried, 'Grieving for a Lost Home', in L.J.Duhl, (ed), *The Urban Condition*, Basic Books, New York, 1963. H.J.Gans, *The Urban Villagers*, Free Press of Glencoe, New York, 1962. J.Q.Wilson, (ed), *Urban Renewal: the Record and the Controversy*, Massachusetts Institute of Technology Press, Cambridge, Mass., 1966.
[5] See: A.P.Solomon, *Housing the Urban Poor*, Massachusetts Institute of Technology Press, Cambridge, Mass., 1974.
[6] The studies which reveal the problems in politics and in inter-governmental relations include: B.J.Frieden and M.Kaplan, *The Politics of Neglect: Urban Aid from Model Cities to Revenue Sharing*, Massachusetts Institute of Technology Press, Cambridge, Mass., 1975, and H.S.Perloff, *Modernising the Central City: New Towns Intown and Beyond*, Ballinger, Cambridge, Mass., 1975. Other studies have drawn attention to combining better housing management techniques in low-income rental housing with rehabilitiation, see: W.G.Grigsby and L.Rosenburg, *Urban Housing Policy*, APS Publications, New York, 1975, and M.A.Stegman, *Housing Investment in the Inner City: the Dynamics of Decline*, Massachusetts Institute of Technology Press, Cambridge, Mass., 1972.
[7] For an account of Danzig's activities see: H.Kaplan, *Urban Renewal Politics*, Columbia University Press, New York, 1963.
[8] Logue's role in Boston is reviewed by: L.C.Keyes, *The Rehabilitation Planning Game*, Massachusetts Institute of Technology Press, Cambridge, Mass., 1969.
[9] A detailed historical account of British rehabilitation policies to 1969 can be found in: K.M.Spencer and G.E.Cherry, *Residential Rehabilitation: a Review of Research,* Centre of Urban and Regional Studies, University of Birmingham, 1970.

[10] The redevelopment emphasis characterises national policy statements in Ministry of Housing and Local Government, *Housing*, Cmnd. 2050,
HMSO, London, 1963.
[11] See Central Housing Advisory Committee, *Our Older Homes: A Call
for Action*, HMSO, London, 1966 and Ministry of Housing and Local
Government, *Older Houses into New Homes,* Cmnd. 3602, HMSO, London, 1968.
[12] A government research project tested some ideas in administering
area rehabilitation. See Ministry of Housing and Local Government, *The
Deeplish Study: Improvement Possibilities in the District of Rochdale*,
HMSO, London, 1966. Other research studies encouraged by the Ministry
tested the feasibility of private enterprise renewal. These reports
(the Halliwell Report and the Fulham Study) discouraged a private
enterprise role. But, as we shall see, circumstances altered in the
1970s.
[13] The Ministry of Housing and Local Government, Circular 36/67
('Housing Standards and Cost Subsidies', 1967) specified obligatory
standards for local authority building and used a yardstick to keep
costs within prescribed limits. The Circular pointed out the comparative high cost of high-rise dwellings and it emphasised, both for
economic and social reasons, the merits of low-rise housing whenever
this was possible. This Circular went on to say that local authorities
must show very good reason for building at very high densities. The
subsidy tables were framed in such a way as to support the views
expressed in the Circular.
[14] Rents in private unfurnished housing were brought under the
regulations of the rent assessment system in 1965, but furnished
accommodation was not included until 1974. High rents in London were
in the furnished sector, which attracted economic returns from housing.
The British system of rent regulation was discussed in Chapters 5 and 6.
[15] See R.M.Kirwan, and D.B.Martin, *The Economics of Residential
Location and Improvement*, Centre for Environmental Studies, London,
1972.
[16] See Department of the Environment, *Final Report of the Working
Party on Housing Co-operatives,* HMSO, London, 1975, and J.Hands,
Housing Co-operatives, Society for Co-operative Dwellings, London, 1975.
[17] London's housing stress has been more vexing than in other cities.
The social consequences have attracted strong political lobbies from
Shelter (a national organisation agitating against homelessness), from
well-organised housing rights groups in London, and from the London
Boroughs. The political pull of this lobbying has led to the creation
of rehabilitation policies primarily matching London's needs, though
grants are still available within GIAs and for individual houses.
[18] J.T.Roberts, 'The Organisation of General Improvement Areas',
Local Government Studies, New Series, Vol.2, April 1975, pp1-14, and
General Improvement Areas, Saxon House, Farnborough, 1976.
[19] N.D.Deakin, 'Some Constraints on Innovation on Social Policy in
London', *Policy and Politics*, Vol.3, March 1975, pp 61-73.
[20] R.McKie, *Housing and the Whitehall Bulldozer*, Institute of
Economic Affairs, London, 1972, and 'Cellular Renewal: A Policy for
Older Housing Areas', *Town Planning Review*, Vol.45, No.3, July 1974,
pp 274-290.
[21] See Department of the Environment, *Inner Area Studies*, HMSO,
London, 1977.
[22] These ideas are discussed at greater length by O.A.Davis, 'A Pure
Theory of Urban Renewal', *Land Economics*, May 1960, pp 220-226, and
O.A.Davis and A.B.Whinston, 'The Economics of Urban Renewal', *Law and
Contemporary Problems,* Winter 1961, pp 105-117.

[23] Not all people on social security live in dilapidated dwellings.
Some single and young unemployed can group into a household and
economise their individual housing costs by sharing a high rent in a
high quality dwelling. This occurs frequently and attracts scorn and
abuse from the popular press.
[24] See R.K.Wilkinson, 'The Income Elasticity of Demand for Housing',
Oxford Economic Papers, Vol.25, No.3, November 1973, pp 361-377.
[25] This is discussed at greater length by M.Whitbread and H.Bird,
'Rent, Surplus and the Evaluation of Residential Environments',
Regional Studies, Vol.7, 1973, pp 193-223, the ideas of which were
reviewed in Chapter 3.
[26] This view of the economics of urban renewal was derived from
discussion with D.Beattie and J.Vipond during 1975 when they were
employed in the former Australian Department of Urban and Regional
Studies as professional economists. They had begun to examine urban
renewal and its impact on the housing opportunities of tenants and
owner-occupiers.
[27] An evaluative review of this literature can be found in C.Pugh,
'Older Residential Areas and the Development of Economic Analysis',
in J.C.McMaster and G.R.Webb, (eds), *Australian Urban and Regional
Economics: A Reader*, Australian and New Zealand Book Co., Sydney, 1976.
[28] See C.Pugh, op.cit., 1976.

REFERENCES (SELECTED)

Anderson, M., *The Federal Bulldozer: A Critical Analysis of Urban
   Renewal, 1949-62.*, Massachusetts Institute of Technology Press,
   Cambridge, Mass., 1964.
Davis, O.A., 'A Pure Theory of Urban Renewal', *Land Economics*, May 1960,
   pp 220-26.
Davis,O.A. and Whinston, A.B., 'The Economics of Urban Renewal', *Law
   and Contemporary Problems*, Winter 1961, pp 105-117.
Fried, M., 'Grieving for a Lost Home', in L.J.Duhl, (ed), *The Urban
   Condition*, Basic Books, New York, 1971.
Frieden, B.J. and Kaplan, M., *The Politics of Neglect: Urban Aid from
   Model Cities to Revenue Sharing*, Massachusetts Institute of Technology
   Press, Cambridge, Mass., 1975.
Gans, H.J., *The Urban Villagers*, Free Press of Glencoe, New York, 1962.
Greer, S., *Urban Renewal and the American Cities: The Dilemma of
   Democratic Intervention*, Bobs Merrill, New York, 1965.
Grigsby, W.G. and Rosenburg, L., *Urban Housing Policy,* APS Publications,
   New York, 1975.
Kaplan, H., *Urban Renewal Politics*, Columbia University Press, New
   York, 1963.
Keyes, L.C., *The Rehabilitation Planning Game*, Massachusetts Institute
   of Technology Press, Cambridge, Mass., 1969.
Kirwan, R.M. and Martin, D.B., *The Economics of Residential Location and
   Improvement*, Centre for Environmental Studies, London, 1972.
McKie, R., *Housing and the Whitehall Bulldozer*, Institute of Economic
   Affairs, London, 1972.
McKie, R., 'Cellular Renewal: A Policy for Older Housing Areas', *Town
   Planning Review*, Vol.45, No.3, July 1974, pp 274-290.
Perloff, H.S., *Modernising the Central City: Newtowns Intown and
   Beyond*, Ballinger, Cambridge, Mass., 1975.
Pugh, C., 'Older Residential Areas and the Development of Economic
   Analysis', in J.C.McMaster and G.R.Webb, (eds), *Australian Urban and*

Regional Economics: A Reader, Australian and New Zealand Book Co.,
Sydney, 1976.

Roberts, J.T., *General Improvement Areas*, Saxon House, Farnborough,
1974.

Solomon, A.P., *Housing the Urban Poor*, Massachusetts Institute of
Technology Press, Cambridge, Mass., 1966.

Wilson, J.Q., (ed), *Urban Renewal, The Record and The Controversy*,
Massachusetts Institute of Technology Press, Cambridge, Mass., 1966.

9   The government and social administration of housing

Any sphere of social policy, and especially something as complex as housing, will very much depend for its effectiveness on the nature of institutional, organisational and governmental structures and qualities. One of the key bases of this study has been that institutions should be considered as an important variable, diverse among the different countries, and influencing self-fulfilment, choice and the wealth and distributional results in housing. As we have seen, the subject of institutional form has been drawn to the centre of modern theoretical and applied studies in welfare economics and public finance. It has always been at the centre of interest in the study of public and social administration, but in recent years intellectuals in these subjects have been more interested in the relative policy effectiveness, distributional consequences and efficiency aspects of institutional, organisational and governmental arrangements. We address ourselves to those sorts of things in this chapter, and discuss them in the context of comparative variations among countries, referring them to emergent policy matters in housing.

The intergovernmental and organisational aspects of housing have received insufficient attention in modern literature. However, as comprehensiveness in housing proceeds, and as urgent priorities of new urban development begin to recede, the intergovernmental and organisational aspects of housing will have greater significance. It is in these spheres that comparative evaluation of experiences in various government systems can be particularly useful. In recent years, considerable change has come about in intergovernmental relations, inter-agency relations and organisation. These developments have been a response to general economic, social and political change; housing and urban requirements have been key factors to induce change. Government activities have expanded in these spheres and additional responsibilities within government have been accompanied by deep changes to the theory and practice of public administration. Interesting results are now emerging. Several modern democracies are now at the point where earlier spontaneous changes and their confusions have been reviewed. Processes of change which used to be haphazard are being made coherent, and are being institutionalised.

We need to define and interpret this process. This chapter offers a framework within which the new change may be understood, and clearly related to housing problems and processes.

The past decade has seen greater interaction between levels of government (vertical interactions) and within levels of government (lateral or horizontal co-ordination). The growth of these suggest that some spheres of public policy ran into problems which could not be solved within narrow divisions of governmental and administrative machinery. However, the inherited structure of public administration was characterised by administrative separatism where agencies of government pursued their own narrow priorities (often written into the statutes) and neglected their impact on others. Under administrative separatism housing and urban and other aspects of public administration lacked overall coherence and effectiveness. The growth of interaction and co-ordination tended to be spontaneous, with little thought for the general implications for intergovernmental and organisational relationships. Sometimes this growth led to overlap, competition and confusion, especially where functions and relationships were not clearly defined. Now some countries are attempting to eliminate the confusions but to endorse and legitimise useful interaction and co-ordination.

Other related changes have occurred in the theory and practice of public administration. New theory and practice in planning has been legion, penetrating public administration on three fronts, and mediated through three professions. The three planning spheres are; social, financial and economic (sometimes referred to as programme budgeting, planning-programming-budgeting-systems, or PPBS) and very much reformed land-use planning. Social planning has been mediated through sociology and social administration, programme budgeting through economics, and land-use planning from the social sciences and reforming elements within the town planning profession. In Sweden, these spheres are now viewed as co-ordinate, and relevant to common problems.

Planning in its various guises has tended to disturb and re-arrange economic, financial, political and administrative accountabilities. In each sphere it has been contentious, theoretically and in practice. Like other aspects of change in government and administration, the new planning has been characterised with considerable confusions and with protagonists intent on winning ground for particular theories, ideologies, experiences and practices. However, in the sense that planning means applying more analysis to public policy, taking account of the future, and programming resources and administrative efforts to achieve objectives, then there has been more planning in public administration. In other words, administration is becoming more analytical, projective and programmatic. Planning has been added to older control (auditing) and management accountabilities rather than replacing them. These accountabilities compete to some extent - for administrative significance and particularly when economic restraint dominates.

Regionalisation represents another dimension of change, one with critical significance in merging intergovernmental interaction, inter-agency co-ordination and planning. In fact, some countries, (e.g., Norway and Sweden) are using regionalisation to bring coherence to some of the other changes. Regionalisation can be understood as a process of developing public administration and community power at a level between central government and local government. The new regionalisation is always administrative, usually executes functions shared with both levels of government, and sometimes has its own institutions, which have important economic, financial and interactive relationships with other levels of government. The interactions produce regional perspectives in local and central administration. Overall, we can classify and describe the processes of developing public administration and community power in terms of localisation, regionalisation and centralisation.

Regionalisation, like the other changes, relates with existing institutions, and with their historical justifications. These historical inheritances frequently include industrial development policies, government assistance to particular regions and so on. Theories of regionalism from geography, economics, town planning and other disciplines/professions overlap and compete with the new justifications, parts of which involve the taking over of regional aspects of housing, urban and other public policies. For example, in urban infrastructure - roads, public utilities, educational services and health services - some economies of scale in providing and administering the services lie in an area which appropriately fits between localisation and central-isation. These services have important efficiency and equity-related consequences for regional-scale communities. Through the externalities influencing housing, it is clear that this function has important connections with regionalisation.

In this study, housing has been discussed and in terms of requiring a simultaneous solution to problems of social equity, programming, differentiated finance and an urban and regional network with complex relationships between housing and other physical, social and economic services. This expresses much of what is meant by comprehensiveness in housing. This conceptualisation has led the study to economics, finance, social policy, urban renewal, land development and social theory. Ultimately, the theories, principles, concepts, and policies must be referred to systems of government and administration. Housing has interdependence with other public policies, with the private and voluntary sectors; its policy needs have forced the breaking down of administrative separatism.

The externalities of housing extend across the neighbourhood, the suburb, the town and the region. These are area-based externalities with connections to neighbourhood amenities, to social characterisation of the neighbourhood, to suburban shops and service networks, and then to wider urban and regional servicing, transportation and recreational facilities. Most of these services and facilities are administered by non-housing jurisdictions and have their own justifications, laws and administrative machinery. However, because of their interdependence with housing and their co-existence in localities and regions, horizontal co-ordination, localisation and regionalisation are needed.

Centralisation in housing owes its justifications to other inter-dependencies, connecting housing to the national economy, central public finance, national legislation and to national policies. Hence, the need for vertical interaction and intergovernmental co-operation in housing.

If our task was to prescribe principles of good administration and government in housing, certain key points would be argued. We would make a case for vertical and horizontal co-ordination, planning, regionalisation and harnessing social and economic objectives to public and private enterprise. Also, we would be concerned with the processes through which policies are shaped and administered through governmental processes. Then, we should anticipate better performances where localisation, regionalisation and centralisation are balanced, and where public administration is relatively enterprising. These things are examined, below, in their comparative context.

COMPARATIVE EXPERIENCE WITH INTERGOVERNMENTAL CHANGE

This section reviews the experience with recent intergovernmental change in federal systems (Australia, the United States and West Germany) and in unitary systems (Britain, Norway and Sweden), the main purpose being to establish the conditions under which the requirements for comprehensiveness in housing can be fulfilled. These conditions vary according to government and social, economic and political change. As we shall see, the difference between federal and unitary systems is not the only significant matter influencing the capacity of a country to adapt to changing needs. Other important factors include: the inherited balance of localisation, regionalisation, and centralisation; the reform approach; and whether the issues are understood and acted upon by the country in question. Most rationality appears to be emerging in West Germany, Norway and Sweden and rather less in Australia, United States and Britain. These comparative differences have implications for the progress of comprehensiveness in housing.

A summary re-statement of the relevant points will be useful to establish the significance of intergovernmental change for housing-related requirements. Housing-related externalities have area significance - hence the interest in regionalisation. These external-ities cover items of urban infrastructure and services administered under non-housing jurisdictions in central, regional, local and specialised government agencies. Hence the interest in vertical and horizontal co-ordination/interaction. The connections between housing and national economic and social policies adds another reason for vertical co-ordination. Intergovernmental transfers of finance, resources and consultative services are often necessary to ensure that housing-related services are adequately resourced. These transfers can include lateral transfers to improve equity between regions. Finally, the more recent justifications for regionalisation are sometimes built on to older purposes, harmonising with housing-related matters. We now have a foundation for an evaluation of comparative experience.

Norway

Norway has a system of government which has traditionally *interlocked* local, regional and central administration. Interlocking occurs when there is cross-representation from one level to another. The *Fylkes* (these are 20 county-regions) were, until 1975, made up of representa-tives from local governments in the region. A *Fylkesmann* was appointed by the Crown to act as a regional governor and to interpret local and regional attitudes to the centre. Local government deals with urban utilities, housing, town planning, some aspects of health and social services, recreation and municipal enterprises. The regional body operated as a secondary local-regional authority dealing with some functions in health, education and forestry which were too awkward for this small, isolated local unit to administer.

The *Fylkes* are organised into a policy making part, the *Fylkesting,* and an executive body, the *Fylkesutvalg*. The *Fylkesting* elects some among its members to serve on the *Fylkesutvalg*, and the *Fylkesmann* was chairman of the *Fylkesutvalg*. Since 1971, the Norwegians have begun the process of revising this system with the objectives of strengthening horizontal and vertical co-ordination, and emphasising localisation. Following reform in 1975, the *Fylkesting* has been directly elected by popular vote.

At the end of the 1960s, the Norwegians saw the need to make horizontal and vertical co-ordination coherent and clear, and to strengthen local administration. This was additional to earlier consolidations of local government which had occurred after 1960. In recognition that these objectives carried strong political implications a royal commission, comprising politicians, was created to review the prevailing arrangements. However, more significantly, alongside this royal commission, and developing an effective technical and administrative role, a *Steering Committee for the Reform of Local Government* has been influencing the process of reform since 1971. The Committee has professional administrators and economists working to create acceptable administrative and intergovernmental change. Its members have closely observed and assessed patterns which are evolving in Denmark, Sweden and other European democracies. The method of work has been to formulate proposals, then to obtain some critical response from varied sources with professional, administrative or political interests, and finally to act.

The action has proceeded in stages, and the crucial step taken so far is that central administration is being regionalised to improve horizontal and vertical co-ordination with the *Fylkesting* and the local authorities. In effect, the *Fylkesting* has been designed as a coherent pivot through which regionalisation and co-ordination will be achieved. These reforms enable Norwegian social, economic and financial planning to be given a more thoroughly regionalised and localised perspective. Furthermore, the system of intergovernmental finance is also being reformed with an emphasis upon giving the local and regional spheres access to financial resources and greater discretionary power in many parts of public expenditure. The organisational aspects are well-designed to achieve co-ordination and to control public expenditure, and this fits the modern needs to attend to housing-related externalities and local housing conditions.

The Norwegian reforms have been facilitated by several factors working in combination. First, Norway inherited the interlocking principle in its structure of government and administration. This has been a useful foundation for building up more planning and some increased vertical and horizontal co-ordination. Second, the approach to reform follows the Norwegian political characteristic of careful deliberation, planning and phasing, negotiation and finally implementation. Third, localism has not felt threatened by the reforms, rather the localities have supported a change which moves some power vertically downwards. Finally, the reform process has been consistent in the pursuit of objectives, but flexible and gradual in the detail of administration.

Sweden

Like Norway, Sweden has been developing regionalisation to achieve co-ordination in housing, urban and social policies. However, our main interest in Sweden for present purposes is to see how its principal metropolitan city, Stockholm, has achieved regionalised urban co-ordination in housing policy development. It will be recalled from the discussions in Chapter 5 that frictions and competition among London's vestries and the Metropolitan Board of Works held back progress in housing policy development. Similarly, London's recent housing policy development has been frustrated by lack of co-operation, and inadequate structuring of relationships among the Greater London Council (GLC) and the London Boroughs[1]. The division of housing responsibilities in

London gives the GLC strategic housing powers and the London Boroughs have concurrent development powers as well as estates management functions. However, a solution to London's housing problems (access to land, elimination of homelessness among the poor, housing improvement and so on) would require co-operation among the Boroughs and co-ordination between them and the GLC. This has not been forthcoming, and central government has not intervened to produce greater effectiveness, but in Stockholm some metropolitan housing problems have been dealt with by local governments working together voluntarily. This began in housing and has spread to housing-related urban functions.

As urbanisation in Stockholm spread during the first decades of the twentieth century, rural local authorities suddenly found they had been urbanised. Also, the Stockholm City Council found its housing and urban responsibilities were being affected by a residential population which lived outside its jurisdiction but was involved in work, recreation and so on throughout the metropolitan region. In 1913-1949, some suburban local authorities agreed to be incorporated within the City of Stockholm. However, after 1938 the issue of metropolitan organisation had a broader and more searching review. For example, the 1944 *Committee for Municipal Co-operation* reviewed several possibilities, including, a federation, a unitary Greater Stockholm Council, and voluntary co-operation among local authorities. The Committee favoured a regional co-ordination policy. During the Committee's deliberations (1938-1947) the suburban councils developed voluntary co-operation. In 1946 they formed the *Co-ordinating Board of the Stockholm Suburbs* to work to resolve urban problems, organise co-ordination and install network services in water supply, sewerage systems and so on. One aspect of the collective interests of the suburban councils was their relationship with the City of Stockholm.

The *Co-ordinating Board* has ranged its interests through virtually all social, economic and physical aspects of urban development, but some of its work has been transferred to new specialist committees and other institutions. For example, in 1958 housing and planning were transferred to the *Greater Stockholm Planning Committee*, and in 1971 the *Stockholm County Council* was created to strengthen strategic metropolitan planning.

Our main interest is in the Greater Stockholm Planning Committee with its origins in attending to housing-related problems. It was established in 1958 and comprised five members from the Co-ordination Boards of the Stockholm Suburbs and five from the City of Stockholm; each section provided half its running costs. The impetus which gave rise to the formation of the Planning Committee was the serious housing shortage in Stockholm, and during the 1960s its most important task was to increase housing production in metropolitan Stockholm. By 1973, the critical housing shortage had been overcome. By 1976 Stockholm's housing problems were associated with 7,000 vacancies in new apartments in some southern parts of the metropolitan region. Housing has been the Committee's main function, with the objective of achieving regional co-ordination of local government housing plans. The Committee develops its own planning information and policy, and from this makes recommendations to local authorities. With the passage of time, the Committee has broadened its planning involvements in regional utilities, traffic management and general urban servicing.

Issues currently occupying the Committee's attention include; the intra-regional equalisation of public finance, regional employment policy, and regional impacts of the growing urban renewal programme. The intra-regional equalisation of public finance has come into significance as metropolitan migratory patterns have taken more affluent households from inner areas to the suburbs. Regionalised employment is a relevant policy matter where the proportion of manufacturing employment has decreased and smaller urban centres have become competitive with Stockholm in land and wages costs. Finally, urban renewal has among its aims the conversion of some inner-urban units to accommodate families. This implies a net reduction of these units and the rehousing of some households in the suburbs. Inducements to re-locate can be made in the form of attractive rehousing dwellings in the suburbs. Accordingly, urban renewal needs to be regarded as part of a metropolitan housing policy.

The work of the Greater Stockholm Planning Committee is a good example of how metropolitan regionalisation can be achieved. It was developed under voluntary collaboration among local governments. Vexation with metropolitan housing provided the impetus for this, but it should also be recalled that the initial response to collaboration occurred in 1946, when a committee of enquiry was reviewing the organisational problems of metropolitan urbanisation. The voluntary initiatives and the subsequent performance can be partly regarded as forestalling more formal actions and sanctions to overcome metropolitan urban problems. In London there have been political obstacles from localism to impede the reform of metropolitan organisation. Metro-politan collaboration needs incentive or sanction, or a blend of both.

West Germany and federalism

Now that Britain is actively interested in devolving some government to Scotland and Wales, the theory and practice of federalism will have more relevance to British policy makers. The distinguishing characteristic of German federalism, compared with Australia or the United States, is that its powers are divided horizontally rather than vertically.[2] This means that the Federal (the *Bund*) and the State (the *Lander*) levels of government have many *concurrent* powers in housing, urban and social policies, whereas the Australian and American patterns of federalism generally allocates all power over some matters to one level of government and all power over other matters to the other level of government. The West German pattern is more suited to intergovernmental co-ordination. Powers are exercised in a generally coherent way on the following basis. The federal level is mainly responsible for providing general framework legislation which expresses national priorities, and the States are responsible for providing supplementary legislation and for administering both the federal and their own legislation.

The States' administrative perogatives are derived from the Constitution and they are jealously guarded by the *Bundesrat* (the German Upper House) which is the State's House. In effect, the *Bundesrat* pro-vides a federal example of the *interlocking* principle. Some of the modern needs for administrative change - more co-ordination, planning, regionalisation, and intergovernmental redistributions of resources - have come into relationship with this horizontal federalism. Although the administrative traditions in West Germany have favoured separatism and formalism, during the last decade horizontal and vertical co-ordination has grown at all levels of administration. Furthermore, adjustments have been made to intergovernmental finance so that each level of government can fulfil its responsibilities, but maintain controls over public expenditure.

Since 1952, the Federal Government has secured a legal entitlement to a share in income taxes, and in 1955 a negotiated agreement resolved the proportionate sharing of revenue from these taxes and set the basis for a process of biennial review. Later, with the growth of the public sector during the 1960s, it became necessary to widen the pool from which the Federal and States' governments share revenue. Accordingly, the value added tax was added to the pool. The general principle in German public finance is that the two tiers will develop their programmes within the level of their own financial resources. Also, the scope for administrative and intergovernmental consultation and co-operation has grown. When greater demands were placed upon government and public administration during the 1960s, the Federal Government appointed the *Troeger Commission* to recommend reforms. Following the Commission's report in 1969, some constitutional amendments were passed which set up a variety of new responsibility sharing arrangements. An Institute for Joint Tasks (*Institut der Gemeinschaftsaufgaben*) was set up to facilitate co-determination in Federal-State policy making in regionalisation, education and other matters.

The initiatives to formulate a new national regionalisation programme began at a conference of Federal and State governments in 1970. It was agreed to create regionalised economic and social development programmes, to improve regional economic balance, to co-ordinate investment planning and to achieve horizontal and vertical co-ordination. The agreement provided for new States' legislation which obliged their local governments to adapt their local plans to regionalised planning. Regional plans were to be formulated and proposed by the States and summarised into authorised plans which were passed to the Federal government for assessing their compliance with Federal planning law. Machinery for intergovernmental consultation and for developing strategic policy making has been created. Thus, West Germany is well-equipped to further the cause of intergovernmental and inter-agency co-ordination in regionalisation and in the provision of urban services which project economic and social value into housing. The Australian and American federations have not been able to adapt their systems in such inventive and useful ways with consequent loss in potential in developing co-ordination in housing, urban and social policies.

Britain

Britain is more centralist than the systems of government in Australia, the United States, West Germany, Norway and Sweden. However, during the mid-1960s, Britain began its interest in reforming its structure of government and administration with a succession of official enquiries covering administration, alteration of boundaries and devolution[3]. Although some reform of local government boundaries was achieved under the *Local Government Act*, 1972, and public administration now does have more planning, it has been confusion, contention and an absence of systematic purpose which have characterised British attempts at reform. Two royal commissions[4] had overlapping roles and both experienced strong dissenting minority reports[5]. In the political sphere, minority nationalist organisations in Scotland and Wales have been able to pull the general political processes towards their priorities.

Viewed from the perspective of the sort of changing requirements in government and administration which are needed for modern housing, urban and social policies, the dissenting reports present more rationality than the majority reports. In his Memorandum of Dissent (Royal Commission on Local Government, 1969) Senior argued the case for regionalised investment planning. To achieve this regionalised investment planning, Senior proposed that thirty-five elected regional authorities be created with functions in physical planning, water, sewerage, refuse disposal, police, fire and educational services. Compared with the thrust of this writing, Senior based his regionalism upon social geography without much significance to scale economies, to horizontal and vertical co-ordination, and to administrative-financial planning.

Crowther-Hunt and Peacock in their latest Memorandum of Dissent (on the Constitution) presented an argument for regionalisation and organisational reform which lies very close to the themes of this book. They favoured seven regional governments, five for England and one each for Scotland and Wales. Their argument for regionalisation centred around:

1. Making some of central government's *ad hoc* decentralisation coherent within common boundaries.

2. Releasing central government's energies for national policy making and for the imminently growing tasks in the European Economic Community.

3. Absorbing functions such as hospitals, some utilities and others which were increasingly being taken from local government and placed in specialist *ad hoc* authorities.

Crowther-Hunt and Peacock also advocated the *interlocking* principle at central government with some reform of the House of Lords (the British Upper House) to achieve regional representation.

These ideas reflected something akin to the West German system of government with a central emphasis on framework legislation and policy making. The regions would execute some nationally significant policy and fill in some administrative detail. Crowther-Hunt and Peacock also advocated other ideas which can be identified with the German system. First, the regional governments would have their own revenue-raising powers so that at least some of their responsibility in finance was clear cut. Second, it was anticipated that Members of Parliament might get themselves involved with detailed policy-making work, critical scrutiny of proposals for new legislation and so on. The German *Bundesrat* (the Upper House) has this sort of characteristic, and so have the parliamentary systems in Norway and Sweden.

In their examination of constitutional change, the majority of the commissioners took a narrower view of their terms of reference[6]. Although their report ranged through general matters connected with parliamentary processes and administration, their recommendations were aimed at devolving some powers to Scottish and Welsh assemblies. However, the commissioners were divided on whether England should be regionalised, and what form regionalisation should take. Compared with regionalisation in West Germany, Norway and Sweden, the British approach has been indefinite.

The problem with British structure of government and administration is that it lacks an overall and general framework for achieving co-ordination and a balance of centralisation, regionalisation and localisation. In the absence of such a general framework, co-ordination tends to grow *ad hoc* and incoherently. Housing provides good examples of this. First, in reviewing the necessity for co-ordinating regional-local housing and social services, the Morris Committee[7] advocated a specific system in these two functions, but there is no system of rules, administration and finance which could make such ideas work *executively*. The co-ordination would be mainly *advisory*, not administratively effective. Second, similar limitations would arise in the implementation of ideas from the Green Paper on housing (1977)[8] which recommended that central-local consultation machinery be established to achieve flexible and comprehensive strategic planning in housing. The British system of government needs more fundamental reforms, along the lines argued by Crowther-Hunt and Peacock. The extension of the comparative review into policy making and the organisation of public administration, below, adds further to the argument for basic structural reform.

THE ORGANISATION OF MODERN HOUSING

As the public demanded better housing performance and government tried to supply it, the governmental and administrative demands on housing have been increasing. Housing is more specialised, diverse and significant in its administrative content. This change influences all sections of housing including policy-making, programming, development, finance, estates management, intergovernmental relations, inter-agency relations, and relations among government, the private and voluntary sectors. Housing needs organising so its specialist administrative needs do not confound each other or clutter up key parts of government and management. On the other hand, the parts need to be co-ordinated, sometimes integrated and always balanced and blended at all levels.

When there is so much change, an evaluative review drawing on comparative experience can be particularly useful. It will cover policy making, central administration, programming, enterprise in housing, and estates management. In many cases, the organisational aspects of these topics complement the earlier discussions. Organisation in modern housing is about adjustment to new administrative processes and about designing suitable structural arrangements, through a period of change. The discussion will proceed by looking at the legacy of organisational theory and practice before the modern changes began.

Some theories of bureaucracy and administrative organisation[9] suggest that housing and other institutions will organise themselves to avoid internal conflict, to protect themselves from outside threats and to advance their own narrowly-conceived interests. Internal administrative structures, routine procedures and formalisation of relationships with the outside world have been partly explained theoretically as protective devices to prevent unwanted incursions by other bureaucracies, critical groups in the community or politicians.

In fact, some housing institutions have established specialist sections to serve as the diplomatic contacts with the outside world. These characteristics point to some degree of insularity and to a wary relationship with other bureaucracies. However, in the modern government and administration of housing, a bureaucracy needs to establish communications with various government institutions, with the general community and with private enterprise. Furthermore, housing institutions will need to expand their activities into areas where the legal authorities are vague or where there is competition with other institutions. Diplomacy is usually better than warfare, and a modern housing institution must determine its role and legitimacy as best it can, where powers are vague or in conflict or competition with other institutions. This continues to be true even if government and administration are doing their best to make accountabilities more clear and compatible.

Traditionally, established bureaucracies have viewed their public administration responsibilities in a narrow sense without much regard to the wider social and economic needs of the community. In a changing society, and particularly in a period of rapid reform, there are considerable problems associated with confined attitudes in bureaucracies, insularity, and the traditional principles and practices of public administration. Ultimately, the restrictive attitudes and inertia can jeopardise a bureaucracy's existence. In recent years public, voluntary and private enterprise sectors of housing have been critically assailed by resident action groups, feminist groups, intellectuals and other proponents of change. It is this process which reforms old bureaucracies, creates new historical justifications, new ways of doing things and new institutions.

Policy making and administration

Though policy making is closely tied up with political ideologies, it should incorporate wider considerations than ideology. Ideologies and basic value principles do not, in themselves, achieve action. Programmes need resources, administration and executive commitment, and they accumulate considerable experience in day-to-day management. All this means that effective policy making involves carefully blending various considerations, from primary value statements, through analyses of historical performance, to some of the pragmatic administrative issues. Furthermore, in spheres such as housing, a diversity of intellectual and professional viewpoints have to be drawn together, particularly economics, sociology, political science and public administration. Some key points of the policy-making process can be located in parliament, in central administration, in consultation with community groups and with research.

In parliamentary processes, according to Johnson[10], the legislatures can either equip themselves with knowledge and information to keep pace with the executive and run the risk of losing political colour; or they can use parliament as a debating arena and challenge executive decisions, but in consequence become hopelessly ill-informed and ill-equipped to understand or to impede executive processes. The Westminster system and its expression in Australia and Britain, is ill-informed and ill-equipped in this sense. By contrast, the committee systems in Norwegian, Swedish and West German parliamentary processes enable detailed scrutiny of policy and specialist interests among members. This clearly assists policy-making. The United States Congress has specialist committees and hearings at which experts present submissions on public policy. However, the dispersion of legislative and executive authority in the American system of government reduces their effectiveness; often they are used to impede presidential objectives rather than to create useful policy.

Sweden, Norway and West Germany provide useful examples of how both policy making and key administrative considerations have plenty of room to develop, yet remain co-ordinated. In Sweden, the ministerial departments with housing and planning responsibilities operate mainly as policy makers with some responsibilities in monitoring relevant statistical information. These departments advise ministers on policy and draft terms of reference for specialist committees/commissions appointed to review policy development. In short, the ministries are not cluttered with detailed oversight of housing and planning. This is the responsibility of national boards which manage, plan and supervise housing and planning in the regions, and locally. These boards also advise the Minister of significant policy aspects of the operating programmes; the difficulties, possibilities for improvement and so on. Both in the ministerial departments and the boards, the administrators' knowledge of key subjects is impressive. Finally, it should be noted that the boards consist of people with useful professional, commercial and administrative experience in the wider community. The experience is useful for direction and guidance, and the presence of an independent board can keep management alert and enterprising[11].

The West German system of government and administration achieves a similar specialisation of policy making and administration, and has interaction between the two. The *Bundestag*, (the Lower House), proposes framework legislation; this is clearly a policy-making role. Ministerial departments mainly work on policy-making, in consultation with the States and with interest groups. Any legislation with administrative implications in the States (and most has) is closely scrutinised by the *Bundesrat*, (the Upper House), which can call on representatives of States' administration to advise specialist committees on any pitfalls of Government proposals. Thus, policy making is influenced by a blend of ideology, consultation, and administrative experience. The Norwegian system with its relationships between the Minister and his department, the Housing Bank and a review Committee achieves a similar blend.

The Netherlands has gone further than most countries in formalising its consultative arrangements. As seen in Chapter 6, housing occupies a very significant social and political role in Dutch society. Under the *Housing Act*, 1965, the Minister of Housing and Planning must consult his Housing Council, made up of representatives from the professions, intellectuals, financiers, developers, women's movements, building materials suppliers and others. The Council has three standing committees with specialist roles in technical advice, financial planning and general policy making. This system has worked well. The Minister gets a reaction to policy proposals before they are presented to parliament and there is an exchange of views before ideas are committed to legislative form.

The discussions on the economics and finance in housing in Chapter 4 drew attention to the growing importance of programming, which has interdependencies with policy making, administration and research. However, like the other aspects of modern administration in housing, programming is best accomplished if held at a distance from the other elements but brought into relationship with them at appropriate times and in key executive decision making. Experience with programme budgeting has shown that it runs into problems when confounded by control, routine and other necessary administrative features. However, programming can be successful when key executives want it, and know how to use it, and when it is given room to develop its analytical features and its internal co-ordination of different sections of administration [12].

To summarise this section, it has been seen that regionalism has a key role in developing governmental co-ordination, and that Norway, Sweden and West Germany have achieved useful structural conditions. These same countries have created committee systems and other instruments which enable policy making to be given greater thought and scrutiny than is common in a Westminster' system. British policy-making procedures consequently have less coherence than Norway's, Sweden's and West Germany's, and so it is not so surprising that British housing policies are less coherent than they otherwise might be.

It remains to discuss policy making at the level of operation, that is, in estates management.

Participation and estates management

Modern democratic societies have been increasingly influenced by citizen participation during the last decade or so. Participation is influencing the administration of housing, town planning practice, social planning and capital-labour relationships. This participation can be regarded at once as representing some demands for self-fulfilment, as overcoming some excessive bureaucratic tendencies and as an evolutionary social response in an increasingly educated society. In housing, the initial phases of participation led to some confrontation with government agencies, with private developers and with voluntary housing developers. As participation developed, administrators and developers altered their practices to meet some demands, and participation itself differentiated among various social groups and social purposes. In housing this has influenced the development process, landlord-tenant relations and tenure -related equity. Participation can take various forms and it can be more or less closely involved in policy making and management. Our main interest will be in co-determination (i.e., sharing decisional and managerial tasks) in housing and estates management.

Co-determination and co-ownership are two things which can be related to modern participation. Another way of looking at co-determination and co-ownership is to view them as ways of institutionalising participation, giving it organisational coherence and sharing out management and economic responsibilities on an agreed and reasonable basis. All of this gives the co-determination and co-ownership principles wide relevance and significance in modern housing. The principles have significance among various types of sponsor-developers and in estates management generally. As the discussion proceeds we shall become more sharply aware of exactly where this relevance and significance lies. Before getting involved in the use of self-help and co-determination in estates management it is appropriate to look more closely at the conditions which bind individuals and households into group interests.

Mutual interests between individuals and an organised group form the basis of co-operative housing organisation. The essential economic and organisational features of this mutuality are as follows. First, a group has at least some economic interest in common. Second, there is an economic need which can be effectively fulfilled by joint action, thus consolidating mutuality and interdependence. Third, it is possible to organise the group interest into an enterprise. Finally, the organised enterprise will promote the joint interests of members. The earlier historical account showed that the presence of housing stress gave impetus for group self-help initiatives. These self-help initiatives enabled co-operators to get access to low-cost non-profit housing, to achieve economies of scale in organisation, to obtain mutual financial security, to mobilise savings, and to accumulate experience in development and estates management. However, although housing vexation and spontaneous mutualities gave the impetus to self-help, it needs something to establish it on a continuing basis. In order to consolidate voluntary group interests in housing it is necessary to establish legally binding relations between individuals, the group enterprise and society at large.

The general principles referred to above can be applied to a wider context than co-operative housing. For example, consider modern estates management in housing, and particularly some modern neighbourhood lay-outs where housing is constructed in groups or clusters with some shared neighbourhood amenities and some shared space. In the introductory analytical discussions we emphasised the principles of area-based externalities and their relationship to housing. These externalities are manifest as the 'public' goods part of housing value. It is possible to influence these values through the form of neighbourhood development or through the activities of public institutions producing physical, social and economic services in the urban/regional environment. Some housing externalities are derived from the immediate group of houses or the neighbourhood, some from the wider district, town or region. An organisation formed to manage the very local mutual interests may then also act as a negotiator for the local interest in wider issues; but its *participatory* basis will remain strictly local.

Economic externality provides a basis for legal expression to be given to shared housing rights, responsibilities and costs. A material interest in a dwelling unit can legally be bound up with neighbourhood amenities and such things as garages, children's play areas, landscaped areas and so on. In private housing a condominium arrangement can ensure that individual properties are bought and sold along with some jointly shared responsibilities. In Sweden, this type of arrangement has been taken further. The Stockholm Savings Bank [13] organises house purchasers into an estates management committee which manages neighbourhood amenities; the costs are borne by home owners, but the Bank will act as the financial manager if the committee so wishes. Some estates management functions (on maintenance and development) are generally accomplished by self-help and some are contracted out where the nature of the work or the economies of scale indicate that self-help would be less efficient and effective. The appropriate legislation for joint-site management was passed in 1966.

The scheme referred to above gives a hint of what can be done in other contexts; for example, in urban renewal and in devolving some responsibilities in public housing. Organisationally the scheme is

rational in dividing out management responsibilities and costs.
Furthermore, the scheme provides a coherent method of institutionalising
some participation. To some extent group self-help in estates management enables a choice on the apportionment of costs by the group on the
one hand and the specialist estates manager. This specialist estates
manager will be housing authorities in some cases, and government
agencies in others. These are significant possibilities in a context
where the costs of estate management have been rising. The apportionment system could also lead to some increased sophistication in the
economics and accounting of estates management services. This is an
aspect of housing management which has received less attention than
other parts of housing (e.g., development) where network analyses,
programming, control budgeting and management accounting have been
extensively used.

We can distinguish the argument for co-ownership in the equity of the
property from that which refers to sharing estates management
responsibilities. However, in actual administration these are not
mutually exclusive, they can occur simultaneously.

In Britain, an official committee[14] has recommended the extension of
the co-ownership idea. The committee envisaged that properties could be
acquired or developed under a joint mortgage with shared equity. The
occupier would purchase a community leasehold which could be sold back
at market value at any time for the market price, less the proportion
owned by the other owner. In the case of countries which have not
inherited a strong co-operative sector, the co-ownership could be shared
with local government, government urban development authorities,
building societies or new institutions set up for this purpose. The
specific sharing arrangements would depend upon the institutional and
legal setting of the particular country. However, it would be
necessary to provide legislation binding relations between individuals,
organised groups and society at large. Generally, such co-ownership
possibilities would achieve the broad social purpose of enabling some
households access to a share in equity. This might appeal to some low
and moderate-income households which could not afford to full equity
owner-occupier tenure. This sort of co-ownership could be used in
housing rehabilitation programmes in inner-urban areas and in widening
the tenure choices in public housing. However, these possibilities
would flourish better in patterns of mixed public-private financing as
discussed in Chapters 4, 5 and 6.

The co-determination and co-ownership ideas fit the modern needs of
policy development in housing. In particular, they could facilitate
the housing management process and the need to give more emphasis to
rehabilitation and the conservation of the existing stock. Also, as
was mentioned earlier, they have considerable potential in achieving
useful estates management opportunities in new medium-density
construction. More generally, in non-housing spheres, there is a modern
surge in interest in co-determination, co-ownership and co-operation in
industry. Some of this interest is derived from worker participation
schemes in continental Europe and from the mood to implement similar
schemes in Britain. But the interest has a deeper and wider source than
the comparative industrial policies in continental Europe. Among
economists and political scientists there is a growing feeling that the
recent economic turbulence of inflation and industrial unrest in Britain
reflects a breakdown of the traditional economic regulators in the form

of fiscal, monetary and incomes policies. The issues can be viewed as a reflection of heightened capital-labour conflicts, the solution to which depends upon re-ordering the capital-labour relationship. Co-operation, co-ownership and co-determination occupy prominent places in the discussions of these issues.

Some of our discussions of urban renewal (Chapter 8) indicated that housing, urban issues, employment and economic problems are inter-dependent. It also seems that self-help, co-operation, co-ownership and co-determination will have a greater significance in future society. Housing is an obvious candidate for this development which can be used in varied ways. Furthermore, it begins to look as though urban renewal and housing rehabilitiation will become the major avenues through which change will occur. This is not surprising; housing reform through urban renewal has deep historical roots. Social housing began as a corollary of nineteenth century slum clearance. More recently, the impetus for social participation and social planning in urban administration grew out of the trauma of urban redevelopment activities in American, British, European and Australian cities. In each historical case the ideas and legacies of change have reverberated through housing, urban and social policies. This time it looks as though the scope will widen and join reforms in industrial organisation. Those housing and urban development instrumentalities which have inherited joint functions in housing and industry will start with some organisational advantages. It is from them that interesting innovation seems likeliest to come.

NOTES

[1] This has been the subject of several critical housing policy evaluations, the most extensive and detailed of which can be found in: M. Harloe, R. Issacharoff and R. Minns, *The Organisation of Housing in London*, Heinemann, London, 1974.
[2] For a fuller account of West German federalism, see: N.Johnson, *Government in the Federal Republic of Germany*, Pergamon, London, 1973.
[3] See: Committee on the Management of Local Government (Maud), *Management of Local Government,* Vol.1, Ministry of Housing and Local Government, London, 1967. Committee on the Staffing of Local Government, (Mallaby), *Staffing of Local Government,* Ministry of Housing and Local Government, London, 1967. *Report of the Royal Commission on Local Government in England*, (Redcliffe-Maude), Vol.1. Cmnd. 4040, HMSO, London, 1969 and Vol.2, *Memorandum of Dissent*, (Senior), Cmnd. 4040-1, 1969. *Report of the Royal Commission on The Constitution*, Vol.1, Cmnd. 5460, HMSO, London, 1973, and *Memorandum of Dissent*, (Crowther-Hunt and Peacock), Cmnd. 5460-1, 1973.
[4] Report on the Royal Commission on Local Government in England, *op. cit.*, (1969). Report on the Royal Commission on the Constitution, *op. cit.*, (1973).
[5] Memorandum of Dissent, (Senior), *op. cit.*, (1969). Memorandum of Dissent, (Crowther-Hunt and Peacock), *op. cit.*, (1973).
[6] Report of the Royal Commission on the Constitution, Vol.1, *op. cit.*, (1973).
[7] See Scottish Development Department, *Housing and Social Work : A Joint Approach*, (Morris), HMSO, Edinburgh, 1973.
[8] *Housing Policy: A Consultative Document*, Cmnd. 6851, HMSO, London, 1977.
[9] Some of the explanations in traditional theories do not fit recent

developments in housing. Writings which give some emphasis to bureaucracy and change include: M.Albrow, *Bureaucracy*, Routledge and Kegan Paul, London, 1970. A.Etzioni, *Readings in Modern Organisations*, Prentice Hall, Englewood Cliffs, 1969.

[10] Johnson, *op. cit.*, (1973), pp.183-84.

[11] Swedish capability and integrity in administration is also encouraged by openness. Documentation is accessible to the public and the press can publish excerpts from documents.

[12] For further elaboration of this point see A.Schick, *Budget Innovation in the States*, Brookings, Washington D.C., 1971.

[13] The full scheme involves: (1) attracting savers to a scheme enabling them to obtain access (after 'waiting' time) to home ownership housing which is partly financed by government loans and subsidies, (2) organising developers to construct group housing meeting the conditions necessary for government financing, and (3) allocating the housing to the savers who have accumulated sufficient 'savings' points.

[14] See Department of the Environment, *Final Report of the Working Party on Housing Co-operatives*, HMSO, London, 1975.

REFERENCES (SELECTED)

Albrow, M., *Bureaucracy*, Routledge and Kegan Paul, London, 1970.

Etzioni, A., *Readings in Modern Organisation*, Prentice Hall, Englewood Cliffs, 1969.

Marris, P. and Rein, M., *Dilemmas of Social Reform*, Routledge and Kegan Paul, London, 1972.

Johnson, N., *Government in the Federal Republic of Germany*, Pergamon, London, 1973.

Schick, A., *Budget Innovation in the States*, Brookings, Washington D.C., 1971.

10   Conclusion: towards a social administration of housing

This concluding chapter summarises some of the key principles to be extracted from the detailed discussions and analyses in earlier chapters, but it also has other messages. Some of the social administration of housing is about moral reflections and vocational commitments as well as utilitarianism and materialism. Administrative housing knowledge obviously involves an understanding of society, policy making, programmatic planning and modern management principles. This knowledge is more readily conveyed than the moral reflections and vocational commitments forming part of housing. Sometimes it becomes clear from examinations of policy that vocational commitments have been omitted or washed out of administration. Housing is a protracted process and is full of personal, professional and administrative interactions from the early ideas on the drawing board to handing over the keys. Housing is also subject to pressures from community groups, politicians, industrialists and financiers, powerful non-housing parts of public administration and from intellectuals. It is consequently vulnerable to administrative slippage and to external pressures. Without some qualities beyond a preference for an uncomplicated life, technical knowledge, and utilitarianism, housing will take the easy way out. Some modern housing in all countries is a masterpiece of technology but does not seem to be cared for by its developers, estate managers, or occupants. Walking around such housing, an intelligent observer sees that its production process and management have been dominated by narrow careerisms and self-interested utilitarianism. It is generally ineffective, but current social and economic changes indicate that some future lower cost housing will have this characteristic.

This study began by asserting that good modern housing policy required a simultaneous solution to problems of social equity, programming, production technology, differentiated finance for production and consumption and an urban and regional network with complex relationships between housing and other physical, social and economic services. Ways and means of meeting that requirement have been the subject of the intervening chapters. The table below (10-1) summarises the key generalisations to be extracted from the study together with the main policy issues. The remaining pages will then attempt to weave these two together to produce a concentrated version of the content of a modern social administration of housing, and then to summarise some answers to the key questions which arise in modern housing policy.

TABLE 10-1

Social Administration of Housing : Summary of Key Issues

Extraction of Key Points from the Study	*Policy Issues*
1. Housing policy is about social justice, resourcing, financing,	1. Self-fulfilment in housing and its implications for social theory,

administrative commitment, professionalism, and structural relations in government and administration.

2. The quality of housing performance depends on the character of institutionalisation, which needs to incorporate social motives, resources, enterprise, experience, commitment and government support. Furthermore, housing institutions perform more coherently if the general social, economic and political context does not produce too much unproductive discord in housing.

3. In contrast to the above statement, at times of great social, economic and political change, progress in housing moves forward when there is a ferment of ideas and some conflict. Such times and places create a folklore of housing and push knowledge forward.

4. During the past decade, there has been considerable social, economic, and political change with direct impacts on housing, which needs to take new directions in housing theory, resourcing, administration and in knowledge-building.

and choice in tenure and dwelling type.

2. Solution to the low-income housing problem, and its connections to urbanisation and social and economic change.

3. Co-ordination in intergovernmental and inter-agency administration, particularly in housing, urban and social policies.

4. Adjustment to the inflation of the 1970s and learning from it.

Housing is about social justice. At each phase of historical reform, explicit and implicit social theory was implanted into housing policies. Utilitarianism, Social Democratic theory, and Conservative theory have all contributed. In addition, the Marx-Engels version of Socialism had specific things to say about housing. A bit of each theoretical stream has been counter-productive to housing. For example, Utilitarianism is far too remote from moral content and social rights. Conservative idealists have been too dutiful and superficial in their belief that class differences can be broken down by the impact of personality, by interaction, and by philanthropy. Social Democratic idealism has bequeathed an exaggerated environmental determinism in politics and in the theory of town planning and social housing. The Marx-Engels version of Socialism lacks width and a thorough intellectual interest in the more pragmatic difficulties of human endeavour.

On the other hand, each theoretical tradition has contributed something of value into housing. Utilitarianism has left useful concepts of economic externality, and a useful practice of approaching social problems by means of social surveys. Social Democratic idealists have achieved social reform, and in housing they have left the idea of non-profit enterprise and co-operative organisation. Though these things have not always worked effectively they have been significant in countries with the best housing policies. The modern democracies generally have much to learn from housing practice in Norway, Sweden and The Netherlands. Conservatives are more useful in housing when they sincerely promote the cause of individual and family self-fulfilment and separate it from aristocratic notions of property and powerful capitalist interests. The Marx-Engels approach advocates 'dialectical materialism', but its thrust towards structural reform (even if not on its own terms) is broadly correct and more direct when housing vexation is deep and protracted.

Sorting out the more useful from the less useful strands of theory adds to the explanation of housing. For the reformer, the dilemma is that ideologies and manifestos come in packages. However, in a comparative study it is possible to find an approximation to the sort of blend and balance which produces useful results. During the 1970's, Social Democrats with their egalitarian ideas, have depended on middle-road support in West Germany, The Netherlands and Sweden. This has produced mixtures of public and private enterprise, more selective and accurate subsidisation and more sense on the home ownership issue. In Norway since 1916 the Labour Party has consistently supported owner-occupier, co-operative and rental tenures. It has not shirked structural reform to achieve national economic and social planning. Norwegians have been radical when the need arose; during the 1920s the Labour Party was more radical than its European counterparts, and in 1946 a group of radicals in Oslo stirred action in housing. However, Norway also has an agrarian Conservative way of life in the homestead pastures, the forests, and the fisheries. This asserts self-determination, self-fulfilment, and even co-operation when the benefits are obvious. It has also given the country some of the most capacious and satisfying physical housing forms in Europe. Thus Norway has a sense of the theoretical and the practical, and a tradition of people's movements. Its housing policies have been blended and balanced better than most.

To be effective, the principles of social justice have to be connected to resources, finance and organisation. Setting aside the organisational issue for the moment, we shall examine resourcing and financing in relation to choice in housing and the low-income housing problem. Choice has been tightly constrained in some countries by absurd theory, by a powerful impetus from narrow financial frameworks and by vested interests protecting the *status quo*. Some processes of social and economic change are dismantling some of the severest constraints on choice. However, policies have not yet fully adjusted to slower demographic growth, more complex patterns of household formation, economic affluence and consumer resistance to some types of housing. The progress towards reform is more readily achieved in some countries than in others.

This comparative study has found that certain social, economic and political structural characteristics inhibit reform. For example, the Westminster governmental system does not produce policy-makers as well informed as those in West Germany, The Netherlands, Norway and Sweden. Structures of government which divide powers vertically do not achieve satisfactory political and administrative reforms compared with countries that divide powers and functions horizontally (e.g., West Germany and Norway). Also, countries which inherit hardened and complicated class systems with a mix of feudal aristocracy, strong materialist capitalism, and socialist thinking which regards modern Social Democratic parties as working class property, achieve neither egalitarianism nor productivity, both important in housing. The real reasons for homelessness in modern Britain can be explained by its inheritance of class, divisiveness and insularity. The Netherlands has a historical inheritance of Jewish entrepreneurship, Catholicism, Calvinism, Socialism, Conservatism, and an international outlook. However, modern Dutch society has retained its useful inheritances and grafted on to them egalitarianism, productivity and wider internationalism. Housing policy development has better prospects in The Netherlands than in Britain, where one of the main policy debates during the 1970s was whether, on the basis of socialist or conservative dogma, public housing should be sold.

The low-income housing problem is not synonymous with working class housing problems, neither is it restricted to providing dwelling units. Housing problems are most acute among low-income families, some new moderate and low-income households, and where urban economic growth is rapid and not shaped by suitable land development policies. Hence, the solutions to the problem lie in the allocation and distribution of housing finance and land. Whether one is inclined to Conservative or Social Democratic attitudes, the low-income housing problem cannot be regarded as just another welfare problem. The real point is that, in the widest and most legitimate sense, in which the term subsidisation can be applied to housing, the middle and high-income groups are getting most of the cake. This is inequitable and has no rational economic or political basis. Furthermore, there are useful opportunities inherent in the solutions. Any reasonable solution requires housing to be a community goal, not residual welfare. Housing finance needs to be reformed. Land development policies need to assert priority for public enterprise in land acquisition and *development* planning, which should be concerned with producing urban environments working efficiently and equitably for housholds so they have convenient access to important housing-related amenities.

Social justice in housing, together with economic resources, can be effective only through organisation and institutionalisation. At the level of central administration, the key point in institutionalisation is to harness suitably designed financial instruments to social objectives. The design of financial instruments should balance allocational, distributional and stabilisation objectives. Some of the recent experience of inflation has highlighted stabilisation issues (i.e., the inflation proofing of public expenditure) and intensified the need to make allocational and distributional reforms in housing finance. This has meant that housing policies have begun to depart from their association with historical cost renting/instalments, an association strongly held in the theory and practice of social housing. However, historical costs have produced vertical and horizontal inequities. The severe inflation heightened them for new households in virtually all income groups. The recent reforming impetus in housing finance is concerned with co-ordinating subsidies and moving closer to problems of tenure-related inequity. The Dutch have attempted to solve this tenure problem by designing a special low-income home-ownership programme, and the Swedes have found a new justification for production subsidies. Before 1968 these had been justified by the need to encourage volume production; by 1975 they were being advocated as a counter balance for the heavy implicit subsidisation which owner-occupiers receive. However, under the Swedish system, it is possible to receive both the implicit subsidisation and the production subsidies. The problem of tenure-related equity remains unresolved, but much in the forefront of modern policy issues.

At the level of operation, institutionalisation works best when it combines enterprise, resources, administrative commitment and experience in the housing process. Enterprise depends on the wider economic and organisational environment which should allow competition between developers. The problem with the public housing approach is that it tends to aim at a section of housing clients instead of more broadly where private voluntary and public developers overlap the various housing demands. Though the post-1964 British approach has three sectors, they tend to serve distinct sets of clients. The financing systems need to be united and re-arranged so that public, co-operative and private developers can each serve most sections of the housing market. In effect, the co-operative housing sector should be organised along the lines of the Swedish HSB model and the basic system of housing finance should *mix* public finance with private finance and make the mixtures accessible to all developers on similar terms. Australia and the United States could also benefit by gradually pulling their financial systems round to something like those in continental Europe. The mixed public-private finance solution obviously needs to assert social objectives and a community housing programme which ought to be differentiated but not stigmatised. In summary, institutionalisation needs to be arranged to bring enterprise in production, choice in consumption and a financial framework into relationship with a comprehensive housing policy.

Under modern conditions, housing has to be thought of and administered in relation to its externalities. Increasingly, housing enterprises are more directly involved in other private and public investments. But sometimes it is a matter of establishing programmatic planning and working relationships with other urban investors. The general point is that urban investments in housing need better programmatic planning and co-ordination. Ultimately, this has wider implications for the quality of inter-governmental and inter-agency relationships, and also for structural coherence in government and administration. Regionalisation can be used to achieve this coherence. Rightly designed, it can allow good lateral co-ordination at regional level, while linking central government roles to very local government and co-operative roles in effective ways, through practical working procedures. All of this helps achieve economic efficiency and equity in programming urban investments and in translating the programming into realistic land use plans.

Social science is most fascinating where there is a concentration of theories, ideas, activities and reactions specific to time and place. Housing has some of this fascination. It is not too difficult to build up a folklore by identifying key situations where society has been challenged to do new things in housing. The discussions in the book have reviewed Vienna and Stockholm in the 1920s, and Glasgow in the 1890s in this light. Vienna had its 'workers palaces', Stockholm its 'magic houses' and Glasgow had genuinely civic purposes.

Vienna revealed some charisma, but also a representation of some invalid social theory. Stockholm's 'magic house' programme may yet prove to contain many of the answers to modern day housing needs. However, this would mean some return to policies which combined cheap and well-serviced land, organisation of the building industry to produce

socially useful products, counsel and experience in developing
individualised housing, and home ownership for those moderate and low-
income groups wanting this. Glasgow needs to revert to some of its
earlier housing activities. The Gorbals slums are now virtually wiped
away; but they have been replaced with slab-blocks, and tower blocks,
symbolising a phoenix spirit of architectural and technical
sophistication rather than effective living for ordinary people. During
the 1890s, the Glasgow Workmen's Dwelling Company pioneered cheap and
useful rehabilitation. It would have been better to have continued this,
rather than to have expressed modern civic purpose in architectural
monuments with plaques on the facades proclaiming the official opening
hand of royalty.

Some of the most interesting features of housing folklore are the
connections between housing, urban and social conditions. The conditions
in Glasgow during the nineteenth century reflected rapid urbanisation,
poverty and housing shortages. It can be shown that housing problems
under such conditions need simultaneous solutions in urban, social and
employment policies.

Glasgow's urban poor needed increasingly productive employment, social
security, cheap land, suitable housing finance and housing
rehabilitation. Modern policies have begun to extend social security to
housing allowances and to review housing finance so that it can meet
allocational, distributional and stabilisation requirements. Glasgow
itself was pioneering housing rehabilitation at early times and
Stockholm City Council was ready to acquire land for new development.
The modern world needs other co-ordinated connections in housing, urban
and social policies, particularly in administration and social
development. It seems all the more remarkable that housing policy
development has not achieved this framework earlier. However, these
studies have shown that irrelevant social theory, limited professional
knowledge, modern technology and historical circumstances overwhelmed
Glasgow's rehabilitation programme of the 1890s and Stockholm's 'magic
houses' in the 1920s. This means that a rational co-ordination between
housing, urban and social policies has to be created, and articulated;
it will not grow spontaneously, except where conditions are fortuitous.

Housing needs intellectual attention. It needs a middle-ground
reasoning, looking at theory and empiricism together, and a language
which can handle concepts of resource allocation and opportunity cost,
and also the social and human purposes which assimilate the domestic
life inside the houses. In some countries housing needs cooler, more
specialist attention from politicians, with less ideological assertion.
Some modifications of the Westminster system may well be needed, to
allow the sensible use of professional skills, and the considerable
degree of bipartisan political consensus, which should in principle
contribute to modern housing policy.

Housing is influenced by intellectual ideas and by political
processes, but the administrators are the people who have to practise
it, and attend to its day-to-day problems. During the past decade,
administration in both the private and the public sectors has
experienced considerable change in co-ordination, the absorption of new
professional expertise, the reform of older professions, altering
characteristics of intergovernmental and inter-agency relations and
administrative re-organisation to fit the new demands of a society which

itself is changing. This means administrators need to understand society, and the history, economics, sociology and the technology of housing. Then, because housing is complex, and vulnerable to error and to loose organisation, it needs a vocational commitment. A social administration of housing is justifiable in principle and in practice.

The study was addressed to a number of modern policy questions, and in conclusion we can give some summarised answers.

The first set of questions: What are the most suitable forms of providing housing assistance? To what extent can social income be relied upon to ensure an adequate standard of housing? How much housing should be provided relatively among government, non-profit housing associations, and private enterprise?

Our seven countries show remarkable variations in the ways they arrange their resourcing, financing and administration of housing. However, in all these countries governments provide assistance via tax policies, attention to mortgaging instruments, direct production subsidies and in a greater or lesser development of housing allowances and for rent rebates. The continental European countries have co-ordinated their recent reforms in housing finance and rent policies, and their policies are more comprehensive than those in the English-speaking countries.

Housing assistance has gone well beyond cash-income provisions to the poor. This is mainly because housing history, housing sociology and housing economics reveal housing as a genuinely 'merit' good. Its benefits are delayed, diffused and complex, beyond the range and effectiveness of purely private markets, and assistance is provided 'in kind' rather than simply in cash support to consumers. Housing poverty and housing inequality overlap other poverties and inequalities, but they do not exactly co-incide. Moreover, the benefits and distributional aspects of housing are important within the family - especially for women and children - as well as among and between broad income and social class groupings.

It is possible to provide housing 'socially' through a diversity of means - entrepreneurial non-profit voluntarism, owner-occupier initiatives, public housing and in a varied private rental stock. Also, it is possible to have sectoral ineffectiveness; for example, the British private rental sector compared with that in West Germany. It becomes more serious if the housing system as a whole fails, and for purposes of evaluation it is necessary to examine housing as a whole, not just within single sectors. Viewed in this way, Norway emerges as the best system. Its central resourcing framework amends market provisions, retains consumer choice in tenure, dwelling type and participation, and the mortgaging and housing allowance structures make standard housing affordable for low and moderate-income groups. In countries where there are sectoral rigidities closely bound up with tenure, problems and conflicts arise in relation to egalitarianism and consumer choice objectives. Britain has those sorts of problems and conflicts, and comparative analysis shows how things might otherwise be different, especially in public housing and in private rental housing.

The second set of questions: How effective and well-directed are existing programmes of housing assistance? What are their effects upon the distribution of income and wealth?

Substantial vertical and horizontal inequity occurs in the housing systems of most countries. It is important to look at this matter with reference to life cycle factors as well as to (cross-sectional) income and class categories. The severe inflation of the 1970s has disturbed and re-arranged tenure-related inequities. Generally, the questions have to be referred to a co-ordinated set of solutions involving: (1) reforming housing finance to cope with inflation, (2) making production subsidies more selective and targeting them to low-income groups and some first-time home buyers, and (3) taxing imputed rental values of owner-occupiers, and providing universal housing allowances. Economic analyses should be used to reveal interactive public-private sector effects of any redesign to subsidies and housing finance, with attention to tenure-related equity. We can provide no general reconstruction and revision for all countries, because their institutional and current resourcing frameworks are very different. However, we can say, again, that Norway, with its generally accessible 'social' mortgaging and housing allowances, has found it easier to adapt to modern social change than other countries where tenure-related consequences draw conflicts and dilemmas. Sometimes these conflicts are sufficient to favour the *status quo* and create an impasse on the tenure-related equity question.

As property, housing has very significant effects on the distribution of wealth and income. In some housing systems, the structural barriers against home ownership and/or the bad arrangements for providing social or private rental housing compound antecedent inequalities. Access to home ownership over long periods of time in Norway and Australia has been a means of more broadly distributing wealth. The same is true of the Scandinavian co-operative organisation in housing. Apart from responses to the particular issues of the 1970s (as discussed in the previous paragraph), it is the longer term institutional arrangements in housing which are crucial. We are not going to solve housing inequality in the short term; it is often a difficult matter in which to get substantial progress. Nevertheless, this comparative study shows that given the right institutional arrangements, in the longer term housing can be used as an equaliser without any deadhand bureaucracy. Yet again, the Norwegian pattern emerges as a useful paradigm. If other countries cannot replicate its results in the short term, they can revise mortgaging and subsidisation so that longer term processes tend to equalise. The same general principle is true for Marxist countries; housing equality takes longer to achieve than other aspects of equality, and it is not simply solved by expropriation and re-allocation in the first few months of post-revolutionary fervour. As we saw in Chapter 2, developed Marxist countries are currently involved with issues similar to those in the modern democracies - making subsidies more selective, gearing loans to capacity to repay, establishing choice in tenure, and reviewing the distribution of costs between individuals and the government. The matter of housing inequality will be around in intellectual debates and in policy relevance for many years.

The third set of questions: How could housing policies be better co-ordinated with environmental and social development policies, and with the provision of infrastructure? What institutional arrangements and organisation are appropriate for administering comprehensiveness in housing? What is the role of localisation, regionalisation and centralisation in housing? What is the role of the community and what methods of consultation should be adopted?

The historical inheritance of social theory and of the relevant professions has been (mainly) bad - a misconceived environmental determinism, an eclectic and often muddled set of social considerations in housing and a lack of intellectural coherence. Our discussions in Chapter 3 outlined the problems of the theoretical weaknesses, and the institutional and historical separatisms which cut across the need for unity in housing, urban and social policies. However, some encouraging signs have emerged during the last decade or so. Sociologists and economists now understand urbanisation and its inequalities much better than they did before the mid-1960s. The institutional inheritance in land development, social development and housing policies remains separatist in many countries, but Sweden stands out as a country where unity is appreciated, and the direction of its reform in intergovern-mental organisation and land policy is progressive to the aim of co-ordination. Outside Sweden, the recent decade has witnessed considerable change and reform in processes, methods and organisation in public administration, but this change has not been consolidated because, during the 1970s, priorities have been redirected to anti-inflationary curbs in public expenditure and public administration. The move towards comprehensiveness in housing demands co-ordination and planning, but the demands have been met only among some continental European countries. In Norway, Sweden and West Germany the various levels of government are *interlocked*, achieving some balance and co-ordination in localisation, regionalisation and centralisation. In The Netherlands, the Housing Minister consults with a broadly representative group of social and economic interests in housing. Housing interest groups in continental Europe have far more influence on policy, compared with Britain where party politics are dominant. This comparative study shows that housing results are better in continental Europe, and this is partly attributable to those conditions from socio-political-governmental structure.

In conclusion, a comparative housing study shows that there are good, bad and indifferent ways of doing things. Housing is sufficiently significant in personal, social, economic and political life for us to aspire to organise it well for everyone. Comparative analysis shows the conditions under which housing can be so organised. For policy significance it is relevant to adopt a broad approach, drawing upon various social sciences and history to give exposition, criticism and appreciation. The design and construction of policy will depend upon how we conceive and interpret housing. This study has argued for social, economic and political breadth, and for comparative assessments of performances in the modern democracies. From comparative analysis, we get to know the conditions under which housing arrangements work effectively for self-fulfilment and social equity.

REFERENCES (SELECTED)

Broady, M., *Planning for People*, Bedford Square Press, London, 1968.
Donnison, D.V., *The Government of Housing*, Penguin, Harmondsworth, 1967.
Grigsby, W.G. and Rosenburg, L., *Urban Housing Policy*, APS Publications, New York, 1975.
Hallett, G., *Housing and Land Policies in West Germany and Britain*,

MacMillan, London, 1977.

Harvey, D., *Social Justice and The City*, Arnold, London, 1973.

Headey, B., *Housing Policy in the Developed Economy*, Croom Helm, London, 1978.

Peston, M., *Public Goods and the Public Sector*, MacMillan, London, 1973.

Richardson, H.W., *Urban Economics*, Penguin, Harmondsworth, 1971.

Stretton, H., *Capitalism, Socialism and the Environment*, Cambridge University Press, London, 1976.

Index

D

Deakin N, 254
De Salvo J, 51, 122
Disraeli B, 22
Donnison D.V., 1-2, 190-191
Downs A, 47, 121
Dutch housing, 55, 109, 118-119, 136, 152, 177-178, 192-193, 197-198,
                210, 219-224
Dynamic rent calculation, 223
Dyos H, 149

E

Egalitarianism in housing, 53-55, 74, 101-118, 209, 213-214, 291-292
EHAP, 105, 107, 111, 114-115, 123, 126, 136, 137-143
Engels F., 25, 30-31
Environmental determinism, 25-26, 34, 37, 38, 61, 64, 71, 74, 92, 130
                            162, 188, 241, 247, 263, 293
Equity in housing, 53-55, 233-236

F

Fabianism, 33, 156, 160-161, 167
Filtration theory, 42, 117-118, 130, 204-205, 257

G

Gans H.J., 6, 71, 75
General Improvement Areas (GIAs), 252-253
George Henry, 230
Glasgow housing, 51-52, 156-157, 188, 252, 289-290
Gough J.W., 48
Greater London Council 190, 272-273
Green T.H., 23-24, 32, 33, 53, 55
Greer S, 249
Grey A, 84-85, 196
Grigsby W.G., 42, 89-90

H

Hallett G, 185, 1 91, 195, 216, 218
Harvey D, 72
Hayek F.A., 49
Head J.G., 5, 47
Headey B, 38
Hill, Octavia, 23, 43, 44, 66, 68-69, 101, 107, 155, 158-159, 160, 161
              162, 166, 167, 179-180, 242

High density living, 34-35, 37-38, 72, 177, 187, 189, 224, 252
Historical costs, 42-43, 109, 110, 116, 118-119, 127-128, 169, 187,
                  202, 208, 211-213, 214, 215, 218-219, 220, 223, 225
                  239, 288-289
Housing Action Areas (HAAs), 194-195, 253-254
Housing allowances, xiv, 5, 100-111, 137-143, 193-194, 198, 203-205,
                  207-208, 212-213, 217-218, 222-223, 250
Housing Corporation, 188, 191
Housing gap, 100-116
Housing markets, 111-116
Housing standards, 64-68, 162, 165, 166
Howard, Ebenezer, 159, 241-242
Huber V.A., 26-27
Human capital, 4
Housing sectors, 7-9, 169, 172, 179, 184, 188, 190, 220-221, 289

I

Inflation, 9-11, 118-119, 127, 132-135, 174, 184, 198, 206, 207-209,
            218, 220, 239, 288-289, 292
Institutional economics, 51-52
Intergovernmental relations, 3, 150, 154, 155, 168-169, 201-202,
                  204, 268-278
Intuitionist theory, 53-54
Isler M.L., 13

J

Jackson D, 4, 5
Jevons W.S., 41

K

Kilroy B, 84-85, 196
Kropp G, 26

L

Land policy, 230-243
London County Council (see Greater London Council), 66, 154, 161, 163-
                  164

M

Marshall Alfred, 41, 43, 101, 157, 159, 179
Marx Karl, 24-25
Marxism in housing, 4, 25, 30-32, 40, 53-54, 71, 72, 80, 86, 286-287
Mao J, 131
McKie R, 255
Mearns Andrew, 150, 192
Menger Carl, 41
Merit goods theory, 5, 46, 50, 105-106, 224
Mill, John Stewart, 23-24, 32, 33, 43, 230
Milner Holland Committee, 189-190
Model dwelling companies, 22, 66, 151-153, 158, 163
Mortgage reforms 132-135, 174-175
Mulhall M, 159-160
Murie A, 7
Murray M, 122
Musgrave R.A., 46, 47
Myrdal G, 21, 45, 178, 210

N

Natural law theory, 21
Needleman L, 130-132
Neoclassical economics, 41-44, 51
Neue Heimat, 28
Nevitt A.A., 87-88, 119, 127, 189-190
New urban sociology, 71
Niskanen W, 78
Nixon, President, 202-203
Norwegian housing, 28, 39-40, 76-78, 81, 85, 110, 175-177, 197-198, 205-210, 287-293

O

Older housing, 128-132, 186, 250
Olsen E.O., 42
Olson, M.,47
Owen Robert, 24-26

P

Pareto, V., 45, 50
Peacock A, 276-277
Pigou A.C., 41, 43-44, 49, 101
Proudhon J.H., 25, 31
Public goods theory, 2, 44, 46, 50-51
Public health reforms, 63-64, 149-150

Steiner P.O., 46, 47
Sternlieb G, 129
Stockholm magic houses, 37, 214-215, 240-241
Stretton H, 72, 73-74, 83
Swedish functionalism, 67
Swedish housing, 28-30, 36-37, 38, 55, 109, 110, 118-119, 152, 167,
177, 178-179, 192-193, 195, 197-198, 210-215, 237-241,
272-274

T

Tarn J, 151-153
Taxation and housing, 10, 119, 126-127, 170, 187, 190, 191-192, 196,
205, 209, 213, 216, 217, 221, 230-231, 232, 236,
241, 242, 257, 263
Tenure, 7-8, 31-32, 37, 39, 50, 79, 80-86, 112, 127-128, 187, 196-197,
200, 206-207, 209, 213-214, 218, 220-221, 282-283, 288-289,
292
Torrens T.M., 154
Tudor Walters Committee, 66, 67, 165

U

Urban renewal, 247-264
Utilitarianism, 19-21, 41, 49, 53-55, 63, 91-92, 286-289

V

Vienna, 38-39, 289

W

Walras, Leon, 41
Webb Beatrice, 167
Welfare economics, 41, 44-46, 50, 51, 122, 137-143
Welfare state economics, 41, 43-44, 100-143
West German housing, 27-28, 110, 118-119, 152, 171, 178, 192-193,
197-198, 210, 215-219
Whitbread M, 72, 73
Wicksell K, 46, 47, 49
Wilkinson R.K. 2-4, 130-132
Winnick L, 41
Wohl A, 150-153
Women and housing, 69, 70, 88, 103, 106, 166, 279

X Y Z

Yates J, 85-86